# Fund Raising

The NSFRE/Wiley Fund Development Series

FUND RAISING
EVALUATING AND MANAGING THE FUND DEVELOPMENT PROCESS
PROCESS
Second Edition

James M. Greenfield

JOHN WILEY & SONS, INC.
NEW YORK • CHICHESTER • WEINHEIM • BRISBANE • SINGAPORE • TORONTO

To my wife, Karen, my constant, without whose generous love, patience, tolerance, and understanding this book could neither have been attempted nor completed.

This book is printed on acid-free paper. ♾

Copyright © 1999 by John Wiley & Sons, Inc. All rights reserved.

Published simultaneously in Canada.

This publication is designed to provide accurate and authoritative information in regard to the subject matter covered. It is sold with the understanding that the publisher is not engaged in rendering legal, accounting, or other professional services. If legal advice or other expert assistance is required, the services of a competent professional person should be sought.

Library of Congress Cataloging-in-Publication Data:
Greenfield, James M., 1936–
    Fund raising : evaluating and managing the fund development
process / James M. Greenfield.—2nd ed.
        p.   cm.—(The NSFRE/Wiley fund development series)
    Includes bibliographical references and index.
    ISBN 0-471-32014-5 (cloth : alk. paper)
    1. Fund raising.   2. Nonprofit organizations—Finance.
I. Title.   II. Series.
HG177.G76   1999
658.15′224—dc21   98-48156

Printed in the United States of America

10 9 8 7 6 5 4 3 2 1

The NSFRE/Wiley Fund Development Series

The NSFRE/Wiley Fund Development Series is intended to provide fund development professionals, volunteers including board members, and others interested in the not-for-profit sector with top-quality publications that help advance philanthropy as voluntary action for the public good. Our goal is to provide practical, timely guidance and information on fund raising, charitable giving, and related subjects. NSFRE and Wiley each bring to this innovative collaboration unique and important resources that result in a whole greater than the sum of its parts.

The National Society of Fund Raising Executives

The NSFRE is a professional association of fund-raising executives that advances philanthropy through its more than 20,000 members in 154 chapters throughout the United States, Canada, and Mexico. Through its advocacy, research, education, and certification programs, the Society fosters development and growth of fund-raising professionals, works to advance philanthropy and volunteerism, and promotes high ethical standards in the fund-raising profession.

1997–1998 NSFRE Publishing Advisory Council

Message from NSFRE's President

Jim Greenfield is one of the fund-raising profession's true stars and has made a significant contribution to the fund-raising profession throughout his career. His calm and professional demeanor hide a passion for fund raising and, perhaps more importantly, for teaching fund raising.

Jim's new volume not only clearly and succinctly discusses the fundamentals of fund raising, but pushes the profession to new levels of understanding through what he terms the "fund development process." It is a book for both neophytes and veterans, and contains both practical hints for developing your donor base and theoretical discussion on the nature of philanthropy.

Accountability is a critical issue facing today's not-for-profit sector. Today's donor wants to know that her or his funds are being used wisely and efficiently. Not-for-profits throughout North America want to ensure that their fund-raising programs are the most effective they can be and organizations are constantly searching for tools to meet this critical need.

This book is an excellent resource for chief executive officers and executive staff that have management responsibilities for the development process within their organizations. Learning how to evaluate the efficiency and effectivness of a fund-raising program is a challenge for anyone outside the profession, and this book provides good tools to assist a CEO in this effort. Jim's easy interpretations of development language and statistics make the evaluation process much more manageable and productive. As a former CEO of a large voluntary health organization myself, I used many of the strategies outlined in this book to assist our organization in evaluating our development program.

This book is a perfect example of setting the course, and now it is up to us in the not-for-profit sector to follow it.

Paulette V. Maehara, CFRE
President and CEO
National Society of Fund Raising Executives

Contents

CONTENTS

List of Exhibits

▼ Foreword

There comes a time in the evolution of any profession when one of its members, suddenly emerging from the pack, steps up to the difficult task of writing a sweeping book, one that embraces and clearly states the fundamental precepts and principles of that profession. Many in the profession marvel at this work, in part out of frustration and dismay at the opportunity lost; perhaps one of them should have been the one to pen the classic. The book is so fundamental: It lays out the elements of what the profession is all about for all to peruse; it endures.

In his book *Fund Raising: Evaluating and Managing the Fund Development Process*, now out in this second edition, Jim Greenfield has performed this task for the fund-raising profession. For fund raisers and others, the basics of the process, the art and science of raising money for charitable causes (*fund development*), are fully yet succinctly laid out—a reflection of this gifted individual's 36 years of experience in the field. For those starting out in the profession, this is *the* place to start. But even old pros do themselves a favor when they dip into these pages for some nourishment, encouragement, or perspective.

Jim guides the reader through the necessary preliminaries: a brief review of philanthropy, some thoughts on institutional leadership, perspectives from the standpoint of the donor and the solicitor, and a general summary of the fund development process.

Then the book is devoted to some subjects usually omitted in lesser efforts of this nature. It offers a summary of what the fund raiser needs to know about the legal aspects of the organization (including its tax-exempt status), reminds us of the leadership role of the board of directors, focuses on development of the "master plan," and states policies and procedures for the solicitation of charitable gifts from the public.

The middle of the book takes the typical fund raiser where he or she usually wants most to go: into the realms of the various fund-raising techniques. The reader is wended through the options: annual giving, direct mail, special events, capital campaigns, planned giving, and estate planning. Jim tackles some tough topics to master: donor clubs, recognition guidelines, and cause-related marketing. He provides useful advice about the seeking of support from corporations (gifts and other funding) and private foundations (grants).

The closing pages yield advice on the actual operation of the fund development office and examine a very pertinent question: Why does someone become a fund raiser?

As a lawyer and not a fund raiser, I have enjoyed this book in its first edition over the years, and have had many occasions to liberally borrow from it in explaining the fund-raising process to clients. (This edition, I am confident, will continue to serve.) I like the scope of the book, the flow of it, the writing in it. Jim is obviously proud of his profession, likes to write about it, and does not hide from being a fund raiser. (None of this exercise whereby fund raisers become advancement officers or consultants or some such thing, like lawyers hiding out calling themselves attorneys.)

Energy is required for this sort of undertaking, and Jim has plenty of it, as reflected in his books and his extensive volunteer involvement with organizations like the National Society of Fund Raising Executives and the Association for Healthcare Philanthropy. Jim's enthusiasm and vision for the fund-raising profession is amply mirrored in this fine book.

This book is, as I said, a classic and belongs on the shelf of every fund-raising professional, not to mention others such as lawyers, accountants, trustees, and key management personnel. Simply put, for fund-raising fundamentals, this is the place to begin.

Bruce R. Hopkins

▼ Preface to the Second Edition

Fund-raising professionals have a lot in common with orchestra conductors: They have to recruit and train the players, select the music, rehearse the group, prepare promotional materials, sell tickets to fill the hall, and entertain guest soloists. The only exception is that fund raisers do not get to conduct the orchestra in front of an audience; they remain offstage and out of sight. In any not-for-profit organization, fund-raising staff identify, recruit, train, and reward volunteers who conduct solicitations and many other fund development tasks. They also explain the purposes for which funds are to be raised, tell this story in multiple media forms, help with any solicitation strategy and execution as needed, and manage a program of positive relations with all donors and volunteers. This is the fund development process at work.

More than 20 years ago, my father suggested that I write a book about fund-raising practice because I was teaching it so often. I had explained to him that few textbooks on fund raising were available and that nearly all instruction was drawn from on-the-job experiences. His reply was, "Then they need your book."

If I had tried to write this text then, I would have failed, as I did not yet understand what I now define as the "fund development process." By that time in my career, I had learned quite a bit about how to raise money from the direct experience of working for four separate not-for-profit organizations over the span of 15 years. I knew well the tasks associated with organizing and managing annual giving programs, including direct mail acquisition and renewal, benefit events, corporate and foundation solicitations, and even three capital campaigns. But the past 20 years were needed to teach me the process for successful fund development, which involves more than mastery of the methods and techniques of fund raising. I now believe that a comprehensive understanding of this process can be used in any not-for-profit organization to produce good results and to improve on them each year. I also have learned that not-for-profit organizations are not the same in how they perform fund raising and that fund raising does not perform the same for every organization. A considerable amount of flexibility is required to design and implement a successful program utilizing established methods and techniques; that's the science of fund raising. The art of it is in how those methods are applied.

Fund-raising textbooks, journals, and training programs are now widely available. Most of this literature continues to stress the "how to do it" skills required for successful application. Fund-raising staff can quickly learn these essential skills and put them to work for their organization, even if they know little about how or why they are effective and what results to expect. To many people—staff, donors, and volunteers alike—this *is* fund raising, and nearly every fund raiser can do it.

To move from fund raising to the fund development process requires more than how-to knowledge—it requires making the multiple forms of solicitation work together in concert, beginning and building a program that understands the essential relationships between *friend raising* and *relationship building,* directing appeals to target audiences that can develop a predictable level of current and future gift income, training and motivating volunteers who are energized by capable and well-prepared leaders, and more. Management skills in several traditional areas also will be employed: accounting, communications, finance, human resources, marketing, planning, and advocacy.

Every type and size of not-for-profit organization can enjoy success in fund development; the degree of success is in understanding all the factors—the working relationships between donors and their favorite charities, the cost-benefit ratio of each solicitation technique, the essential need for matching institutional priorities to urgent, relevant public needs, the overarching fact that leadership is the key to success in volunteer management, to name a few. Proper application of the fund development process can define an organization's potential for public support and the direct means to achieve it, and can realize, even predict with reliability, the income an organization can expect at any given time. Today's professional fund-raising executives need to know how to evaluate their results with the same skill as they manage their implementation; understanding performance is the guide to continued success, increased productivity, and profitability.

This book is designed to address this level of management skill. Several areas of application are featured, from planning and marketing to community relations and public relations, from managing volunteers and donors to fund-raising staff, and all with an emphasis on friend raising and relationship building. A fund development program is dedicated to the long haul, to building increasing capability and capacity to address today's needs with an eye toward those coming tomorrow. The nature of philanthropic practice is much more than the exchange of money; it is really about what that money can do to benefit others.

Academic institutions across North America are exploring a new field of instruction and research—philanthropic studies. The importance of not-for-profit organizations in society is becoming better understood, as is the need for people who can enter this career field prepared to provide leadership and direction. There also is a growing interest in studying the relationships between for-profit and not-for-profit business practices, including accounting, finance, asset management, human resources, and more. Actual practice is not the same in both instances, and what is different is important to study and understand. One goal of this understanding is a greater appreciation of how these practices influence a not-for-profit organization's ability to succeed in recruiting and retaining public gift support.

Today more than 1.2 million not-for-profit organizations are raising friends and funds across North America. The concepts and the successful practice of philanthropy are rapidly spreading around the world. More people are becoming personally involved in giving and in asking for gifts from others. New as well as old causes are receiving serious attention, not as alternatives for delivering programs and services to the public that government either shares or cannot support, but as essential components of a civilized community. Public awareness can be increased, followed by public participation. But leaders also must be found, trained, and supported in repeat successes. Not-for-profit organizations also must direct their abilities to define public needs more broadly and address them successfully, thus improving their own communities on a broader scale. It is not enough for one program to succeed if the others fail. Business, government, and not-for-profit organizations can achieve great things if they will work together as partners.

Despite the growth in the number of not-for-profit organizations in America and a corresponding growth in giving, peoples' needs go unmet. Too many children get sick or die for lack of food and adequate healthcare facilities. Too many adults go hungry for lack of help in finding work. Primary and secondary educational institutions are hindered from providing quality education by old facilities in need of repair and renovation. In addition, there remains a need to continue newly defined research studies on the basic nature of philanthropy and its practice. The people involved in giving and getting funds for charitable purposes need to understand this bountiful tradition better, to enhance it for today's needs and to grow and preserve it for tomorrow's. For all of us, there is the current need for a better understanding of how the fund development process can best be utilized and improved so that community benefits can be realized with adequate funding. This book is intended to be a contribution to that end.

James M. Greenfield
Newport Beach, California
October, 1998

Acknowledgments

Writing books takes one's time and attention away from everything and everyone but makes one quite dependent on others at the same time. I wish to acknowledge those who have contributed to my on-the-job experiences over a 35-plus-year career as a fund raiser that allowed a pattern of constructive trial-and-error learning—making all the mistakes over and over to find what will work and how to make it succeed. My thanks go, in order of appointment, to the University of California, Riverside; California Institute of Technology; Claremont University Center/The Claremont Colleges; Children's Hospital Medical Center, Boston; University Hospital/Boston University Medical Center; The Cleveland Clinic Foundation; and Hoag Memorial Hospital Presbyterian in Newport Beach, California. Secondly, my appreciation goes to my many friends and colleagues in the Association for Healthcare Philanthropy and the National Society of Fund Raising Executives for giving me so many opportunities to learn from them, to test my ideas with them, and to share the results with others in conferences and workshops.

I also am indebted to the capable team at John Wiley & Sons for their continued support of this second edition along with my other books they have published. They translate these words and ideas into a winning combination of good English, readable exhibits, and handsome texts. In particular, I wish to thank Martha Cooley, Editor, for her patience and counsel, Tony Callihan, Copy Editor, for his many improvements, and Greg Everitt, Production Manager, for turning a cut-and-paste reworking of an eight-year-old text into this new, good-looking book.

Lastly, to Bruce Hopkins, my good friend and mentor in all these book projects. Bruce provided the original invitation to submit my ideas to John Wiley & Sons, convinced them a book on fund-raising practice was worthwhile, then convinced me I could do the work and enjoy it, too. He was right. His Foreword to this second edition is gratefully acknowledged as is his constant encouragement that has been so instrumental in fulfilling my father's wish of 20 years ago—my dad and I remain most grateful.

J.M.G.

1 ▼ Giving Money to Charity: An American Tradition

When Americans are asked to support their favorite charitable organizations, how much do they give? Total contributions increase each year and now exceed the operating budgets of most nation-states. In 1997, for the first time in history, Americans gave over $150 billion to charity.

Is fund raising so simple that all the charities have to do is ask? How is so much money raised? More important to this book, what methods are used to raise it, why are those particular methods chosen, and how do they work? The answers lie in the "fund development process"—understanding philanthropy, knowing how to ask for gifts, and being sensitive to donors' decisions.

Gifts of money and assets to not-for-profit organizations are but one form of philanthropy, in America and elsewhere. Volunteerism is pervasive, whether for civic or political causes, as are other forms of people helping people. Philanthropy cannot be understood by counting the money or by studying where the money goes and how it is used. Philanthropy is a human experience; perhaps only a needy recipient fully appreciates it and only a giver knows its benefits.

Giving for charitable purposes can also be a function of foundations and corporations. As institutions, they lack human motives for giving but their participation is carefully selected and their resources have great value and impact.

Not all charitable organizations provide public benefits. Some engage in self-serving work that benefits only a few people or proprietary public services. For example, credit unions and cemetery companies can be not-for-profit entities. An understanding of the breadth of philanthropy is essential to engaging in it intelligently, not intuitively, and to encouraging others to practice it skillfully.

COMMUNITIES IN NEED: RETURN OF CIVIL SOCIETY

> Community is a phenomenon that occurs most easily when free people with some sense of equal worth join together voluntarily for a common enterprise. Great leaders create a sense of freedom, voluntariness, and common worth.[1]

Philanthropic practice is synonymous with civic-mindedness. To understand community needs is to appreciate human aspirations for equal opportunity; fair employment; freedom to speak, write, and worship; the "good life"; and the opportunity to care for others. All are important but it is caring for others that actualizes the spirit of philanthropy by inviting those who enjoy the good life to give something of themselves to aid others less fortunate. Such caring activity exemplifies Robert Payton's definition of philanthropy: "voluntary action for the common good."[2]

Philanthropy is basic to community because it can be the source of action that addresses human as well as community needs to build, or rebuild, a civil society. Feeding the homeless and healing the sick are one type of community response to one's neighbors, be they nearby or across the world. The libraries, museums, and performing arts centers that provide education and access to culture to young and old are valued community assets as well. However, valuable as these institutions are to every community, they may fail to address the root causes of community problems and fall short of the goal of making a better life for every citizen. Peter Drucker suggests that an even greater effort to achieve community is called for:

> Civilizing the city will increasingly become the top priority in all countries and particularly in the developed countries such as the United States, the United Kingdom, and Japan. The chaotic jungle into which every major city in the world has now degenerated needs, above all, new communities. And that, neither government nor business can provide. It is the task of the nongovernment, nonbusiness, nonprofit organization.[3]

---

[1]Clifford Pinchot, "Creating Organizations with Many Leaders," in *The Leader of the Future,* ed. Frances Hesselbein, Marshall Goldsmith, and Richard Beckhard. (San Francisco: Jossey-Bass, 1996), 28.

[2]Robert L. Payton, *Philanthropy: Voluntary Action for the Common Good* (New York: Macmillan, 1988).

[3]Peter F. Drucker, "Civilizing the City," in *The Community of the Future,* ed. Frances Hesselbein et al. (San Francisco: Jossey-Bass, 1998), 1. This entire text on community is worth careful study.

The communal instinct is common to most higher life forms. It is normal for human beings and many animals to seek out one another, to choose to live together in groups, to care for one another, and, as a community, to provide shelter and security to all. Humans also coexist in sophisticated relationships with one another as marriage partners and family members, colleagues in the workplace, neighbors, customers and clients, and as members of civic, professional, and social associations. These arrangements are human creations, structured enterprises that invite cooperation in working for goals of common benefit. Participants value group effort, success, and teamwork, and, perhaps most important of all, relationships themselves.

To achieve community requires a civil society. A civil society requires that people respect one another, as evidenced in decent behavior and observance of common law. This same society must care for its institutions as well as the diversity of its members, including its churches, schools, government, and businesses. It also must care for the air, land, and water that sustains its life. When society fails to meet these universal goals, it is the community that must act through its members to resolve each deficiency. Stephen Covey identifies four principles necessary to achieve this perhaps ideal community:

1. One standard: principle-centered goodness
2. One heart: vision and direction
3. One mind: purpose, mission and unity, not uniformity; oneness, not sameness
4. Economic equality: no poor among them[4]

To complete this design for the civil community of the future, there must also be a commitment to common values. According to Dave Ulrich, "six practices may be used to create communities of values and also build a stronger community overall." Those practices are as follows:

1. Forge a strong and distinct identity.
2. Establish clear rules of inclusion.
3. Share information across boundaries.
4. Create serial reciprocity.
5. Use symbols, myths, and stories to create and sustain values.
6. Manage enough similarity so that the community feels familiar.[5]

[4]Stephen R. Covey, "The Ideal Community," in Hesselbein et al., *The Community of the Future*, 54–55.
[5]Dave Ulrich, "Six Practices for Creating Communities of Value, Not Proximity," in Hesselbein et al., *The Community of the Future*, 157–158.

UNDERSTANDING PHILANTHROPY: NEEDS AND CAUSES

> Hence also it is no easy task to be good. For in everything it is no easy task to find the middle, . . . or to give or spend money; but to do this to the right person, to the right extent, at the right time, with the right motive, and in the right way, that is not for everyone, nor is it easy; Wherefore, goodness is both rare and laudable and noble.[6]
>
> ARISTOTLE (384–322 B.C.)

Aristotle got the concept right. We can also thank the ancient Greeks for the word we use to describe the concept: philanthropy, which means "love of humankind." Nearly every recorded culture has considered it noble to help someone else, especially when the giver expects nothing in return. Altruism, a devotion to others or to humanity, places the notion of giving to benefit others on a lofty level. However, to achieve such nobility, something of value has to be given away, and giving away money is not the easiest idea to accept, despite Aristotle's belief in universal generosity.

Philanthropy has become much more than simply asking for and receiving money, or setting up and supporting charitable causes and purposes. Philanthropy is larger than the good works it performs, and, because it has become an American tradition, its pervasive presence is largely taken for granted. Today, philanthropy promotes the quality of life, is carried out in a variety of ways, includes the concepts of charity and love toward strangers, and requires voluntary actions for the benefit of others.[7] Philanthropy, Arthur Frantzreb suggests, is something we should celebrate:

> Let us be proud of philanthropy—the word, the spirit, the act, the result. Let us understand that philanthropy is a sublime demonstration of man's caring for his fellow man. Let us reach and teach others that sharing our resources, be they small or large, is a demonstration of true caring. Let us disown proclamations that generous giving is the result of greed, guilt, fear, ego, recognition.[8]

[6] Aristotle, "Ethica Nicomachea," Book II, Chapter 9, in *Introduction to Aristotle*, ed. Richard McKeon, trans. W. D. Ross (New York: Random House, 1947), 346.

[7] The study of philanthropy has begun in earnest, thanks to hard work by academic scholars who have labored in sometimes unpopular research on not-for-profit management, donor and volunteer motivations, giving trends, government policy, tax law, and more. The Association for Research on Nonprofit Organizations and Voluntary Action (ARNOVA) is the principal source of most of this good work.

[8] Arthur C. Frantzreb, *Not on This Board You Don't: Making Your Trustees More Effective* (Chicago: Bonus Books, 1997), 67.

The practice of philanthropy includes volunteer service in addition to gifts. Causes such as the rights of animals, environmental protection, and preservation of historic landmarks, among others, offer opportunities for advocacy, a basic freedom guaranteed in the U.S. Constitution. In practice most causes continue to heed fundamental issues that seek to enhance the quality of humankind through expressions identified with religion, education, health, art and culture, civic duty, public welfare, and similar pursuits. The formal (and formidable) charitable organizations that now exist to accomplish these goals receive the extra encouragement of government endorsement through an allowable deduction for charitable contributions. Government money is thus made available to traditional not-for-profit organizations, a further testimony to their assured place in our society's priorities for human service. Philanthropic practice is not a direct response to needs or desperate conditions, although these truly exist; it is an opportunity to alleviate such problems or to ensure protection against them by improving the quality of life.

The practice of philanthropy cannot take place in isolation. It must be guided by a clear purpose articulated in statements of organizational mission, vision, and values. It must be carried out by a host of people who serve various roles on behalf of the expressed mission—board members, management and professional staff, employees, donors and volunteers—who all share its vision and values. "Philanthropic behavior," writes Kay Sprinkel Grace, "is motivated by values. Board members' commitment to serve and ask, volunteer enthusiasm, and a funder's sense of satisfaction in giving are based in an implicit search for ways to act on their values. Matching volunteer, funder, and institutional values is a critical practice of successful nonprofit organizations."[9] An organization's all-encompassing statement of mission, vision, and values must be shared with all who are involved and interested in the organization and the benefits it delivers back to the community it serves. The mission statement is the declaration of the organization's cause, or purpose, for being, and serves as a rational argument for voluntary giving of time, talent, and treasure by the public. It is the "case statement" inviting the public's active participation and financial support. "A motivational, honest case statement will transform apathy for every organization into a cause that moves people into action. When done and done properly, the case can challenge the entire organization toward greater service and en-

---

[9]Kay Sprinkel Grace, *Beyond Fund Raising: New Strategies for Nonprofit Innovation and Investment* (New York: Wiley, 1997), 3.

thusiastic support in fulfilling its vision, mission, founding purposes, and humanitarian results."[10]

Some scholars hold that the role of philanthropy is to meet community needs outside of government, that gifts pay for services the government would otherwise provide and are, therefore, public funds. Government's basis for granting the privilege of a tax deduction for gifts to charity is the premise that donors are, in effect, deciding on the proper use of public money. Despite this argument's conflict with the separate role of religion in our society, a pluralistic society includes needs and causes that are apart from government interests and responsibility. The tax deduction motive for giving is a valid assumption, but philanthropic practices existed long before they were sanctioned by the state. Giving of one's personal resources includes giving of time, energy, and talents as well as treasure; to help another person or to advance a cause that benefits others is more than a simple "quid pro quo" exchange supported by government policy. The principle of tax deductibility has its place, even if every citizen does not have access to its benefits each year. And, while it is reasonable to assume that the annual total of gifts made by Americans would not be as generous without government's endorsement, it is just as unreasonable to conclude that philanthropy is simply an alternate revenue source to fulfill government obligations.

A proper role for government in endorsing philanthropic behavior is to enact laws that regulate charitable organizations in a legitimate manner and to provide tax-exempt benefits to aid each organizations' formation and stability and to encourage the public's participation. "Legal tax avoidance" is a positive principle of government because it fosters acts for the public good. But government also modifies, enhances, and removes these same laws, causing the public as well as not-for-profit organizations to be confused, and stifling rather than encouraging philanthropic practice.

Several other classes of voluntary organizations, called *"noncharities,"* are given tax-exempt privileges under these same tax laws. Gifts to these organizations are certainly welcomed by each recipient, but the gifts are not deductible from donors' income taxes. Representing a broad cross-section of nongovernment enterprise, these organizations include such diverse enterprises as social welfare organizations, business leagues, chambers of commerce, social clubs, trade associations, labor organizations, agricultural organizations, title-holding corporations, local employees' associations, fraternal beneficiary societies, cemetery companies, credit unions, teachers' retirement fund associations, mutual insur-

---

[10]Frantzreb, *Not on This Board,* 158.

ance companies, veterans' organizations, political organizations, and homeowners' associations.[11] The public is quite confused about the charities/noncharities distinction, but continues to give money and volunteered time even when informed that their gifts are not deductible. The tax deduction is not their primary motive for supporting these enterprises.

Philanthropy is more directly beneficial to the community and to donors when it involves the 650,000-plus not-for-profit corporations that are classified under the Internal Revenue Code as "501(c)(3)" tax-exempt charitable organizations. Gifts to these organizations qualify for income tax deduction, and the money is used to help fulfill their mission, purposes, goals, and objectives. Contributions are used for community benefit as defined in their annual operating expenses and most organizations could not provide their public benefit services without them. For some larger, long-established charities, gifts are "extra" funds that make a difference in their quality or breadth of service, or in expansion of their facilities and professional staff. In either situation, contributions are the means to greater ends, which is why they have such leverage upon the organizations that receive them.

When a not-for-profit organization is seeking to be incorporated, it must submit a mission statement that explains its purposes, goals, and objectives. The mission statement must describe why this institution or agency was founded and what it is committed to accomplish. The statement of mission "reflects the dominant values of the organization and is a cogent argument as to why those values should be served, expanded, strengthened, and multiplied."[12] The organization's basic purposes must be of public benefit to qualify as a tax-exempt charitable organization under the law. Each charitable organization also is required to have a legitimate legal structure, with a voluntary board of directors that takes responsibility that all services provided will be faithful to the mission and that all funds received will be used in fulfillment of that mission and not for the private inurement of any board member, employee, client, or other person involved. Other privileges associated with legal status as a not-for-profit corporation include exemption from paying income, sales, and property taxes. These privileges are currently receiving increased scrutiny as government at all levels looks to not-for-profit organizations as a possible source of additional revenue.

[11] Bruce R. Hopkins, *A Legal Guide to Starting and Managing a Nonprofit Organization,* 2d ed. (New York: Wiley, 1993), 37–53.

[12] Henry A. Rosso, *Rosso on Fund Raising: Lessons from a Master's Lifetime Experience* (San Francisco: Jossey-Bass, 1996), 14.

The articles of incorporation must list the specific charitable purposes as set forth in the mission statement. These purposes, which represent the uses for public gifts that qualify the organization for tax exemption, can be quite different from agency to agency. For example, the purposes for a public college include teaching, research, and public service. Museums maintain their collections for public edification. A not-for-profit hospital defines its purposes to include caring for its patients as well as offering charity care for those who cannot pay. Other groups work to preserve the environment for public use and to foster better health. An assessment of the organization's mission and operating criteria, using a form such as that shown in Exhibit 1.1, will confirm that, among other things, it has the appropriate legal structure, fulfills a charitable purpose, completes annual reporting requirements, has tax-exempt status, and that its day-to-day operations are within legal requirements.

America's not-for-profit organizations have prospered not only because they could receive funds but also because volunteer leadership and commitment have expanded their quality and service. All not-for-profit

EXHIBIT 1.1 Assessment Criteria for the Mission

	Score				
	Low				High
1. Fulfills a "charitable" purpose.	1	2	3	4	5
2. Completes annual public reporting requirements.	1	2	3	4	5
3. Provides high quality of service.	1	2	3	4	5
4. Offers accessibility to service.	1	2	3	4	5
5. Increases public awareness of the cause.	1	2	3	4	5
6. Addresses five advocacy measurements.	1	2	3	4	5
7. Adequately uses audits and auditors.	1	2	3	4	5
8. Is financially accountable.	1	2	3	4	5
9. Stimulates innovative ideas.	1	2	3	4	5
10. Provides programs of value to the public.	1	2	3	4	5
11. Develops new leadership.	1	2	3	4	5
12. Is guided by written policies and procedures.	1	2	3	4	5

Median Score:

Reprinted from James M. Greenfield and John P. Dreves, The Nonprofit Handbook: Fund Raising, *2d ed. (New York: John Wiley & Sons, Inc., 1997), 134. Used with permission.*

organizations are required to elect a volunteer board of directors whose prime responsibility is stewardship of all funds received, held, and spent. These volunteers receive no pay for their work and no direct benefit from the organizations they serve. They are expected to give of their "time, talent and treasure"—to be public stewards of the organization's funds, to provide leadership and direction, and even to give direct financial support. The general public is willing to support an organization and to give it money because of the public trust in the volunteer board, which has been charged to do the right thing. When abuse or a scandal occurs, all charitable organizations as well as philanthropy itself are tainted. The public and the government regard the stewardship responsibility as an obligation of the highest order and expect proper conduct. Keeping the public trust is worthy of each organization's attention. A fragile or tarnished trust could lead to possible loss of a tax exemption privilege or intermediate sanctions.

To succeed in its mission, every charitable organization needs public participation, in the form of voluntary service or gift support or both. Each donor, whether an individual, foundation, corporation, or association, can select the institution, agency, cause, or need that it wishes to support with its own funds; can determine the amount, extent, and frequency of its gifts; and can specify the uses to be made (unrestricted or restricted purposes) of funds given. Donors can and should request an accounting of how the organization has used its funds for public benefit, in keeping with the mission of the organization.

Philanthropy in practice today thus incorporates noble purpose, community benefit, government endorsement, legal structure, formal mission, voluntary leadership, and stewardship of funds, all of which are carried out openly. Because this "critical mass" permits public solicitation of contributions support, all these components should be in place before an organization begins to ask for money.

INSTITUTIONAL LEADERSHIP AND PROFESSIONALISM

Many people do not realize it, but the largest number of leadership jobs in the United States is in the nonprofit, social sector. Nearly one million nonprofit organizations are active in this country today, and they provide excellent opportunities for learning about leadership. The nonprofit sector is and has been the true growth sector in America's society and economy. It will become increasingly important during the coming years as more and more of the tasks that government was expected to do during the last thirty or forty years will have to be taken over by community organizations, that is, by nonprofit organizations.[13]

PETER F. DRUCKER

Preparations that are required to organize and direct any enterprise become more intense when others are being asked for money to support it. Great ideas, causes, and even burning issues need to be assembled into institutions that perform functions in an organized manner to accomplish objectives. Even after the legal work has been completed, the board members have been elected, and a staff has been hired, much more is required. Completion of a mission, vision, and values statement constitutes a definition of the purposes of the organization, and, while most essential, must be followed by hard work to implement these writings and turn their words into deeds. Each goal and objective needs to be given a priority and a timetable for action. In combination, the mission, purpose, goals, and objectives provide a road map to keep everyone involved moving in the right direction.

Unexpected events can occur or outside forces can cause even the best of plans to be modified. Therefore, management skills are as necessary to not-for-profit organizations as are boards of directors and mission statements. The curricula in colleges and professional schools have only recently begun to offer courses in not-for-profit management. Many employees in not-for-profit organizations today received their training through on-the-job experience in the field. Recognizing this shortcoming, some foundations and corporations are willing to make grants to not-for-profit organizations for training of their administrative and supervisory staff in professional management skills. In our ever more complex society, not-for-profit organizations will not long survive without expert skills in all areas of management and administration.

Board members' and administrators' responsibility for management of financial affairs extends to more than approving budgets and accounting for funds. It appears at times that the nature of not-for-profit organizations is to be fiscally imperiled or at the brink of financial ruin—at least that is how they sound. "Balancing the budget," "meeting payroll," and "ending the year without a deficit" are phrases not often heard around the boardrooms or executive suites of Intel or Microsoft. Not-for-profit organizations *can* make a profit; they *can* finish their fiscal year with an excess of revenue over expenses. In fact, "profits" are the sign of management success. Charitable institutions or agencies can be cited as models of

---

[13]Peter F. Drucker, "Not Enough Generals Were Killed," in Hesselbein, Goldsmith, and Beckhard, *The Leader of the Future*, xiv.

management expertise because they can and should operate their annual financial affairs using good business principles. To do so requires skill in managing operating money and assets, and the board of directors must also be a resource for this skill.

Special knowledge and management skill at the board and executive level are needed for supervising the fund-raising programs and the professional staff hired for fund development. If the directors and managers lack this skill, the fund-raising program will be handicapped by a poor understanding of how it should be working, what it should be doing, and how its results should be measured. This book will provide some guidance, but those serving as directors must acknowledge that the responsibility to learn and to supervise this area lies with the board and senior management, not with the fund-raising staff.

Another responsibility essential to each not-for-profit organization is community leadership, an interaction that works both ways. Not-for-profit institutions and agencies must be part of their community if they expect public participation and support of their mission, cause, or issue. Many institutions and agencies are so buried in their own issues and concerns, so focused on fiscal survival and coping with overwhelming public needs, that they are often unaware of the changing world outside their front door. Their voice is needed in public debate about solving community problems, even if philanthropy itself is not the solution to the problem. They should worry less about being part of the "right" solution and concern themselves more with being part of the debate. Who is better qualified to suggest some solutions to public challenges than leaders in organizations whose purpose for being includes this assignment (i.e., public service) and whose daily attention is given toward the same end? Colleges, hospitals, national health agencies, social and welfare organizations, and cultural institutions are among those collective groups that have formed associations to advocate their special needs and do battle with legislative and regulatory threats to their ability to fulfill their mission and purposes. In the future, similar coalitions of not-for-profit organizations will be needed to take responsibility for areas of concern that are underserved, and to provide qualified representation on complex issues such as tax-exempt status or the indigent.

One example of an underserved area is American public education, from kindergarten through the end of high school. Children are learning less and are finishing school poorly equipped to meet the challenges of adult society. Some school systems are nearly nonfunctional; teachers are overworked and underpaid, and school plants need extensive renovation, repair, or rebuilding. The problem is too complex to be solved by just increasing taxes or selling public bonds to finance some repairs; money alone is not the solution. An overhaul of the entire system, underwritten by the time and talent of all our institutional leaders, is needed—an effort that requires the combined contributions and commitment of community leaders and every segment of our society working together. Board members and executives in our not-for-profit organizations bring experience in collaborative enterprise to the table when they join other professionals from corporate, legislative, and public education fields to define and implement such massive solutions.

No single not-for-profit organizational structure can address such an enormous and complex issue, but the solution is likely to be the result of a design that is intrinsic to any not-for-profit institution or agency. Observe what America has done with its exceptional system of private higher education, which is also supported by the public. Not-for-profit organizations are pervasive throughout our society. Each has expressed, through its mission, purpose, goals, and objectives, what it believes can be realized by teams of people who work together and are committed to solutions they believe are correct.

THE DONOR: FROM ASPIRATIONS TO INSTINCTIVE REPLY

> Giving is not an obligation, a requirement, or a responsibility. *It is a privilege.* If people give to your organization, they are exercising that privilege, and they are paying tribute to your mission and to the value of your programs that are serving the public good.[14]
>
> HENRY A. ROSSO

Each gift decision requires some thought by the donor, who must first be satisfied that the request is legitimate. Donors usually have personal reasons for choosing to support particular charitable organizations. They may respond to a request and continue to support that charity faithfully for many years, not once visiting the institution or participating in its activities. Many donors designate only local organizations for support because they know of their work first-hand, recognize one or two board members by name, derive a positive image from local media coverage, or may have used their facilities or participated in their programs.

Street-corner panderers are not charitable organizations but are quite adept at public solicitation. Is not placing a coin in their tin cup an act of

---

[14]Rosso, *Rosso on Fund Raising*, 56–57.

charity equal to placing that same coin in the Salvation Army Santa's red pot? A donor who decides to give the coin to the street vagrant may reason that the Salvation Army can ask other donors for money to help its programs, but the utility of the gift to the vagrant is more direct and almost identical: feeding and housing the homeless.

To make any gift decision, whether a spur-of-the-moment or a more deliberate contribution, requires sorting out quite a lot of information. Who is asking and for how much? Why me? For what purpose? Why now, and how soon again? Some donors try to estimate the income tax implications of their decision, which guides them in how much, using which asset, and when to give. With so many factors affecting a donor's decision, approaching him or her requires considerable skill. The following are 10 points to consider before asking a donor for a contribution:

1. People want to belong, want to be part of the solution of a perceived need, part of a successful venture.
2. People must be convinced of the need, the logic of the program to meet the need, the confidence in the governing board and in the administrators to use funds properly, and the importance of their investment.
3. People are complimented by being asked to give at a level and at a time which complements their estimate of interest, concern, and potential impact of their leadership position to act first.
4. People who are not asked to give in accordance with their own estimates of their capacity immediately know that the asker either:
    *   is not convinced of the importance of the project;
    *   has not given himself/herself;
    *   has not done homework as to the prospect's potential or importance; or
    *   does not have a carefully studied financial support plan.
5. People who are the potential donors are the only ones who decide just what their gift is to be in the final analysis.
6. People who are substantial prospects for above-average gifts merit a personal call by at least one person and may be turned off from major gift participation by letters, phone calls, written proposals, and/or expensive printed publications.
7. Prospects for substantial gifts should not be visited by more than two persons except in most unusual situations.
8. Substantial gift prospects determine their participation in terms of their estimate of their part of the total fund goal.
9. People respond to goals and deadlines.
10. It is far more important to consider what happens after a solicitation which does not result in an immediate, signed commitment.[15]

[15]Frantzreb, *Not On This Board You Don't*, 152–153.

Donors also have habit patterns: They make regular gifts of the same amount of their favorite organizations. For example, attendance at weekly religious services affords an opportunity for weekly giving, which may be a learned experience. This donor's decision is visible to others when the collection plate or basket is passed. Preparation involves deciding when to attend, the amount of the gift, and the method to be used (visible cash or coins, or a sealed envelope). Regular churchgoers usually make gifts of the same amount and for the same purpose each week. They are also quite unlikely to respond to other requests, even from other churches. Their commitment is based on prior association (membership) and personal experience (attendance) and supports their perceived values and benefits (faith). Most donors make their gift decisions in the privacy of their homes without external pressures and are guided by a variety of motives including personal convictions, available cash, family priorities, and their own spirit of altruism. To secure a first gift or repeat gifts is to "invade" the home and is a major challenge for every not-for-profit organization.

Independent Sector biennial national surveys on giving patterns by Americans based on household income reveal that

> since 1989, households with income over $100,000 increased slightly from 4 to 5 percent of all households, but the proportion of total contributions represented by this group nearly doubled from 12 to 22 percent. Conversely, the share of total contributions from households with incomes of $50,000 or below, representing about three-quarters of all households, declined from 51 percent in 1989 to 43 percent in 1993. Since 1989, the average percentage of household income contributed declined for most income groups with the most notable exception being for households with incomes of $100,000 or more. The steepest declines are among lower income households. Until 1993, respondents from contributing households with average household incomes below $10,000 gave a higher percentage of household income than any other group.[16]

Despite the decline in contributions made by households in most income groups, it is encouraging to know that, for the past decade, nearly three-quarters of all households report making some charitable contributions.

Independent Sector studies also reveal that the highest percentage of household income contributed came from persons who were retired, over 65 years of age, and living in households with an income of $100,000 or

[16]Virginia Ann Hodgekinson and Murray S. Weitzman, eds., *Nonprofit Almanac 1996–1997: Dimensions of the Independent Sector* (San Francisco: Jossey-Bass, 1996), 67–68.

more. The explanation appears to be that the elderly, having prepared for their retirement and possessing ingrained habits of giving, possess the best-developed altruistic motives, whereas younger people are still in pursuit of their fortune and are leveraging their finances to other objectives. Add to this finding the reported "generational transfer" within the next 15 years of an estimated $10 trillion in assets held by individuals aged 65 years and older, and clearly not-for-profit organizations should appeal for some of these funds held by seniors to help meet future demands for quality programs and services.

Most contributors plan their gifts according to their means and motives for giving, sometimes aiming toward long-term goals. Each gift may be modest but the amount has been thought about in advance and supports an intention to continue giving faithfully. Some not-for-profit organizations recognize these regular contributions as cumulative gift decisions that build to quite large sums over time and give donors an extra measure of satisfaction for achieving their targeted performance. Charitable organizations need to recognize their pattern donors, thus cultivating their long-term interests, and to encourage other donors to consider similar patterns of giving that encompass both their occasional and their faithful giving.

When groups of donors can be mobilized to support a single program or a multiyear project, an organization has the potential for significant support and a "campaign" is born. Donors known to have valuable assets, property, or investments should be invited to plan their larger gifts toward an objective suitable for their resources, such as to fund a major project or to establish a permanent endowment that will sustain their favorite project in perpetuity. A donor can also arrange for specific long-term goals through a bequest of some or all of an estate to favorite charitable organizations, to continue faithful support for years to come. Charitable organizations, for their part, must respect their donors' wishes with the same faithfulness (see Exhibit 1.2).

From his research, Paul Schervish has identified a number of variables as influencing giving in general regardless of how wealthy the donor is. These eight variables are as follows:

1. *Communities of participation.* Groups and organizations in which one participates.
2. *Frameworks of consciousness.* Beliefs, goals, and orientations that shape the values and priorities that determine people's activities.
3. *Direct requests.* Invitations by persons or organizations to directly participate in philanthropy.
4. *Discretionary resources.* The quantitative and psychological wherewithal of time and money that can be mobilized for philanthropic purposes.

EXHIBIT 1.2 A Donor Bill of Rights

A Donor Bill of Rights

PHILANTHROPY is based on voluntary action for the common good. It is a tradition of giving and sharing that is primary to the quality of life. To assure that philanthropy merits the respect and trust of the general public, and that donors and prospective donors can have full confidence in the not-for-profit organizations and causes they are asked to support, we declare that all donors have these rights:

I.
To be informed of the organization's mission, of the way the organization intends to use donated resources, and of its capacity to use donations effectively for their intended purposes.

II.
To be informed of the identity of those serving on the organization's governing board, and to expect the board to exercise prudent judgment in its stewardship responsibilities.

III.
To have access to the organization's most recent financial statements.

IV.
To be assured their gifts will be used for the purposes for which they were given.

V.
To receive appropriate acknowledgment and recognition.

VI.
To be assured that information about their donations is handled with respect and with confidentiality to the extent provided by law.

VII.
To expect that all relationships with individuals representing organizations of interest to the donor will be professional in nature.

VIII.
To be informed whether those seeking donations are volunteers, employees of the organization or hired solicitors.

IX.
To have the opportunity for their names to be deleted from mailing lists that an organization may intend to share.

X.
To feel free to ask questions when making a donation and to receive prompt, truthful and forthright answers.

DEVELOPED BY
AMERICAN ASSOCIATION OF FUND RAISING COUNSEL (AAFRC)
ASSOCIATION FOR HEALTHCARE PHILANTHROPY (AHP)
COUNCIL FOR ADVANCEMENT AND SUPPORT OF EDUCATION (CASE)
NATIONAL SOCIETY OF FUND RAISING EXECUTIVES (NSFRE)

ENDORSED BY
INFORMATION
INDEPENDENT SECTOR
NATIONAL CATHOLIC DEVELOPMENT CONFERENCE (NCDC)
NATIONAL COMMITTEE ON PLANNED GIVING (NCPG)
NATIONAL COUNCIL FOR RESOURCE DEVELOPMENT (NCRD)
UNITED WAY OF AMERICA

Design Lipman Hearne/Chicago

Please help us distribute this widely

From James M. Greenfield, Fund-Raising Fundamentals: A Guide to Annual Giving for Professionals and Volunteers *(New York: John Wiley & Sons, 1994). Reprinted by permission of John Wiley & Sons, Inc.*

5. *Models and experiences from one's youth.* The people or experiences from one's youth that serve as positive exemplars for one's adult engagements.
6. *Urgency and effectiveness.* A sense of how necessary and/or useful charitable assistance will be in the face of the onset of an unanticipated or previously unrecognized family, community, national, or international crisis.
7. *Demographic characteristics.* The geographic, organizational, and individual circumstances of one's self, family, and community that affect one's philanthropic commitment.
8. *Intrinsic and extrinsic rewards.* The array of positive experiences and outcomes of one's current engagement that draws one deeper into a philanthropic identity.[17]

Not-for-profit organizations must *ask for* the funds they need. This obvious fact explains why it is so critical to ask well. To paraphrase a famous political admonition, fund raising is the art of asking early and often. If volunteer solicitors were subject to the statistical measures used for baseball players, most would have batting averages of .200 or below, which means they are successful less than once in every five tries. People do give when asked, but no one can support every cause. Volunteer batting averages will improve when the givers are selected through better methods and the askers are better trained.

Most charitable organizations concentrate their fund-raising activities on annual giving methods. Used once a year or on a regular schedule throughout each year, these methods can include multiple forms of asking—usually for modest gifts of whatever spendable cash the donor or prospect has available at the time. In their quest to acquire an increased number of new contributors each year, charitable organizations might overlook their current donors, who are supporting them faithfully. Donors are the best prospects for repeat gifts as well as for new gifts, larger gifts, and estate gifts. Neglecting donor relations is perhaps the greatest sin of omission within fund development programs.

Donors' rights include an expectation that the organization will keep accurate records of their support and will offer them appropriate acknowledgment and perhaps even recognition. Donors also expect to receive a report on how their funds were used, an invitation to the institution's public events, and access to information about the organization's programs, services, and financial affairs. Donors may not be clear about

---

[17]Paul G. Schervish, "Inclination, Obligation, and Association: What We Know and What We Need to Learn about Donor Motivation," in *Critical Issues in Fund Raising,* ed. Dwight F. Burlingame (New York: Wiley, 1997), 112–113.

what is due them from the organization or what the organization is going to do with their money. Internal Revenue Service regulations require "gift substantiation" in the form of an official letter or receipt from the charitable organization for any gift valued at $250 or more. Also, IRS says that donors who purchase tickets to benefit events for $75 or more must be notified *at the time of invitation* what amount or percentage of their ticket price is not deductible, reflecting the quid pro quo estimate of the value of goods and services (food and drink, etc.) they will receive at the event. Time and money, within limits, also should be spent on donor relations. Because donors are the most promising prospects and current donor gifts are essential to fiscal well-being, a well-conceived and well-executed program of donor relations is a correct and worthy use of some of an organization's operating income. How much? The Internal Revenue Service suggests as much as 2 percent of the original gift value, which is a calculation linked to the commercial or material value of the recognition that is selected. Thank-you letters are the best form of acknowledgment and, excepting a postage budget, there is no limit to how many times and in how many forms an organization can say "thank you."

Donors are the best friends any organization can hope to have. They will not only give early and often; they will talk about "my favorite charity" to friends and neighbors and will encourage others to joint them in active support. Donors are also the best pool for voluntary services of all kinds and can become major contributors of their time and talent as well as of their treasure. Some may rise to a role of leadership on the board of directors. This pattern of ascendancy is not accidental and should be a direct result of efforts planned by the organization to inform and enthuse donors by inviting them to increase their participation wherever and whenever they can. If donor enthusiasm has a measure, it is the number of zeros following the digits on regularly received checks. Each time another check arrives, current donors are confirmed as best prospects. Many current donors become future leaders and major investors, but only if an organization plans for this future outcome.

THE SOLICITOR: A JOB TO BE DONE WELL

Organized fund raising is a discipline that requires cooperation from each component of the organization that is endeavoring to support its programs through volunteer gift giving. It cannot be the total effort of one person. The task is too complex. The organization seeking the funds must put its support behind the person charged with the responsibility to prepare the plan and to administer the action required by the plan.[18]

HENRY A. ROSSO

True leadership inspires others to action. Only a few people like to ask their friends for money, so a lot of leadership is needed to persuade people to do this job and to motivate them to do it well. Yet, volunteer solicitors who have been properly recruited, educated, cultivated, recognized, and rewarded can raise millions of dollars for any cause. Beyond adequate tools for carrying out their assignments and motivation to complete their work on time and with energy and enthusiasm, volunteer workers need preparation for the rejection they will experience from many of the people they approach.

All charitable organizations have plenty of donors and prospects waiting to be asked; what they lack are numbers of askers. Successful preparation of volunteer solicitors requires training, careful thought, effective materials (worker kits), professional staff support, and the all-important leadership. The skills necessary to be a productive volunteer solicitor must be learned. Professional training should be provided by the organization; it should be organized by the fund-raising staff and modeled by board members.

Perhaps the most important motive for becoming a successful volunteer is commitment to an organization, cause, or project. A "believer" makes his or her own gift first, before asking anyone else to give. When a volunteer who is a donor asks a friend to support "my favorite charity," the request will more often be successful when the solicitor exhibits belief in the charity's mission, purposes, goals, objectives, and benefit to others in the community, and has made a personal gift to support it. The value of the gift is not in its amount but in the fact that it has been given; the personal conviction communicates to others the credibility of the cause. A further enhancement is that the solicitor has nothing to gain personally from the reply of the person asked.

How does it feel to be solicited by a friend who is enthusiastic about a worthy project? Nearly everyone should have this experience at least once! The prospect may never have heard of the organization, may be indifferent to its purpose, and may know nothing about how it functions. But a friend who has invited the prospect to lunch proceeds pointedly to describe "my favorite charity." Because they come from a friend, the information and intent are trusted to some degree. The commitment and energy of the solicitor are most impressive, if not persuasive, and the

---

[18]Rosso, *Rosso on Fund Raising,* 9.

prospect may then consider a decision to join in and help if possible. At this instant, the solicitor has succeeded in convincing the prospect of the merits of the appeal. How much the prospect might give or what else the solicitor might do to facilitate a gift follows upon this initial persuasion that the cause is worthwhile.

The volunteer who solicits his or her friend intuitively realizes that fund raising is about relationships. Kay Sprinkel Grace has compiled an eight-point list that speaks to the relationship-building aspect of fund raising:

1. Donors do not give to organizations because organizations have needs: they give because organizations meet needs.
2. Fund raising is less about money than it is about relationships: in the words of a Stanford Centennial Campaign volunteer, "Fund raising is a contact sport."
3. Philanthropy is defined by Robert L. Payton (1988) as a participatory and democratic process which involves giving, asking, joining, and serving. It is *not* "multiple choice." In a vigorous society, people must engage in each aspect of the process.
4. There are three levels of involvement and practice for staff and volunteers: philosophical, strategic, and tactical. Successful organizations operate at all three levels.
5. There is no such thing as a "quick fix" in the philanthropic sector. Organizations that experience immediate or unexpected success still must create the systems and structures that will endure over time. Otherwise, they will find they have built a roof without creating a foundation or walls.
6. Based in values, philanthropy is the context for values-driven development and fund raising.
7. Stewardship is a neglected and misunderstood function. It must be practiced as diligently for the donor as it is for the donor's gift.
8. The process of asking for contributions to a nonprofit organization should be one in which the asker feels the pride of inviting investment and in which the donor feels not pressure, but release.[19]

Motives for giving are as numerous as donors; those of individuals are quite different from those of foundations and corporations. Individual donors report their motives to be among the following: charity, ego, respect, religion, recognition, participation, joining with others, helping others, and many more. But the reason most often cited by individuals is because they were asked. Foundations exist to give money away, but they decide how much to give, when, and to whom, based on carefully prepared policies and procedures linked to their own mission, purposes, goals, and objectives. They seek a "match" with their purposes from

[19]Grace, *Beyond Fund Raising*, 1–2.

among the applications they receive. Corporations have a history of following a quid pro quo exchange, which has been dignified by being called "enlightened self-interest" in recent years. Corporate gift decisions often require a prior justification in terms of a visible benefit to the company. The concerns and inquiries of stockholders, who might well prefer these funds were paid to them as higher dividends, are part of any corporate giving decision.

The lists of motives for giving only confirm that there is no single reason why people or institutions make gifts, but motives are important to study because they trigger the gift response (see Exhibit 1.3). Once a prospect decides a cause or appeal is worthwhile, he or she must choose how much to give and when. If any one factor is dominant in this decision, emotion appears to be the clear winner. A telephone call from a college alumni friend stirs good memories and can stimulate a positive reply arising from warm feelings and the emotional tug of the "good old days." An earthquake inspires people to want to help the victims, even at a distance, by sending money to an emergency fund or by donating blood to the American Red Cross to help with medical relief. Emotion may be the most consistent motive when individuals make gift decisions.

Donors also will be motivated by confidence in organizations that perform visible good works seen as benefits to the community; public image and reputation are significant factors in these gift decisions. Consequently, newer and less popular causes find it especially hard to gain their fair share of attention and support without extra efforts. However, Americans are willing to trust every not-for-profit organization, regardless of its history or its purposes. They will consider supporting a new cause or even a controversial or uncommon one, once they grasp the need behind the plea. For example, before the entertainment industry went public in support of AIDS, not many people listened to appeals for AIDS funds.

Public confidence and trust are essential to successful solicitation for charitable giving. The few who would abuse this basic public trust, by fraudulent solicitation for personal gain or improper use of funds raised, do great harm to the public's inherent faith in charitable activity. For this reason, such illicit acts are abhorrent to philanthropy's image and justify the existence of laws, regulations, and penalties. A delicate balance of trust exists between the giving public and the asking organization. It is the duty of charitable organizations, with the visible help of community members who volunteer to serve, to perform all their activities with the highest standards of behavior and professional conduct, in order to preserve this public trust. To that end, the selection of volunteers invited to serve not-for-profit organizations must include a review of their ability, by association, to inspire public confidence.

EXHIBIT 1.3 Framework for Determining Why People Give

Internal Motivations	External Influences
Personal or "I" Factors	*Rewards*
Acceptance of self or self-esteem	Recognition
Achievement	Personal
Cognitive interest	Social
Growth	
Guilt reduction or avoidance	*Stimulations*
Meaning or purpose of life	Human needs
Personal gain or benefit	Personal request
Spirituality	Vision
Immortality	Private initiative
Survival	Efficiency and effectiveness
	Tax deductions
Social or "We" Factors	*Situations*
Status	Personal involvement
Affiliation	Planning and decision making
Group endeavor	Peer pressure
Interdependence	Networks
Altruism	Family involvement
Family and progeny	Culture
Power	Tradition
	Role identity
	Disposable income
Negative or "They" Factors	
Frustration	
Unknown situations	
Insecurity	
Fear and anxiety	
Complexity	

Reprinted with permission from Principles of Professional Fundraising *by Joseph R. Mixer (San Francisco: Jossey-Bass Publishers, 1993), 14.*

Volunteers' motives often coincide with those of donors. They seek the same warm feelings of satisfaction and they respond similarly to the respectability attached to participating in a success. Joining is a strong motive, which points again to the validity of friend raising and relationship building before asking for money. Volunteers are pleased by recognition and reward and, while they may not openly seek it, they expect some form of appreciation from the organizations they have served. Volunteers working for charitable organizations are not accidental walk-ons. They deserve careful consideration and may require a fair amount of "people stroking." An organization that needs or depends on voluntary workers for any purpose must give them the attention they require and fully deserve or it will lose them.

Perhaps the volunteer motive least talked about is fear. Most people dread asking someone else for money, even if the gift is for a worthy cause, because they are afraid they will be turned down (rejection). But they also fear failure in front of others whom they respect or whose respect they crave (loss of face). A curious phenomenon is that those who, if left alone, would fail to act, out of fear of rejection, will do what is asked of them or what they agreed to do, so as not to risk being a nonperformer in front of their leaders. Fear as a motive can be a hindrance in many human endeavors, including fund raising, but it seems able to be an incentive here as well.

The choice of the leaders who will recruit and direct volunteers is one of the most important decisions any not-for-profit organization can make. Leaders should be selected before attempting to gather volunteers, to afford them maximum flexibility in selecting those who will work with them. Leaders often recognize who will perform and can be relied upon, just as each person chosen no doubt knows what will be expected of them if they agree to serve.

Volunteers can perform many other functions quite valuable to fundraising success besides asking their friends for money. Volunteers who are uncomfortable with such personal contact can give their time and talent to preparing materials, organizing meetings, or even stuffing envelopes. They will perform any task rather than solicit their friends for money, and a place should be made for everyone who wants to help. They can also identify other potential donors or solicitors. They can gather information about prospects and donors that will assist in their solicitation—personal preferences, prior gifts to other causes, current financial circumstances, how much to ask for and when, recognition preferences, and similar data.

Many charitable organizations hire professional fund-raising executives to organize and direct their fund development efforts. Some volunteers might think that they are no longer needed after the "pros" take charge, or that they cannot expect to perform as well as paid staff, with whom they must now compete. Both assumptions are incorrect. The job of paid staff often is not to solicit. Even if it were, the paid staff, no matter how many or how talented, could talk to only a limited number of prospects and donors in a week. A group of 25 to 50 volunteers will call upon five times as many prospects, will bring back a higher number of gift decisions, and will raise more money than staff professionals. Why? Because donors and prospects more readily respond to volunteers who are friends and neighbors than to paid staff. Every organization is constantly in need of more volunteers who are willing to ask their friends for money, but professional staff are essential to organize, train, and guide the volunteers to be successful askers. A team effort works the best.

UNDERSTANDING THE "DEVELOPMENT PROCESS"

> [W]e must—as researchers in philanthropy and philanthropic fund raising—assume at least two crucial roles. First, we must accept the role of *teacher*. We must share the tenets of life-enabling education with professional colleagues and fellow citizens. Robert Bellah and associates have suggested that this life-enabling education could promote a "society with a healthy sense of the common good, with social morale and public spirit, and with a vivid memory of its own cultural past." . . . Second, we must assume the role of *rhetor*. We must understand our responsibility, in the traditional sense of rhetor, as one who "leads a public conversation, appealing to traditional sources and contemporary inventions on behalf of shared purposes and goals." . . . As teachers and rhetors, we position ourselves in the places and contexts where public discourse and accountability must be promoted, challenged, nurtured—made a genuine part of our democracy.[20]
>
> PAUL PRIBBENOW

Fund raising is a unique form of communication: It promotes a cause and asks for the order at the same time. "Fund raising," or "development," was perhaps first defined by Harold J. "Si" Seymour, in his 1966 primer in the field, as "the planned promotion of understanding, participation, and support."[21] Another, more recent definition from Kathleen Kelly is helpful: "Fund raising is the management of relationships between a charitable organization and its donor publics. I conceptualized the process of fund raising and titled it **ROPES**. It consists of five steps: **R**esearch, **O**bjectives, **P**rogramming, **E**valuation, and **S**tewardship."[22]

[20]Paul Pribbenow, "And We Will Teach Them How: Professional Formation and Public Accountability," in Burlingame, *Critical Issues in Fund Raising*, 3–4.

[21]Harold J. Seymour, *Designs for Fund Raising* (New York: McGraw-Hill, 1966), 115. A second edition of this exemplary text was reissued in 1988 in paperback by The Fund Raising Institute, Ambler, PA.

[22]Kathleen S. Kelly, *Effective Fund-Raising Management* (Mahwah, NJ: Lawrence Erlbaum, 1997), 40, 391–443.

The one common feature among all fund-raising methods is asking for gifts. Asking is simple; there are only three basic ways: by mail, by telephone, or in person. Mail solicitation is 16 times less effective than personal solicitation but most fund raising uses this most impersonal of approaches. The conduct of fund raising by not-for-profit organizations is far too complex to rely on just one method of solicitation; simultaneous application of many methods of asking is often required in order to be successful. Each technique has separate performance characteristics and should be evaluated for its suitability, acceptability to the public, potential or capacity for success, and cost-effectiveness. Performance evaluations, to be fair, must distinguish among the fund-raising methods used and allow for their separate performance characteristics.

The several methods of fund raising can most easily be understood by dividing them into three levels of activity: annual giving, major giving, and estate or planned giving. Exhibit 1.4 illustrates the methods used at each level and the steps in the development of a donor's commitment. Each method has a greater potential when it is well-coordinated with other methods. Successful activity follows a logical process:

1. Maximize the use of each method as a separate fund-raising technique;
2. Coordinate several methods, to develop a greater interest and involvement by donors beyond just a single gift each year;
3. Offer additional methods of asking; always beginning at the annual giving level, encourage donors to grow in their commitment and enthusiasm and to reach the investment decision level.

Most organizations can raise the money they need for annual operating purposes by using the annual giving methods at the bottom level of the pyramid; others try to use as many of the higher and more complex varieties of asking as will work for them. Mature fund development offices have designed their total fund-raising program based on the pyramid plan. In a highly coordinated effort, they use several fund-raising methods simultaneously. They understand their capacity to succeed in gaining a limited share of public contribution support, and they work toward realizing that potential.

Some organizations and their leaders become impatient for quick results and will pressure volunteers and staff, even entertaining somewhat unethical fund-raising gimmicks that appear to offer a "quick buck." Such methods have never developed faithful, repeat donors, nor will they ever produce more than a few one-time gifts at best. Although resorting to gimmicks to raise dollars is inexcusably bad practice, it is important to understand the forces in today's not-for-profit environment that make

EXHIBIT 1.4 The Pyramid of Giving

From James M. Greenfield, Fund-Raising Fundamentals: A Guide to Annual Giving for Professionals and Volunteers *(New York: John Wiley & Sons, 1994), 12. Reprinted by permission of John Wiley & Sons, Inc.*

those shortcuts appear so attractive. As Margaret Duronio and Eugene Tempel point out, several factors now make fund raising more challenging than ever:

> In the 1990s, critical factors in the nonprofit environment have profound implications for fund raisers. These factors include:

- Increased scrutiny and critical judgments of nonprofit management and spending
- More donor solicitation with a corresponding increase in donor sophistication and awareness
- Greater dependence on private support for many nonprofit organizations and more competition for philanthropic dollars
- The anticipated transfer of trillions of dollars in private wealth as baby boomers approach retirement age
- The growth in numbers, size, and resources of many nonprofits, and the increased complexity of managing them—resulting in, among other things, higher salaries for some nonprofit executives.

Because of these factors, the work of fund raising has never been more demanding, more challenging, or more important. Fund raisers, who create the bridge between mission and market-place, are among those who must mediate these issues and concerns with the donative public, while experiencing increased pressure to reach higher goals with fewer resources to apply to fund raising.[23]

It is unreasonable to expect that a new fund development program will produce big gifts from the top level of the pyramid. Major gift decisions are comparable to investments made by an individual or corporation. Each investment requires considerable research and study before the decision to act. In the development process shown in Exhibit 1.4 an investment-minded donor progresses upward from identification, information, interest, and involvement to investment. New donors are unlikely to make the biggest gift of their life to an organization they just heard about. Time (three years at a minimum), energy, work, and budget are all required to build a broad base of reliable annual donors. As Jerry Mandel notes, the institutions most successful at building awareness and support are those that employ the following discipline:

> The advancement efforts of the successful institutions were focused: they knew what they were about; their efforts grew from an understanding of institutional aims; they were marked by organized staff and volunteer efforts; they acknowledged the importance and worth of the people—volunteers and staff— charged with securing philanthropic dollars. In short, successful advancement programs were *managed* across the range of organizational needs; their dollar expenditures were rationally directed; their internal and external relationships were carefully—even artfully—designed. By way of comparison, the operation of the less successful organizations conveyed a slap-dash quality; "hit and miss" appeared to be the dominant strategy. They moved in a crisis state.[24]

[23]Margaret A. Duronio and Eugene R. Tempel, *Fund Raisers: Their Careers, Stories, Concerns, and Accomplishments* (San Francisco: Jossey-Bass, 1997), 16.

[24]Jerry E. Mandel, foreword to *The Effective Advancement Professional: Management Principles and Practices,* by Duane L. Day (Gaithersburg, MD: Aspen, 1998), xi.

Donors cannot be pushed or prodded into making gifts; they must be ready. Rushing them will result in smaller gifts as well as unhappy donors who might never give again. Similarly, it is important not to place too much emphasis on only money, which can be a danger signal to donors. No one likes to be "taken." Besides, pressure tactics and arm-twisting send the wrong messages to donors. They will question the leadership of the organization and their confidence in making a gift decision will be shaken.

Fund-raising staff and volunteers should study the pyramid of giving to gain an accurate appreciation of how, with time and dedication, all the levels of giving can be developed for any not-for-profit organization. Reports on the numbers of generous donors and volunteers whose active participation and support have made an effort a success can have a reinforcing effect. As Kay Sprinkel Grace suggests, staff and volunteer *participation* in donor development (friend raising and relationship building) is the key to their developing confidence in their roles as askers:

> People who participate in donor development and relationship building grow in their willingness to play a role in fund raising. They see how potential donors, and current donors with greater potential, derive pleasure from involvement with the organization. As the relationship grows, staff and volunteers move naturally to the next step: inviting potential funders to make an initial or increased gift. This transition, from reluctance to confidence in asking, is the principal result of a changed attitude. It requires the following:
>
> 1. *Pride in the achievement of the organization.* Communicate accomplishments and surround them with information about what resources are required (human and financial) to further strengthen the programs and services.
> 2. *Involvement and communication.* Board members, other volunteers, and program staff need to be kept informed about accomplishments and concerns, and be invited to participate in celebrations and problem-solving.
> 3. *A belief that the donor, not the organization, is the center of the marketplace.* The donor's and the community's needs, not the organization's, are paramount. Their interests, enthusiasm, attachments, and concerns must be the focus in determining the potential relationship.
> 4. *An overriding conviction about the value and impact of services.* Overall, this is the key to confidence in the organization and the process of development and fund raising. It is the key to innovation and changed practices.
>
> The tin cup attitude can and must disappear as organizations are increasingly positioned as investments that reflect donor and community values. A passive donor-institution relationship will not provide the active partnership needed within our communities. The dynamic donor-investor relationship must be created.[25]

[25]Grace, *Beyond Fund Raising*, 34–35.

Details about how each of the several methods of fund raising is integrated into the "fund development process" are provided in later chapters. What is essential to understand from this introduction is that a basic program design is required for all-fund-raising activity. The design must stimulate a series of multiple, continuous, positive, asking situations that offer donors repeat opportunities to fulfill their personal giving aspirations by supporting their favorite charitable organizations.

ACCOUNTABILITY, ETHICS, AND STEWARDSHIP

The not-for-profit organization holds the most serious of responsibilities in exchange for its multiple privileges. It is obligated to fulfill its mission to the community and to remain true to its vision and values. It must demonstrate an exacting accountability for delivery of quality programs and expanded services; for ethical conduct in all its relationships, be they with clients or customers, board members or employees, donors or volunteers; and for stewardship of its assets, including all funds raised and received as well as its people, facilities, and equipment. There can be no substitute for the highest standards of conduct in every area of a not-for-profit organization's daily activity, because, in the end, it is the public's confidence and trust that enables the organization to operate. Without such a commitment by the public to give of their own time, energy, talent, and personal funds, an organization cannot long survive.

Therefore, the organization must operate in full public view, with open and complete disclosure of all its activities, financial affairs, commitment to excellence, and dedication to serve every purpose defined in its mission as its reason to exist. To be accountable to these precepts is also to practice actively, at the minimum, the 10 ethical precepts in the Donor Bill of Rights (Exhibit 1.1). Each donor's first right to open and complete disclosure is "To be informed of the organization's mission, of the way the organization intends to use donated resources, and of its capacity to use donations effectively for their intended purpose." Failure to observe each of these 10 fundamental precepts is a major transgression of stewardship responsibility. Each such blunder also is a demonstration by those involved—board member or staff manager, employee or volunteer—of a lack of professional conduct and personal commitment to high ethical standards. Such errors lead quickly to charges of fraud and deception and become scandals that can affect the confidence and trust of donors to other organizations as well. "What we all have in common is a responsibility to play our roles well. For nonprofit practitioners, conscientious volunteers, and foundation grantmakers, the concept goes to the heart of professionalism. Easy to miss, however, and a source of profound confusion, is the difference between *role* responsibility and *ethical* responsibility—a difference that, as Aristotle suggests, is hardly 'an easy matter.' The difference is important because of the deceptively easy substitution of role-playing for truly ethical behavior."[26]

Stewardship includes the obligation to report back to donor-investors on results and performance, which can be measured against the organization's stated mission, vision, and values. It is also a means to preserve or enhance a donor-investor's confidence and trust in the organization's use of his or her contributions. Kay Sprinkel Grace offers 11 basic principles to guide the preparation and management of a strong stewardship program:

1. Begin involving donors in the stewardship program with their first gift.
2. Alternate messages to your donors.
3. Allocate budget to stewardship activities.
4. Be sure the stewardship practice is appropriate to the amount of the gift and the budget and image of the organization.
5. Determine what kind of involvement your major gift and planned gift donors, some of whom may be very busy with other organizations and their own professions, want.
6. Coordinate stewardship and cultivation outreach, so that current donors have an opportunity to convey their enthusiasm and commitment to prospective donors.
7. Tie stewardship outreach to the organization's mission.
8. Focus on intangible, rather than tangible, benefits.
9. Maintain stewardship with long-time and generous donors, even when their giving flags.
10. Keep all previous large-gift donors informed and part of your database, even those who make what seems to be a "one-time-only gift," unless and until you hear they no longer want to hear from you.
11. Establish relationships between donors and program staff whenever possible.[27]

The final word on this all important obligation—stewardship—and its relation to ethical fund raising is from Hank Rosso:

> If we accept the philosophy that stewardship flows from our common value system, then it is clear that ethical fund raising simply surfaces these values

[26] Albert Anderson, *Ethics for Fundraisers* (Indianapolis: Indiana University Press), 1996, 1.
[27] Grace, *Beyond Fund Raising*, 169–173.

and illuminates them. That is why a sensitive presentation with an emphasis on *vision* and *mission* will supersede manipulation any day. Sincere passion reflecting the solicitor's commitment and respect for the purpose of the work and its meaning to the civic community will stimulate more interest and desire to give than any contrived maneuvering to induce the gift.[28]

DONOR RECOGNITION

The last discussion in every chapter of this book will be about recognition. Fund raising concentrates too much on asking for money. More time and attention should be given to the relationships needed to sustain donor interests. If the only current reason to treat donors better is to ensure their gift again next year, then a program for annual donor recognition should be defined and implemented. But there is so much more to donor relations that can and should be done. Donors are the essence of fiscal well-being to not-for-profit organizations; their health and welfare are the organizations' concern and their willingness to be generous and committed deserves appropriate recognition.

[28]Rosso, *Rosso on Fund Raising,* 152.

▼ 2 Readiness Tests

If it is to be successful, a new fund development program requires that several preparatory tasks be undertaken in the correct sequence. Legal status must be established, a proper board election held, policies and procedures firmly stated and implemented, and financial controls instituted to fulfill generally accepted business practices. Relevant committees must be formed and given accountabilities. Solid short- and long-term plans for annual operations must realistically estimate income and expenses because contributions will be the primary means for accomplishing both current and future goals. Even before the program is launched, and certainly during its early stages, market research can be done to reveal what the public thinks about the organization and its intended use of their contributions. Ample evidence of community need for its proposed programs and services must be collected and analyzed to help plan how the organization can deliver appropriate benefits to the community. Knowing what the public thinks about the organization *before* it begins asking for contributions can help with decisions on what methods of solicitation to use and what results can be expected from each. Plans for the future also should be part of a program's design. Donors want to know that the organization will be around for a while, that it knows where it is headed, and that its programs are capable of making a difference. They will then join in more willingly to help make that future happen. "Fund raising relies on the building of a structure," writes Henry A. Rosso, "The building blocks are analysis, planning, execution, control, and evaluation. Analysis and evaluation are sciences. In between them comes the art. The genesis of fund raising demands serious thought before a plan can be reduced to writing. Every practitioner should keep in mind the axiom, 'It's what you do up front that counts.' "[1]

---

[1] Henry A. Rosso, *Rosso on Fund Raising: Lessons from a Master's Lifetime Experience* (San Francisco: Jossey-Bass, 1996), 120.

Because charitable organizations cannot raise money for the private inurement of any individual, they must be set up as legitimate charitable organizations, which includes incorporation and filing an application for a certificate of tax exemption and an identification number from the Internal Revenue Service (IRS). As part of its application for approval to solicit, the organization must submit its articles of incorporation and bylaws to the IRS and state authorities, nominate and elect its voluntary board of directors and its officers, and fulfill local regulations. Only after being fully chartered can the organization begin active fund raising.

LEGAL ORGANIZATION AND TAX-EXEMPT STATUS[2]

Fund development usually is correlative with deductible charitable giving and, for a gift to be deductible as a charitable donation, it must be made to a qualified organization. The law, both state and federal, has much to say about the meaning of "qualified."

Here are the four steps for achieving not-for-profit, tax-exempt, charitable status for an organization:

1. Selection of the appropriate legal form
2. Preparation and adoption of the necessary documents
3. Preparation and filing of an application for recognition of tax-exempt status
4. Securing comparable tax-exempt status under state law (if available)

Thereafter, the organization will be expected to file federal annual information returns and perhaps state reports; if fund raising, the organization will likely be expected to register and report pursuant to one or more state charitable solicitation statutes.

Legal Form

Before an organization can be eligible to receive deductible contributions, it must be legally established as a not-for-profit organization. What

[2]This section of the text was written by Bruce R. Hopkins, Esq., with the law firm of Polsinelli, White, Vardeman & Shalton in Kansas City, Missouri. His contribution is gratefully acknowledged.

is construed as a not-for-profit organization basically is a matter of state law. Occasionally, an organization will be chartered by the U.S. Congress.

Just because an organization is not for profit does not mean that it cannot generate a "profit" (in the sense of revenue in excess of expenses). A not-for-profit organization is entitled to earn a profit; the concept of "not for profit" focuses on what is done with that profit. A for-profit organization is expected to earn profits for its owners; these profits, often in the form of dividends, inure to the owners (usually stockholders). By contrast, the profits of a not-for-profit organization are not supposed to inure to the benefit of private persons but are to be used for program and other organizational activities. Thus, in not-for-profit organizations, profit may occur at the organizational level but not at the ownership level. (Moreover, there rarely are "owners" of a not-for-profit organization.)

A not-for-profit organization will be one of three types: a corporation, a trust, or an unincorporated association. The choice will depend largely on the extent to which liability is a factor and the stringencies of state law. However, most contemporary not-for-profit organizations are corporations.

Necessary Documents

A not-for-profit organization is created by the execution of what the federal tax law terms "articles of organization." For a corporation, this document is known as the articles of incorporation. For a trust, the document is a declaration of trust or a trust agreement. For an unincorporated association, the document is a constitution. Each of these documents is signed by those who establish the organization. Articles of incorporation are filed with the appropriate state office(s), which issues a certificate of incorporation.

Once incorporated, the not-for-profit organization must comply with appropriate state law; the filing of annual reports is commonly required. State law may also impose reporting and other requirements on trusts and/or unincorporated associations.

Following formation, the not-for-profit organization should adopt, as soon as possible, its rules of organization and operation. Usually termed "bylaws," this document should contain details as to the responsibilities, composition, and terms of office of the organization's directors, the responsibilities and terms of office of its officers, its committee structure, its fiscal year, any indemnification arrangements, procedures for amending the bylaws, and more.

The bylaws should be adopted at an organizational meeting and memorialized in a well-written set of organizational minutes. The minutes should reflect adoption of the bylaws, election of directors and officers, selection of one or more financial institutions, and authorization of someone to proceed with the tax-exemption and other legally required processes.

Tax-Exempt Organizations: Federal Law Requirements

Several categories of not-for-profit organizations qualify for tax-exempt status under federal law.[3] Some of these organizations will also be eligible for exemption from one or more state taxes, such as sales, use, tangible personal property, intangible personal property, and/or real property taxes.

In general, the only type of not-for-profit, tax-exempt organization that is pertinent to the fund development process is the "charitable" organization, which includes organizations that have purposes that are educational, religious, scientific, and the like.[4] Specifically they include churches, colleges, universities, schools, hospitals, other health-care entities, private foundations, certain membership associations, and other public charities.[5] Contributions to these organizations are deductible as charitable gifts.[6] Other organizations that are eligible to be charitable donees are certain veterans' organizations, fraternal organizations, and cemetery companies.[7]

There are several other categories of tax-exempt organizations. These include social welfare and other types of advocacy organizations,[8] labor unions and like organizations,[9] trade and professional associations,[10] and social clubs.[11] Although contributions to these entities are not deductible, they often have related "foundations" to which deductible contributions can be made.

---

[3] In general, tax exemption under the federal tax law is authorized by the Internal Revenue Code (IRC) of 1986, as amended, Section 501(a).

[4] These organizations are described in IRC § 501(c)(3).

[5] IRC § 170(b).

[6] IRC § 170(c)(2), except for organizations that test for public safety, as described in IRC § 509(a)(4).

[7] IRC § 170(c)(3)–(5).

[8] IRC § 501(c)(4) organizations.

[9] IRC § 501(c)(5) organizations.

[10] IRC § 501(c)(6) organizations.

[11] IRC § 501(c)(7) organizations.

Meaning of "Charitable"

The term *charitable* in the federal income tax setting embraces a variety of purposes and activities. These include relief of the poor and distressed or of the underprivileged, advancement of religion, advancement of education, advancement of science, lessening of the burdens of government, community beautification and maintenance, promotion of health, promotion of social welfare, promotion of environmental conservancy, advancement of patriotism, care of orphans, maintenance of public confidence in the legal system, facilitation of student and cultural exchanges, and promotion and advancement of amateur sports. These categories are reflected in the federal income tax regulations, IRS rulings, and court opinions.[12]

Thus, the term *charitable* as used in the federal tax context is not as broad as the term *tax-exempt*, and certainly not as inclusive as *not-for-profit*. Stated another way, not-for-profit organizations are not necessarily tax-exempt and tax-exempt organizations are not always charitable ones.

Public Charities and Private Foundations

The federal tax law divides charitable organizations into two categories: public charities and private foundations. The law presumes that a charitable organization is a private foundation,[13] requiring a charity to rebut (if it can) the presumption of private foundation status. There is no advantage to classification as a private foundation; to the contrary, the federal tax law imposes many stringent regulations on those entities that are categorized as private foundations,[14] including less-favorable charitable contribution deduction consequences.[15]

Many institutions are automatically exempted from classification as a private foundation because of the nature of their activities, such as by being churches, educational institutions, or hospitals.[16] This classification is not predicated on the manner in which these organizations are funded.

By contrast, some organizations avoid private foundation status because they are publicly supported. There are two categories of publicly

---

[12]This aspect of the law is discussed in Bruce R. Hopkins, *The Law of Tax-Exempt Organizations*, 7th ed. (New York: Wiley, 1998 and annual supplements).

[13]IRC § 509(a).

[14]E.g., IRS §§ 4940–4948.

[15]The charitable deduction rules are the subject of Bruce R. Hopkins, *The Tax Law of Charitable Giving* (New York: Wiley, 1993 and annual supplements).

[16]IRC § 509(a)(1). Hopkins, *Law of Tax-Exempt Organizations*, § 11.3(a).

supported organizations. One is the organization that normally receives a substantial part (at least one-third) of its financial support (other than income from the performance of an exempt function) from governmental agencies and/or contributions from the general public.[17] The other is the organization that normally receives more than one-third of its support from a combination of (with a variety of limitations) contributions, grants, membership fees, and/or revenue from the performance of exempt functions, and normally receives no more than one-third of its support in the form of investment income.[18]

Another category of public charity is the supporting organization. This type of organization is an entity that is sufficiently related, structurally or operationally, to one or more of the automatically exempted institutions listed earlier or publicly supported organizations.[19] A supporting organization must be organized, and at all times operated, exclusively for the benefit of, to perform the functions of, or to carry out the purposes of one or more public charities. The supporting organization must be operated, supervised, or controlled by or in connection with one or more public charities. Examples of supporting organizations include advocacy or social welfare organizations, labor organizations, and business or professional associations.

The Application Process

The federal tax law provides for eligibility for tax-exempt status. The IRS grants recognition of tax exemption. Only charitable organizations and certain employee benefits organizations are required to obtain recognition of tax-exempt status.

The application process for charitable organizations is commenced by the filing of an application for recognition of tax exemption (Form 1023).[20] The application requires the organization to reveal a wide range of information concerning its program activities, fund-raising program, sources of financial support, board of directors, officers, relationship with other organizations, and much more. If the application process is successful,

[17] IRC §§ 170(b)(1)(A)(vi) and 509(a)(1). Hopkins, *Law of Tax-Exempt Organizations*, § 11.3(b)(i).

[18] IRC § 509(a)(2). Hopkins, *Law of Tax-Exempt Organizations*, § 11.3(b)(iv).

[19] IRC § 509(a)(3). Hopkins, *Law of Tax-Exempt Organizations*, § 11.3(c).

[20] Hopkins, *Law of Tax-Exempt Organizations*. Sample answers for preparation of the application appear in Bruce R. Hopkins, *A Legal Guide to Starting and Managing a Nonprofit Organization*, 2d ed. (New York: Wiley, 1993), 82–85.

the IRS will issue a "determination letter" that classifies the organization as a charitable one, both for tax-exemption and deductible-giving purposes.

This determination from the IRS also contains the classification by the IRS as to the applicant organization's non-private-foundation status (if any). Where the organization qualifies as a church, college, university, school, hospital, or other similar institution, or as a supporting organization, the determination as to non-private-foundation status is termed a "definitive" ruling. If the organization is endeavoring to qualify as a publicly supported charity, the IRS will issue an "advance" ruling, which will subsequently ripen into a definitive ruling once the organization is able to demonstrate that it is in fact publicly supported.

In addition to receiving tax-exempt status under federal law, the organization may be eligible for tax-exempt status under state law. The state law exemptions may relate to income, sales, use, tangible personal property, intangible personal property, and real estate taxes; contributions to the charitable organization may be deductible under state law.

Reporting Requirements

Nearly all tax-exempt organizations are required to file an annual information return with the IRS.[21] For most of these organizations, the return is on Form 990.

This return must reflect the organization's items of "support and revenue" (such as gifts, grants, dues, program service revenue, other public support, revenue from the sale of assets, rents, and investment income). The return must also reflect disbursements (such as grants made, compensation, other employee benefits, professional fund-raising fees, legal and accounting fees, and the costs of occupancy, travel, conferences, and supplies). Expenses must be categorized by function, namely, program services, management and general, and fund raising. The return includes a balance sheet showing assets, liabilities, and net worth.

A tax-exempt organization must make its three most recent annual information returns available for inspection by anyone at its principal office during regular business hours. The penalty for failure to provide copies of the annual information returns for inspection, in the absence of reasonable cause, is $20 per day with a maximum penalty per return of $10,000.

---

[21]Hopkins, *Law of Tax-Exempt Organizations,* § 24.3.

Failure to file the information return on a timely basis or failure to include the requisite information, without an exception or reasonable cause, can give rise to a $20-per-day penalty, payable by the organization for each day the failure continues, with a maximum per return of the lesser of $10,000 or 5 percent of the organization's annual gross receipts. Organizations with gross receipts in a year exceeding $1 million can face a penalty of $100 per day, to a maximum of $50,000 per return. A person failing to respond to an IRS demand for a return can be subject to a penalty of $10 per day, to a maximum of $5,000 per return.

Other federal and state filings can include the unrelated business income tax return, reports of gift property sold by the charity, state annual reports, and the reports required by the various state charitable solicitation acts.[22]

There may also be annual reporting requirements pursuant to state law.

Fund-Raising Regulation

The process of fund raising for charitable purposes is regulated by the states, by application of "charitable solicitation acts."[23] At the present, there are 49 of these statutes; approximately 36 of them embody general regulatory provisions. These laws impose registration, reporting, recordkeeping, and other requirements on charitable organizations that solicit within their respective jurisdictions; in many instances, these laws are also applicable to professional fund raisers and professional solicitors.

Federal law also regulates the fund-raising process. This is done through disclosure requirements for both charitable and noncharitable organizations,[24] the exemption applications procedure,[25] the reporting procedure,[26] current audit guidelines,[27] application of the unrelated business income rules,[28] and the charitable deduction rules.[29]

---

[22]Hopkins, *Starting and Managing a Nonprofit Organization*, 96–99.

[23]Bruce R. Hopkins, *The Law of Fund-Raising*, 2d ed. (New York: Wiley, 1996 and annual supplements); Hopkins, *Starting and Managing a Nonprofit Organization*, 120–128.

[24]Hopkins, *The Law of Fund-Raising*, § 6.2, 6.5.

[25]Ibid., § 6.7.

[26]Ibid., § 6.8.

[27]Ibid., § 6.1.

[28]Ibid., § 6.6.

[29]Ibid., § 6.13.

Day-to-Day Operations

Once all legal organizational requirements, including acquisition of recognition of tax-exempt status, have been satisfied, the not-for-profit organization must thereafter operate in conformity with them. The requirements emanate from many sources: the language in the organization's articles of organization and bylaws, and the law concerning tax-exempt status, charitable giving, and fund-raising regulation.

The Federal Tax Code regulates the ongoing operations of the charitable organization for exempt (charitable, educational, scientific, and so on) purposes. The law bars the organization from operating for the benefit of persons in their private capacity (including "private inurement" of net earnings), curbs the ability of the organization to engage in lobbying activities, and prohibits the organization from involvement in political campaigns.

The organization should be managed properly. While the law has little to say about management as such, it is important for the organization to, when required, hold its board meetings, conduct elections, file financial and other reports, and use the services of professionals (lawyers, accountants, and fund raisers, for example).

The board of directors of the organization is expected to set policy and oversee the entity's operations. Day-to-day operations are generally the province of officers and staff, but lines of demarcation are often difficult to draw.[30] For example, as to the matter of fund development, the board should set the overall policy, such as the purpose and timing of a capital campaign or the basic elements of a planned giving program; officers, staff, and volunteers would implement the policy.

The board of directors of a charitable organization is, notwithstanding the title given to them, a "board of trustees." They are trustees in the sense of fiduciaries; they are stewards of the organization's assets and revenue and should always act in a way to preserve and enhance those resources. They should avoid conflicts of interest and function on the organization's behalf, rather than their own.

Liability Issues

In this litigious age, charitable and other not-for-profit organizations, and perhaps the individuals who manage them, are more likely than ever to

---

[30]See Hopkins, *Starting and Managing a Nonprofit Organization*, 18–24.

face a lawsuit. There are several ways to protect against successful litigation. The principal one is to avoid conduct that might be the basis for a suit; a related one is to keep adequate records.

One author offers this list of directors' responsibilities, which, if adhered to, will eliminate or at least minimize personal liability:

- Make certain that all technical requirements of law have been met before the organization commences operations.
- Keep informed of the general activities of the organization and the general field of interest in which it functions.
- Assure complete and accurate disclosure of the details of all transactions, such as the sale of securities.
- Avoid self-dealing in any matters relating to the organization's operations.
- Attend directors' meetings regularly; if meetings must be missed, be certain that the minutes reflect a valid reason for the absence.
- Register dissent when in disagreement with board action; be certain that it is made a matter of record in the minutes of the meeting and that the accuracy of the minutes is checked.
- Have a complete and competent knowledge of the duties of the office.
- Avoid any contract to serve personal interests or to assume any position that would bring personal interests into conflict or competition with the interests of the organization.
- Keep informed of the provisions of the documents creating the organization and setting forth its rules of operation that relate to the powers and duties of the directors.
- Exercise the utmost good faith in all dealings with and for the organization and be prepared to prove good faith if necessary.
- Obey all statutes and other forms of law that prescribe specific duties to be performed by directors.[31]

There are other defensive actions that can be taken. One is to incorporate. As a general rule, incorporation confines any liability to the organization, deflecting it from directors, officers, staff, and/or volunteers. Some individuals' actions, however, like crimes and forms of negligence, cannot be shielded from liability through incorporation.

Another defensive action is to purchase insurance. This displaces the risk of liability for personal injury, property damage, officers' and directors' actions, defamation (if the coverage can be found), and the like. Another method of shifting this risk is indemnification, whereby the organization agrees to use its resources to defend certain claims against those individuals who are charged with the wrongdoing. Insurance shifts the risk to a third party; indemnification shifts it to the organization. Of

---

[31]George D. Webster, *The Law of Associations* (New York: Matthew Bender, 1965), § 2.07[2].

course, the indemnity provided by the organization is only as viable as the resources that stand behind it.

Some states have adopted immunity statutes: By law the directors and officers of the not-for-profit organization are made not liable for certain types of actions under certain conditions. These actions and conditions vary, so a review of applicable state law on this point is essential.[32]

Intermediate Sanctions

The law concerning "intermediate sanctions"[33] is applicable with respect to all charitable organizations, with the exception of private foundations. Intermediate sanctions are penalties that may be imposed on trustees, directors, officers, key employees, members of their families, certain controlled entities, and other persons who engage in inappropriate private transactions.

Persons subject to these rules are termed "disqualified persons." In general, a disqualified person is someone in a position to exercise substantial influence over the affairs of the organization. This law applies to a person who was in a disqualified status at any time during the five-year period ending on the date of the transaction in question.

The primary concern of this body of law is the "excess benefit transaction." In that transaction an economic benefit is provided by a charitable organization directly or indirectly to or for the use of a disqualified person, where the value of the economic benefit provided exceeds the value of the consideration received by the organization for providing the benefit. The likely focus of the intermediate sanctions rules is unreasonable compensation—usually where an individual's level of compensation is found to be in excess of the value of the economic benefit derived by the organization from the individual's services. An economic benefit may not be treated as compensation for the performance of services unless the organization clearly indicated its intent to do so at the outset.

The concept of the excess benefit transaction includes any transaction in which the amount of any economic benefit provided to or for the use of a disqualified person is determined in whole or in part by the revenues of one or more activities of the organization, where it would otherwise be private inurement. A transaction of this nature is known as a "revenue-sharing arrangement." (This rule may have significance in the realm of percentage-based fund-raising compensation.)

[32]Ibid., 10–11.
[33]IRC § 4958. Hopkins, *Law of Tax-Exempt Organizations*, § 19.11.

A disqualified person who benefited from an excess benefit transaction is subject to an initial tax equal to 25 percent of the amount of the excess benefit. The excess benefit must be returned to the charitable organization, as part of the process of "correcting" (undoing) the transaction. An additional tax, at the rate of 200 percent, may be imposed on a disqualified person where the initial tax was imposed and a timely correction did not occur.

If a transaction creating a benefit was approved by an independent board, or an independent committee of the board, a presumption arises that the terms of the transaction are reasonable. The burden of proving excess benefit would then shift to the IRS. This rebuttable presumption may cause a restructuring of the boards of directors or trustees of some charitable organizations to achieve adequate independence.

Unrelated Business Activities

The federal tax law imposes a tax on the net income derived by a charitable organization from the conduct of unrelated business activities.[34] A fund-raising activity, such as a special event, may qualify as an unrelated business. For an activity to be taxed, it must be a "business"—that is, an activity "regularly carried on" to produce revenue from the sale of goods or services. Generally, a business undertaking must be conducted with a profit motive.

If the business activity is "substantially related" to the achievement of charitable purposes, the net income associated with it is not taxable. To meet this criteria, a "causal relationship" must exist between the conduct of the business and the fulfillment of exempt ends, and the relationship must be a substantial one.

Many exceptions exist for types of income and activities. Several of them are directly pertinent to charitable organizations and their fund-raising activities. Some special events escape treatment as taxable businesses on the grounds that they are not regularly carried on. These tend to be annual events, although if the organization spends considerable time preparing for the event, the IRS will take that time into account and conclude that the event is regularly carried on and thus taxable.

Other exceptions can shelter fund-raising operations from taxation: businesses where substantially all of the work is performed by volunteers, businesses carried on primarily for the convenience of the charitable organization's students or patients, sales of items that were donated

---

[34]IRC §§ 511–514. Hopkins, *Law of Tax-Exempt Organizations*, Part Five.

to the organization, receipt of qualified sponsorship payments, rental and exchanges of mailing lists, and the offering of low-cost premiums as inducements to charitable giving. There are still other exceptions, such as for fairs, expositions, and trade shows.

For the most part, a charitable organization's investment income is not taxed. Thus, in general, interest, dividends, rent, annuities, royalties, and capital gains are not taxed. At the present, the exception for royalty income is the most controversial, as organizations are attempting to structure cause-related marketing, affinity card programs, insurance endorsement efforts, and the like in an effort to generate income in the form of royalties.

Conclusion

Once the proper legal structure and tax-exempt status has been secured, the organization should be operated "like a business," in the sense of adherence to the organizing documents, regular meetings of the board and committees, development of personnel policies and a benefits package for the employees, and the like. Charitable organizations should follow professional management practices; like their for-profit counterparts, they should observe business procedures for daily operation, entrust decisions to employee managers, have checking and savings accounts, payrolls, accountants, and so forth.

Not-for-profit organizations differ from for-profit ones in their purposes and missions. However, simply because an organization exists to help others, advocate a cause, or encourage a particular practice does not mean that it should not be well run. Charitable and other not-for-profit organizations seek success in financial operations, along with quality services. These goals require attention to technical, legal, and sound business requirements, whether they apply to fund raising or other operational aspects.

POPULAR MYTHS ABOUT NOT-FOR-PROFIT ORGANIZATIONS

One myth about not-for-profit organizations is that they do not need "all this legal stuff" to go into business or to ask for gifts. Wrong! To do otherwise is against the law. "Scam" charities have been used as easy-money operations, victimizing a trusting public. Federal and state laws are designed to protect the public from fraud and abuse and to keep reputable charitable organizations above suspicion. Another reason to observe proper legal procedure is to maintain the tax-exempt privilege.

A second myth about charitable organizations is that they are poorly managed but that mismanagement is permissible because they are obligated to "lose money" as proof of their not-for-profit status. However, as the previous section stressed charitable organizations are expected to use professional business practices. The volunteer board members are responsible for leadership and direction that will result in professional management and successful fiscal operations. For example, not-for-profit boards require a budget plan that has a break-even-or-better financial operation as the annual goal, and they need to keep a tight rein on expenses through monthly reports that monitor revenue and expense performance. Today, many college and university professional schools offer graduate level curricula in not-for-profit management for executives and managers who may not have had previous training in this specialty or in the differences between for-profit and not-for-profit management.

A third and pervasive myth is that the executives and staff of charitable organizations do not deserve to be taken as seriously in their roles as leaders and managers as their counterparts in for-profit corporations. If they work for an organization that "loses money," their positions are probably career stopovers and their responsibilities casual and unmotivated. Organizations that endure disprove this myth by demonstrating competency through efficient institutional management.

WHY PLANNING IS IMPORTANT

Leaders of charitable organizations must define their directions each year, prepare written goals and objectives, and measure outcomes quarterly or semiannually. Such strategic planning is needed to define where to go and how to get there—a suitable exercise for both the organization and its fund development program. Moreover, the not-for-profit organization faces a recurring need to assess all its income sources, not just contributions. Equally important is the need to study the results of its efforts, including the outcomes of the programs and services it provides the public along with the operating expenses incurred to deliver them. A not-for-profit organization's leaders also should plan to deal with a number of contingencies that will affect its ability to succeed in its fund development program. A list of these contingencies is presented in Exhibit 2.1. Functional committees are needed to meet the planning and operational

EXHIBIT 2.1 Why Do Strategic Planning for Fund Raising?

- The organization is in the process of developing a full strategic plan, and it has become evident that substantially greater resources will be required to implement the plan.
- The organization desires to develop new programs or to put more money into existing programs.
- The organization has experienced the loss of a major contributor whose long-time support has undergirded the development program and, indeed, the organization's operating budget.
- The vulnerability of existing streams of income—contributed or earned—is recognized.
- The organization has a new CEO or director of development.
- New members, who have an interest in fund raising, are added to the board.
- The organization observes that competitors are beginning to receive a larger share of the philanthropic pie.
- The organization experiences changes in the demographics of its constituency or in the community's economic well-being.
- It has been four or five years since the organization has looked at where its money comes from and the methods it uses to foster giving.

Reprinted from Kimberly Hawkins with Elizabeth M. Lowell, Edith M. Pearson, and Nancy L. Raybin, "Strategic Planning for Fund Raising," in The Nonprofit Handbook: Fund Raising, *2d ed., ed. James M. Greenfield (New York: John Wiley & Sons, 1997), 13. Reprinted by permission of John Wiley and Sons, Inc.*

needs of the organization, and enough board members who have the right expertise should be elected to cover all committee assignments. Because contributions from the community will be asked for, individuals who are experienced with fund raising and are considered "movers and shakers" should be invited to serve; their names on the board roster alone will prompt contributions. Most voluntary organizations conduct their business via committee work. The board should establish policy and supervise its faithful observance, permitting the hands-on activity to take place in committees that work with professional and management staff. The key committees relating to fund raising are nominations, finance, investment, fund development, and donor relations. Fund raising should be a conscious part of the work of the board and all of the committees, not just the fund development committee. Candidates for board election should be considered for their ability to help raise money (by giving or getting funds, or both). The finance committee, which controls fiscal activity, should be kept informed about fund-raising performance. Its function is not simply to count gift income. Both the finance and the investment committees must ensure that restricted funds are properly accounted for and used only for their restricted purposes, that funds held as endowments are professionally invested, and that charitable trusts are managed with faithful payments and other required services to their donors.

The committee on fund development oversees all aspects of fund raising. Committee members are responsible for evaluating prospects' giving potential, defining realistic expectations for each method of fund raising used, approving the budget, monitoring performance (including cost-effectiveness analysis), assisting in hiring and evaluating professional fund-raising executives and consultants, and reporting progress at board meetings. Fund development committee members also need to provide personal leadership and direction to each fund-raising program, beginning with their own personal gifts. Given the importance of contributions income to fiscal well-being, the management of fund raising is an important area of responsibility at the board level.

LEADERSHIP FROM THE BOARD OF DIRECTORS

Nothing of importance in fund raising will happen until the organization's elected or appointed leaders take action. The many duties and responsibilities of board members can be summarized as follows:

- An emphasis on mission and purpose at all board and/or committee meetings and in all institutional decisions
- A commitment to passionate pragmatism throughout the life cycle of the organization
- Leadership succession planning, including enforcement of board member evaluation and limits to years of board service
- Regular evaluation of the executive director/CEO
- One hundred percent financial participation by the board in all fund-raising campaigns
- One hundred percent participation by the board in donor and fund development activities
- Early and thorough attention to budding program or people problems (board, other volunteers, or staff), which could grow and overwhelm the focus on mission
- A focus on solutions, not problems

- Respect for staff, board, and other volunteers as partners who share a mutual dedication to the organization and the mission[35]

An examination of these duties will conclude that the board's primary responsibility is the organization's financial security. Because management of fund development operations requires a high sense of duty, it should be assigned to the board, not to volunteers or staff. The board should appoint one of its members to serve as chairperson of the fund development committee. The chairperson should then select volunteers to work on the committee and should report to the board regularly. This chain of command permits the fund development committee to operate all fund-raising activities, to establish policies and procedures, to set annual goals and objectives, to review and approve job descriptions (for subcommittees as well as their chairpersons), to approve all fund-raising program plans, to set deadlines, to evaluate performance of volunteers, staff, and each individual fund-raising activity, to approve budget requests—in short, to establish an accountability that everyone involved will observe and respect.

Leadership, however, is more than being assigned to a committee. It requires being a dedicated advocate, making personal gifts and soliciting a few others, and serving as an example to others who are involved. Not everyone has the time this job requires, and some people lack the talent to lead others. For example, Arthur Frantzreb writes that "[s]eldom is a trustee who serves as a volunteer leader adequately prepared to serve in the public role as a dedicated advocate of the mission and services of the organization."[36] Leadership for fund raising demands some qualities that can be acquired, but mostly it asks for genuine commitment and enthusiasm. An ideal board member will possess many of the following abilities and attributes:

What Board Members Do	*What Board Members Are*
Make personal contribution	They are rich.
Make strategic plans	They have "clout."
Create development plans	They are generous to lots of
Add to the mailing list	causes.
Identify and evaluate	They are well liked.
prospects	They are true believers in the
Cultivate prospects	project

[35] Kay Sprinkel Grace, *Beyond Fund Raising: New Strategies for Nonprofit Innovation and Investment* (New York: Wiley, 1997), 38–40.

[36] Arthur C. Frantzreb, *Not On This Board You Don't: Making Your Trustees More Effective* (Chicago: Bonus Books, 1997), 11.

Make introductions
Write annual appeal letters
Write supporting letters
Plan special events
Make acknowledgments
Accompany on an ask.[37]

They are well organized.
They are good speakers.
They are fearless.[38]

What Their Attitude Can Be

They know it is hard work, but it is worth it.
They are passionate about the causes for which they are raising money.
They come not as beggars, but as individuals offering others rare opportunities to invest in the future of their communities.
They are the catalysts for converting citizens to donor-investors in the organizations whose values they share.
They find the process to be satisfying and gratifying.
They see it as a way of involving people known and unknown to them in organizations that are making a difference in their communities.[39]

Men and women are available with these talents, but they have to be found and then either brought into the organization as volunteers through the committee system or invited directly to the board. Professional staff can assist in many ways, but their chief purpose is to work with and help each of their leaders to succeed.

MISSION

The board of directors can find guidance for achieving readiness for operations and fund raising in the organization's mission and purpose. Further board responsibilities, including setting strategic goals and program objectives plus the annual operating budget, are also guided by the mission statement. All of these should be written down. Reasonably frequent assessments of the organization's mission, vision, and values plus its purpose, goals, and objectives should ideally be carried out every three years—and certainly no less frequently than every five years. Boards of

[37]Fisher Howe, "The Board's Role in Fund Raising," in Greenfield, *The Nonprofit Handbook: Fund Raising,* 2d ed., 230–231.
[38]Irving R. Warner, *The Art of Fund Raising* (New York: Harper & Row, 1975), 24–25.
[39]Grace, *Beyond Fund Raising,* x.

directors should revise and rewrite their mission in order to reflect environmental change, demographic shifts, marketplace priorities, and economic cycles that affect those whom the organization is dedicated to serve, or as the result of evolutionary changes, maturity, technological improvements, and even local disasters.

The external factors listed above and board members' response to them also affect fund-raising performance although board members may prefer to believe unrealized expectations were the fault of other volunteers and fund development staff rather than less-than-effective board leadership. In projecting the organization's potential for public support, board members need to be alert to external forces as well as internal factors that affect results. A not-for-profit organization is seldom "one of a kind," alone in its community with a unique mission and minimal competition for friends and funds. In order to ensure that the not-for-profit organization remains vital, the board needs to evaluate its members' own performance annually in five key areas: advocacy, financial accountability, charitable purpose, leadership development, and written policies and procedures. The board's performance in the annual budget exercise is an inadequate measure of all its duties plus its handling of the internal or external factors that have such an impact on the success of both operations and fund raising.

The Independent Sector, in its mission to aid all not-for-profit organizations to benefit the public good, has proposed a program of "measurable growth" as a national objective. To that end, it developed the following checklist to define what board members can do to monitor faithfulness to the mission (see also Exhibit 1.1 on page 8) and successful performance, as well as to define what benefits they can achieve from concentrating on measurable growth toward fulfillment of purpose, goals, and objectives. The following 10 recommendations can serve the board well as a checklist for improving both mission achievement and organization management by concentrating on fund-raising performance:

1. The board should set fund raising goals for next year and five years that are realistic, but which stretch the Board and everyone else in the organization.
2. The board must commit a significant portion of the resources of the organization, including their own time, to the pursuit of the fund-raising goals. For most organizations, it will take a minimum of 20 percent of the organization's time and money to develop significant fund raising. This is fully justified if, in the long run, the organization will be able to do more in the fulfillment of its program mission.
3. Similar goals and commitments should be made to increase volunteer participation.

4. The board should devote a portion of almost every meeting and at least one full meeting to evaluating progress toward the goals. It should resolve to make these goals central to everything the organization does.
5. Make fund raising and the effective utilization of volunteers every bit as important and prestigious as the most important program activities of the organization.
6. Encourage the board and staff to participate in training efforts to improve fund raising skills and effectiveness in recruiting and involving volunteers. Where necessary, help create such training opportunities by working with experienced and successful volunteer and staff leaders from other organizations.
7. The organization's communications to current volunteers, members, contributors and others should emphasize the message of "fiving" and the importance of all people being engaged in active citizenship and personal community service. Pay first attention to those who are already involved. They offer the greatest potential for increased participation.
8. Help to develop a local coalition of churches, other volunteer organizations, funders, media and others to build interest and awareness of "fiving" and a spirit of contributing back to the community through support of the causes of one's choice.
9. Honor the strong contributors and volunteers. Make it clear that the organization is aware and appreciative of how special they are.
10. Elevate the good volunteers and fund raisers to the board. Make it clear that their performance is what the organization respects.[40]

THE INSTITUTIONAL MASTER PLAN

Before the organization's leaders can spend much time on long-range planning, the annual operations must be made to work reliably, within the current operating budget. Most organizations annually repeat this struggle to survive—a fine objective, because survival is the primary priority. But growth to maturity requires lifting one's head up now and then for a look ahead. A view of the horizon suggests a need to plan for the future. This plan or "vision" of the board and chief executive officer tells a great deal about their commitment to achieve exciting and worthwhile goals that address community needs and deliver measurable benefits back to their community. The vision also can be described to the public to develop their enthusiasm and inspire them to be instrumental in bringing the vision to life.

[40]Independent Sector, *Daring Goals for a Caring Society: A Blueprint for Substantial Growth in Giving and Volunteering in America* (Washington, DC: Independent Sector, 1986), 11–12.

A long-range plan must begin with the vision of top leadership, whose duties include providing credible answers to donors who ask, "What's the money for?" This master plan should be written down and circulated appropriately. It should include

- Details about current programs plus any new services to be offered that will improve the quality and breadth of present activities to benefit others
- A financial plan, calculating the finite fiscal resources required to pay for the programs and services that will meet future public needs
- A description of capital and equipment needed to provide the facilities that will allow planned programs and services to be carried out

Long-range planning also requires an honest commitment from top management and needs professional guidance.

Programs and Services: The Vision

> The future environment of nonprofit organizations almost certainly will feature less governmental support, greater reliance on earned income and other private sources, and a more demanding public. These constituents will insist that nonprofits manage their scarce resources with increasing effectiveness. In this context, research on the critical issues of resource management can make an exceedingly important contribution to the health and productivity of nonprofit organizations and their constituents in the decades ahead.[41]
>
> DENNIS R. YOUNG

The complex forces of today's changing world pressure not-for-profit organizations to be flexible, more cognizant of and responsive to evolving human needs, and ever eager to act upon new challenges to better serve their communities. Managing change while preserving financial stability is a major challenge. Government funding priorities continue to change, reducing support in traditional areas such as human services, education, health care, and the arts, adding stress to fiscal planning and resource development. Alternative revenue sources must be explored including for-profit enterprises, joint ventures, collaborative grant seeking, and increased fund-raising productivity. Traditional stewardship issues of profit, debt, equity balances, and investment performance are increasing in complexity today and require new levels of expertise from board mem-

---

[41] Dennis R. Young, "The Management of Nonprofit Organization Resources," in *Critical Issues in Fund Raising*, ed. Dwight F. Burlingame (New York: Wiley, 1997), 31–32.

bers. A "global society" will follow on the heels of already instant global communications. Many U.S. not-for-profit organizations are becoming alert to the worldwide applications of their expertise as well as their attractiveness to foreign clients, customers, patients, and causes.

Given the factors listed above, what is the not-for-profit organization's vision for the future? What confluence of external factors will it follow? What values will it observe when revising and creating programs and services to meet changing needs? Answers will be found by paying attention to the world outside the organization's walls, and by not relying completely on those inside who lead and serve it daily.

Charitable organizations define their current position in the marketplace by the reach of their services, the types of services offered, geography, fiscal resources, and other factors. Marketplace conditions change quickly because they reflect variations in economics, demographics, environment, and government policy. The marketplace should be measured often (every other year), to estimate the demand for services that meet public needs and to know the competition. The data gathered will affect current services, staffing levels, income and expense estimates, and other operating details driven by market conditions.

Market research is valuable in placing an organization on the proper grade level in the "School of What's Happening Now." Who are the people served? Where do they come from? What motivates them to seek the services? Why do they come to one organization and not to another offering similar services? What services do they seek that are not offered now but might be added? What is the present level of quality of services and how can they be improved? To forecast a future "menu" of community needs for service, each organization must conduct market research and make plans based on accurate interpretations of present conditions and reasonable estimates of future public needs.

Growth can be managed only to the extent that changing conditions can be anticipated. Crisis decisions cannot be managed. No one can adequately anticipate a crisis—certainly not early enough to permit the fund-raising program to satisfy all of the emergency's needs and mobilize philanthropic sources that will cover any further unforeseen events. The exception is the American Red Cross that is already prepared with its appeal for funds to air on radio and on television within 24 hours after any disaster; that is the organization's crisis fund-raising plan. Other organizations also may be well prepared with disaster plans to add their services when needed, but are not prepared to ask for contributions. Their future disaster plans also should include appeals for funds. Fund development must have lead time, before the actual need for cash, to develop the necessary levels of public understanding, participation, and support, which are linked to how the money will be used. The great benefit from planning is that contributions are more likely to be delivered when needed.

Growth and change can be anticipated in a long-range plan. With advance warning, fund raising can mount its solicitation programs early, match new funds with expanding needs, and deliver the money on schedule. A management dictum of "no surprises" can help fund raising because a plan to expand operations and anticipate change offers to annual donors the best evidence that their regular gifts are making improvements possible.[42] The best plan for the future is to set aside some funds raised this year as a reserve for next year's expenses. However, current programs and services can consume every dollar raised, on the day it arrives.

Financial Plans and Reality Tests

Financial planning is just as essential as program planning, but must follow program decisions. What is financial planning? Essentially, it is a study of revenue sources and of changing patterns to determine whether adequate income will be available to meet predicted operating expenses. Prices can be expected to increase; even a limited expansion will probably nearly double expenses but never seems to double revenues. The public expects charitable organizations to improve their management skills, especially regarding fiscal affairs. "Profit" is neither illegal nor a bad word to use, even when disguised in not-for-profit accounting jargon as "excess of revenue over expenses." Profits are a sign of success, and success helps to build donors' confidence that the best use is being made of their gift dollars.

Good management of assets includes adding to those assets new forms of gifts (real estate, charitable trusts and annuities, in-kind gifts, etc.) that can be converted into cash or set aside as endowment. Receipt of these types of gifts helps build equity and permits greater financial flexibility to meet future operating needs, but the decision to set aside these funds has to compete with the demand for cash for current operating programs. Some balance between fund-raising time and budget allotted to current expenses and that allotted to future expenditures is needed, otherwise future assets are not likely to be developed at all. Short-term think-

---

[42] These exact needs constitute the best list of annual giving projects "for sale" because they clearly reflect growth in programs and services that justifies asking for increased annual contributions support.

ing (survival again) is a natural by-product of concentrating on annual operations but will be less in conflict with long-range planning if asset development has been established as a goal.

Alternative sources of revenue should be studied. Good management of the annual budget may produce a slight "profit" (2 or 3 percent of budget), which can be used to fund depreciation or (more likely) new services, renovations, equipment replacement, and the like. Where else can new funds be developed? Investment earnings will help but first there must be an endowment with funds to invest; and before that, there must be requests for bequests and gifts restricted to endowment. Not-for-profit organizations may engage in a limited amount of for-profit enterprise, and any net revenues can be used for any purpose within the mission. However, entrepreneurship is difficult to manage with much success, is limited to less than 15 percent of the operating budget, and is vulnerable to a government decision to tax the realized income as unrelated business income. What other sources of new revenue are available? Philanthropy, cash from charitable contributions, and loans. To borrow money is a last resort; borrowing may be valid for major capital and equipment needs but is most unwise for annual operating purposes. Given these limitations, fund raising for new endowment and cash represents *50 percent* of the options to increase revenues. The gift dollar is a highly leveraged dollar indeed; it becomes all the more valuable when compared to what it takes to realize that same dollar as a net of the operating budget.

Facilities Planning for Capital Needs

Facilities planning is a must for every charitable organization. Good maintenance and repair of existing buildings and equipment are annual expenses and can be designated as annual gift opportunities for donors. Not-for-profit accounting rules permit depreciation of buildings and equipment over time, to encourage building up replacement funds, but not every organization can or will fund its depreciation allowance because of the constant pressure for cash for current programs and services. Older institutions face a choice between renovation of existing facilities or new construction; the cost today is about the same for either option. Tax-exempt bond sales or other borrowing methods can be considered for construction, renovation, and equipment projects, but lenders and investors make decisions based on sound current finances and the absence of budget deficits in prior fiscal years—and they expect to be paid back on time. Favorable interest rates for such not-for-profit loans have allowed access to capital but their debt service is added pressure to the already burdened operating budget and is not a good goal for fund raising.

Long-range plans for programs and services, finance, and capital needs are, therefore, ingredients of the complete master plan for each charitable organization. When such documentation is in place, fund raising can begin with a better expectation for success.

The Case for Giving

Henry Rosso describes the language of fund raising as "the gentle art of persuasion."[43] Experienced fund-raising practitioners, either volunteer or staff, realize that money is not given; it has to be raised. Harold Seymour's declaration that "fund raising or development is the planned promotion of understanding, participation and support" speaks to the three tenets of fund development and their right order of application.[44] Kathleen Kelly has added, "Fund raising is the management of relationships between a charitable organization and its donor publics,"[45] incorporating Rosso's and Seymour's definitions into a purpose statement. Newcomers to the field should appreciate that asking for money is secondary to what may be best described as "friend raising" and "relationship building" between people in the community and the causes and organizations they care about. Indeed, caring is a big factor in most gift decisions and requires that donors have more than casual knowledge and appreciation of the cause each contribution is intended to address. What each decision comes down to most often are the facts of the story itself. Why does this organization exist? Whom does it serve? Are these services necessary, perhaps urgently needed, in this community? How are they valued by the recipients? Is this organization delivering its programs effectively (with quality) as well as efficiently (by staff at reasonable expense)? Each is a tough question; each needs an unequivocal answer before even the first words asking for support of the enterprise are spoken or written.

The case for giving, or case statement, is both an intellectual conviction and an actual document based on the ingredients of the institutional

---

[43]Rosso, *Rosso on Fund Raising*, 134.

[44]Harold J. Seymour, *Designs for Fund Raising* (New York: McGraw-Hill, 1966), 115.

[45]Kathleen S. Kelly, *Effective Fund-Raising Management* (Mahwah, NJ: Lawrence Erlbaum Associates, 1998), 8.

master plan. It must contain the essential facts about the organization, the community needs it serves, its vision and values, and how charitable contributions make a difference to those served as well as benefit the prospective donor (see Exhibit 2.2). The case for giving, when written, might contain all or nearly all of the following elements:

1. The problem (or opportunity) to be addressed
2. Trends affecting the problem (or opportunity)
3. Your response to the problem (or opportunity)
4. Role of the prospective donor
5. Your mission
6. Your history, track record, and marketplace position
7. Goals, strategies, and objectives
8. Organizational resources
9. Accountability and evaluation
10. Future organization plans.[46]

EXHIBIT 2.2 Questions to Be Addressed in Creating a Case Statement

- What is the purpose of the organization?
- When was the organization founded?
- What is the structure of the organization? Is it composed of volunteers only, or does it have professional staff?
- What are the key needs that must be met in the community served by the organization?
- What does the organization plan to do to meet these needs?
- How will it accomplish these tasks? Who will carry them out?
- Why is this organization best qualified to undertake these services?
- How do you define success for the program? What criteria will you use to evaluate success?
- How will success enable the organization to continue or to grow?
- What is the funding need for the program? How will the organization meet ongoing funding needs once these dollars have been raised?
- What is expected of donors? How can the donors give?

From John Hicks, "Grass-Roots Fund Raising," in The Nonprofit Handbook: Fund Raising, *2d ed., ed. James M. Greenfield (New York: John Wiley & Sons, Inc., 1997), 563. Reprinted with permission of John Wiley & Sons, Inc.*

---

[46]Simone P. Joyaux, *Strategic Fund Development: Building Profitable Relationships That Last,* ed. James P. Gelatt (Gaithersburg, MD: Aspen, 1997), 201–202.

The Role of Philanthropy

Philanthropic dollars are a revenue source that can be molded to meet the needs listed in the master plan. The cost of the total list will most likely far exceed the projected income from present fund-raising efforts. Even Harvard University, with its billions in endowment, must raise $200 million each year to maintain its programs at the standards of quality that have been set. If philanthropy is to be maximally successful for an organization, a selection process or priority ranking of the total needs list is necessary. The timetable for completion of events in the master plan should be reviewed and shared with potential donors. If they can give where the need is greatest, donors enjoy the reassurance that their gift made a difference and helped the organization toward realizing its planning objectives. Expressing the master plan's priorities in annual terms alerts everyone to the sequence in which projects will be undertaken and identifies the next set of annual gift priorities. Larger capital needs, with their multiyear construction schedules, are better suited to highly selective, major gift solicitations and capital campaigns. New program areas that will take two or more years to implement are appealing to corporations and foundations that award grant support. Endowment building takes time and patience and is well matched to the fund-raising methods of planned giving and estate planning solicitation efforts. The relationship between defined needs and the role of philanthropy provides clear answers to "What's the money for?"

Measuring Fund Development

Because philanthropy requires vigorous volunteer participation and public solicitation, its results should be assigned where they can best serve the current and future needs of the organization. Each fund-raising method's plan for growth should define its own capacity to provide numbers of donors and increased income each year. Progress should be monitored through regular evaluations of performance. For example, a quick review of percentage rate of return and average gift size will signal any change in public acceptance of the appeal message. Annual giving programs, layered in sophistication from direct mail and support groups to benefit events, annual solicitation committees, and donor clubs, are well suited to the promotion of constant levels of annual giving. These programs are reliable producers, but they cannot grow rapidly or develop large amounts of new income because they are recruiting new donors and renewing prior donors in the bottom tier of the pyramid of giving, which is not where large contributions come from.

Market Research as Measurement Tool

Market research surveys are quite valuable to planning the fund development program. They help define audiences of potential volunteers and likely new contributors by estimating their responses and projecting their potential for dollars given in response to selected priority projects. These professional surveys also can sense the public's moods, inquire into their perceptions of the organization's value, tabulate their impressions of current and projected programs and services, capture their thoughts about the organization's leaders, tally their acceptance of current fund-raising methods, and much more. The use of market research surveys to aid the design of fund-raising plans can provide more reliable forecasts of future gift results than simple analysis of prior giving performance alone.

Marketing the Not-for-Profit Organization

Translating survey data into a coherent strategy of marketing, communications, and fund development objectives is the next step. Each of these areas supports the others; each depends upon the others' results to realize its own goals and objectives. The organization can evaluate this essential linkage using Exhibit 2.3 to determine where it stands in each of these three target areas.

Marketing, by itself, is mutually beneficial to both the organization and the public; it is the strategic application of knowledge about customer needs merged with organizational capability to deliver "the voluntary and purposeful process of developing, facilitating, and executing exchanges to satisfy human wants and desires."[47] Building relationships with a variety of public constituents, sometimes over great distances, is not easy. Each party may have different, even opposing, motives for participation that guide the level and extent of its response. Marketing is an essential function of modern organizations, as Philip Kotler and Alan Andreasen explain:

> Marketing is not a peripheral activity of modern organizations but one that grows out of the essential quest of modern organizations to effectively serve some area of human need. To survive and succeed, organizations must know

[47]Michael P. Mokwa, William M. Dawson, E. A. Prieve, and Steven E. Permut eds. *Marketing the Arts* (New York: Praeger, 1980), 15.

EXHIBIT 2.3 Analysis of Coordination of Marketing, Communications, and Fund Development Goals and Objectives

	Score				
	Low				High
Marketing Objectives					
Identify target markets	1	2	3	4	5
Establish an image	1	2	3	4	5
Create clients for programs	1	2	3	4	5
Elicit a positive response	1	2	3	4	5
Stimulate the public to act	1	2	3	4	5
Communications Objectives					
Inform and educate	1	2	3	4	5
Tell a story; repeat it often	1	2	3	4	5
Report results, deeds, outcomes	1	2	3	4	5
Build confidence and trust	1	2	3	4	5
Build community consensus	1	2	3	4	5
Fund Development Objectives					
Friend raising and relationship building	1	2	3	4	5
Develop a willingness to volunteer	1	2	3	4	5
Develop a willingness to give	1	2	3	4	5
Develop gifts to meet priority needs	1	2	3	4	5
Provide continuous contact with donors	1	2	3	4	5

their markets; attract sufficient resources; convert these resources into appropriate products, services, and ideas; and effectively distribute them to various consuming publics. These tasks are carried out on a framework of voluntary action by all the parties.[48]

As an example of the value of market research and its applications in strategic marketing activities, consider the following list of marketing goals (this list can be thought of as a marketing plan in itself):

1. *Definition of the constituent groups (sometimes called "stakeholder groups") that will be served.* If there is agreement on the organization's mission through an analysis of constituent perceptions and feelings, the effect can be a powerful catalyst for the organization to achieve its goals.

[48] Philip Kotler and Alan R. Andreasen, *Strategic Marketing for Nonprofit Organizations,* 3d ed. (Englewood Cliffs, NJ: Prentice Hall, 1987), 36.

2. *Identification of the needs of the constituents and the community that will be satisfied by the not-for-profit organization.* The organization must know what criteria individual and multiple stakeholders are using to judge the success of its performance.

3. *The ultimate strategy by which the needs of the constituency will be satisfied.* The strategies and philosophies used by the not-for-profit must be in keeping with its core set of values; otherwise, there is little chance of achieving stakeholder satisfaction.[49]

An organization will need to use communications strategies to help meet its marketing objectives. Communications strategies traditionally are public relations activities to manage public information and publications. A more inclusive term than public relations is *corporate communications*. This type of communications begins with good writing techniques, builds upon expertise in advertising and media relations management, designs and tracks public responsiveness, coordinates "high-tech" multimedia campaigns with production and distribution of collateral materials, and manages data from marketplace and customer surveys into an organizational message designed for its effect on each audience. Kathleen Kelly explains how an organization can use a communications strategy called "symmetrical public relations" to build the best possible relationships with the publics it serves:

[O]rganizations succeed and survive in environments made up of publics that affect or are affected by the organizations' behavior. Public relations helps manage these interdependencies by controlling strategic publics through persuasion or manipulation (asymmetrical public relations) or by adaptation through collaborative negotiation and strategies of conflict resolution (symmetrical public relations). Symmetrical public relations, which J. E. Grunig (1992) argued is synonymous with excellence, contributes to organizational effectiveness by using research to not only manage communications with strategic publics, but also to counsel senior management on adjusting the organization's behavior when it is in disharmony with the needs and interests of those publics. Its functional purpose is to establish two-way dialogue with publics from which mutual understanding will emerge.[50]

Given this much awareness, image building, and advance information, the challenge for fund development is neither to identify and inform

[49] Barry J. McLeish, "Marketing Strategies in Development," in Greenfield, *The Nonprofit Handbook: Fund Raising,* 2d ed., 34.

[50] Kathleen S. Kelly, *Effective Fund-Raising Management,* 10. See also J. E. Grunig, ed., *Excellence in Public Relations and Communication Management: Contributions to Effective Organizations* (Hillsdale, NJ: Lawrence Erlbaum Associates, 1992).

prospects nor to build their confidence. The challenge is to demonstrate through clear messages, consistent with the story already told to already known target audiences, the "call to action" based on the value of public participation in a charitable cause or project. And, building upon the public's trust, to openly disclose operating details along with the mission, purpose, goals, and objectives in an invitation to them to share their time, talent, and treasure with confidence that these resources will be well used for community benefit.

Demographics and Diversity

Author, fund raiser, and teacher Dr. Judith Nichols helps us understand that one of the forces driving constant change in our society is diversity.[51] We are all not the same in how we think and act (thank goodness!) and our diversity is increasing. This becomes especially clear when one studies the generations that make up the U.S. population. Dr. Nichols segregates the population into five age groups and identifies their distinct personalities for the purposes of fund-raising messages (see Exhibit 2.4).

We are also a culturally and ethnically diverse society. The United States has been the melting pot of Western civilization for most of its history and is still the destination of choice for many immigrants. The balance among cultural and ethnic groups continues to change. Hispanic Americans will become the largest minority group in the United States by 2020, representing up to 30 percent of the U.S. population (an estimated 90 million people). The Asian American population is increasing less rapidly but is distinct in its geographic location, mostly along the West Coast, and is the most highly educated of all ethnic groups. The population of black Americans is growing nearly three times faster than the white population. Black Americans are generous with their contributions, which are, as a percentage of income, greater than those of non-Hispanic whites. White males, who today occupy many seats of power and influence, will be a shrinking minority in the year 2020. Communications with these diverse groups is necessary for not-for-profit organizations to cultivate the time, talent, and treasure of each, according to its generational attributes and

---

[51]Judith Nichols's books, all available through Bonus Books, include *Changing Demographics: Fund Raising in the 1990s* (1990); *Targeted Fund Raising: Defining and Refining Your Development Strategy for the 1990s* (1991); *Pinpointing Affluence: Increasing Your Share of Major Donor Dollars* (1994); *Growing from Good to Great: Positing Your Fund Raising for BIG Gains* (1995); *Global Demographics: Fund Raising for a New World* (1996), and *Strengthening Fund Raising through Evaluation* (1998).

EXHIBIT 2.4 Generation Gaps in Values

Depression Babies   The Civics
(Born prior to 1935)
                          "We fought for it."
                Money personality: "Save, save, save"

World War II Babies   The Silents
(Born 1935–1945)
                          "We earned it."
           Money personality: "Save a little, spend a little."

Baby Boomers   The Idealists
(Born 1946–1964)
                          "We've owed it."
          Money personality: "First spend, then save for it."

Baby Busters   The Reactives
(Born 1964–1977)
              "We deserve it, but probably won't get it."
              Money personality: "It's hopeless."

Boomlet   The Civics
(Born 1978–1994)
                   "We'll be taken care of."

---

*Reprinted with permission from "Demographics: Our Changing World and How It
Affects Raising Money" by Judith E. Nichols, in* The Nonprofit Handbook: Fund
Raising, *2d ed., ed. James M. Greenfield (New York: John Wiley & Sons, Inc., 1997),
153.*

perceptions. By neglecting diversity in its communications strategy, an organization runs the risk of offending much of its constituency.

THE FUND-RAISING ENVIRONMENTAL AUDIT

The internal and external operating environments of a not-for-profit organization exert significant influences on its success in fund raising. Internal
factors (such as board background and attitude) are easily recognized but

hard to change. External factors—what the public thinks and believes about the organization—are more likely to affect results because they do change. An audit of these two broad areas that looks at 30 distinct elements adds a dose of reality to readiness preparations and defines what is reasonable and what is possible (see Exhibit 2.5 for a sample audit scoring form). The combined score of both types of factors provides a qualitative and quantitative assessment to aid the organization in evaluating how ready it is to invite the public to participate in its mission, vision, and values. Understanding the internal and external factors that affect fund-raising success also increases the organization's awareness of its potential for improvements that will increase results.

Each environmental factor has value and exerts an influence. In general, external environmental factors influence fund-raising performance, whereas internal factors affect fund-raising success. A study of the entire environmental spectrum reveals that not-for-profit organizations are *not* the same in how they perform fund raising, nor does fund raising perform the same for *every* organization. Comparative analysis between not-for-profit organizations is especially difficult and more often than not is neither an equitable nor impartial contrast. No two charities of the same kind with the same history in the same community are likely to invite the same people to give to the same project at the same time using the same volunteers and solicitation methods. Therefore, each organization must assess its own results and potential by studying its own strengths, weaknesses, opportunities, and threats (known as a SWOT analysis). It should establish its own set of standards of performance by measuring its results, program by program, method by method, and using three or more years of experience data to establish reliable patterns of giving and volunteering. Such a comprehensive audit will yield an improved grasp of true philanthropic potential.

Group A: External Environmental Factors

Clear Mission, Purposes, Goals, and Objectives

An exceptional example of a clear statement of mission, purpose, goals, and objectives is found in the nine-word statement of Mothers Against Drunk Driving: "To prevent drunk driving and care for its victims." Many not-for-profit organizations retain the mission written at the time of their founding unchanged; however, these words are not inscribed in stone and can be modified as necessary as long as the organization retains its "charitable purpose." The text of many statements consists of long, cumbersome paragraphs attempting to cover a whole waterfront of

EXHIBIT 2.5 Environmental Audit of Fund-Raising Potential

	Score				
	Low				High
Group A: External Environmental Factors					
Clear mission, purposes, goals, and objectives	1	2	3	4	5
Vision and values	1	2	3	4	5
Competition, image, and market position	1	2	3	4	5
Public confidence in programs and services	1	2	3	4	5
Board leadership and competency	1	2	3	4	5
Management leadership and competency	1	2	3	4	5
Fiscal management and profitability	1	2	3	4	5
Overall economic conditions	1	2	3	4	5
Overall political and government conditions	1	2	3	4	5
Geographic location (urban or rural)	1	2	3	4	5
Accepted style of local fund-raising practice	1	2	3	4	5
Media attention to fund-raising scandals	1	2	3	4	5
Median Scores Subtotal:					
Group B: Internal Environmental Factors					
Type of not-for-profit organization	1	2	3	4	5
Written long-range and strategic plan	1	2	3	4	5
Board leadership, background, and attitude	1	2	3	4	5
Ethics and professionalism	1	2	3	4	5
Employee wages and benefits	1	2	3	4	5
Status of debt financing	1	2	3	4	5
Pressure for cash	1	2	3	4	5
Commitment to develop an endowment	1	2	3	4	5
Volume and variety of fund-raising practices	1	2	3	4	5
Leadership development program	1	2	3	4	5
Volunteer recruitment and training	1	2	3	4	5
Availability of new prospects	1	2	3	4	5
Existing donors for renewal and upgrading	1	2	3	4	5
Access to wealth	1	2	3	4	5
Focus on major gift cultivation and solicitation	1	2	3	4	5
Professional staff and fund-raising counsel	1	2	3	4	5
Appropriate space, budget, and systems	1	2	3	4	5
Donor recognition program	1	2	3	4	5
Median Scores Subtotal:					
Group A & B Median Scores Total:					

Reprinted with permission from James M. Greenfield, "Fund-Raising Management,"
in The Nonprofit Handbook: Management, *2d ed., by Tracy Daniel Connors (New*
York: John Wiley & Sons, Inc., 1997), 498.

causes and needs to be sure to appeal to every source of money. Simple and precise language with noble aims that deliver benefit to the community will carry the day every time. Mission, vision, and values come first and statements of purpose that define specific goals and objectives are next. The mission statement must provide great answers to two of the most critical questions for fund raisers: "Why do we exist?" and "What's the money for?" Without truly great answers, the public's willingness to give generously will not be motivated.

Vision and Values

A vision is a conceptualization of what an organization desires to become. Neither fantasy nor science fiction, a vision is a statement of dreams and aspirations based on the mission. A vision statement encapsulates what the organization's leaders care about, how they feel, what they perceive is possible. And, most important, a shared vision is a means to build consensus, to generate enthusiasm that will attract others to join the cause and the excitement, and to share in the efforts required to achieve something of value.

An organization's values are statements that signal its inner culture, its beliefs. They are guideposts for the organization's behavior toward everyone it contacts, serves, and employs. Everyone associated with the organization should be informed that these are the values it will adhere to in its daily operations; everyone involved should also be invited to make them part of his or her life as well. Sharing the vision and values is part of the fund-raising story, adding strong answers to the two questions posed earlier about mission and purpose: why do we exist? and what's the money for?

Competition, Image, and Market Position

No matter who or where you are, whether your organization is new or old, large or small, for profit or not, it is in competition with other organizations for everything. Not-for-profit organizations compete for clients, patients, students, board members and other volunteers, donors, and money. Image and reputation are crucial to the public's response, which depends on much more than whether they "like" the organization or "like" its visible leaders and employees. Quality sells because it is a real phenomenon based on each constituent's direct experience, not because it is the result of marketing strategies, advertisements, or other clever message mediums.

Public Confidence in Programs and Services

If an organization is not good at delivering its programs, is not effective at providing its services, and is not efficient in using its funds raised, it does not deserve public support. It's a rare organization that can survive if the public loses confidence in the quality of programs and services it delivers daily for community benefit. How does the organization stand today in the eyes and minds of community residents? Market research studies provide the truthful answers, both positive and negative.

Board Leadership and Competency

The public is watching all the time. It entrusts "its" charitable organizations to a few of its own whose duty it is to lead as well as fulfill the mission to deliver programs and services back to the community. Board members have serious duties and responsibilities—honest obligations that require attention and effort. If a board member cannot perform them, he or she should step aside in favor of someone who can. The public has the right to expect quality leadership just as it expects quality programs and services.

Management Leadership and Competency

The board is responsible for hiring and firing the administrator, executive director, or CEO. Top management and professional staff are highly visible in the community. They represent their organization and personify its vision and values every day. They are expected to be community leaders and examples to others, and they are called to a higher standard of behavior and performance than other executives because they work in a charitable enterprise that requires public confidence and trust in their behavior as well as their performance to succeed.

Fiscal Management and Profitability

The board of directors and management are expected to operate a successful organization, to demonstrate efficient and effective use of organization resources, to be faithful to the public's trust that its funds are used for charitable purposes only, and to run a successful business using standard business practices including competent management of the annual operating budget without deficit spending. A "profit" is allowed, encouraged, and perfectly legal so long as any excess of revenue over expenses is used exclusively for charitable purposes and not for anyone's personal inurement. Profits are a sign of success but they do not eliminate the need for contributions.

Overall Economic Conditions

In today's world, it is not uncommon for entire nations to experience dramatic economic upheavals and for the global markets to change overnight. Not-for-profit organizations, being good stewards of their funds, should invest in a variety of monetary markets using conservative, "risk-averse" policies. Even then they will experience the ups and downs of the world economy. Posting investment returns is a good idea; they are of high interest to donors, especially those who may be asked to entrust their personal assets to this same organization. In an economic downturn, fund-raising performance may suffer because of donor concerns about the economy and constraints on their assets and available income.

Overall Political and Government Conditions

Elections usually are followed by revisions in public policy and adjustments in budgetary priorities. It is never safe to assume that the generosity of government is permanent; it is better to anticipate funding cuts. The 1980s and 1990s were witness to many cutbacks, including the elimination of selected government-sponsored support for the arts, education, and health, social, welfare, and other public policy programs. Alternative revenue sources available to each not-for-profit organization must be identified, budgeted, cultivated, and invested in prior to political change so as not to become too dependent on any single source at any time.

Geographic Location (Urban or Rural)

Demographic studies have shown that population concentrations and diversity—including sheer numbers—affect any fund-raising activity. For example, most community hospitals offer all the basic services, but rural hospitals are less likely to be able to afford the latest state-of-the-art medical technology because of their small population served and limited access to sources of contributions compared with their counterparts in large metropolitan centers. There also may be a limit to how many charities a local community can support, but this theory has yet to be demonstrated.

Accepted Style of Local Fund-Raising Practice

The rich social and business fabric of America includes diversity in culture, tradition, and "how things are done." The local "style" affects how well certain types of fund raising perform, usually because both volunteers and donors are familiar with established and acceptable practices; they know what reply can be expected from the donor. Hollywood's glitzy parties would not perform as well in conservative New England, nor would New England's soup-and-sandwich luncheons fit the Los Angeles "power-lunch" lifestyle. Fund-raising professionals must be flexible enough in their planning to adapt proven methods and techniques to local situations and local styles.

Media Attention to Fund-Raising Activities

The organization also must take time to build its relationship with the media. It is often difficult to get the local media to pay attention to "good news" stories because they are not as juicy as scandals, scams, fraud, and abuse. A story about an illicit fund-raising practice or unlawful use of funds raised usually receives front-page treatment. Donors and volunteers are rightly concerned, especially if the story is about their favorite charity. The 1990s experienced a few but highly visible media events labeled as fund-raising abuses (e.g., William Aramony's compensation and use of United Way of America funds, the Ponzi scheme perpetrated in William Bennett's New Fund for Philanthropy, and Watson & Huey's direct ownership and abuse of donor lists in the United Cancer Council case). These were, more accurately, stories about unlawful or unwise use of funds raised, not improper public solicitation activities. When the story breaks, such details seldom stand in the way of headlines.

Group B: Internal Environmental Factors

Type of Not-for-Profit Organization

Annual contribution data for several classes of not-for-profit organizations have been published by the American Association of Fund Raising Counsel for more than 35 years in its annual report, *Giving USA*. Every year the champion recipient of gifts is the same, *religion*, which receives 44 to 48 percent of all funds raised. At the next level of support, receiving 8 to 12 percent of all gifts each, are *education, health,* and *human services*. The *arts* and *culture* receive from 6 to 8 percent annually, and *public* and *civic benefit* causes receive 2 to 5 percent. Together, the total value of gifts made was $150 billion in 1998.[52] Based only on these data, an arts organization, for example, when setting its contributions goals, should appreciate that competition exists as well as does a potential limit to the amount of community support it may expect, compared with churches, colleges, hospitals, or the local United Way. Unrealistic and unrealized expectations will

---

[52]American Association of Fund Raising Counsel, *Giving USA* (New York: AAFRC Trust for Philanthropy, 1997), 16–19.

weaken volunteers' and the public's confidence in fund raising as a viable source of revenue and can cripple a fund-raising program.

Written Long-Range and Strategic Plan

The absence of a written plan for the future means that possible supporters can investigate only a single criterion: the organization's annual budget performance. More important, without a long-range plan, there is no evidence the organization has any "vision" for the future and no fiscal assurance that it has the ability to continue to provide even present-day programs and services beyond one year. This absence of plans for the future will inhibit a donors' decision to make any sizable investment or commitment, whether of "time, talent, or treasure," and thus prevents any significant progress in fund development.

Board Leadership, Background, and Attitude

Giving USA reports that individuals make 88 to 90 percent of all gifts to charity each year, whereas foundations and corporations together give between 10 and 12 percent. But most board members come from a for-profit business background and may believe that most gifts come from foundations and corporations. Their value to fund raising will lie in their using their prestige and contacts to influence *individuals* who can give or can get important gifts. Board members also may arrive with preconceived attitudes about how to manage a not-for-profit organization, derived from their for-profit training and experience. Organizations that provide their board members with well-prepared orientation and training activities (including training in their role in fund raising) will likely retain them and, with their help, grow and prosper. No fund-raising program ever achieved success without effective leadership from the board. To be effective, board members first have to provide the necessary staff and budget as well as accept the personal responsibility to assist. When board leadership is lacking, good donors and volunteers become discouraged about any future service.

Ethics and Professionalism

Not-for-profit organizations and individuals associated with them are asked to observe a very high standard of institutional conduct and personal behavior. Acceptance and observance of the Donor Bill of Rights (see Exhibit 1.2, page 16) as a board-approved policy is first recommended, followed by fund-raising staff's adherence to the Standards of Professional Practice and Code of Ethical Behavior of the National Society of Fund Raising Executives or similar code of conduct. There is no substitute for absolutely unimpeachable behavior regarding observance of the law; equally resolute should be everyone's conduct when soliciting the public and using its money to provide quality services.

Employee Wages and Benefits

Salaries and benefits at not-for-profit organizations often lag behind those of private business, but, to their credit, many not-for-profit employees bring to their job a sense of commitment to the cause and an honest concern for their clients. However, positive working conditions and benefits are needed to attract and retain competent managers, professional and technical staff, and trained employees at all levels. Fair wages, comprehensive benefits, and safe working conditions are required, and although their offerings will not match for-profit business packages, not-for-profit organizations can and should be fair and equitable.

Status of Debt Financing

Government regulations permit not-for-profit organizations access to tax-exempt bond financing, usually for capital needs. Often possessing limited capital assets of their own, organizations can meet urgent community needs through borrowing. However, the debt service becomes a burden to the operating budget, already strapped to provide basic programs and services, and can dissuade donors from making gifts. More important to donors is limited debt as an example of astute fiscal management. Donors prefer to invest in successful, fiscally healthy, and well-managed not-for-profit organizations.

Pressure for Cash

One of the most difficult areas of fund-raising practice is to meet the need for cash on schedule. Not-for-profit organizations can spend every dime raised, today, but gifts do not occur on this schedule and not all are cash. The pressure for cash to meet payroll and to pay contractors, vendors, or suppliers can be so great as to divert fund-raising efforts from deliberate friend-raising and relationship-building activities to "hustling for dollars." The organization finds itself relying on high-cost methods of solicitation (e.g., acquisition mailings, telemarketing, benefit events, and pressured requests to board members and current donors) because there is no time for the cultivation and solicitation necessary to procure major gifts from individuals, corporations and foundations. Organizations that operate "hand-to-mouth" are too dependent on immediate results from abbreviated fund-raising efforts, forever hobbling their fund development program and preventing it from fulfilling its potential for true success.

Commitment to Develop an Endowment

Another by-product of the pressure for cash is absence of the ability (and the resolve) to set aside a reserve, fund depreciation, or develop an endowment to meet future needs. One example of an endowment-building practice is a board policy directing that each unrestricted bequest be kept as unrestricted endowment. These gifts are precious indeed, not only because they occur once in each donor's lifetime, but because when they are kept as a board-designated endowment fund, the board retains the right of access to the principal should that absolute need ever occur. The best endowment fund-raising method is a planned giving and estate-planning program, which requires a minimum of five years of investment in staff and budget to begin to mature. These gifts are often reserved in advance with irrevocable contracts to become endowment funds. When they do arrive, they are magnificent!

Volume and Variety of Fund-Raising Practices

To meet their operating cash needs, most not-for-profit organizations engage in two or more forms of annual solicitation to acquire and renew donors' annual contributions. A broad base of volunteers and supporters must first be built to yield desireable, predictable levels of contributions to cover annual operating purposes and special-project funds when necessary, and to elicit major gifts for construction, renovation, and equipment, and even endowment funds. To reach all areas of potential public support and to develop volunteers and donors over time from interested participants to significant investors requires an organization to integrate the entire scope of fund-raising methods and techniques, and operate them according to a dependable design for maximum success (see the Pyramid of Giving, Exhibit 1.4, page 26).

Leadership Development Program

Because leadership of volunteers, committees, and the board of directors is absolutely essential to the success of a not-for-profit organization, it must define and conduct a leadership development program. Leaders have to be identified, recruited, trained, put to work, evaluated, appreciated, and rewarded. Individuals do not arrive at your door already prepared to help your organization succeed. Even people with volunteer experience at other not-for-profit organizations will want to learn your organization in detail in order to be able to apply their skills where they can best be used. A simple way to start leadership development is to require the appointment of a vice chair with every chair position of each committee or volunteer group, as a planned training experience. The job description for the vice chair might state, "Pay attention; you get the chair's job next year." Without such a commitment, an organization forever will be lacking in the talent and direction it absolutely needs.

Volunteer Recruitment and Training

You can never have enough volunteers. Any expansion in philanthropic potential depends upon the number of volunteers and the extent of their knowledge, experience, and commitment. Volunteers, like leaders, have to be identified, recruited, trained, put to work, evaluated, appreciated, and rewarded, which may include promotion to any number of leadership positions. A corps of experienced volunteers is a true army that stands ready to accomplish multiple tasks at the asking. They are advocates and translators of your mission and purpose; they espouse your objectives and future plans to family, friends, and neighbors; they stand ready to write letters, get on the phone, or appear in front of any audience to sing your praises and advocate your cause. They also are the arms and legs of every fund-raising method and technique you can offer; and they are the key to continued financial success and worth every penny and second of time spent in working with them.

Availability of New Prospects

No organization can expect to meet the needs of the community by depending on only a few loyal friends. People change their priorities, move away, grow old, retire, and die. Every not-for-profit organization has a geographic range or boundary, even if its appeal is global, within which it can effectively concentrate its search for new friends and funds, be they suspects or prospects. This appeal is tied to image and the extent of the organization's programs and services. Serious time and expense must be invested in identifying and recruiting prospective donors as well as new volunteers. It is best to begin with those nearby who are now, have been, or will be served by the organization. Participants will "care" about an organization based on their personal experiences—a definite recruiting advantage. People who live farther away, have never been clients, and are not involved in any way are much less likely to care and to give.

Existing Donors for Renewal and Upgrading

Great wealth resides in the current donor pool. The best "prospects" are those who already support the organization, so they must not be taken for granted, despite their faithful commitment. They must forever be cultivated, communicated with, and rewarded. Continuous efforts to preserve and increase donors' current participation and encourage their potential for even greater support in alternate ways (time, talent, and treasure are all available) will always succeed by far greater measure than similar efforts to win over suspects and prospects who have not yet begun to give. For example, an invitation to a donor to increase the size of his or her annual gift has between a 10 and 15 percent rate of success (more income from the same source at no increased cost to solicit). But more important to overall results this year and in the future, most donors who are invited to "upgrade" their gift will agree to continue at their present level (reliable income at no increased cost to solicit). Donors will always be the best prospects because they believe in the mission and want to be a part of its success.

Access to Wealth

Attention to those few wealthy people whose ability to participate is greater than that of others must be among the organization's priorities. A comprehensive program of major gift solicitation has specific objectives, including to identify a certain number of qualified prospects, to arrive at a strategic plan for each, to match legitimate major gift projects with relevant needs, to actually make contact, and to use the best form of "ask." People are not likely to make large, investment-level decisions with their assets in favor of a not-for-profit organization before both parties engage in an extensive dialogue and get to know one another well. For this program to work, wealthy individuals must be available and within reach.

Focus on Major Gift Cultivation and Solicitation

Even if it has success with annual giving programs, an organization still must devote time and attention each year to the development of patrons and benefactors—those few "best friends" whose capacity for six-figure (and up) contributions is crucial for the present and the future of every not-for-profit organization. As noted in the previous section, identification and invitation, recruitment and cultivation, and solicitation and recognition of only a few candidates for significant gifts from individuals, corporations, and foundations must become annual priorities. The attention of these donors must be directed toward the not-for-profit's "vision" and the long-range plan that they can and will help complete. They must come to know and appreciate that each major gift they make will help to bring that vision to life in a way that allows their own aspirations to be matched and fulfilled, for the use of their money is much more important than the size of any gift they can make.

Professional Staff and Fund-Raising Counsel

Success in fund raising is more likely to occur with an organized program led by a professional fund-raising executive (more than likely one with a Certified Fund Raising Executive [CFRE] certificate). Gone are the days when volunteers could raise the funds needed by staging a benefit or not-for-profit organizations could rely on the board of directors to make up the difference needed to balance the budget at the year's end. Modern organizations increase their potential for success through the use of trained, experienced people hired to manage and direct the fund-raising program. That potential can be further improved upon by using professional fund-raising counsel. Counsel adds professionally proven methods for recruiting and training staff, increasing board and management involvement (and comfort) in solicitation, building adequate levels of support systems, designing recognition programs, and improving performance in other areas. When best used, these expert advisers define specific programs with detailed plans, prepare everyone to conduct the effort, provide supervision or "coaching" along the way, evaluate results objectively, and demonstrate personal conviction on how to proceed with an expectation of success. Most important, their guidance helps everyone avoid distractions and misdirections and concentrate on the task of raising money, which promotes success.

Appropriate Space, Budget, and Systems

The not-for-profit organization needs adequate support in the form of office personnel, space, budget, and modern systems for managing data. Location is less important than competence. It costs money to raise money: Reasonable cost levels are routinely targeted for each individual solicitation program, but there are also costs for management functions, equipment, computers, publications, research, support personnel, and continuing training programs, all necessary for success today and in the future.

Donor Recognition Program

Recognition is important to volunteers and donors, no matter how they protest to the contrary. A program of recognition guided by board-approved policy and procedure (see Appendix A, Section J) addresses how current volunteers and donors are treated at *all* times, including after their gifts have been received. Recognition must be visible so that donors (and those who aspire to increased giving) can see that their support is honestly appreciated, is valuable, and has been publicly declared to have been significant and worthwhile. Moreover, hard evidence is needed to demonstrate to prospects how donors are treated, how their names will appear on buildings, plaques, or donors' walls, and how prominently their recognition will be displayed. There are many ways to say thank you to donors and volunteers; use as many as you can and look for more.

Bringing the External and Internal Factors Together

When the scores for this extensive environmental audit are tallied, if more than 15 factors score below a 3.0, the potential for fund-raising success may be seriously handicapped; a more thorough analysis of areas of weakness to find improvements or correct deficiencies should be done immediately. An overall, average score of 3.5 or better suggests readiness exists with some potential for success. Conducting this audit with several volunteer and staff groups annually will track improvements. After three years of well-defined efforts, the average score should be 4.0 or better. In conclusion, no score will predict how much money will be raised, how many volunteers are needed, which solicitation programs will perform better than others, how big a staff is needed, or what budget is needed. Fund-raising results are the consequence of effort, and if the effort is well defined in light of an understanding of probable outcomes, the results are likely to be within the range of reasonable expectations.

FUND-RAISING PRODUCTIVITY ANALYSIS

A fund-raising productivity analysis is not the "big finish" wrapped up with a simple answer of what is the reasonable cost for fund raising. In this section, performance evaluation methods are offered to help demonstrate the productivity and "profitability" of fund development activities. This section answers questions on what to measure, shows how efficient and how effective each solicitation program is, and demonstrates the efficiency and effectiveness of volunteers in completing their assignments.

If fund-raising productivity were only a simple comparison of revenue received against cost to raise it (the "bottom line"), it would illustrate only a single money-raising ratio and would fail to show any amount of program effectiveness or efficiency. This oversimplified measurement will also fail to assess any progress toward the potential that may exist or the extent of the public's capacity for giving to the organization to satisfy its present needs and fulfill its future plans. There is much more to fund raising than raising money, and there is much more to its productivity assessment than simple bottom-line analysis.

Fund-raising departments are engaged in a variety of methods and techniques to raise the money needed by their not-for-profit organizations. They have goals and objectives that go beyond how much money is raised in a single fiscal or tax year. They employ these same fund-raising methods to communicate information, to cultivate positive relationships, and to solicit a variety of positive responses in addition to money. They produce ever larger numbers of suspects, prospects, and donors, stimulating their active participation as well as their fiscal support. They inform and enthuse, build confidence and trust, offer new and old friends important roles to play and valuable work to be done, and, using gifts as but one exchange medium, bond all these supporters ever more tightly to the organization and its mission, purposes, goals, and objectives.

Time and energy are necessary to support fund raising, which must be understood to be an investment decision and a firm commitment. Each budget dollar spent and each gift received should be appreciated for its cost-benefit ratio and for its long-term return on investment, which aids in the institution's own advancement. It takes years of investing in time and energy, plus budgeting, to build a successful development program that meets planned needs for the future. One year's budget and its results can and should be measured for direct performance, but they should also be measured for their contribution toward an increase or return on the next year's and future years' results as well.

Most professional fund-raising executives employ the image of a pyramid (see Exhibit 1.4 on page 26) to illustrate the design for the overall fund development program. The pyramid shows each fund-raising method available, how each relates to the others, and at what levels performance should be measured. Management tools are available to measure each fund-raising activity. Murray identified the purposes for such evaluation as follows:

Evaluation has four purposes:
- To identify what is being done well and to confer suitable rewards
- To identify areas where improvement is possible and desirable
- To assess the entire planning process and its critical assumptions
- To develop future plans, objectives, and standards[53]

[53] Dennis J. Murray, *The Guaranteed Fund-Raising System: A Systems Approach to Planning and Controlling Fund Raising*, 2d ed. (Poughkeepsie, NY: American Institute of Management, 1994), 47.

Fund-raising productivity analysis is the means to examine how to measure, to explore what to measure, to explain how it should be performed, and to become educated in what the outcomes may mean. Fund raising has been defined by Seymour as "the planned promotion of understanding, participation, and support."[54] Peter Drucker has stated that "performance in the nonprofit institution must be *planned*. And this starts out with the mission . . . [f]or the mission defines what results are in this particular nonprofit institution."[55] Murray's definition adds that "fund-raising management . . . is proactive and results-oriented."[56] Each of these concepts (promotion, planning, results) can and should be measured. The results of their assessment will add a better understanding of their contribution to the overall success of a comprehensive fund development program and the not-for-profit organization it serves.

Results measurement begins with adequate preparation to ensure (1) access to valid statistics and their fair comparison and (2) an easy-to-understand report format for every audience intended. Nick Costa, in his thorough study of fund-raising cost performance in health-care institutions, defined the following criteria for compiling and comparing statistics to ensure the integrity of their results:

- Establish clear and decisive standards for recording data for each of your reports
- Maintain the standards you establish
- Use the reports to simplify, clarify, and educate
- Seek a uniform standard of measurement when using external statistics[57]

EVALUATING FUND-RAISING PROGRAM EFFECTIVENESS

Comparative analysis between not-for-profit organizations, even those using the same fund-raising methods, is never fair. No two not-for-profit organizations are identical in how they provide programs and services,

---

[54]Seymour, *Designs for Fund-Raising*, 115.

[55]Peter F. Drucker, *Managing the Nonprofit Organization: Practices and Principles* (New York: Harper Collins, 1990), 109.

[56]Murray, *The Guaranteed Fund-Raising System*, 7.

[57]Nick B. Costa, *Measuring Progress and Success in Fund Raising: How to Use Comparative Statistics to Prove Your Effectiveness* (Falls Church, VA: Association for Healthcare Philanthropy, 1991), 7–8.

including how they conduct and track costs for their fund-raising programs. Organizations do not solicit at the same time and in the same way any more than they reach the same donors and prospects, have the same volunteers and leaders, possess the same history with prior donors, operate with the same budget and staff configurations, and so on. Consequently, their results always will differ. What is similar and worth studying is how each solicitation activity performs measured against its own results from prior years. This comparison leads to an accurate understanding and appreciation of how existing solicitation activities are working to achieve their potential, what improvements can be made based on previous results and changing conditions, and what expectations can be made for higher levels of productivity and profitability with reliability.

Fund-raising practice does not have a uniform standard of measurement, although many solicitation methods use similar ingredients (lists, volunteers, events, requests by mail). A nine-point performance index can be used to evaluate the unique performance of each fund-raising method based on its results (see Exhibit 2.6). Measuring each solicitation activity with the same index provides a uniform grid for comparative analysis. Each of these nine elements is, in itself, an indicator of performance success. Together they provide more than adequate detail to allow not-for-profit organizations to interpret their results and estimate future income with reliability based on how well each solicitation method has proven its mix of ingredients for success. The nine elements of the performance index are presented in two sections. Group A provides the three data elements—number of participants, income received, and expenses—that are required to complete the six performance measurements in Group B.

Group A: Basic Information for Measurements

(1) Participants

Each solicitation method is designed to stimulate a number of responses. Decisions on how many prospects to ask to make a gift are tied to how many responses are likely to be received, which helps the solicitors determine whether the group(s) solicited were the best ones to ask. The number of participants provide evidence of the degree of acceptance of the appeal's message. Tracking the number of participants from each group solicited helps to decide whom to ask again. Because success depends on stimulating numerous replies, what rate of response is required for success? This answer will be different for each fund-raising method used and can range from 1 to 25 percent or higher.

(2) Income Received

In addition to stimulating responses, each solicitation also is expected to produce revenue. How much income depends on several factors. Most annual giving solicitations offer donors a range of gift sizes (e.g., $25, $50, $100, Other: $_____). The objective is to tell those being asked for money how much is being requested, or what level of gifts are considered appropriate responses. The amount of income received is directly linked to these suggestions. Gifts above $100 can be requested when prospect research or other information suggests a pool of candidates capable of giving more than $100 is available. Results also can be influenced by the urgency and relevance of the appeal message (giving to the American Red Cross is greatest after a disaster), who does the asking, timing, follow-up, and more.

To avoid making faulty assumptions, you should not rely on the performance ratio of number of gifts to number of prospects solicited until after two or more solicitations of the same group are complete. The actual results establish the willingness and generosity of each likely donor *at that point in time.* For example, if the request is an invitation to attend a black-tie dinner dance priced at $100 a couple, the number of reservations

---

EXHIBIT 2.6 Nine-Point Performance Index

Basic Data
1. Participants   = Number of donors responding with gifts
2. Income   = Gross contributions
3. Expense   = Fund-raising costs

Performance Measurements
4. Percent Participation   = Divide participants by total solicitations made
5. Average Gift Size   = Divide income received by participants
6. Net Income   = Subtract expenses from income received
7. Average Cost per Gift   = Divide expenses by participants
8. Cost of Fund Raising   = Divide expenses by income received; multiply by 100 for percentage
9. Return   = Divide net income by expenses; multiply by 100 for percentage

---

received will be linked to the invitation list and ticket price, *plus* the quality of the location, its reputation for food and service, quality of the entertainment, prior experience from attending events produced by this organization, effective volunteers who sell tickets, and more.

(3) Expense

The budget or cost required to conduct a fund-raising activity should be estimated in advance. Budget dictates how much effort will be put into every solicitation. When reasonable expense levels are allocated for each solicitation activity, reasonable rates of return can be expected. However, the cost-to-return ratio will not be the same for each solicitation method used. This lack of uniformity is not due to any failure among the separate solicitation activities; rather, it is a function of the type of solicitation used and the external environment in which the organization must solicit, as well as its image and reputation, prior fund-raising history, volunteer leadership, urgency and relevance of the project, prospect understanding of public benefits to result, and much more.

Group B: Basic Performance Measurements

(4) Percent Participation

The number of replies received is a percentage of all who were invited to participate. Percent participation first indicates acceptance of the message. As an example, 1,156 replies from 80,575 prospects after two mailings is a 1.43 percent response rate, whereas one renewal letter sent to these same 1,156 donors the next year that results in 602 new gifts represents a 52 percent response rate.

Sample calculation:

	Acquisition Mailing	**Renewal Mailing**
Divide number of responses received by the number of solicitations made	$\dfrac{1{,}156}{80{,}575} = 1.43\%$	$\dfrac{602}{1{,}156} = 52\%$

This result may suggest all acquisitions mailings are a waste of time and money, but a 1.43 percent response rate is considered above average for a first-time donor acquisition effort. By comparison, the letter sent to all 1,156 donors a year later that produced a 52 percent response would be considered as eliciting only an average level of participation.

(5) Average Gift Size

How much each donor contributes is a valuable indicator of the program's financial success. Gift size is important to donors; they give what they can afford at the time. Size is also an indicator of whether the solicitation method, prospect list, and amount requested were well matched, as well as how worthwhile donors believed the project to be, either for themselves or for others in the community. In the preceding direct mail example, the 1.43 percent response rate is considered successful. But, if the average gift was $5, the solicitation would have failed to raise enough money to pay for the cost of mailing the request. Similarly, if prior donors who made an average gift of $100 last year were to give only $52 this year, this mailing also would fail by losing half the donors and half the money raised previously.

Sample calculation:

	Acquisition Mailing	Renewal Mailing
Divide total contributions received by number of donors	$\frac{\$5{,}758}{1{,}156} = \$5.00$	$\frac{\$31{,}304}{602} = \$52$

(6) Net Income

Net income is sometimes neglected in reports of fund-raising success because focusing attention on gross revenue makes results look as good as possible. True success is net income the not-for-profit organization can use for its programs and services *after* deducting the costs of solicitation.

Sample calculation:

	Acquisition Mailing	Renewal Mailing
Subtract solicitation costs from total contributions received	$35,758 −32,641 =$3,117	$31,304 −1,625 =$29,679

Focus on net income reveals profitability as well as the efficiency of the prospect list chosen and solicitation method used. Renewal mailings are more profitable because those who are asked are already donors; acquisition mailings have to be sent to a large number of nondonors because, at the normal 1 percent response rate, not many donors will be acquired unless the mailing goes to thousands of prospects. Also, renewal solicitations with prior donors should be expected to cost less because a lot fewer people have to be asked. It should become a matter of concern to the organization when renewal percent participation falls below 50 percent and when average gift size drops.

(7) Average Cost per Gift

How much does each gift cost to solicit? What is the reasonable guideline for expense? Average cost per gift helps to confirm the relationship between net income and cost to produce it. Using mail program results again, an average gift of $30.93 was realized at a cost of $28.24 per gift from acquisition, while renewal gifts were produced at an average cost per gift of $2.69 to realize an average gift of $52.

Sample calculation:

	Acquisition Mailing	Renewal Mailing
Total fund-raising costs divided by number of donors	$\dfrac{\$32{,}641}{1{,}156} = \$28.24$	$\dfrac{\$1{,}625}{602} = \$2.69$

Comparing the mailings, 1,156 new donors were realized first at a much higher cost per donor, and, after expenses, net profits of only $3,117 were available compared with renewal's net return of $29,679. All four measurable criteria (number of donors, average gift size, net income, and average cost per gift) are quite revealing in evaluating whether this mail solicitation effort was successful. Combining acquisition with renewal results each year is the final program performance measurement for the overall direct mail program.

(8) Cost of Fund Raising

The cost-effectiveness of each fund-raising method is a bottom-line measurement of overall profitability and productivity. Acquiring new donors is more expensive than renewing prior donors, but new donors must be found in order to have candidates to renew later. In addition, not all donors renew each time they are asked, further reducing the pool of best prospects. If regular investments are not made in acquisition, the donor pool will shrink more rapidly and net proceeds will drop quickly.

For a comparison, what is the reasonable cost that a for-profit business will spend to acquire a new customer? Depending on the product for sale and other factors (marketplace, competition, advertising and promotion, etc.), the answer is often as much as $4 to $5 to raise $1, because the executive knows that profits are the result of customers buying their product many times again.

In the not-for-profit world, the guideline for reasonable cost to acquire new donors by mail is $1.25 to $1.50 for each $1 raised. Is this not more efficient than the for-profit world? Board members and management staff who challenge these expense levels need to be encouraged to compare the investment standard in the business world with the performance of the not-for-profit world when using the same method (acquiring customers by mail). Also, it is worth emphasizing the equal expectation of higher profits from investing time and attention in building relationships with prior donors and asking them to give again and again in the future.

Sample calculation:

	Acquisition Mailing	Renewal Mailing
Fund-raising expenses divided by total contributions received;	$\dfrac{\$32{,}641}{\$35{,}758} = 0.9128$	$\dfrac{\$1{,}625}{\$31{,}304} = 0.5191$
multiply by 100 for a percentage	$\times\ 100\ = 91.28\%$	$\times\ 100 = 5.191\%$
(Expressed as cost to raise one dollar)	($0.91)	($0.052)

(9) Return

Budget dollars spent in solicitation activity always should be able to demonstrate success in positive terms. Results ought to be expressed as the direct relationship between the investment made and its result (another term would be "profit," not necessarily a comfortable word for not-for-profit executives). Actual performance will vary from year to year among solicitation methods, but each should be able to improve on previous results and, over time, provide reliable levels of efficiency and profitability.

The larger the number of active donors available for renewal, the greater the net return they will provide. Continued success for annual giving depends not only on the choice of solicitation method but also on whether community needs are perceived as urgent and relevant as well as whether energetic, well-trained volunteers use efficient and well-managed fund-raising solicitation methods.

To return to the direct mail examples, even a "cold call," first-time acquisition effort, as previously shown, produced a 1.43 percent response rate and an average gift of $30.93. This performance was achieved at an average cost per gift of $28.24 to produce a net "profit" of $3,117. The cost to raise $1 was $0.91 and this fund-raising program achieved a 9.55 percent rate of return within two to three months. By comparison, renewal data demonstrated a remarkable return rate of 1,826 percent; where can you achieve this level of performance in the for-profit world?

Sample calculation:

	Acquisition Mailing	Renewal Mailing
Net income received divided by fund-raising expenses,	$\dfrac{\$3,117}{\$32,641} = 0.095$	$\dfrac{\$29,679}{\$1,625} = 18.26$
and multiplied by 100	$\times 100 = 9.55\%$	$\times 100 = 1,826\%$

Reasonable Fund-Raising Cost Guidelines

Completing the nine-point performance index for each fund-raising method identifies a variety of performance qualities to be tracked each time those methods are employed. Analyzing the data for a minimum of _three_ successive years will yield information on public acceptance, growth in giving statistics, and enough data to forecast future performance. Inevitably, much attention will focus on the overall bottom-line cost percentage for the fund-raising program. Bottom-line analysis adds together the results of each solicitation method to illustrate the profitability and productivity of the overall fund development program. A caution: An organization should _not_ rely on the bottom line as its only measurement of fundraising effectiveness or efficiency. Looked at by itself, it can lead to erroneous conclusions about the performance levels of each of the fundraising methods in use. For example, if overall fund-raising costs are under $0.25 to raise a dollar because two new foundation grants were credited at full value (but each has a three-year payment schedule) and two bequests were received in this same year, the $0.25 does not accurately reflect actual performance for the year for either foundation work or planned giving efforts, and the program may be unable to repeat this performance next year.

The fund-raising profession lacks industry-wide guidelines and standards for both performance and reasonable cost. But some entities have published their own recommended guidelines. For example, the Philanthropic Advisory Service of the Council of Better Business Bureaus recommends a 35 percent fund-raising cost guideline,[58] while the National Charities Information Bureau advocates 40 percent or below.[59] Several national

[58]Council of Better Business Bureaus, Inc., _Standards for Charitable Solicitations_ (Arlington, VA: Council of Better Business Bureaus, 1982).

[59]National Charities Information Bureau, _Standards in Philanthropy_ (New York: National Charities Information Bureau, 1988).

associations, notably the Council for Advancement and Support of Education (CASE)[60] and United Way of America, have developed data-collection tools for comparative results analysis among their groups of not-for-profit organizations, but these tools cannot serve as guidelines for every class of organization. In 1998, the American Institute of Certified Public Accountants (AICPA)[61] released revised guidelines on joint-cost allocation, but these, too, fall short of serving as a uniform standard because they address only direct mail applications. The Research Council of the National Society of Fund Raising Executives (NSFRE) has recently invited the Center on Philanthropy at Indiana University and the National Center for Charitable Statistics at the Urban Institute to develop a national survey instrument to gather data directly from every class of not-for-profit organization. Based on these results, it hopes to be able to offer applicable industry-wide guidelines. We remain hopeful these efforts will succeed.

In the interim, preliminary cost guidelines for each fund-raising method are available from several sources to serve as a pilot. Exhibit 2.7 illustrates guidelines based on the results and experience of several programs. These percentages should be applied to fund-raising programs only *after three years of active operation* and consistent data collection. Note that these guidelines are based on reasonable performance and can be improved upon when favorable environmental conditions, such as strong leadership, access to wealth, experienced volunteers, positive economic conditions, quality projects linked to multiyear strategic plans, and well-managed solicitation programs are brought together.

BUDGETING AND ACCOUNTING FOR FUND-RAISING SUCCESS

One of the more perplexing areas of fund-raising management is the relationship between operating expenses (budget) and use of contributions

[60] Council for Advancement and Support of Education and the National Association of College and University Business Officers, *Expenditures in Fund Raising, Alumni Relations, and other Constituent (Public) Relations* (Washington, DC: Council for Advancement and Support of Education and the National Association of College and University Business Officers, 1990).

[61] American Institute of Certified Public Accountants, "Accounting for Costs of Activities of Not-for-Profit Organizations and State and Local Governmental Entities that Include Fund Raising," Statement of Position 98-2, New York, 1998.

EXHIBIT 2.7 Reasonable Cost Guidelines for Solicitation Activities

Solicitation Activity	Reasonable Cost Guidelines*
Direct mail (acquisition)	$1.25 to $1.50 per $1.00 raised
Direct mail (renewal)	$0.20 to $0.25 per $1.00 raised
Membership associations	$0.20 to $0.30 per $1.00 raised
Activities, benefits, and special events	$0.50 per $1.00 raised (gross revenue and direct costs only)†
Donor clubs and support group organizations	$0.20 to $0.30 per $1.00 raised
Volunteer-led personal solicitation	$0.10 to $0.20 per $1.00 raised
Corporations	$0.20 per $1.00 raised
Foundations	$0.20 per $1.00 raised
Special projects	$0.10 to $0.20 per $1.00 raised
Capital campaigns	$0.10 to $0.20 per $1.00 raised
Planned giving	$0.20 to $0.30 per $1.00 raised

Reprinted with permission from Fund-Raising Cost Effectiveness: A Self-Assessment Workbook *by James M. Greenfield (New York: John Wiley & Sons, Inc., 1996), 281.*

Sources: For direct mail guidelines—Direct Mail Marketing Association. For planned giving—Norman S. Fink and Howard C. Metzler, The Costs and Benefits of Deferred Giving *(New York: Columbia University Press, 1982). For capital campaigns—American Association of Fund Raising Counsel, New York. The balance are derived from the author's direct experience, research, and publications.*

†*Benefit event cost allocations: To calculate bottom-line total costs and net proceeds from a benefit event, calculate and add the indirect and overhead support expenses to direct costs incurred and subtract from gross revenue.*

received (accounting). Annual budgets often result in a competition between departments within organizations that allocate the majority of their resources correctly to support their programs and services and fulfill their mission. That is, administrative costs are "overhead" expenses, and, while they are necessary to every organization, they take second seat to programs and services. Budgets for fund-raising activities and business office operations have to compete with necessary expenses such as those for auditing, legal counsel, consulting, planning, marketing, public relations, human resources, and the needs of senior administrative officers. As a result, these latter support areas "make do" with less support than may be appropriate.

Accounting guidelines for all not-for-profit organizations were revised substantially by the Financial Accounting Standards Board (FASB) in 1993,[62] with follow-up audit guidelines published by the American Institute of Certified Public Accountants (AICPA) in 1995. A major focus of these revisions is the accounting and reporting of contributions received; therefore all not-for-profit organizations who had to comply were forced to modify their internal accounting systems, creating additional operating costs as well as more than a bit of confusion over interpretations of how to count and how to report results. Richard F. Larkin notes, "Because the new accounting standard is that unconditional gifts (included pledges) will be revenue when the gift or pledge is first received, many not-for-profits will record some of their revenue sooner than they do now. This means usually higher revenue, larger excess of revenue over expenses, and larger fund balances (net assets). These organizations will appear to be in better financial condition than heretofore and thus will sometimes present fund raisers with the additional challenge of convincing prospective donors that new gifts are truly needed."[63]

Budget preparation processes remain unchanged, and should be directed by business officers and internal guidelines. This once-a-year exercise is a good opportunity to review and discuss performance, but that opportunity too often abdicates to the practical task of justifying the budgetary requirements of ongoing activities (requesting a 3-to-5 percent increase for labor and nonlabor, for instance). Fund-raising budgets should be reviewed with both income and expenses in mind:

> The end results of proper budgeting are the realization of the anticipated revenue and the control of expenses. Budgeting is a major leadership task of fund-raising professionals, an essential process that consumes the time and talents of staff and volunteers. Budgets are both evaluation and planning tools, designed to measure the fiscal performance of fund-raising efforts. A budget may be an important part of other administrative tasks, such as the formulation of grant proposals, determining program support, and establishing new programs and campaign efforts. A budget may also serve as an occasional reference on program progress or as a step-by-step guide for financial development.[64]

[62] Financial Accounting Standards Board, *Statement of Financial Accounting Standards No. 116: Accounting for Contributions Received and Contributions Made*, No. 127-A (Norwalk, CT: Financial Accounting Standards Board, 1993); and Financial Accounting Standards Board, *Financial Statements of Not-for-Profit Organizations*, No. 127-B (Norwalk, CT: Financial Accounting Standards Board, 1993).

[63] Richard F. Larkin, "Accounting for Contributions," in Greenfield, *The Nonprofit Handbook: Fund Raising*, 2d ed., 654.

[64] James E. Connell, "Budgeting for Fund Raising," in Greenfield, *The Nonprofit Handbook: Fund Raising*, 2d ed., 51.

In preparing budgets for fund-raising activities, keep in mind that each fund-raising method performs at a different level of efficiency and effectiveness, as shown earlier in Exhibit 2.8, Reasonable Cost Guidelines for Solicitation Activities. Some activities (direct mail, membership programs, donor clubs, and benefit events) have large numbers of donors, receive modest-sized gifts, and require more budgetary support for annual operations. By comparison, volunteer-led solicitation activities as well as foundation relations, capital campaigns, and planned giving activities receive much fewer gifts (all larger by comparison) each year and cost less to operate. Although some methods appear to be less efficient (raise less money) or more expensive (require more budget) by comparison, they should not be deemed failures. Their effectiveness is in finding and retaining donors who will become reliable sources for major gifts in the future.

Finally, the budget for fund-raising activities should be prepared as a "profit center"—that is, details about revenue to be received (forecast) should be included with the corresponding budget necessary to deliver those revenues. Thus, one can see the projected return on investment. Prior performance figures in the form of a report that displays gifts received alongside the prior year's budget and the actual budget expended for each solicitation method are quite helpful when preparing a new budget (see Exhibit 2.8). In addition, these figures supply a performance indicator—that is, cost of fund raising for each activity—quite useful in evaluating results and in planning the next year's activities. Submission of a combined revenue and expense budget also is a superb opportunity to educate volunteer leaders and the board of directors with details about how fund raising performs. For many, this once-a-year exercise is the single opportunity when prior performance and proposed activities are given serious attention. A summary budget (see Exhibit 2.9) should include labor and nonlabor costs plus projected revenues, net revenue expectations, cost of fund raising, and the return so that the overall investment principle can be visibly demonstrated.

POLICIES AND PROCEDURES FOR PUBLIC SOLICITATION

The final area of readiness involves the preparation of written policies and procedures for all areas of fund development. Guidelines are important because they provide the board, the committee on fund development, donors, volunteers, and staff with rules that will assist them in their

EXHIBIT 2.8 Cost of Fund-Raising Report by Solicitation Method

	Gift Amount	Budget Approved	Budget Expended	Cost of Fund Raising(%)
A. Annual Giving Programs				
Direct mail (acquisition)	$35,500	$14,500	$14,798	42
Direct mail (renewal)	76,500	1,500	1,620	2
Membership dues	48,500	550	585	1
Benefit events (3)	59,600	20,000	21,747	36
Volunteer-led solicitations	82,000	1,200	1,250	2
Subtotal	$302,100	$37,750	$40,000	13
Direct Costs: Annual Giving				
Labor/payroll		$62,000	$63,050	
Non-payroll costs		37,750	40,000	
Subtotal		$99,750	$103,050	34
B. Major Gifts Programs				
Corporations	$45,500	$3,500	$3,250	7
Foundations	65,000	3,500	2,015	3
Individuals	145,500	3,800	4,200	3
Bequests received	45,000	200	1,850	4
Subtotal	$301,000	$11,000	$11,315	4
Total	$603,100	$48,750	$51,315	9
Net Income	$471,985			
Direct Costs: Major Gifts				
Labor/payroll		$18,000	$16,750	
Non-payroll costs		11,000	11,315	
Subtotal		$29,000	$28,065	9
C. Expense Summary (A + B)				
Direct Costs (labor/payroll)		$80,000	$79,800	
Indirect Costs/Overhead (non-payroll)		$48,750	$51,315	
Total		$128,750	$131,115	22
Return				360

Reprinted with permission from Fund-Raising Cost Effectiveness: A Self-Assessment Workbook *by James M. Greenfield (New York: John Wiley & Sons, Inc., 1996), 249.*

EXHIBIT 2.9 Summary Budget Request with Estimated Expenses and Revenue

	Previous Year	Last Year	Current Fiscal Year	Coming Fiscal Year
Budget				
Labor costs	$66,009	$74,164	$79,800	$90,259
Nonlabor costs	43,594	50,026	51,315	50,000
Total budget	$109,603	$124,190	$131,115	$140,259
Gift Revenue				
Gross revenue	$342,738	$563,384	$603,100	$655,000
Minus expenses (budget)	109,603	124,190	131,115	140,259
Net revenue	$233,135	$439,194	$471,985	$514,741
Cost of fund raising	32%	22%	22%	21%
Return	213%	354%	360%	367%

Reprinted with permission from Fund-Raising Cost Effectiveness: A Self-Assessment Workbook *by James M. Greenfield (New York: John Wiley & Sons, Inc., 1996), 24.*

operations decisions. Policies should be written regarding solicitation activity; annual and multiyear priorities; the use of funds raised; handling gifts of securities and of personal and real property; operating rules and procedures for subsidiary organizations (support groups); special events; review and approval of planned gifts; gift acknowledgment; and honors and recognition, including the naming of facilities (see Appendix A).

Brief explanations of the content of each of these policies are given here.

Solicitation Activity

The fund-raising methods authorized for use and who has the authority to select them should be defined, with specific supervisory responsibility assigned to each board-appointed volunteer subcommittee for an area of fund raising. The written guidelines should include protocols for setting annual goals, performance evaluation, budget and cost-effectiveness measurement, and descriptions of the reports required and of their content and frequency. Handling of all cash received should be defined step by step from the moment of receipt until deposit in the bank (audit trail), with adequate security and proper accounting procedures provided throughout. Instructions should restrict any use of the official name or logo of the organization (or any popular abbreviations), especially by any outside organization raising money on its behalf. If federal, state, or local laws and regulations apply to planned activities (raffles, bingo games, Las Vegas nights, and so on), documentation of internal program approvals, permit applications, payment of fees, and filing of financial statements and other reports should be carefully described.

Annual and Multiyear Priorities

The annual procedure for submission and approval of projects assigned as fund-raising priorities must be defined in detail because projects that are not on the approved list are ineligible for fund-raising staff, time, or budget. Priorities recommended will require board endorsement; they are likely to be closely tied to the annual operating budget based on long-range and strategic plans, financial and facility plans. The committee on fund development should have the opportunity to review the priority list, for recommendation of the projects most likely to stir the minds and hearts of donors and prospects and for estimation of how much is likely to be raised by each.

The Use of Funds Raised

Many fund-raising programs have failed because of control problems—internal conflicts over how the money was going to be used, in advance of raising it. Money is a political weapon within every organization; the same battle lines are drawn in laying claim to future gift income as declaring a right to the funds in hand. Approved programs and goals should be defined at the board of directors level in advance of fund raising; a directive should specify how funds raised will be deposited within existing financial systems and how access can be achieved through normal fiscal procedures. Professional staff have been known to view gift dollars as "extra" money, exempt from normal budget restrictions and to be coveted and protected. Some staff may attempt to solicit gifts on their own, instructing each donor to direct the money into their special fund account by name. The board must retain administrative control over all gifts received from any source and for any purpose.

Gifts of Securities and of Personal Property

Definition of proper procedures for handling of assets that are readily marketable is critical; the method for determining their value for tax deduction purposes should be specified. Securities and Exchange Commission (SEC) procedures require brokers and agents to set up accounts for the transfer, receipt, and sale of securities given to not-for-profit organizations. Internal organizational policies should be written to specify minimum values for any personal property gifts to be considered; require gift substantiation; define procedures for the sale of assets received; identify the authority for sale of securities received and the method to value stock gifts; describe how to value personal property, real estate, and gifts-in-kind for accounting purposes; and give clear instructions on the costs for transportation, storage, maintenance, and repairs of items accepted.

Operating Rules and Procedures for Subsidiary Organizations (Support Groups)

The organization's relationship with each support group authorized to raise money in its name should be clarified regarding membership categories and dues amounts, approval of annual elections and appointments to the board of directors and committees, duties of officers and committees, annual meetings, control and accountability of all funds, use of the organization's name, and so forth. In effect, procedures to act as a separate set of bylaws governs each group authorized within the tax-exempt privileges of the parent. These groups are entitled to use the name of the parent, to extend tax deduction privileges for all gifts made in its name in the form of membership payments and event ticket sales (minus the value of goods and services received), to use third-class bulk-rate mailing, and to be exempt from taxes on their activities, depending on local regulations.

Special Events

Ideally, the policy for special events should read "No event shall be conducted unless the net profit realized will be 50 percent or more of its gross proceeds." Events have merit and fit within the fund development program plan, but they consume an inordinate amount of time for their net results. Events should be approved only when they can demonstrate profitability, availability of volunteers to do the work, valid marketing and public relations value, a likely audience who will attend, potential sponsors and underwriters, opportunities for cultivating major gift prospects, and limited conflict with other activities. Each event proposal should be reviewed by the fund development committee following submission of a budget that includes projected income and expenses and estimated net proceeds. All contracts for services made in the name of a support group or the charitable organization should be subject to approval by an official of the organization, because liability falls to the sponsoring organization and ultimately to the parent, not to volunteer workers. Events sponsored by groups outside the organization should be subject to these same criteria, with the addition of prior approval of all solicitation materials and service contracts and a complete accountability for all funds through frequent progress reports.

Review and Approval of Planned Gifts

Planned gifts are legal contracts that bind the organization to extensive legal and fiduciary obligations. The planned giving program should state minimum levels of age and gift size; net present value; payout rates; trustee preferences; selection and supervision of the investment manager retained; and expectations regarding preparation of income checks, audits, and tax return preparations. An attorney who is an expert in charitable trusts and estate planning should be retained to review each trust document prior to acceptance and to certify that the agreement is correct in all details, including all of the charitable organization's obligations as trustee and remainderman.

A few professionals in estate planning, attorneys, stockbrokers, financial planners, insurance salespeople, and others are "marketing" planned gifts as tax shelters and "shopping" them to charitable organizations for fees and commissions. Serious questions have been raised as to whether these clients are donors at all, because charitable intent to the recipient organization must be demonstrated. A board policy should guide everyone against dealings with "con artists" and bad gifts and should address the issue of any fees or commissions to be paid vendors for such gifts, if at all.

Gift Acknowledgment

Those responsible for gift processing, as well as the manner and form of official acknowledgment by board members, committee chairpersons, or

senior management staff, should be carefully designated. The time required for processing all gifts should not exceed 48 hours; it is important
that donors be thanked properly and quickly. The responsibility for maintenance of all gift records and for preparation of all reports to the IRS and
other authorities that require disclosure of details on fund-raising performance should be assigned to particularly reliable persons. Good donor
relations is like insurance; you invest ahead of need (see Exhibit 2.10).

Honors and Recognition

Practicing the art of donor relations, or giving deserved attention to generosity, is both necessary and enjoyable. The written policy should set out
the qualifications, recommendations, review and decision procedures,
and methods of recognition for all available honors and recognition, including titled positions, named chairs, and the naming of endowment
funds, buildings and property, and departments. Addition of qualified
donors to existing recognition systems, such as donor walls, deserves

---

EXHIBIT 2.10 Opportunities for Good Donor Relations

1. Listen to what donors say.
2. Visit with donors whenever possible to discuss their ideas about the
   organization's programs.
3. Send donors your quarterly or annual financial statements; enclose
   information about the scope and effectiveness of your programs and
   about "what's new."
4. Schedule periodic forums to brief donors on program progress and to
   ask for their questions and ideas.
5. Telephone donors periodically—although not too frequently—to tell
   them of new developments that may interest them.
6. When you see something in the newspaper or on television about
   donors or their children, give them a call or write a pleasant note.
7. Knowing what donors' interests and needs are is important, but it is
   more important to hear what their *wants* are.
8. Break your back to send a gift acknowledgment within 24 to 36 hours. If
   you cannot do this, telephone your major donors as soon as you receive
   their gifts. Make it a friendly, pleasant call. It makes a good impression
   on the donor. It is a way to keep your friends.

Reprinted with permission from Rosso on Fund Raising: Lessons From a Master's
Lifetime Experience *by Henry A. Rosso (San Francisco: Jossey-Bass, 1996), 67–68.*

equal attention. The board should reserve all rights to the conferring of honors and recognition, measuring each decision for the visibility and prominence accorded to the honoree as well as for the benefits derived by the organization from the gift. The elements to be used (certificates, plaques, identification cards, even VIP parking privileges, as well as the form and style of awards and citations) should be tasteful. Details of public announcements, publicity given to dedication ceremonies, and receptions should be matched to various gift levels. All qualified donors should receive a particular manner of continued communications. The fund development department should be assigned to supervise the faithful observance of the honors and recognition program.

STEWARDSHIP

The final area of accountability for all not-for-profit organizations is stewardship—stewardship of funds, of course, but also stewardship of the mission, vision, and values; of multiyear plans and strategic purposes; of annual goals and objectives; and (always) of the highest quality of programs and services delivered to the community in exchange for their support. "Stewardship," writes Henry A. Rosso, "is a reflection of many values critical to the practice of philanthropy and its working partner, fund raising. Stewardship is trust, responsibility, liability, accountability, integrity, faith, and guardianship."[65] Stewardship is increasingly important in fund raising, for it is the essential link in the exchange between donors and their favorite charities. According to Kathleen Kelly, "The fund-raising process is not complete without stewardship. Obligations and responsibilities to the donor must be met. Furthermore, the last step proves an essential loop back to the beginning of the process for new efforts. . . . The stewardship step in ROPES consists of four progressive elements requiring fund raisers' attention and action: (a) reciprocity, (b) responsible gift use, (c) reporting, and (d) relationship nurturing."[66]

Kay Sprinkel Grace advocates a board-approved, formal stewardship program guided by the following basic principles:

1. Begin involving donors in the stewardship program with their first gift.
2. Alternate messages to your donors.
3. Allocate budget to stewardship activities.

---

[65]Rosso, *Rosso on Fund Raising*, 145.
[66]Kelly, *Effective Fund Raising Management*, 433–434.

4. Be sure the stewardship practice is appropriate to the amount of the gift and the budget and image of the organization.
5. Determine what kind of involvement your major gift and planned gift donors, some of whom may be very busy with other organizations and their own professions, want.
6. Coordinate stewardship and cultivation outreach, so that current donors have an opportunity to convey their enthusiasm and commitment to prospective donors.
7. Tie stewardship outreach to the organization's mission.
8. Focus on intangible, rather than tangible, benefits.
9. Maintain stewardship with long-time and generous donors, even when their giving flags.
10. Keep all previous large-gift donors informed and part of your database, even those who make what seems to be a "one-time-only gift," unless and until you hear they no longer want to hear from you.
11. Establish relationships between donors and program staff whenever possible.[67]

To engage in daily fund-raising operations and to plan for their optimal use in the future, preparations are necessary. They should be based on correct legal form and operation, on readiness drawn from an environmental audit, on demonstrated performance, and on written guidelines issued by the board. Because charitable organizations exist to provide valued services that benefit others, the role of philanthropy is to encourage and allow others to join in the cause. Fund development is the "process" whereby community support and generous funds are stimulated to enable the organization to reach its fruition.

[67]Grace, *Beyond Fund Raising*, 169–173.

3 ▼ Pyramids Are Built from the Bottom Up

Fund raising does not begin at high levels of performance. A fund development program's primary design is to secure a dependable, adequate income from *annual giving,* the bottom tier of the giving pyramid and a fund-raising area that offers variety, excitement, creativity, and instantaneous results. Annual giving also is about mass communications, attempting to reach a variety of people using multiple channels. This basic form of fund development is a lot like vegetable gardening. Careful soil preparation and the planting of seeds come first. Radishes appear almost overnight. Tomatoes, carrots, and squash require the entire growing season. Patience is required to realize the full benefits of fund-raising victory gardens. Wise organizations first become radish experts. Then, with patience, hard work, and help from others they prepare to harvest the prized vegetables for maximum yield. And, at years end when all is done, they prepare to repeat the entire process again next year.

THE ANNUAL GIVING PHENOMENON: A NECESSITY AND AN OPPORTUNITY

Income for current purposes is most often the highest priority for a fund development program. Annual support is required to fund daily programs and services that meet public needs, a constant assignment to produce cash quickly. Most annual giving programs supplement other revenue sources to help meet an organization's budget requirements; others may constitute most, if not all, of the money needed for its annual operating budget or for a special project, such as to introduce a new program or service, replace or renovate one of its facilities, or to buy a new piece of equipment. Several fund-raising methods can be used, usually in combination and all within 12 months, to find new donors and to renew and upgrade prior donors, all the while yielding reliable amounts of cash for current needs without fail, year after year. Nonetheless, annual giving is not just about money—it must remain true to the organization's mission and values, as one expert points out:

> The case for fund raising is primarily the fact that the organization needs money, needs it badly, and "By gosh, everybody should give. Give or our organization will have to stop doing good in service to the community." This is a down-to-earth basic budget appeal, a plain pitch to the guts, a sales appeal with no heart in it. It makes no reference to the human or societal needs that justify the existence of the nonprofit, no reference to its mission, its vision, and its program goals and objectives.[1]

The annual giving program, and the mass communications that are part of it, yields other benefits besides necessary cash: opportunities for volunteer recruitment and training and for leadership development, recruitment of new clients, improved market penetration, expanded public exposure, increased business contacts, and improved community relations. Annual giving also enlists faithful, committed donors, most of whom will give again next year. In time, these faithful donors may commit assets acquired over their lifetime to the organization through major gifts, endowment gifts, planned gifts, and bequests from their estate. All these good things become possible from a comprehensive program of annual giving.

When several methods of annual giving solicitation are conducted each year, their management requires simultaneous use of several means of communication, efficient assignment of volunteer help to various campaigns, and adherence to an overall, sometimes overlapping schedule. Managers are accountable for programs' performance and must recognize the separate characteristics that enable the success of each method of fund raising. Most factors affecting success are outside the direct control of the not-for-profit organization (see Exhibit 2.5, page 65, for a list of 30 external and internal environmental factors that affect performance). The role of volunteers and professional staff requires their best estimates of potential results, to enable the organization to plan its expenditures with confidence in the outcome of its several revenue-producing operations. Criteria used in estimates include public acceptance of the message, a

---

[1] Henry A. Rosso, *Rosso on Fund Raising: Lessons from a Master's Lifetime Experiences* (San Francisco: Jossey-Bass, 1996), 18.

99

sense of urgency in the project that needs funds, a sufficient number of participants who have appropriate giving levels, the suitability and time-liness of each method of solicitation for a particular community, and a cost-effective performance. The effort required to raise predictable amounts of money year after year, trying always to increase annual performance and productivity, is an extraordinary challenge; annual giving is not an easy business.

Annual fund-raising programs can occur once a year or all year long. Many organizations utilize two or three methods of solicitation each year (e.g., mailings, membership recruitment, and benefit events), strategi-cally staging them months apart because the same audience will be asked to reply to all three. Other organizations seem to be constantly ask-ing for money, using either one method of solicitation or many. Board members and volunteers often express concern at a high volume of ask-ing and may suggest some restraint if they believe overly aggressive be-havior might offend those being solicited and hurt the organization's chances for raising the money it needs. The main defect in their argu-ment is that they have misunderstood annual giving. It does not mean only one gift each year; if valid needs exist, its true purpose is to ask for multiple gifts throughout the year. If an organization can raise all the money it needs with one solicitation, then a single appeal may suffice. But only a few organizations today can do that; multiple methods, used throughout the year, are necessary for the rest. Volunteers should be re-minded that other charities also will be asking the same donors and prospects for support throughout the year and might well receive gifts from them. The answer to the debate over the potential for a saturation that will halt public giving is that it has yet to occur because not every-one is giving. Givers seem to appreciate that public needs continue to ex-pand and far exceed the amount of public support being provided. Donors expect requests and each prospective donor has the right to choose to whom, when, how much, and how often he or she gives. Giv-ing *is* voluntary.

Asking has many values for fund raising. Each request can produce some reply—friends or funds and usually both. The direct relationship between asking and giving has been proven many times over. Asking can be by mail or telephone, and can be done by a friend, neighbor, business colleague, or other volunteer. The invitation can be to give $100 as a mem-bership fee in a group supporting the not-for-profit organization or to buy tickets to attend a social or sporting event held for its benefit. Or a volun-teer may ask for a commemorative gift in someone's memory or to honor their accomplishments. Each of these contributions may be made to the same organization.

Three Objectives in Annual Giving

- Acquire new donors
- Renew current donors
- Maximize the method used for both

These basic objectives—*Acquire*, *Renew* or *Retain*, and *Maximize* (ARM)—will indeed ARM an organization by funding its immediate needs and preparing it for the future. From acquiring and renewing donors will come the identification of future leaders, a cementing of relations between donors and the organization, and the education of the public about the cause. These are the by-products and consequences of the practice of mass communications throughout the year. Annual giving not only provides cash for current purposes but also attracts committed donors who are a resource for meeting future needs.

Annual giving is the lifeblood of most not-for-profit organizations; it transfuses the annual cash that is most urgently needed. But a "quick fix," based on a one-time fund-raising scheme, is not enough. Ask yourself: Can this same amount of money be raised again next year using this same form of solicitation? Will these same donors be willing to give again? Will they increase their gift's size? Will they respond to additional appeals to help the organization in other ways, including asking others to give? The best way to transform quick fixes into true annual giving programs is to constantly acquire new donors and renew the ones you have using proven, traditional methods.

The basic value of an annual giving program is its ability to deliver *predictable* levels of cash each year. Success in achieving those levels requires maximizing all fund-raising methods and resources. Volunteers must be willing to ask their friends for money, a pool of prior donors and eligible prospects must be kept current, and professional staff managers must have a budget that is adequate for organized direction of the entire enterprise. More important, institutional needs must be valid, priorities must be firm and clear, and solicitation methods must be proven and sensitive, but not uncreative.

Needs and Priorities

Every not-for-profit organization has the capacity to consume every dollar it receives by supporting, expanding, and rewarding its operations and personnel. However, its mission statement calls for meeting these needs to the best of its ability and performing services that fulfill community needs and are directed toward public benefit. Many organizations are known only to local residents. Their fund-raising efforts are conducted within the same community that needs and uses the services their own gift funds will provide. Therefore, each proposed project must be seen as essential and must register a high level of public acceptance and trust in the organization's ability to deliver promised benefits. One project can become everyone's goal for their annual gift.

But there is never only one project. The planning staff must identify all likely funding requirements for the next few months or year and present each project as one of a series of needs, a specific current objective in a continuum of annual giving priorities. As these projects come to life each year, the community will have constant proof that its contributions are working and will more easily accept the next request.

More and more, donors prefer specific projects, tangible items, and results whose value they can appreciate. Annual giving programs targeted to these kinds of needs are more likely to capture wide acceptance and be successful for both first-time and repeat donations. Annual giving is designed to provide funds quickly. It inspires confidence when the project that receives the funds can be completed in the next 12 months or less.

Constituency

Donors appreciate the immediate use of their funds when a plan to address a need or solve a problem is the appeals focus. This type of appeal has to be directed to those who are most likely to respond and who have funds to share, which is not everyone. Not-for-profit organizations should study their constituency, whether it is entirely local or extends beyond state borders to national and even international audiences, in order to identify those for whom their mission has appeal. And, once identified, they must pay attention to the steps necessary to develop that constituency of donors, volunteers, advocates, board members, and leaders (see Exhibit 3.1). Unfortunately, most organizations do not give much time or thought to identifying their more likely constituents as potential partners and candidates for active participation. Nor do they make an effort to understand their needs, wants, and desires to learn if the organization's mission, vision, and values are a match. The all-too-common shortsighted view is just to ask as many people for money as you can afford to and do it as quickly as possible.

Solicitation Methods

Mass communication opportunities are numerous throughout the year. The public can be provided with many occasions to learn something about the organization and the valid services it provides. A prospect's

EXHIBIT 3.1 Ten-Step Constituency Development Process

The Steps	The questions to answer
1. Identify the predisposed and decide if they might become constituents.	*What makes them a good candidate?*
2. Inform constituents.	*What do they know about us?*
3. Get to know your constituents.	*What do they want?*
4. Identify potential relationship between prospect and your organization.	*Is there an intersection?*

If there is an intersection, continue the constituency development process. If not, stop the process. Do not consider the constituent a prospect.

5. Develop the relationship.	*Are they involved, committed?*

Continue building the relationship. If at a point you determine that there isn't enough interest on the part of the prospect, discontinue the attempt to develop the relationship.

6. Evaluate the prospect's interest, readiness, and capacity.	*Is the constituent ready?*
7. Design the ask.	*What is the right ask?*
8. Ask.	*Was the ask effective?*

If the prospect gives, acknowledge and recognize. If the prospect refuses, acknowledge, and decide if you should cultivate more or discontinue the process.

9. Evaluate the prospect within constituency development process.	*What next?*

Move the prospect into maintenance or upgrade tracks.

10. Enhance the relationship.	*How can you build the relationship?*

Strengthen the constituency development process by continuously moving the donor through steps 3–10.

fuzzy image of the organization as an institution or an employer or even a remote force for good can be enhanced by positive images of what benefits it provides to others in his or her community. Recognition is essential when people are asked to give.

Being a frequent asker validates an organization's need, especially when the funds are used exactly as advertised, within a short time. Having a reputation as a competent asker is equally desirable. A study of some fund-raising materials received from other organizations can be valuable. What reactions do they produce? Are they poorly written, shabby in appearance, unclear about their need or about what they will do with the money received? Or, do they look too good to be truly in need of money? The public allows each organization individuality in the manner and style chosen for fund-raising solicitations, but it demands believability and competence.

Mass communications can have several valuable by-products. Community awareness of the organization, its mission, its goals, and its services to the public will increase—a necessary first step in building the trust and confidence that are essential for continued public gift support. Each opportunity for community contact needs to be matched with the appropriate fund-raising method. What are other charities in the community using? How successful are these same methods for them? When they use them, who is asked to give? The same community residents are available to all charities for solicitation; poor timing can result in requests from donors to stop asking for money.

Organizations can use, either separately or in combination, as many methods of annual giving as they choose. Consider the following mix suggested by Henry Rosso:

> Programs approved for fund raising by the development director and the development committee use direct mail for acquisition and gift renewal purposes, first-class mailings for gift upgrading, and a judicious number of special events. In addition, the fund raising agenda includes solicitation of special purpose gifts from individuals, foundations, and corporations. This mix offers abundant opportunities for generating financial resources to support operating programs.[2]

The most common methods of annual giving are

- Using the mail for acquisition and renewal
- Telephone and telemarketing
- Benefits and special events

[2]Ibid., 20.

- Support group organizations
- Donor clubs
- Volunteer personal solicitation campaigns.

There are other ways to raise money, but they do not lend themselves easily to a managed program for repeated use, nor are they reliable for raising friends as well as funds each year. These other options include advertising and coupons, affinity cards, commemorative giving, commercial sales and cause-related marketing, door-to-door and on-street solicitation, gambling (sweepstakes and lotteries, Las Vegas and Monte Carlo nights), federated campaigns, and more. Each of these will be discussed following the traditional methods later in this chapter.

Annual giving must be annual. If solicitation is suspended even for one year, restarting the program and bringing it back to its former level of productivity can take two years or more. Each year's effort repeats many of the tasks of soliciting for the first time: finding new prospects to begin their gift support; recruiting and training volunteers who will ask their friends for money; and preparing solicitation letters, case statements, and worker information kits. Some tasks, however, happily build upon the previous year's success, such as soliciting prior donors to continue (or upgrade) their levels of annual gift support. The key to succeeding in these efforts year after year lies in the ability of the organization to achieve coordination, cooperation, and communication between the volunteers and the organization and to maintain an astute awareness of donors' receptivity. Fund raising involves diverse activity, large numbers of people, and simultaneous appeals to the same available audience. Only a highly coordinated team effort can make it effective (see Exhibit 3.2). As a bonus for success, it can all be experienced again the following year.

Goal Setting for Annual Gift Results

Goal setting for annual giving requires careful analysis of prior results, attention to changes in the local community and the not-for-profit organization, and an excellent understanding of donors. The institution's needs must be balanced realistically against what it can raise in the current year, given the maturity of the organization, the productivity of each annual giving method in use, and how well these factors are working together.

Forecasts should be based on accurate analyses of the methods in use and their results. Performance measurement can provide considerable insight for this purpose. Organizations perform differently, even when they use the same methods of fundraising; another organization's productivity

EXHIBIT 3.2 Elements of a Successful Annual Campaign

1. Board leadership
2. Participation by volunteer teams
3. A plan
4. A goal that is realistic but a "stretch"
5. A carefully constructed list of prospects
6. Strategies that include all donors in a continuum of investment opportunities
7. Energize the volunteers with training and "product news"
8. Be sure support staff and materials are ready to enhance the volunteer experience

Reprinted with permission from Beyond Fund Raising: New Strategies for Nonprofit Innovation and Investment *by Kay Sprinkel Grace (New York: John Wiley & Sons, Inc., 1997), 138–144.*

may be unattainable for no apparent reason. Much depends on volunteers, individually and collectively, who can have uneven success from one year to the next. They cannot be pushed too hard or treated like employees, whose performance is linked to monetary reward. Volunteers' continued enthusiasm for public service and motivation to improve their performance are not to be taken for granted. As an example, if only 15 volunteers are available to solicit 450 "best donors," loading each volunteer with 30 assigned prospects is unrealistic; all 450 donors would not be seen and asked under the best circumstances, and placing the entire burden on so few volunteers may cause them to quit. They will think their best efforts failed the organization, and failure is not a motive for continued service.

Income sources from previous years must be reviewed: Were they onetime successes or annual, dependable producers? A local repertory theater may have arranged a premiere opening and raised a net total of $10,000. Will they want to do it again? Will the play and the cast selected this year draw the same size audience again? Will the sponsors and underwriters pay for the cost of invitations, tickets, and programs again? Has another organization approached the theater for a similar event? Each of these questions must be resolved favorably before the $10,000 can be forecast for the current year. Some other event may have to be created; whatever the source, the organization needs the same $10,000.

Goals must be understood by management and volunteers as target objectives, not fixed figures. They are a "package" of priority needs and dollar objectives, public benefit and fiscal goals and the *combination* must be the point of focus and measurement, not the amount of money realized.

Timing of requests, except for disaster relief, also has to make sense. Donors are not likely to respond to arbitrary schedules invented by not-for-profit organizations. They must first appreciate the results they can make possible. If they feel that every dollar raised will be put to the best use possible, they will encourage others to join in and give too. Whenever possible, visible projects—for example, new equipment or buildings, new programs that serve more people, and scholarships—should be selected for public giving campaigns, timed with public awareness of the need for the project that will benefit others and that can begin as soon as the funds are received.

If one definition could bring all these elements of annual giving together, it might read as follows:

> Successful annual giving is the planned use of proven methods of solicitation designed to produce the required results consistent with public recognition of a need, the maturity of fund-raising methods in use, and the reliability of volunteer leadership and performance.

Goal setting directly affects volunteer groups. They also must agree that the targets set can be achieved and even exceeded in a team effort, and that their accountability for the fund-raising results is valid. If volunteers believe the goal assigned them is beyond their capacity and best efforts, they will lose confidence in the design plan and in their ability to succeed, and the entire program can fail. The formula for setting good goals for annual giving programs is to establish objectives that are based on careful and critical measurement of prior results, include a realistic analysis of current conditions, and create a new goal that can be achieved and exceeded, even if it is higher than last year's team effort. Volunteers are quite willing to work hard to meet objectives they know are attainable; they often commit to beating last year's results. Competition against a past goal is enormously valuable and can spark the extra enthusiasm that leads to success.

Goals and objectives can be developed by the entire fund-raising team by allowing everyone to join in the analyses of the previous year's results and present conditions and in the decisions on final goals. A process of annual consensus that allows volunteer participation is quite valuable and can be helped by written guidelines from the board, outlining the steps to follow in setting each year's annual goals and objectives.

Each annual giving method used requires three to four years to reach a level of maturity at which predictable levels of annual net income can be forecast. During those years of building, you must maintain a positive environment, a belief that every effort will meet or exceed the previous year's performance regardless of changing circumstances. Every successful program or event nurtures volunteers' confidence in their ability to perform and in the methods used. The result is a willingness to continue next year, perhaps in a leadership role. Success fuels the potential for ever greater levels of commitment.

What to Use in Making Annual Gifts

Exactly how do people make a gift that may also qualify as being tax deductible? Depending on what they have to give, people give cash and currency, pledges, securities, personal property, and gifts-in-kind.

Cash and Currency

Cash, checks, and money orders have been in use for years; charges to credit cards have now been added as a means of donation. There is a small service fee (up to 3 percent) for the use of "plastic" but the donor acts *now* on a gift decision, the charity receives full value (less the fee) right away, and the donor pays for it later under the terms of the charge account. Amounts claimed as charitable contribution deductions are currently limited by federal law to be available only to those taxpayers who file an itemized ("long form") return. (Non-itemizers lost their deduction for gifts to charity under the 1986 Tax Reform Act.) More recent IRS regulations require written documentation from the organization for all gifts of $250 or more, plus substantiation in the letter of the material value of any goods or services received by the donor that reduces the deductible value of the gift. The text of this declaration might read as follows: "In accordance with IRS regulations, this letter will substantiate that the value of your contribution for income tax purposes is $250.00. Furthermore, I can advise you that no material goods or services will be received by you as a result of this gift. If you itemize your taxes, please keep this letter as evidence of your claim for a charitable contribution tax deduction in the _____ tax year." Donors who qualify may claim the value given (less the value of any material goods or services received) up to a maximum of 50 percent of adjusted gross income. Donors whose gift total exceeds 50 percent may carry forward the unused portion of their deduction as a credit or credits on tax returns filed during the next five years as a carryover.

Pledges

Pledging for annual gifts is less common than currency donations but may be necessary if a solicitation is performed over the telephone or on radio or television, or if payment is made via payroll deductions by employees. (United Way encourages this simple but effective method.) Annual giving, by its nature, requires a short pledge period that ends on December 31 or on the fiscal year-end date of the organization. Pledges are an administrative burden; they cost the organization money for record-keeping, billing, and collections. They also carry an increased potential for some amount of nonpayment. Most annual giving programs prefer cash to pledges because the organization will use the money as soon as it is received.

In 1993, the Financial Accounting Standards Board (FASB) amended the accounting guidelines for pledges, which are now called "unconditional promises to give." According to the new provisions the full value of the pledge amount must be entered as revenue in the fiscal year the pledge is received. Furthermore, it must be treated as an asset with a corresponding liability and the option to pursue for collection. This final action is considered by most organizations to be too threatening to use with multiyear donors without full disclosure to the donor of these conditions at the time a written pledge is executed. Just how organizations will account for formal, written pledges in the future may vary. One option is the use of a lesser method—a "conditional promise to give" or an "intention," whichever removes the threat of going to collections. As to FASB's stipulation that the pledge's full value be recorded in the same year it is received, calculation of the pledge value to be entered on financial statements can be discounted in both of the following ways: first, by imputing the time value of money over the pledge period (two years or more) using current inflation rates, and second, by applying a discount based on the organization's history of past pledge collections (e.g., 92 percent). This dual procedure will reduce the figure or gift amount in financial statements from that which was negotiated with the donor.

Securities

Stocks and bonds are assets that have changing market value. Securities with appreciated values are subject to capital gains tax if they are sold, but if they are given to a qualified not-for-profit organization, the donor may claim the current market value as a deduction in the year of the gift and avoid payment of any capital gains tax. The method preferred by the IRS to document the contribution value has three steps:

1. Calculate the mean average price of the stock on the date when ownership was transferred to the charity.
2. Verify the calculation with a broker *and* in the next business day's edition of a newspaper that carries the stock exchange listing, as does the *Wall Street Journal,* the *New York Times,* and the like.
3. Confirm the gift value in writing to the donor and include the gift substantiation language described in the "Cash and Currency" section above.

Individuals who are active in financial markets know when to make a gift using stock and most often will choose to act when stock values are up. Securities gift decisions can be deferred until market conditions are favorable. Most annual gifts involving securities are modest in size (under $5,000 in value) and occur before the tax year ends. The donor expects that the stock will be sold and the proceeds will be used toward annual giving priorities.

Personal Property

Goodwill Industries, the Salvation Army, the St. Vincent de Paul Society, and thrift shops derive substantial annual support from gifts of tangible personal property. Other organizations may receive such gifts but often cannot match any direct use for them to their mission. When an item is not directly usable, the donor's deduction value is limited to a maximum of 30 percent of adjusted gross income; when it is usable, the donor may claim a deduction of up to 50 percent of adjusted gross income. Donors can deliver or drop off used clothing, furniture, appliances, and other personal effects or, in some areas, can ask to have the articles picked up by the charity.

Many donors have an incorrect impression that gifts of personal property have an important deduction value (not to mention the value of their being rid of unused items from their attic or basement). Tax deduction amounts claimed for gifts of personal property are strictly between donors and the IRS. Donors who ask the recipient charity to provide a statement of value are put off when told that the charity cannot verify value and often become angry when advised that the IRS requires the donor to arrange and pay for a qualified written appraisal of the property given. However inconvenient, these procedures are the law. A few gifts may be lost when donors learn that the not-for-profit organization can provide only a receipt certifying what was received and when, but the IRS believes (quite correctly) that charities are unqualified to place a value on personal property given to them.

The IRS has specific procedures for placing a deduction value on gifts of property. Claims for deductibility for property valued at $5,000 or more must be authenticated in writing by a certified professional appraiser, at the donor's expense, and a copy of the appraisal attached to IRS Form 8283 must accompany the donor's annual tax return. (Even if a copy of the appraisal is given to the charity, it can verify only that it received the property.) The Form 8283 also must be signed by the organization, to verify that it has received the property and date of receipt. If the organization sells the property within two years, it is required to submit IRS Form 8282 describing the date of sale and the price received. The IRS can compare these two transactions, and, if the sale price is substantially lower than the original amount claimed as a gift deduction, the IRS may audit the donor to challenge the donor's claim of the original deduction. If the property is held by the organization for two years and a day, the comparative period expires and no Form 8282 is needed.[3] Gifts of personal property need to be handled knowledgeably.

Gifts-in-Kind

Some donors are in a position to give goods and services that can be used for charitable purposes in lieu of cash, securities, or personal property. Gifts-in-kind can be valuable when they are directly usable for the mission of the organization or can be used in direct support of a benefit event. Examples are free or reduced-price printing of invitations, programs, or tickets by a professional printer; decorations and flowers from a florist; food from a caterer or wholesaler; table favors from local merchants; and wine and similar items from appropriate sources. Gifts-in-kind can help to reduce the direct costs of staging an event and thus mean greater net proceeds for the not-for-profit organization. Tax deductibility claims for gifts-in-kind valued by the donor at $5,000 or more, as with gifts of personal property, must be documented with a complete, certified appraisal to verify the exact amount to be claimed as a deduction, plus IRS Form 8283 signed by the donor and the charity, both to be submitted to the IRS with the donor's annual income tax return.

Credit and Count: How to Report the Value of Gifts

An important distinction must be made between how gift values are recorded in donors' gift histories and how they are recorded on financial

---

[3]For a full discussion of appraisal requirements, see Bruce R. Hopkins, *The Law of Fund Raising*, 2d ed. (New York: Wiley, 1996) § 6.13(i) at 511–516.

statements. Accounting guidelines specify how each contribution is to be recorded on financial statements and annual audits for all not-for-profit organizations. Fund development offices should follow those guidelines, but there may be exceptions due to *credit and count*. *Credit* is the value of the charitable contribution deduction claimed by the donor and recorded in the donor's gift history for cumulative tracking and donor recognition purposes. *Count* is the figure entered on all financial statements. These figures may differ, as the following two examples illustrate:

> Mr. Jones makes an annual gift of 100 shares of stock, which is verified to have a fair market value of $1,050.25 on the date ownership of the stock is transferred to the organization. The organization's gift substantiation letter reports this value as the correct amount for the donor to claim for income tax purposes. This same amount is entered in the donor's gift history and the donor is notified his contribution qualifies him for membership in the President's Circle for annual donor recognition purposes. The organization sells the stock the next day through its broker and, after commission, Securities and Exchange Commission fees, and taxes, the net amount is $995.75, which is the value recorded as revenue received on financial statements. Both figures are correct for their separate purposes, as credit and count, respectively.
>
> Mrs. Smith makes a five-year capital campaign pledge of $100,000, payable at $20,000 a year, and is accorded donor recognition credit at the Benefactor level for donors giving between $100,000 and $250,000. The chief financial officer and the auditor record this pledge at full value in the year it is received, *minus* a discount for the time value of money over five years (an average of 3 percent per year using current inflation rates) and *minus* a discount based on the organization's history of past pledge collections (92 percent), and enter the pledge value at $87,000. Again, both amounts are correct for their respective uses, as credit and count.

The prior examples illustrate the importance of communication within the organization between the chief development officer and the chief financial officer or business officer about how contributions are recorded for donors' income tax purposes and donor recognition purposes, as well as how the same contributions are reported for financial and audit purposes. Reconciliation of fiscal records between the fund development office and the accounting office is made possible when accurate records are shared, when both parties appreciate the need to report their separate figures for separate purposes, and when both parties explain their use of these separate figures to board members, donors, volunteers, and others in a spirit of open and full disclosure.

Asking for Annual Gift Money

Asking for gifts is quite simple because there are only three ways: by mail, by telephone, or, the most successful way, in person. Personal solicitation is not popular with volunteers because they have to ask their friends for money. Direct mail, the most impersonal method, is the least efficient. Mail solicitation is estimated to be at least 16 times less effective than personal solicitation; yet most annual giving solicitations are still performed by mail. When compared with managing the recruitment, training, motivation, and supervision of volunteer solicitors, which takes a lot of time and energy, use of mail solicitation is easier for fund-raising staff. Organizations that have no volunteers can send out appeal letters and get immediate results.

The fund-raising methods most often used in annual giving programs, in their *ascending* order of cost-effectiveness and productivity, are:

- Direct mail acquisition, renewal, and upgrading
- Telephone solicitation
- Visual media
- Benefits and special events
- Support group organizations
- Donor clubs and associations
- Volunteer committees who will personally ask their friends for money each year

Each method is discussed in this chapter.

USING THE MAILS TO ACQUIRE AND RETAIN DONORS

Solicitation by mail may be less effective than personal solicitation but it is by far the most popular method of annual giving practiced in America today because, for most not-for-profit organizations, it works. Any organization can market its programs and services by mail to large numbers of people who may be possible clients for the services as well as potential contributors. The unit cost is low and new revenue may be stimulated within days after a mailing is "dropped." However, direct mail solicitation is neither simple to perform nor easy to operate at a profit. Experts in the field estimate that mail solicitations directed at nondonors who are being asked for their first-ever gifts have a rate of return of between .005

and .010 percent, or a 1-in-100 chance of receiving money. To achieve even these performance levels, list selection is critical and more than one appeal must be sent to the same people; a single letter will not carry the day.

"Direct response advertising" is the classic title for mail solicitation that has become better known as "junk mail." Use of the mails for fund raising is an extremely complex arena and requires years of experience to master; volumes of performance data are available along with an almost equal number of "experts." Given its marginal success rate and high potential for disaster, a direct mail program should not be begun without professional help, nor delegated to volunteers, unless their professional experience includes direct mail management. An organization must secure a permit from the local post office for the use of third-class, bulk-rate privileges when mailing 200 or more pieces (all identical, none personalized). This privileged arrangement reduces postage costs to about one-third of the rates for first-class service. The post office that issues the permit is the site where the letters must be delivered. Advance payment of the anticipated cost of the entire shipment must be received three days prior to the drop, and the entire mailing must be bundled, tied, and bagged in presorted nine-digit ZIP code order, according to specifications of that post office. If the mailing is not completely correct in all respects, it will not be accepted and no mail will be delivered.

Direct mail consultants advise separating the plans to identify and acquire new donors (friend raising) from the plans to renew prior donors (relationship building). The strategy for each is quite different although many details are shared in common.

Success in direct mail fund raising is tied closely to mailing lists— names of qualified suspects and prospects. The first goal is to use the mail to find new donors and stimulate their first gift. Selection of viable lists is critical to success.

Each time letters are sent out, the mailing "package" (see Exhibit 3.3) offers multiple choices regarding mailing lists, an outer envelope, the letter or message, an insert (brochure, postcard, copy of newspaper article), a response form, and a reply envelope. Each choice is important to the effort; failure to weigh the relationship among the choices can spell disaster.

Acquiring New Donors by Mail

Mailing Lists

Rosters of names and addresses, sorted by region, field of interest, specialty, age, income level, and so on, can be bought, rented, or leased from list brokers. Volunteers may be able to supply the names of their business

EXHIBIT 3.3 Components and Options in the Direct Mail Package

Basic Components	Options
Mailing lists	Prior donors
	Members and volunteers
	Prospects and suspects
	Clients and neighbors
	Rented/leased/purchased lists
Outer envelope	Addressee information
	Complete return address
	"Address Service Requested"
	Indicia/stamp/metered postage
	Special "teaser" message
Appeal letter	Official stationery
	Personalized salutation
	Personal message style
	Persuasive wording
	Request for a gift amount
	Typed/printed/computer-output text
	"P.S." message
Enclosure	Brochure, card, or giveaway
	Photograph and message
	Reprinted news article or ad
Response form	Donor's name, address, phone number
	Gift amount options
	Gift club option
	Information for inquiries (on wills, bequests, special gifts)
Reply envelope	Preprinted and preaddressed
	Space for return address
	Postage (blank/metered/stamped)
	Combination response form/envelope (business reply envelope)

Reprinted with permission from Fund-Raising Fundamentals: A Guide to Annual Giving for Professionals and Volunteers *by James M. Greenfield (New York: John Wiley & Sons, Inc., 1994), 39.*

clients, membership rosters from their country clubs and social or civic organizations, or even personal holiday greeting card lists of family and friends. Names and addresses can be copied from the telephone book and from reports of other not-for-profit organizations that publish the roster of all their donors. Finding lists is not difficult; the problem is how to select qualified donor-candidates from all the available sources. Lists must be sorted into suspects, prospects, and donors (see Exhibit 3.4). Two crucial questions apply to each list: Who is likely to reply favorably to a first-time request? Who is likely to respond to a request made by mail? The names selected in answer should be kept and the others discarded.

Lists from brokers, sellers, or services may be an organization's best source because they include performance data on prior use of the lists, which will not be available for newly compiled lists. Volunteers will urge use of their personal lists because they are "free," but an organization usually gets what it pays for.

Testing is only slightly less crucial than list selection. Only 5,000 names are needed to test any list, although usually more than one list is tested at one time. A test mailing is split equally according to some element of the

---

EXHIBIT 3.4 Likely Candidates as First-Time Donors

Suspects | People living nearby.
| People who have been served.
| People to whom service is directed.
| People who work for suppliers.
| People who respond to invitations.
| People who respond to media messages.
| People who respond to similar causes.
| People identified by selection criteria.

Prospects | All the above suspects.
| People who participate in similar causes.
| People who currently participate in the organization.
| People identified by others who are involved.
| People buying tickets to activities.
| People of influence.
| People with proven leadership skills.
| People who were donors in prior years.

Reprinted with permission from Fund-Raising Fundamentals: A Guide to Annual Giving for Professionals and Volunteers *by James M. Greenfield (New York: John Wiley & Sons, Inc., 1994), 36.*

package or its contents—the charity's name on the outer envelope or not, a message on the outer envelope or not, a different color for each group, one page or four pages of text, an insert or none, a postage-paid reply envelope or none. Note: Test only *one* variable at a time. The combination that works best, measured by results and not feelings or preferences, should be used for the entire list.

Outer Envelope

In addition to the sender's and the addressee's full name and address, this envelope has room for a message to stimulate the recipients to open the package. Direct mail experts report the most critical period in the life of a letter appeal is when people sort their mail (usually over a trash basket). If an envelope does not survive this initial screening (less than five seconds), the wonderful words inside will never be seen or read. Given this precarious moment, how important is it to place the name of the not-for-profit organization on the outer envelope? Should a message, or a color, or a logo, or even a photograph be added to pique the recipients' curiosity? The chances that new prospects who may not recognize the organization or know its purpose will interrupt their mail sort above the trash basket to open one particular appeal envelope are slim at best. The appearance of the envelope may save it from the "junk mail" conditioned reflex (trashing). At this moment of decision, having an *exactly* correct name and address for the recipient and sender can be a crucial factor.

Appeal Letter

Mail experts advise that the letter must capture the readers' attention quickly (perhaps within only 15 seconds). The first paragraph and the "P.S." message are the two key attention getters. Few readers are likely to read the contents of the package in its entirety; for those who do read, a four-page letter achieves a higher rate of response and a larger average gift than the more common single-page letter. An exception to these rules appears among elderly recipients. They are apt to read nearly everything they receive because they have leisure time to do so, and their average response is equal to or a little better than that of other age groups; but their average gift is smaller because they have less spendable cash available. Age grouping also should be considered before selecting informational and educational communications to be included in a mailing package.

Enclosure

Adding any insert—a photograph, a reprinted newspaper article, a generic brochure about the institution, or a specific flyer about the project needing funds—will increase the printing costs of a mailing. If the insert brings the package weight above eight ounces, postage is also increased. Inserts should be looked upon as "trade-off" items tied to the message in the letter, the lists being used, and the follow-up letters. A general guideline may help. When a mailing is to people who know about the organization, information can be given in the letter, which has a higher chance of being read anyway. For people who are not yet donors and who know little or nothing about the organization, an informational insert may assist their decision to become donors. List selection remains the primary factor every time.

Response Form

A response form is the action item contained in the package. Most response forms are preprinted with the name and address of the recipient and ask for any necessary corrections. The reply is easy for the recipient to fill out and is used by the organization to confirm or update active files. The recipient can be invited to participate in the mailing by checking a choice of specific gift size, a preference for how the money should be used, and an option to request more information, (e.g., procedures for making a bequest or special gift). The response form should contain codes to identify the list used and other data that will aid in analysis of all replies.

Reply Envelope

The reply envelope is a convenience, to help make responding as easy as possible. No one knows how many appeals fail for lack of a handy envelope, but mail experts can document increased replies when the envelope is added. Risk of wrong delivery is avoided because the full name and mailing address of the organization are printed on the reply envelope. Surprises arrive occasionally in the reply envelope—a request to be taken off the mailing list, statements of strong views about the organization's cause, reactions to the environment of giving or to the general public need—all inspired by the arrival of the letter. These requests should be honored, especially any "do not mail." instructions. These missives also make for interesting reading, especially those that are not "hate mail." They sometimes offer quotable passages for future mailing pieces.

A debate continues among direct mail experts over whether to provide a postage-paid envelope or to ask the donor to pay the return postage by adding a first-class stamp. In the author's experience, limited-size mailings (under 300,000 pieces) have yielded no conclusive evidence either way. Postage-paid business reply envelopes require special handling by the post office at a cost of $0.55 per envelope, which cuts into the mailing's net proceeds. Donors can appreciate the validity of being asked to add their own stamp to save costs; it suggests a sensitivity toward making the best use of their money in helping others.

Much more information is available on direct mail; most of it focuses on acquisition efforts and measurement of results. Direct mail acquisition is without question the most expensive area of fund raising: A mailing that spends no more than $1.25 to $1.50 to raise $1.00 is considered a success. The "profits" are in renewing and upgrading donors by mail. Direct mail acquisition also can be profitable, with good list selection. As another benefit, the not-for-profit organization finds and recruits new friends who can become donors over time, and who, if expertly managed, may develop a loyalty that will make them volunteers, leaders, and major gift contributors. The first letter and the first crop of radishes are the beginning of everything.

Renewing Prior Donors by Mail

The primary purpose of acquisition direct mail is to find and develop new, first-time donors. But the next step, donor renewal, is much more profitable. To evaluate overall direct mail fund-raising success, acquisition and renewal efforts first must be analyzed separately, then measured together. Three years of continuous mail experience will be required in most instances to demonstrate the productivity and profitability of the combination. Fund-raising by mail is an investment strategy: Each group of new donors represents predictable rates of future annual gift revenue at a low unit cost through renewal.

Asking a prior donor to give again is simple compared to the effort that went into acquiring the donor. This person made a favorable decision in giving money, was thanked properly and promptly, and, through continuing communication, learned something about the organization and about the first gift's positive effect in helping others. Can there be a better prospect for another gift?

But renewal is not automatic. Each donor has to be asked for his or her next gift, and therein lie three challenges: How to ask well, when to ask, and how much to ask for. Before the renewal letter is prepared, consider the many similarities to the acquisition mail effort that captured the first gift. The message of needed support and the project to be supported again are probably identical. The same method (mail) is being used to ask for the gift. The timing, the organization, and even the author of the letter may be the same.

What's different is the text of the letter. Renewal letters to donors can presume a lot: the donors were pleased with the last giving experience, the project was successful thanks to donors' help, the people in need were served well, more work remains to be done, and it is all right to ask for help once again. In renewal solicitation, the letter, not the list, is the most important piece in the mailing package. The renewal mail package has the same ingredients as the acquisition package, but with subtle changes, as the following discussion shows.

Mailing Lists

A renewal list should be considered current and accurate, but there are donors and there are *donors*. Those who gave for the first time last year and have made no other gifts of any kind will need to be treated differently from prior donors whose annual giving history goes back several years and who make other gifts during each year. Lapsed donors, inactive last year or even for two or three years, are better prospects than nondonors but will need some extra coaxing to restart their giving. Each renewal begins the same as an acquisition; donors are segregated into groups and each group is addressed separately, according to its donors' different gift history, gift size, and length of experience as a giver. Renewal letters, all personalized, can be tailored to fit each segment of the donor list for maximum results.

Outer Envelope

The envelope must show the organization's name, preferably on the front, because name recognition has a better chance to save the letter from being trashed on arrival. A message is likely to be noticed, but more important is how the donor's name appears. The use of labels or a similarly impersonal method can hurt response; the donor expects (rightly) the organization now knows who they are. The letter should look like and imitate in every way a personal communication. If feasible, the author's name should appear at the upper left-hand corner of the envelope, above the organization's return address.

Appeal Letter

The art of writing personal letters shines here. Personal letters need to be correct in form but friendly in tone. The text, written as one friend writes to another (not to thousands), should use personal pronouns. Renewal appeal letters are an organization's "love letters." Brief but never curt, they should refer to the last gift and cite the numbers of other donors who also replied and joined in making last year's project a success. After mentioning the services and progress made by the institution and the benefits delivered to others, the text must ask for another gift and may even specify the amount of the last gift for a repeat donation. Encouraging consideration of a slightly higher amount this year if possible (upgrading) is appropriate because as many as 15 percent of those approached this way will respond favorably; others will send the amount they gave last time.

Enclosure

An insert is quite easy to add, and inexpensive, given the smaller number of renewal letters, and, if the material is relevant, it could help to ensure the renewal gift. However, to print something special or separate just for prior donors may be seriously questionable from a cost standpoint.

Response Form

The response form can be simple and direct because donors have seen it before. In a renewal mailing, the form can ask for information from donors and can encourage them to ask for specific materials (which reveals their particular interests). This is an opportunity to invite them to become involved as participants in other programs or to receive information about adding the organization as a beneficiary in their will and about other options. The form can introduce the higher gift ranges that are linked to donor recognition or donor club qualifications. It should be an instrument for stimulating more action by recipients and for making the exchange of mail more interesting for them and as positive an experience as possible. Requests made by donors on the form must be fulfilled promptly, to keep credibility and ensure the donor's next gift.

Reply Envelope

The reply envelope is still necessary, postage-paid or not, because of its convenience. If the letter comments on efforts to conserve on costs in conducting fund-raising programs, the donor can be asked to add a stamp. Some people keep unused postage-paid reply envelopes for years and may eventually send money.

Donor renewals also must be multiple-letter appeals. Persistence helps convince both prospects and donors that their gift is valuable and is needed right now. All mailings should be concentrated in the "best times" to mail (September to November and March to May). The period between appeal letters can be from four to six weeks. Direct mail campaigns should have start and end dates consistent with the calendar year, fiscal year, or any other deadline that will be respected and can help stimulate a reply.

Success in the first and second renewal following the first gift is cru- cial to keeping a donor for several years. Between solicitation campaigns, newsletters, annual reports, invitations, and whatever other communica- tions make sense and are cost-effective will increase donors' knowledge of and respect for the organization. Reports should tell donors how their money was used, how valuable their gift was, how many other people joined in, and how the funds were beneficial to others. Each renewal mes- sage is a golden opportunity to build the relationship toward more infor- mation, interest, and involvement. Being part of something successful and worthwhile is the best reason to give again. Seeds for giving must be cultivated all year long.

Nine-Point Performance Analysis of Direct Mail

The complete direct mail program should be analyzed as well as each of its components: testing, acquisition, renewal, and upgrading. Why the emphasis on renewal as well as acquisition? As this author has written elsewhere,

> What is most important about the results of a mail program is what the orga- nization does with its many newfound friends and donors. The keys to effi- ciency and profitability are in the follow-up, not in the acquisition. Donor re- lations is an active program to be managed to use mail communications as the means to stimulate personal interaction between donors and not-for- profit organizations. To realize the maximum potential from a mail solicita- tion program, time and attention also must be given to cultivating the donors acquired by mail to higher levels of involvement with the organization.[4]

As a sample analysis, Exhibit 3.5 shows a nine-point performance index applied to a two-year-old direct mail program. In the program, the initial test mailings were sent to eight lists (30,000 names), and the full "rollout" mailing went to the best-performing four of the eight lists tested (300,000 names). The following outcomes were demonstrated:

(1) The test mailing demonstrated a 1.43 percent response rate, an av- erage gift size of $30.93, and fund-raising cost of $0.91 per dollar raised. Four lists demonstrated the potential for good results and the full mailing of 300,000 letters was sent to these four. Test responses from the other four lists were below 1 percent with average gifts below $20 and a fund-

---

[4]James M. Greenfield, *Fund-Raising Cost Effectiveness: A Self-Assessment Workbook* (New York: Wiley, 1997), 41.

EXHIBIT 3.5 Nine-Point Performance Index Analysis of Direct Mail

	Testing		Full Mailing		Renewal		Totals
Participation	1,156	+	3,653	+	914	=	5,723
Income	$35,758	+	$116,911	+	$31,064	=	$183,733
Expense	$32,641	+	$99,000	+	$1,827	=	$133,468
Percent participation	1.43%	+	0.92%	+	60.77%	=	1.20%
Average gift size	$30.93	+	$32.00	+	$33.99	=	$32.31
Net income	$3,117	+	$17,911	+	$29,237	=	$50,265
Average cost per gift	$28.24	+	$27.10	+	$2.00	=	$23.32
Cost of fund raising	91%	+	85%	+	6%	=	73%
Return	10%	+	18%	+	1600%	=	39%

Reprinted with permission from Fund-Raising Cost Effectiveness: A Self-Assessment Workbook *by James M. Greenfield (New York: John Wiley & Sons, Inc., 1996), 42.*

raising cost of nearly $2 to raise $1. Limited budgets for testing and acquisition dictate using the best performing lists for the full "rollout" mailing.

(2) The full mailing achieved 3,653 new donors at a 0.92 percent response rate and average gift size of $32. A net profit of $17,911 was realized after direct costs of $99,000—a higher-than-normal level of performance, which demonstrates the validity of testing and choosing lists that perform with high returns. The 1,156 donors from testing and 3,653 new donors from the full mailing (a total of 4,809 people!) now become the focus of concentration as they are more likely to remain donors and move up the pyramid of giving.

(3) The first renewal mailing to the 1,156 donors from test mailings achieved a 60.77 percent response rate, quite good. However, this means that nearly 40 percent of the original donors failed to renew, suggesting at least one more mailing to them later on will be beneficial. The average gift increased to $33.99. The direct costs of $1,827 were modest, and the $31,064 in net proceeds amounted to a 1,600 percent return. The cost of fund raising was $0.06, or 6 percent. The organization's continued investment in these new donors will be essential to realize their potential over the long term (many years). There is every expectation that, if renewed for a second time, they will remain mail-responsive donors for an additional five to seven years.

(4) Taken together, the three mailings demonstrated a response rate of 1.20 percent and an average gift of just over $32.00. The total of 5,723 new donors is a splendid start for this direct mail program, but the overall cost of $133,468 may be more than most organizations can afford to invest, despite a net profit of $50,265.

Direct mail is proficient at building a donor file quickly, but it is not the most efficient form of fund raising available and should not be used exclusive of all others.

TELEPHONE SOLICITATION

The advantage the telephone has over mail is personal contact—a big edge and possibly eight times more effective than the mails. Personal conversation is extremely important in a fast-paced society whose people have limited time for reading. The telephone is a splendid instrument for solicitations of all kinds, because of its direct interaction, which is why it has become the medium of choice for many business purposes and has even spawned a new word to describe its use—*telemarketing*. The telephone is best used by not-for-profit organizations for donor relations, to maintain close contact with valued donors. It is also appropriate for "thank-you" calls to major donors on the day their special gift arrives and for recognition purposes to express appreciation for volunteering, to announce an award, or invite someone to a special gathering. However, like the mail, some people resent its intrusive nature, a sensitivity that not-for-profit organizations must respect when they consider using the telephone for raising the funds they need. The telephone is less appropriate (and more expensive) to use for cold calls that attempt to acquire a first-time donor than it is to call lapsed donors to ask them to renew their support.

Perhaps the most important aspect of any telephone solicitation is the caller. There is some debate among fund-raising professionals on the merits of using volunteer callers versus paid, professional callers. At issue is who is likely to perform better and be more cost-effective. But perhaps the ideal candidate is not to be found because volunteers are less effective by comparison but professional callers cost more. Each organization will have to decide the issue for itself in the way that best suits its needs.[5]

Donor renewal efforts by telephone can be difficult when prior donors' annual giving was done through a different fund-raising method. For example, attempting to renew all direct mail donors by telephone alone may be neither efficient nor effective, although it is appropriate for donors who belong to a membership program, donor club, or support group. The difference is due to the nature of the latter donors' relation-

---

[5]For a complete discussion of telephone solicitation, see "Telemarketing" by William Freyd and Diane M. Carlson, in *The Nonprofit Handbook: Fund Raising,* 2d ed., ed. James M. Greenfield (New York: Wiley, 1997) 317–328.

ship with the organization through those special fund-raising techniques. Mail donors have no special allegiance or relationship to the organization; their connection is rather tenuous. But membership implies a link to the organization that includes member benefits and privileges. Similarly, belonging to a donor club is a special relationship deriving directly from the donor's prior gift size, which also includes special benefits and privileges. A support group is a semiautonomous entity that combines features of a membership program and a donor club; its tie to the organization is based on a combination of annual dues and the implied obligation of active participation by all members.

Nine-Point Performance Analysis of Telephone Solicitation

An analysis comparing the results of using the telephone to renew donors whose affiliation is either via direct mail, membership, donor club, or support group organization may be seen in Exhibit 3.6. The largest list for renewal belongs to the mail program, and although the telephone campaign succeeds with 75 percent of its prior donors, participation by direct mail donors lags behind that of the other three donor constituencies. Most noticeable is the contrast in average gift size, which relates directly to the $100 annual membership or donors' gift level required to belong to the other three groups. Tracking these programs and their renewal statistics

EXHIBIT 3.6 Nine-Point Performance Index Analysis of Telephone Solicitation

	Direct Mail Donors	Membership Donors	Donor Club Donors	Support Group Donors
Participation	2,005	225	231	233
Income	$57,038	$18,900	$29,915	$19,700
Expenses	$16,970	$4,750	$4,750	$4,750
Percentage participation	75%	82%	87%	85%
Average gift size	$37.92	$102.16	$148.83	$99.49
Net income	$40,068	$14,150	$25,165	$14,950
Average cost per gift	$8.46	$21.11	$20.56	$20.39
Cost of fund raising	30%	25%	16%	24%
Return	236%	298%	530%	315%

Reprinted with permission from Fund-Raising Cost Effectiveness: A Self-Assessment Workbook *by James M. Greenfield (New York: John Wiley & Sons, Inc., 1996), 92.*

for three or more years will be essential. Here is an analysis of one year's renewal activity:

1. Successful 75 percent of the time, telephone renewal of direct mail donors proved more effective than the renewal letters seen in the earlier analysis (see Exhibit 3.3), which had a 60.66 percent success rate. Average gift size and net proceeds were improved as well.
2. Telephone calls to membership donors resulted in an 82 percent renewal rate and an average gift of $102.16, above the $100 minimum dues level, at a reasonable fund-raising cost of $0.35.
3. The renewal rate of donor club members via the telephone hit 87 percent with an average gift of $148.83, the best performer in this illustration.
4. Support group participants renewed at 85 percent over the telephone, not unusual for this type of program that concentrates more on personal volunteer involvement in the group than on giving.

THE AGE OF VISUAL MEDIA

The most startling new development in fund raising in the past decade has been the blossoming of media use in solicitation. Multimedia combinations using radio and/or television with direct mail and/or the telephone have shown dramatic increases in response rates. To hear on radio or TV over a weekend that a letter will arrive on Monday, and to have it arrive as promised, personally and correctly addressed, commands the highest reader attention and response. Such instant exchanges create a strong sense of urgency; donors have no time to delay and no place to hide.

Use of multimedia in mass communications has only begun. The media of the twenty-first century will be predominantly visual and delivered directly into the home—network and cable television, satellites and downlinks, sophisticated telephone options, video cassettes, fax messages, and computers with modems linked to worldwide communications systems and to financial resources that offer conveniences such as electronic funds transfer (EFT). Messages will pour in on donors. Not-for-profit organizations will need to work hard to learn how to use all these methods as well as to define the public image they seek in these new media. They must also develop new skills with computers, to utilize visual media that can compete with other charities and with commercial funds outlets in new ways and to gain a kind of "brand name" recognition. Prospective donors will have even greater flexibility in choosing the means to receive (and respond to) fund-raising information. Mastery of these new technologies will be essential if not-for-profit organizations are to get their message through to their prospective giving audiences. Public response to all these multimedia stimuli will be well conditioned by their commercial users. Not-for-profit organizations will be hard pressed to match their levels of creativity and inventiveness without incurring equally high costs. How will not-for-profit organizations get their message into the hands and minds of the donors they need?

The greatest danger from these technological advances is not the overwhelming abundance of choices, which will surely happen, but the massive impersonalization that will follow. Will a not-for-profit organization that depends on wide audience attention be able to compete with professional advertising and marketing programs that are supported by bigger budgets? In one expert's opinion,

> Our focus must become one of understanding our donors, their needs, beliefs and attitudes. We need to get close to donors to aid their trust in our organizations and our programs. To succeed, we must master computers and the art of talking in the style of one-on-one dialogue with everybody.[6]

The success of "televangelism" has already moved some organizations to begin to perfect their use of visual media. Churches have prospered for centuries because of the charismatic appearance and effective messages of their leaders. They already use mass media to expand their appeal and instantly reach vast numbers of people across the country and even beyond its borders. No longer does a person need to attend services at a local place of worship; the services come right into their homes in live broadcasts via satellite and telephone line, and maybe by a personal videotaped message or interactive communication via voice or keyboard. Who can compete with this level of personal "high touch"?

Few not-for-profit institutions or agencies, except religious organizations, have made much use of these media methods to raise money. Television is a prohibitively expensive medium unless the TV industry selects a not-for-profit for attention. A few organizations (NFL charities and United Way, for example) can purchase air time. Cable and videotaped programs, on the other hand, cost much less and are perfectly matched to mass media communications. Their added advantage is that the tape can be sent to prospects and donors in the form of a personal message. A

---

[6]John R. Groman, "Fund-Raising in the '90's; Five Key Changes to Make or Break Success," address to Breakfast Plenary Session, NSFRE Orange County Chapter Conference "Fund-Raising Day," Anaheim, CA, October 16, 1989. For a complete discussion of "Technology applications" by Tom Gaffny, vice president and senior creative director, Epsilon, see Greenfield, *The Nonprofit Handbook: Fund Raising*, 2d ed., 627–641.

medium that is lower in cost and simple to implement is audio cassettes, for those times when people are not in front of a TV screen (in their car, jogging, or commuting). Public service announcements (PSA) remain available to not-for-profit organizations.

Media Options

Five means of visual and sound communications can be used in combination with direct mail or direct video to effect fund-raising results: advertising, radio, television (including cable and video cassettes), the computer, and the telephone. Their use by not-for-profit organizations will vary greatly because budget is a significant constraint. Charities that have money to spend on television and radio will dominate the airwaves for years; others can only use alternate means or wait for the cost to come down. Image and name recognition figure prominently in audience response. An example is the billboard advertisements carrying the highly recognized United Way message. Because they appear in many cities, the result is a thousand times more effective than if the same message were attempted on a single billboard by a lesser-known organization, even one that is an affiliated United Way agency.

Advertising

Promotions, ads, coupons, and the like in newspapers and magazines reach substantial audiences but enjoy only limited responses; the money raised is even less than the one-half of one percent statistics for acquisition direct mail. The action is left to the reader to perform: cut out a coupon, make a telephone call, or address and mail an envelope request. People are not so easily stimulated to give their money away. The use of newspaper and magazine advertising is best directed at providing information, aiding in "brand name" recognition, and piquing a bit of curiosity. Similarly, messages on billboards, bus backs, taxicabs, and bumper stickers offer brief opportunities to catch the public eye but have a limited ability to prompt action unless used simultaneously with other media. Each needs a personal follow-up on the airwaves, by mail, or both, to produce gift revenues.

Radio

Radio is not a forgotten medium but it is no longer the predominant source of information in today's world. Programming features talk shows, all-music and all-news stations, sporting events, and, except for National Public Radio's broadcasts during morning and evening "drive-time" hours, a limited number of current affairs presentations. Interesting station managers in programs related to not-for-profit organizations or their public benefit activities is a challenge. The one exception may be the foreign language stations whose faithful audiences depend on the stations for much of their daily information. PSA spots are often available on both AM and FM stations. How much money can be raised by radio? Not much, if any. The best use of radio may be in support of other mass communications outlets being used.

Television

Television is predominantly the most effective communications medium in our society today and will be for the immediate future. Cable television, delivering satellite broadcasts on 250 or more channels at a reasonable cost of access, and the vast array of video cassettes on just about every subject make the TV/VCR combination the predominant message transfer medium. How well this medium will be used by not-for-profit organizations remains to be seen. The field is wide open and the public is receptive.

The Computer

The personal computer is an instant source of vast information—fast, interactive, and the medium of choice for millions of people. Computer technology has other unique attributes: a capacity for instant access to even more information than is available from network and cable television and from video cassettes; interactive capabilities with modem access to nearly any database worldwide; self-directed education at work and at home; communications that are accessible to nearly every member of the family every minute of the day; links to TV sets that allow live exchanges at multisite video conference broadcasts.

The personal computer also provides direct access to people through people-to-people interactions (e-mail and chat rooms) similar to those that ham radio operators have enjoyed for decades. Service-directed not-for-profit organizations can look toward college classes and library research via video and computer keyboard access; communication to physicians and hospitals on patients' vital signs and instant transmittal of laboratory data on disease characteristics, probable diagnosis, and treatment options; and museum and gallery tours and lectures that open every collection to the public at a fingertip's request.

These developing technologies will not feed the hungry or house the homeless, but ownership of personal computers by more than 50 million Americans reflects their financial ability as qualified prospects, once they understand the need for and the value of their support. "The message is the medium" for charitable purposes, provided not-for-profit organizations can learn how to interact personally with their publics through this new method of direct response communication.

The Telephone

Direct dialogue remains key and the telephone remains of great value to fund-raising practice. Other mass communication methods (except interactive computers, most of which, for the time being, have no video camera link) deliver one-way messages. The telephone permits one-on-one and multiple-party (conference call) conversation in which asking can take place directly. Mobile and car phones link people together at nonstationary locations. Fax machines allow complex information transfers and written exchanges to occur nearly simultaneously, with the option for an immediate reply. Visual transmission and reception over fiber-optic telephone lines or via satellite, now on the horizon, promises fund-raising "visits" that will be as near to face-to-face personal solicitation as is technologically possible. Many other advantages for fund raising will result from this technology.

Will the need for direct human contact be eliminated in the next century? Given a transition to impersonal styles of communication, not-for-profit organizations must pay attention to giving people the increased "high touch" that will be valued in a "high-tech" society.

SPECIAL EVENTS AND BENEFITS

Volunteers are expert in this subject. How many times have the following suggestions been made in response to the need for new money? "Let's have a bake sale!" "Let's have a car wash!" "Let's have a concert!" "Let's have a dinner dance!" Not all events are created equal, however, and not all events are worth the time and energy needed to hold them. Should they be held even if they do not raise a lot of money? The answer is yes, no, and it depends, but the amount of money they raise will not change.

Volunteers have their own ideas on what special events and benefits are and their value; contributors often have favorites to which they are strongly attached. Fund-raising staff usually do not like the events even when they raise money, because of the amount of effort and the many details involved. Given such disparity, the definition here is an objective one. A special event or benefit is a social, educational, or sporting activity or other occasion for which admission tickets are sold and both sponsorships and underwriting gifts are solicited to produce revenue in excess of the event's direct cost, with any net proceeds delivered to a charity.

The first great truth about special events and benefits is that they do *not* raise much money in the form of net proceeds. The second great truth is that they consume enormous amounts of time and energy and require spending half or more of all the money raised. Add the direct and indirect expense to the not-for-profit organization of supporting each event (the overhead of staff time and operating budget) and the estimated value of the time given by volunteers who do all the work to stage the events, and it's a wonder that they make any money at all! Unless carefully managed every step of the way, they are losers, not winners.

The third great truth is that events are not equally popular everywhere in the country—nor are they equally successful for every not-for-profit organization. Only Hollywood or New York can charge $1,000 to $5,000 per couple for a celebrity black-tie dinner dance and produce real celebrities who help to sell out a 1,000-seat ballroom in the biggest hotel in town! Only a city like San Antonio can charge $50 a person for a chili cook-off, country music festival, and amateur rodeo, all happening in one evening, and sell over 1,000 tickets and several cases of antacid tablets. Can anyone estimate the net proceeds each event will produce? Could another city attempt the same combination, sell the same number of tickets, and make as much money? Probably not.

Fund-raising professionals across America have the same dream every time a volunteer suggests a new benefit event—a scene in which volunteers realize that events do not raise much money as net proceeds for all the work involved; and in which they decide to put as much effort into asking their friends for money. This dream is doomed never to come true because volunteers have too much fun putting on events; how nice that they raise money too! Fund-raising executives know and appreciate the value of volunteer time and energy; if they could only find a way to motivate volunteers to ask their friends for money with even half the amount of commitment, dedication, and enthusiasm that is applied to staging events.

Although they do not raise much in net proceeds, special events and benefits have other values. They should realize enough total revenue to be able to give at least half as their net profit to the charity, no easy task indeed. Their other values, in no particular order, include

- Increased public visibility for the sponsoring charity
- Active roles for volunteers who work for the organization
- Opportunities for leadership training and development

- Opportunities for "friend raising," cultivation of new prospects, and donor relations
- An occasion for public education about the charity and its mission, usually through a printed program, a few speeches, and media coverage

The most important ingredient in a successful special event or benefit is that everyone should have a good time. Getting lots of volunteers to do all the work can be the second best ingredient. A fund development staff of three or four people cannot create an event without sacrificing aspects of other projects and putting themselves at risk with everything else going on in the department and an increase in burn out. A myriad of tasks accompanies each event, beginning with the critical decisions of where and when to hold it, who or what will be the attraction, and how the tickets will be sold and the necessary sponsorships secured, to raise as much net profit as possible (50 percent is the minimum goal). If its volunteers are not well organized and self-managed, or if they lack the ability to sell tickets and secure underwriting and gifts-in-kind, the organization faces a high probability of near failure and minimal net proceeds. Employees in a not-for-profit organization, regardless of their high motives and willingness to make the sacrifices required, have full-time job responsibility to other fund-raising areas that they know are more profitable for their employer. They also may not have the expertise required for successful special and benefit event production. Most volunteers also have full-time jobs. To provide enough time to get all the work done, a partnership is necessary.

There are at least three models for conducting successful benefits and special events:

1. A strong, well-managed volunteer group operating within the organization as a membership organization, support group, or similar entity that is controlled to some degree (its mission and goals are to aid the organization) and able to conduct the event with high efficiency
2. A combination of an adequate number of competent volunteers and fund-raising staff who can work well together
3. An outside organization that commits to manage the event but is not under the organization's control. A Rotary Club, Lions Club, Assistance League, Junior Chamber of Commerce, Junior League, or similarly reputable local organization can usually be trusted to succeed with an event

Each not-for-profit organization has the right to insist on control over every special event or benefit held in its name, especially regarding all the funds raised and spent. IRS regulations and tax-exempt privileges are sufficient reasons to retain full fiscal responsibility. The not-for-profit organization also is the contracting agent responsible for liability protection for those who need to be hired for their services (hotel employees, printers, musicians, caterers, and the like). A good budget is necessary (see Exhibit 3.7) and must be followed. Enthusiastic volunteers have been known to make a few changes along the way "to make it look better," but they may have sacrificed net proceeds in the process.

Why this negative approach to a popular fund-raising method? Because events can be a cause for mischief, poor management, and financial losses—all in the name of the charity. A committee member may be tempted toward private inurement by "throwing a little business" to a friend whose catering or floral costs are known to be above market prices. The decorations chairperson's efforts may draw kudos in the media and red ink in the decorations budget. The reason for staging the event (to raise money for charity and have a little fun doing it) can become distorted, and at the expense of the not-for-profit organization's reputation.

Some commercial entrepreneurs become involved in events only to gain access to an organization's mailing list and to have a showcase occasion for friends and donors; their own future sales and profits are their only motive. Such events are promoted by art galleries, restaurants, or merchants' associations. No charitable purpose is intended, nor is there any consideration of the relationship of the proposed event to the mission of the not-for-profit organization. The offer of a 5 or 10 percent gift from their sales proceeds is not a good deal for the charity (why not 50 percent if they really want to help?) and donors' and friends' experience of the event's commercial slant may make invitations to the organization's own events unwelcome. Another version of this method, called "cause-related marketing" (discussed in Chapter 4), is designed to enhance and stimulate profits for business enterprises, not to cause donors to make gifts directly to charitable organizations.

Organizations should beware of professional solicitors who promise to conduct an entire event and to remit all the proceeds after subtracting direct expenses and their professional fees. Their enterprise could possibly be illegal and a scam; their goal is making money for themselves, not raising friends or funds for the organization; and their return is usually less than 20 percent of gross revenue to the charity as its net proceeds.[7]

---

[7]Office of the Attorney General of Connecticut, *Paid Telephone Fund-Raising in Connecticut in 1997,* 11th annual report (Offices of the Attorney General and the Department of Consumer Protection of the State of Connecticut, 1998).

EXHIBIT 3.7 Special Event or Benefit Budget Worksheet

	Approved Budget	Actual Expenses
A. *Projected Cash Receipts (Revenue)*		
Ticket sales (400 at $100/couple)	$40,000	$42,000
Sponsor gifts ($250, $500)	6,750	7,500
Underwriter gifts ($1,000, $2,500)	10,000	8,000
Auction receipts	4,000	4,350
Raffle receipts	1,500	1,250
Contributors	1,000	500
Donated materials (gifts-in-kind)	(3,500)	(2,250)
Subtotal	$63,250	$63,600
B. *Projected Cash Expenses (Costs)*		
Cash expenditures (itemized list)		
Printing	$7,650	$7,880
Postage	450	365
Facility use fees	1,000	1,000
Food and beverages	9,500	10,555
Decorations	2,500	1,800
Flowers	1,000	<800>
Favors	1,000	<1,000>
Entertainment	3,500	3,500
Miscellaneous costs	1,000	350
Auction/Raffle prizes purchased	1,000	<450>
Temporary staff hired	-0-	600
Consultant fees	-0-	-0-
Subtotal	$28,600	$26,050
C. *Projected Net Proceeds (A minus B)*	$34,650	$37,550
D. *Percent Proceeds (net of expenses)*	55%	59%

Guidelines and Instructions

The Budget Worksheet is designed to assist benefit committees in achieving *successful fiscal management,* which is defined as achieving net income for a benefit equal to at least 50 percent of the gross proceeds for the benefit, after excluding contributions and donated materials, in-kind gifts, and so on, from gross income.

(continued)

EXHIBIT 3.7 (continued)

Definition of Terms

Benefit budget	An estimate of all planned income and expense categories, prepared and submitted for approval by the board of directors, to represent projected income and expenses required for the benefit to function successfully.
Cash receipts	Direct income from ticket sales plus donations from those unable to attend.
Sponsors and underwriters	Donors who make a special-level gift and qualify for visibility in the official program, on the invitations, at the benefit site, and so on. The benefit committee sets the levels (there can be several), and this revenue counts in the 50 percent test.
Auction receipts	Auction revenues shall be reported in the amount of actual receipts at the auction. The purchase of auction prizes is not recommended.
Raffle receipts	Tickets purchased for raffle sales shall be reported as raffle revenue. If raffle prizes were purchased (which is not recommended), these costs shall be treated as expenses. Donated prizes shall be treated as donated (gifts-in-kind) materials.
Contributors	Donors who "purchase" an item on the expense budget as their special contribution, either with cash or an in-kind gift. The value does *not* count as gross revenue.
Cash expenses	Items bought or directly paid for out of the benefit expense budget, in direct support of the benefit.
Temporary staff	Benefit chairpersons and committees may require direct staff support that exceeds the time available from employees to support the benefit. The decision to hire temporary staff will be considered by the board and development officer. If approved, staff will be hired by the development officer and all expenses for their employment will be added to the benefit budget as an expense.

(continued)

EXHIBIT 3.7 (continued)

Consultants	If professional experts should be required to supplement volunteer and staff talents in order to succeed with a benefit, the hiring of any consultant shall be with prior approval of the board and the development officer, and shall be engaged in a written agreement (fee payment basis only), with all costs added to the benefit budget as an expense.
Miscellaneous costs	Staff time (salary, benefits, and so on) and other expenses incurred by the organization in support of benefits are considered "indirect costs" and are not billed against benefit budgets. These hours and costs will be applied to the annual productivity analysis of all activities, benefits, and special events.

Data Summary is reprinted with permission from Fund-Raising Cost Effectiveness: A Self-Assessment Workbook *by James M. Greenfield (New York: John Wiley & Sons, Inc., 1996), 101. Guidelines and definitions of terms are reprinted with permission from* Fund-Raising Fundamentals: A Guide to Annual Giving for Professionals and Volunteers *by James A. Greenfield (New York: Wiley, 1994), 247–248.*

Small, new organizations may complain that they cannot raise money without hiring outside help in the form of a professional solicitor who is not a fund-raising executive or a professional consultant. One of the primary responsibilities of every board member in any not-for-profit organization is to initiate professional fiscal methods and controls. Hiring out this responsibility is a mistake and a lapse in stewardship.

Special events and benefits, like every other method of fund raising, take time and expertise. There are no easy dollars or quick fixes. Poorly run events will not build the organization's good reputation, nor will they motivate a cadre of committed volunteers and donors to return for a repeat event next year.

Special events and benefits can be a successful part of a fund development program and add a quality component to an annual giving program if they receive quality direction and professional management. The most likely path to building an annual roster of successful special and benefit events that have a reputation for providing a good time and making at least a 50 percent profit for charitable purposes is with the help of a support group organization.

Nine-Point Performance Analysis of Special Events and Benefits

> Evaluation sounds like a technical exercise and usually implies work. Consider the possibility that you just might want to produce your event again. For events, it's not uncommon to begin to plan for the next event as soon as the first is completed. You'll find that many areas will need to be evaluated, which means contact is imperative with those people who were deeply involved. No doubt, they have already been thinking about how things could be better accomplished the next time around. Consider giving them the opportunity to share their ideas and suggestions with you.[8]
>
> BARBARA R. LEVY AND BARBARA H. MARION

Measurement of benefits and special events can be done in a variety of ways, thanks to the volume of quantitative and qualitative data that is generally available. However, because special events and benefits fit no specific mold they are difficult to evaluate against one another, even in the same community. It is more fruitful to compare the same event against itself over multiple years. For example, one can measure the number of invitations mailed compared with tickets purchased and actual attendance for the same event for three years or more to help gauge public interest (i.e., the popularity of the event) as well as actual participation. Tracking the number of volunteers involved and their performance is also helpful. The key to profitability for these events lies in securing sponsorships and underwriting gifts, which also can be measured from year to year. Monitoring expenses is certainly valuable as well, especially the costs of printing, food and beverages, decorations, and entertainment—all of which can easily get out of control.

Exhibit 3.8 provides an evaluation of three types of events conducted by the same organization using the familiar nine-point performance index. Note that the events themselves are quite different in nature and do not lend themselves to fair or equitable comparison. Each should be measured in its own right for effectiveness and efficiency and the results used to guide volunteer leaders and their committees and staff in planning the same events in the future. A summary of the performance analysis follows:

(1) Column 1 contains results from the annual meeting of a membership organization. This is a necessary event to elect new officers and

---

[8] Barbara R. Levy and Barbara H. Marion, *Successful Special Events: Planning, Hosting, and Evaluating* (Gaithersburg, MD: Aspen, 1997), 220.

EXHIBIT 3.8 Nine-Point Performance Index Analysis of Activities, Benefits, and Special Events (Single-Year Results)

	Annual Meeting	Fishing Tournament	Black-Tie Dinner Dance	Total
Participation	545	182	450	1,177
Income	$32,500	$90,176	$159,336	$282,012
Expenses	$29,850	$26,008	$92,651	$148,509
Percent participation	21%	82%	19%	41%
Average gift size	$59.63	$495.47	$354.08	$239.60
Net income	$2,650	$64,168	$66,685	$133,503
Average cost per gift	$54.77	$142.90	$205.89	$126.18
Cost of fund raising	92%	29%	58%	53%
Return	9%	247%	72%	90%

Reprinted with permission from Fund-Raising Cost Effectiveness: A Self-Assessment Workbook *by James M. Greenfield (New York: John Wiley & Sons, Inc., 1996), 104.*

directors, conduct special recognition of major donors, and confer awards for volunteer service. While not a command performance, attendance by 545 members and guests is an excellent turnout and represents 21 percent of those invited. Although this activity is not a true benefit, its volunteers set a goal to "break even" and succeeded in making a slight profit of $2,650.

(2) The second event, a fishing tournament, is limited by its nature to attendance by those who have boats and can afford the entry fee of $300 for a party of three at $100 each. Revenue received and average gift size suggest several sponsors and underwriters participated along with in-kind gifts of direct cost items, all of which helped post a net income of $64,168. The fund-raising cost of $0.29 is evidence this was a highly profitable if not an uncommonly successful example of a charitable sporting event.

(3) The traditional black-tie dinner dance was well attended at a price of $300 per couple but expenses of $92,651 "ate up" the favorable income ratio from paying guests, sponsors and underwriters, yielding a net income of $66,685 at a cost of fund raising of $0.58. Some effort to control these expenses and increase sponsorships and underwriting will be required next year to achieve the desired 50 percent profit level.

(4) In combination, these three events attracted 1,177 paying guests and achieved $133,503 in net proceeds for the organization. Can each event repeat this performance next year? The annual meeting and fishing tournament are quite efficient already and, given the data provided for

the black-tie dinner dance, perhaps only this event contains any potential for fiscal improvement.

SUPPORT GROUP ORGANIZATIONS: "FRIEND RAISING"

Support group organizations are commonly affiliated with churches, colleges, hospitals, arts groups, and other charities. They are semi-independent, self-managed groups of individual volunteers assembled for the purpose of aiding their sponsoring not-for-profit organization. Their purposes include providing annual gift support through membership dues, benefit events, and direct gifts designed to assist the organization in fulfilling its mission, goals, and objectives. They function as friend raisers; they permit their members a high degree of personal interaction with potential and actual volunteers. Their mission may include legislative support, community education, and other valued support services that the not-for-profit organization cannot afford to staff on its own. Some examples of typical support groups are Town and Gown societies, alumni associations, hospital auxiliaries, technical or professional advisory councils, guilds for the performing arts, membership groups at different cost levels, and benefit and special event sponsors.

Legally, because these groups exist under the "umbrella" of the not-for-profit organization they support, they do not need the formal structure and operating style required for a separate tax-exempt organization. Their "bylaws" are more correctly operating rules and procedures approved by the parent organization that permit them to raise money in its name. They usually have their own board of directors and committees and are self-governing in their operating decisions. All funds are raised in the name of the charity, are deposited with the charity, and remain under its control. The uses of funds raised are often selected jointly with the parent organization from the list of current priority needs. The support group then commits to "sponsor" that project as its special contribution and sets for itself the goal of raising the necessary funds.

Support groups are not to be confused with donor clubs or donor associations, despite their similar sounding names. The chief difference is that support groups exist to get people actively involved through membership and voluntary service; donor clubs are a means to recognize donors for their annual gifts without requiring additional participation.

Donor clubs conduct no events, organize no activities, and perform no services other than recognizing individuals who make an annual contribution, in an effort to retain their interest and continued gift support. Not-for-profit organizations can elect to confer on annual donors whatever privileges and benefits are considered appropriate for the size of their gift and the program it supports. Grouping all donors together creates an additional form of bonding that helps preserve their loyalty and their annual gift.

What is the value of two separate paths to what appears to be the same basic objective? Some people want to give but do not want to have to do anything else; others seek the volunteer activity offered by support groups. Not-for-profit organizations that encourage both paths offer their constituents some variety in how they choose to participate. There should be no limit to the number of ways people can be associated with a charitable organization.

Great value can result from an organization's active sponsorship of one or more support groups. They can attract a number of people who become involved participants; they offer opportunities that demonstrate volunteers' leadership skills; they fulfill needed tasks that have high visibility; and their dues, although minimal, reinforce volunteers' commitment to an annual gift. Membership in the group can be a strong link to the parent organization, especially if the group is considered a premiere force in the community and publishes its roster of members each year. In addition to membership dues, revenue from support groups is realized through event net proceeds and extra giving opportunities (beyond dues and event tickets) offered to all members each year.

Support groups are a highly effective means to invite others into the organization, to acquaint them with its purposes and the value of its services, and to encourage their active participation in advancing its mission and goals. The key to support groups' success may lie in a combination of self-management and volunteer-led participation. They offer their volunteers a great many opportunities to participate and lead, from serving on a variety of active committees to serving on the board (see the sample organization chart in Exhibit 3.9). Every function, assignment, activity, benefit, and special event can be facilitated through one or more of the support group's active committees, which also offer a variety of subcommittees to support their overall assignment. A support group is like a major league baseball club's Triple-A farm team where players can try out their expertise, interest, and willingness to join in a common effort. The parent organization, like the big-league club, scans the roster of players to find those with proven talents for leadership plus energy committed to the cause, and a thirst for greater participation. Support groups provide

EXHIBIT 3.9 Sample Support Group Organization Chart

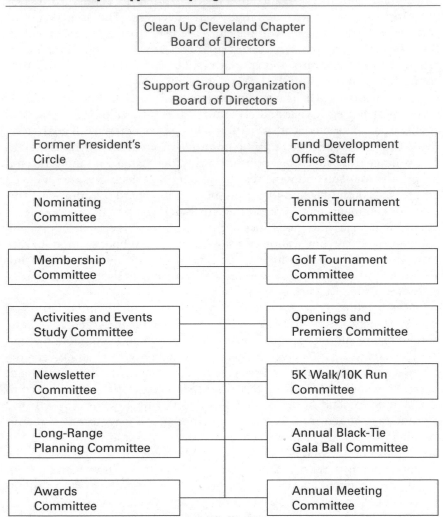

Reprinted with permission from Fund-Raising Fundamentals : A Guide to Annual Giving for Professionals and Volunteers *by James M. Greenfield (New York: John Wiley & Sons, Inc., 1994), 202.*

one of the best opportunities to discover the valued, competent, and motivated volunteers every organization needs to build its secure future.

Most support groups are largely self-governing. The annual routine of a support group begins with the close of the term of office of current officers (some of whom may be board members), the installation and orientation of their successors, the appointment of committee chairs and then committee members, and the beginning of annual operations. Committee tasks are made known. The group may publish three to four issues of its own newsletter each year and an annual directory. Two or more special events or benefits events are scheduled, to help meet the fiscal goal set by the board. Each event has a full committee of volunteers whose assignments range from soliciting sponsors and underwriters, in-kind gifts, and ticket sales to menu and wine selections. All event decisions are reviewed first by the committee and then presented to the board for approval. This chain of command may be extended further, if the parent organization's operating policies and guidelines impose additional levels of supervision and control. Early preparation of a full budget should be required, to estimate anticipated revenue and expenses from all possible sources and projected net proceeds. (A goal of at least 50 percent net profit to the charity is recommended for each event.)

Membership recruitment and renewal are equally important. The quality of members as well as their numbers must be preserved. Members' donations are support groups' most cost-effective and profitable method to raise money; their 80 percent average productivity level far exceeds the cost-per-dollar-raised ratio of special events and benefits. But recruitment of new members takes effort. Sending invitations to prospects is a commonly used method of direct mail solicitation, but it yields only a 1 or 2 percent rate of return. More personal methods are required to recruit members who will become active participants and add to the vitality of the organization. "Mixers" that bring people together in the name of the organization are more effective than invitation letters. These activities can be restaurant openings, theatre parties, movie premieres, group attendances at ball games or cultural events, or any similar occasion that gives current members an easy opportunity to invite their friends to join them and become acquainted with the organization and its supporters in the process. Special events and benefits offer membership enrollment opportunities but the combined annual cost of event tickets and membership dues can be prohibitive. In a more creative approach, a portion of the event ticket can be a "credit" toward payment of the first year's membership dues.

A membership brochure should be available that includes an application and response form and a brief summary of the purposes of the organization and benefits of membership. Sponsorship by a currently active member should ease entry. Membership levels can be equal for all members or graduated ($100 = Bronze Member; $500 = Silver Member; $1,000 = Gold Member; $5,000 = Life Member). Each successive level can mean increased benefits from the organization as recognition of its greater income to the charity. Periodically, it can be announced publicly that the primary purpose of each support group organization is to raise money for its parent charity.

Renewal cannot be taken for granted and requires an annual solicitation; but the expectation of success is high (80 percent retention rate or better). If involvement, education, interest, and enthusiasm have been hallmarks of the past year of membership activity, then renewal is likely to be assured—even at higher giving levels, when they are requested at the time of renewal. The membership device, especially if the annual roster of members is published, works to its greatest advantage with renewals because a link to other members has been formed. Peer pressure, guilt, and embarrassment are legitimate motives for giving, and the charity is the winner every time.

How much independence should support groups have? Each support group must commit its first allegiance to its parent not-for-profit organization. The support group's reason for being is to enhance the image and reputation of its sponsor and to raise friends and funds to aid in the fulfillment of the sponsor's mission. Constant communication, coordination, and cooperation between both entities are therefore essential. In a consistent joint effort, they should develop and retain volunteer leadership, reward those whose service is distinguished, find other important voluntary assignments for proven leaders, and make available the opportunity to be considered for service on the board of directors of the parent organization. Both organizations need one another and should operate at all times as partners.

However, support groups should bear an honest degree of responsibility for their own conduct, for the choice of their leaders and committee chairpersons, for the selection and quality of their events and publications, for productive uses of the funds they work so hard to provide to the not-for-profit organization, and for charting their own destiny and their future plans for success. Given their value to the parent organization, they are entitled to a confidence in their own value as a key source of future volunteer leaders.

If allowed to police their own operations, they must be prepared to make tough decisions. They must select the best candidates for board leadership and committee work who will place the needs of the whole above all else and will not use the appointment for self-promotion or personal financial gain. They must take responsibility for evaluating a need to change any of their plans when the best interests of the charity may require such action, or when their activities or events conflict with calendar priorities of the parent organization. They must be exacting in management of all funds within their purview and ensure that no member gains financially from access to funds donated for the exclusive use of the not-for-profit organization. They must take steps to ensure the continuity of their organization so that it will retain (and even increase) its ability to raise friends and funds for the benefit of its sponsoring organization.

Nine-Point Performance Analysis of Support Groups

The semiautonomous nature of support group organizations offers three main areas for performance analysis: membership, volunteer participation, and fund-raising results. If any support group is to thrive and serve its parent not-for-profit organization well, it must have active volunteers who lead its membership in their select areas of activity, and who engage successfully in each of the fund-raising enterprises they take on. Exhibit 3.10 shows an analysis of three support groups using the nine-point performance index. Here are some findings based on the data presented in the exhibit:

EXHIBIT 3.10 Nine-Point Performance Index Analysis of Support Group Organizations

	Support Group A	Support Group B	Support Group C	Total
Participation	255	1,085	455	1,795
Income	$48,500	$385,400	$97,850	$531,750
Expenses	$23,445	$87,950	$27,650	$139,045
Percent participation	66%	73%	79%	73%
Average gift size	$190.20	$355.21	$215.05	$296.24
Net income	$25,055	$297,450	$70,200	$392,705
Average cost per gift	$91.94	$81.06	$60.77	$77.46
Cost of fund raising	48%	23%	28%	26%
Return	107%	338%	254%	282%

Reprinted with permission from Fund-Raising Cost Effectiveness: A Self-Assessment Workbook *by James M. Greenfield (New York: John Wiley & Sons, Inc., 1996), 77.*

(1) Support group A has the highest fund-raising cost ratio at $0.48 and the lowest average gift size at $290.20, both of which may be due to its small size (255 members) as compared with the others. The group's membership retention rate of 66 percent needs bolstering; it lost a third of its members this year and must give major attention to finding their replacements next year.

(2) Support group B has the highest average gift size at $355.21, which accounts for its having the lowest cost of fund raising at $0.23. This group also appears to be the most mature of the three; it is likely that several membership levels are offered. However, even as the most profitable group of the three, there are areas for improvement. For example, that it has expenses of $87,950 and an average cost per gift of $81.06 suggests operating costs are a drain, part of which may be due to membership size—1,085 participants.

(3) Support Group C demonstrates the best membership retention rate at 79 percent. An average cost per gift of $60.77 is the lowest, suggesting some success with sponsors and underwriters for its events. Although its membership is 455 strong, it could improve that number with continued efforts at recruitment, perhaps offering graduated annual dues levels or a lifetime membership option.

(4) In combination, these three groups are providing excellent returns to their parent not-for-profit organization. Their 1,795 members deliver an average gift of nearly $300 plus a total of $392,705 in net proceeds. A "bottom-line" cost of $0.26 also converts to a 282 percent return on investment in 12 months. Excellent, indeed.

DONOR CLUBS AND ASSOCIATIONS

Each annual giving method discussed so far in this chapter (direct mail, telephone, visual media, benefit events, and support groups) can offer its own program of recognition. A donor club, the recognition of a distinguished group of givers, adds a quality of recognition that, by itself, can develop more committed donors and can yield separate, extra, or larger gifts each year.

The first purpose of donor clubs and associations is to convey gratitude for higher contribution levels; they must then perpetuate a privileged association with the organization in order to encourage faithful participation each year. Donor clubs represent one of the best means to demonstrate an institution's commitment to expressing honest gratitude. Offering a list of benefits and privileges to donors whose annual gifts begin at $1,000 gains their appreciation, helps to retain their interest, and cultivates the potential for other gifts in the future. But effective donor recognition is much more.

The names or labels used for donor clubs and associations should give them a separate, meaningful, and even prestigious identity. The names can suggest a personal, almost private association with key people in the organization. The President's Club or Chancellor's Circle offers meetings with the chief executive officer to all those who qualify. The Century Club identifies a minimum level of giving (usually $100)—one of the critical functions of any donor association program—and encourages escalation of future gifts by attaching advantages to gifts ranging from $100 to $100,000 or higher. Certain privileges should be granted to entry-level donors, but a gift of $1,000 or more should offer additional benefits, to encourage larger gifts. Donors should be informed of all levels and privileges when asked to make their first gift and the information should be repeated often. Names such as The Ambassadors or Society of Fellows suggest that activities may be involved, perhaps representing the institution to others or joining with other equally select members of a parallel society in a collaborative realization of other benefits (see Exhibit 3.11).

Some organizations plan activities for donor club members. The Friends of the Library will be invited to attend functions that are of special interest to bibliophiles. Members can easily be asked for recommendations on speakers or subjects for these activities, a valuable task that requires little time. Friends of the College of Medicine or School of Law can have access to professionals in specific disciplines; the Boosters Club can have privileged seating (or at least privileged access to tickets) at football or basketball games and opportunities for direct association with coaches and players. Each activity chosen should be designed by the organization to stimulate gifts by other prospects as well as current donors. Activities that mix donors who give at various levels can create an incentive among lower-level givers to gain the right to associate with more prestigious givers through larger donations.

Privileges and benefits reward donors for their extra level of generosity; they must also encourage their continued interest and gift support. Various ideas can be used to good effect: a tasteful, jewelry-quality pin to identify donor club members; a published roster of annual members; a separate newsletter; addition of their names to an engraved plaque at the institution, and a small replica to take home; invitations to an annual lunch or dinner with the CEO and to other special events and activities; VIP parking privileges; and discounted services.

The IRS began in 1988 to increase its surveillance of "give backs" that donors receive for their contributions. The threshold that could disqualify

EXHIBIT 3.11 Donor Club Annual Giving Benefits and Privileges

Gift Amount*	Club Name	Benefits and Privileges
$100	Circle of Champions	Quarterly newsletter Annual report Invitations to benefit events
500	Ambassadors	All of the above *plus:* Name listed in annual report donor roster
1,000	Friends	All of the above *plus:* Name added to main Donor Wall VIP identification card with 10 percent discount in gift shop Invitation to annual meeting

2,500	Sponsors	All of the above *plus:*
		Name added to Sponsors plaque
		   at main entrance
		Invitation to annual recognition
		   luncheon
		Subscription to *President's Letter*

5,000	Patrons and
	Life Members
		All of the above *plus:*
		Name added to Life Member
		   plaque at main entrance
		Two tickets to annual black-tie
		   ball
		Personal gift

Multiple gifts within the same year will be counted together in order to qualify the donor at the highest level of donor privileges achieved through cumulative giving. The donor will be honored throughout the following year at this cumulative total.

Reprinted with permission from Fund-Raising Fundamentals: A Guide to Annual Giving for Professionals and Volunteers *by James M. Greenfield (New York: John Wiley & Sons, Inc., 1994), 194.*

a portion of the gift is tied to the market value of personal gifts or items of real value that are offered back to donors; if not more than 2 percent of the value of the original gift, they appear to be of no concern to the IRS. If the value of the privileges and benefits exceeds this level, the deduction claimed by the donor in the year of the gift may be reduced accordingly. Most donors prefer their funds not be used for items of any value. Not-for-profit organizations value the maintenance of an advantaged form of communication and association with their best donors; the last thing they want to do is cause an IRS challenge of a portion of a generous gift because of enthusiastic and well-meaning benefits given back to the donor in the name of donor recognition.

Donor clubs can become a helpful source of annual gifts when offered as a part of the annual giving package. Direct mail can promote donor clubs by name and report the minimum amount to qualify as the top of the suggested giving levels. Telephone and media donors can be stimulated to increase their response when special privileges through a donor association are described. For special events and benefits, extra privileges in addition to complimentary tickets—preferred seating locations and prominent positions in the official program—can be offered to those who purchase entire tables, become sponsors, or make underwriting gifts. Support groups can add donor club status and other forms of recognition for higher levels of membership giving or a life membership plan. The rule of thumb is to add recognition when it will help to raise funds and to renew similar gifts the next time they are requested.

A well-planned policy and procedure guide (see Chapter 2, pages 89–96 and Appendix A, section J) will help ensure that all members are treated equally, no matter what fund-raising program qualified them for the donor club. The size of an annual gift may have brought them these special privileges, but a wise organization keeps track of cumulative giving totals for each donor. When all gifts are tabulated on a historical basis, they can be linked to a permanent recognition for total or consistent giving achievements. Many donors make multiple gifts during any one year. Rewarding their grand total when it reaches a new donor club plateau affords additional recognition and permits them to "move up" and join others who have qualified for the same special privileges.

Nine-Point Performance Analysis of Donor Clubs

Because donor clubs are charged with such a big share of "friend raising" and "relationship building" for their not-for-profit organization, analysis of their performance has to review the level of giving as well as the number of participants and other factors. The four separate donor clubs analyzed in Exhibit 3.12 are indicative of the creativity with which an organization can define for its important donors a special relationship for areas of their highest personal interest. The members of these clubs are among the best friends their respective organizations could hope to achieve. Their support is faithful and generous, as their participation percentage

EXHIBIT 3.12 Nine-Point Performance Index Analysis of Donor Clubs

	Friend of the Library ($100/yr.)	Friends of Law School ($250/yr.)	Boosters Club ($500/yr.)	Ambassadors ($1,000/yr.)
Participation	118	225	485	140
Income	$11,800	$81,250	$255,500	$180,000
Expenses	$2,525	$8,225	$38,500	$24,800
Percent participation	82%	73%	91%	79%
Average gift size	$100.00	$361.11	$526.80	$1,285.71
Net income	$9,275	$73,025	$217,000	$155,200
Average cost per gift	$21.40	$36.56	$79.38	$177.14
Cost of fund raising	21%	10%	15%	14%
Return	367%	888%	564%	626%

Reprinted with permission from Fund-Raising Cost Effectiveness: A Self-Assessment Workbook *by James M. Greenfield (New York: John Wiley & Sons, Inc., 1996), 62.*

and average gift size illustrates. The following are some observations that emerge from analysis of their performance:

(1) The Friends of the Library has the lowest operating expenses ($2,525) and average cost per gift ($21.40) of the group. However, its average gift size is only $100 and its net income delivered to aid the library is only $9,275, which raises an important question: If this club cannot attract more members and perform at higher levels of net income, despite its otherwise efficient style, is it worth the time and effort required to keep it going?

(2) The Friends of the Law School is the most cost-effective unit in this group and delivers the highest return at 888 percent. However, at 225 members it has room to grow. Compared with the Boosters Club and Ambassadors, with their $500 and $1,000 minimum annual gifts, the Friends of the Law School can add more net income by concentrating on expanding its membership.

(3) The Boosters Club has the enviable advantage of offering privileged seating at sporting events and direct contact with players and coaches. While it is true that the Friends of the Library and the Friends of the Law School can offer their own special privileges and direct contact with their key figures, they cannot compete with sports. At 91 percent retention and an average gift above the $500 minimum annual gift, the

Booster Club produced a total net income of $217,000 for athletic programs at a fund-raising cost of $0.15.

(4) The Ambassadors program rewards donors of $1,000 or more with a lot of personal attention at minimal expense, as its $0.14 cost illustrates. Its annual gift requirement causes some attrition among its members, an area of concern. Remedies may be found in analysis of expenses for current benefits and privileges plus a review of renewal solicitation methods (Are volunteer members conducting direct, face-to-face visits or are they using the telephone for these important solicitations?).

THE VOLUNTEER PERSONAL SOLICITATION CAMPAIGN: THE "COMMITTEE OF ASKERS"

In the analogy of the victory garden, fund raising begins by planting the seeds—a variety of proven fund-raising methods. Each sprout is tilled, watered and fertilized, protected, and encouraged equally. The radishes are harvested in response to the first appeal; with the volunteer-led annual giving campaign, the harvest time for the tomatoes, carrots, and squash arrives.

Annual giving begins with identifying suspects and prospects and continues with recruiting and renewing donors. Renewal donors already *know* about the not-for-profit organization. But informative communications continue; donors begin to appreciate the mission, purposes, goals, and objectives of the charity they are supporting. Invitations to public activities, special events and benefits, and functions that offer new acquaintances and new friendships lead to donors' being asked to *participate* more personally in the life of the organization, perhaps on one of its committees. A transformation has begun.

When a donor accepts an assignment that has responsibility attached, he or she is responding positively to becoming involved. Indeed, the donor becomes part of the organization, identified more with those who run it than with those who simply belong to it.

Now comes a major test. Is the donor ready and willing to ask others to join in personal financial support of the organization's cause?

If donor development has been well planned, a series of naturally progressing steps brings donors to this decision point. They believed in the organization's services enough to aid it with repeated contributions. They gave their time and talents to help with projects and to serve on committees. They may have been directly involved in a project, taken a leadership role in organizing others, and brought their friends to a benefit event or open house. Their involvement increased without much prodding on the part of the organization, but all according to the development plan (see Exhibit 1.4, The Pyramid of Giving, page 26).

There is nothing sinister or cynical behind a development plan; it has no hidden agenda. People want to help; organizations have to show them how that willingness is best converted into success for their mission and purpose. Building a partnership with donors takes time, care, and attention; it is not accomplished by accident and no eventuality can be taken for granted. The development plan recruits the interest and involvement of people whose personal goals include giving of themselves to this same purpose.

However, even an organization's best friends and donors can grow shy and reticent when asked to ask their friends for money. They know the money is needed and good use will be made of it. They endorse the organization and its good works enough to give it their own time and money. They have talked about it with their friends and neighbors and have even encouraged them to join and share in its activities. Why is soliciting funds so difficult for them? The answer is something of a mystery at times but it is also as plain as day.

Donors' own interest and enthusiasm have been carefully developed as a result of "planned promotion of understanding, participation and support."[9] The next step, personally asking for money, is quite logical and donors may be as well prepared as is possible. Still, they may be hesitant because the experience of asking for money is new and they feel uncomfortable. That's understandable. Or, perhaps they have asked for funds before but were turned down and never quite overcame the bad feelings that resulted from the rejection. Whatever their perception, the organization has an opportunity to teach them how to ask for money and how to make it a successful and positive experience. They have performed everything else asked of them until now. All that remains is to remove the stigma attached to personal solicitation and to build their confidence that the asking experience will be as positive as the other experiences they have had with the organization.

Every person who donates to an organization could become one of its solicitors. Making that happen is a major opportunity and a major challenge for each not-for-profit organization. Favorable results from requesting people to ask their friends for money will be any organization's most important success. The amount of funds raised using all of the annual giving methods described earlier will always be limited; the methods are

[9]Harold J. Seymour, *Designs for Fund Raising*, (New York: McGraw-Hill, 1966), 115.

reasonably reliable, singly and in combination, but they represent the most expensive means to raise dollars an organization can mount: Personal solicitation performed by the members of the volunteer-led, annual giving campaign committee, the "committee of askers," yields nearly the full dollar amount to the organization.

People who are willing to ask others for money open the door to each organization's future. They allow it to break out of the bottom third of the pyramid of giving and to move upward in its fund development efforts toward the acquisition of major gifts. Productive solicitation programs begin the achievement of the larger gift income levels that each organization needs.

Is this an overstatement of how much is riding on the success of the annual giving campaign committee? No. The committee harvests the final crop from the fund-raising victory garden; theirs is the best produce in terms of sale price, net revenues, and lowest cost. Successful annual giving committees allow all the fund-raising programs in the upper two-thirds of the pyramid of giving to begin and to flourish.

To operate successfully, the annual giving committee must put its volunteers' time and talent to the best use. For personal solicitation to be successful, each of the following components must work well and must be coordinated well with the others:

- Volunteer leadership
- Organization and structure
- Goals and objectives
- Donors and prospects
- Research
- Information and orientation
- A timetable from start to finish
- Reports and accountability
- Professional staff support
- Recognition

Volunteer Leadership[10]

Every fund-raising activity has an absolute need for volunteer leadership. Without someone to recruit others, conduct the meetings, provide direction (and respect), keep the program on track, and insist on performance

[10]For a full presentation on the merits of volunteers and their leadership traits, see Walter P. Pidgeon, Jr., *The Universal Benefits of Volunteering* (New York: Wiley, 1998).

and success, the entire effort is lost. True leaders are rare in all enterprises; not-for-profit organizations are no exception. However, the experience of leading may be more exciting for those who work for not-for-profit organizations because the organizations' friends and donors are people who care and whose motives are altruistic. Leaders who communicate a caring attitude are possibly the sole reason organizations can anticipate success with a high degree of confidence. Caring leaders ensure success in finding others to share in leadership, in recruiting required workers, and in finding others who will take their turn next year. If people truly believe in something, their belief is contagious; they willingly share their feelings with others and spread their enthusiasm broadly and rapidly. If they also happen to possess qualities of leadership—visibility, respectability, clout, wealth, and a willingness to take responsibility over others—and are fearless when it comes time to ask for money,[11] they are perfect candidates for leadership of the annual giving committee. (For a thorough discussion of the activities, attributes, and attitudes of leaders as they apply to the volunteer board of directors see the section "Leadership from the Board of Directors" in Chapter 2 of this book, pages 47–49.)

Organization and Structure

Groups of people will more easily agree to serve if they have confidence in the leadership that has been appointed. They will also respect an assignment if it has been organized and structured to assist them in their success. Annual giving committees usually need only the few layers of organization shown in Exhibit 3.13.

This simple design permits a clear picture of authority (who reports to whom), definition of the task each level has to perform, an equal and fair share in the burden of the work required, an accountability for performance, and the assurance that no worker is without help and support from others on the committee. Most annual giving committees are successful because they spread their work around. Each volunteer worker is assigned only three to five prospects to solicit; each team captain supervises only three to five workers. The design also contains the ingredients for success in future campaigns because volunteers, after gaining sound experience and guidance, can move up to the team captain level and team captains can look forward to becoming vice chairpersons in a year or two.

---

[11] Irving R. Warner, *The Art of Fund-Raising* (New York: Harper & Row, 1975), 24–25.

EXHIBIT 3.13 Organization Chart for Volunteer-Led Annual Giving Campaign Committee

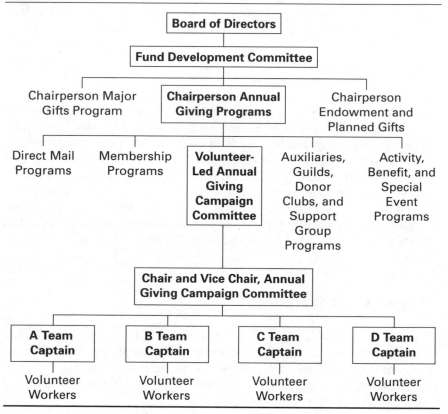

Reprinted with permission from Fund-Raising Fundamentals: A Guide to Annual Giving for Professionals and Volunteers *by James M. Greenfield (New York: John Wiley & Sons, Inc., 1994), 286.*

The vice chairperson is often the best trained candidate to serve as chairperson next year. Annual giving campaigns greatly need a steady progression by volunteers up through the ranks.

Goals and Objectives

Goals and objectives, as discussed earlier, are important to the annual giving campaign committee for several reasons. They provide targets to be met such as number and percentage of calls made, number of new prospects seen, average gift size, number of new volunteers recruited, and number of workers attending training sessions and campaign meetings. All of these items are working parts of an annual giving campaign committee's vehicle for a successful performance.

Goals are also dollar amounts to be raised for specific purposes that have been given institutional priorities. The best objective for the money to be raised is something visible; volunteers can talk about it and both workers and donors can see it happen, preferably within a few months after they have provided the funds required. A valid case for giving or a "for sale" project is a necessary key to success in any fund-raising program (see Exhibit 3.14). Because volunteers will be meeting with donors and prospects to talk directly about the project, it must seem credible on

---

EXHIBIT 3.14 Key Elements in a Successful Volunteer-Driven Annual Campaign

1. Understand and define the culture of the not-for-profit and adapt the campaign to fit its traditions.
2. Understand the traditional role of volunteers in the not-for-profit and measure its effectiveness in raising funds.
3. Ensure that the leadership, both volunteer and professional, understands and approves of a volunteer-driven campaign.
4. Develop a sound volunteer-driven annual campaign before embarking on other campaigns.
5. Secure the best-qualified annual campaign chair even if an external search is necessary.
6. Develop a schedule of highly charged meetings and rallies that lends excitement and fun to the process.
7. Develop a volunteer recruitment plan that encourages retention of successful solicitors and maintains an open environment to encourage new volunteers to join the process.
8. Create and maintain a close team effort between volunteers and the not-for-profit's professionals.
9. Understand the important role of recognition in the attraction and retention of volunteers.
10. Maintain a quality-evaluation component for the annual campaign that reviews volunteer performance based on individual success.

Reprinted with permission from Walter P. Pidgeon, Jr., "Volunteer-Led Solicitations," in The Nonprofit Handbook: Fund Raising, *2d ed., by James M. Greenfield (New York: John Wiley & Sons, Inc., 1997), 357.*

its own, be perceived as a necessary benefit to the community, and have an urgency that requires immediate attention and action (gift support). A bonus exists: In the course of marketing the project by word of mouth around the community, a number of influential people will become educated regarding the organization's commitment to improving its programs and services.

What happens if the goal is not achieved by the deadline? Campaign leaders and volunteers can mount a telephone campaign right away (if planned for and if adequate preparations have been made). A direct mail effort can be addressed to those who did not reply when first asked or those who were never seen or asked (there are always some). Or, annual giving campaign committees can reorganize and hold another campaign after a few months. These extra efforts will get results, perhaps enough to meet the goal, but they might backfire because they may send the wrong message to the community, to committee members, and to donors who have already "bought into" the project with their gifts. Goals must be carefully studied and set, based strongly on analyses of prior years' performance, at an amount that is likely to be exceeded rather than just met, provided that the actual dollars raised will meet the financial needs of the organization. Goals set for annual giving committees need to be viewed as part of a series of years of effort. Each goal may be able to exceed the goal before it but none will be able to jump ahead to a higher goal any faster than volunteer and donor efforts will allow. The methods of fund raising described earlier in this chapter should be used as part of the overall annual giving plan each year. Multiple programs avoid burdening one fund-raising method with the impossible task of raising all the money needed. Goals should not be treated as such absolutes that failure to meet them spells a form of disaster that will discourage the organization, its volunteers, and its donors. Overnight, all the goodwill and public confidence previously gained by years of successful performance from solid annual giving campaign committee work can be negated.

Donors and Prospects

Annual giving committees should concentrate on the best prospects for new and additional gifts and group them by potential gift size. Prior donors are the best of all prospects but not all may be suitable for this level of personal attention. The committee should select for visits those who are most important to the organization. The purpose of visiting these donors and prospects is to get them to realize their potential for an amount of giving this year and next. Each member of the committee needs to appreciate his or her responsibility for the worth of the donors and prospects assigned for visits.

The size of prior gifts is a useful qualifying factor for personal solicitation. Donors who gave $500 or $1,000 during the past year send out an important signal: They care about the organization a lot! And, because they are sending such a strong signal, they deserve the time and attention of a volunteer or two to meet with them at least once a year to discuss how their prior gifts were used, the progress achieved by last year's program and by the organization since their last gift, current and future plans and needs, and the value of all their prior contributions. The difference between an important annual donor and an important major-gift donor is almost imperceptible and will only become known when a volunteer goes to visit that person.

Other potential donors may merit a personal visit by reason of their position, wealth, political influence, connections, or other qualification. The time and effort spent on the peer-to-peer method of contact can prove valuable. Nearly everyone can respect a friend or colleague who takes the time to arrange a meeting to discuss a cause that is of importance to him or her. Whether the prospect can answer the request is secondary to successfully drawing the prospect's attention to the cause for a moment or two. Adding a few high-status prospects to the annual giving campaign each year will stimulate success and bring in some important new donors—and create an occasion to make new friends for the organization.

Research

A volunteer solicitor should know a small amount of basic information about each donor or prospect assigned to him or her: the correct name and address, phone number at home and at work, prior record of association with and participation in the organization, and prior giving history, especially the person's annual appeal response last year. Volunteers do not need a complete biography; nor can they use a portfolio of data on children's interests and status in school and the brand of scotch the person prefers, or a complete summary of the person's business and professional career. Besides, the volunteer frequently already knows the individual and is fairly comfortable setting up a meeting in order to ask for renewed support. More important for the volunteer is knowing how much to ask for as a gift this year and how that amount was derived.

Information and Orientation

Before volunteers begin calling on their friends for money, they will need to be oriented to the task at hand. Two preparatory meetings should be held before the solicitation begins, and each volunteer should be required to attend at least one of them. Individual meetings can be planned for added training or for those unable to attend a training session. Volunteers who say that they do not need to take the time for training because they already know what to do are a risk. Unless their prior experience (and success) in personal solicitation is well known, they should not be excused from the training meetings; they may not want to take the time to complete their assignments either. Attendance at one of the meetings makes volunteers accountable to the committee. They will have met with someone and agreed to perform a task. If they do not perform it, they will have to explain why they did not, which may be most uncomfortable.

The members of the annual giving campaign committee require a complete "worker kit" of information to assist them in their meetings with donors and prospects. The kit should provide the information they will need to give full details about the organization and the support items they will need to complete their assignment. The packet on the organization should include a fact sheet about the project that will benefit from the funds being raised, a summary of the prior year's accomplishments, a selection of printed handouts (annual report, case statement), a roster of board members, and perhaps a copy of a recent newspaper article that reported on one of the organization's successes relating to this year's appeal project. Their assignment packet should contain the roster of donors and prospects they are assigned to call on, with background research on each; the committee's organization chart, showing the names and telephone numbers of the team captain and other team members; the schedule of committee meetings and deadlines; an easy-to-complete contact report form for each prospect assigned; a generous supply of response forms (or pledge forms, if appropriate); and preprinted reply envelopes for mailing in both money and contact reports. These enclosures will allow solicitors to function without further help.

Orientation meetings should go beyond showing the contents of a kit and instructing volunteers on what each piece means and how to use it. Orientation should tell them how to make appointments with their assigned donors and prospects, how to conduct a solicitation meeting, and, the hardest part, how to ask for the gift. Many volunteers fail because they do not know how to ask someone for money. Some people see soliciting as a form of confrontation, an imposition; others feel that asking for money is demeaning, like begging; others fear failure and dread being told "no." A few volunteers will be quite unhappy with this entire assignment and probably will not perform very well. A well-prepared, well-executed orientation program can dispel most of these fears and obstacles; without such a program, however, all the fears will likely come true.

A Timetable from Start to Finish

Volunteers need timetables that specify when the work begins and when it ends; they like to know how much time a task will take and usually base their decision to work on this fact. Timetables require preparation and realistic scheduling so that volunteers' time and effort can be put to their best use during their brief period of intense work. Volunteers gain in self-confidence if some "backup" is available, if the leaders they respect are actively involved, if their kits are complete and orderly, if the orientation meeting is useful, and if the data are accurate.

An annual giving campaign's timetable must be coordinated to the best time for an appeal and must allow an adequate amount of time for performance. Most overall annual giving programs schedule their annual campaign in the fall, between Labor Day and Christmas. The term of the campaign should be only four to six weeks. Solicitations should be finished prior to Thanksgiving because the year-end holidays command personal time and attention. Exhibit 3.15 shows a typical schedule for an annual giving campaign.

A "kickoff" meeting, necessary to get things started, can add some of the fun that is needed too. A kickoff can build enthusiasm and a sense of belonging to the "group" involved in the enterprise. Group interaction and competition help volunteers to gain self-confidence and greater awareness of the task and its deadlines. Report meetings should be held during the campaign, especially for the captains, so that their progress to date and the performance of their workers can be monitored.

A final report meeting should be staged when the campaign is scheduled to conclude. The event creates a deadline for completion of all calls. Deadlines are a wonderful motivator for volunteer action; no one wants to be embarrassed (whether they are present or not) when performance is made public in this final meeting.

EXHIBIT 3.15 Staff Schedule (Timeline) for Annual Giving Campaign

April 15	Begin analysis of last year's effort.
May 15	Hold budget meetings; set goals and objectives for the campaign. Begin identification and recruitment of campaign leadership.
June 15	Complete leadership appointments; draft text and design for all campaign documents.
July 15	Complete recruitment and appointment of leadership team; hold first meeting to plan campaign. Resolve campaign dates, including kickoff function date and site; reserve facility for kickoff event.
August 15	Complete approval of all campaign plans and support documents. Begin volunteer identification and recruitment, beginning with team captains. Schedule orientation and training sessions; resolve contents of volunteers' information kits.
September 15	Complete recruitment and appointment of team captains, followed by recruitment and appointment of volunteer solicitors. Prepare donor prospect cards; circulate to entire committee to select preferred assignments. Complete preparation of orientation and training sessions. Expect delivery of all campaign documents for volunteers' information kits.
October 1	Begin campaign promotion and publicity. Complete assignments to all volunteers. Conduct volunteer orientation and training sessions before October 15.
October 15	Conduct campaign kickoff event. Begin all solicitations.
November 1	Conduct first report meeting for all volunteer solicitors. Report gift results. Recognize those who have completed their assignments.
November 15	Conduct second report meeting. Report gift results. Recognize those who have completed their assignments.
November 30	Conduct third report meeting. Conclude active solicitation campaign. Report all campaign results, including overall volunteer performance. Recognize those who have completed their assignments.

(continued)

EXHIBIT 3.15 (continued)

January 15	Complete preparation of all reports for gifts received as of December 31. Complete donor recognition. Conduct victory celebration and reward leaders and volunteers.
January 30	Complete thank-you letters to all volunteers. Publish results. Prepare final accounting report. Conduct critique meeting with campaign leadership. Prepare and submit critique report with all performance details to board of directors. Include nominations for next campaign's leadership.

Reprinted from Fund-Raising Fundamentals: A Guide to Annual Giving for Professionals and Volunteers, *by James M. Greenfield (New York: John Wiley & Sons, Inc., 1994), 290.*

Reports and Accountability

Weekly or biweekly progress reports from the chairperson to team captains and volunteers keep everyone posted on the progress of the group, the teams, and the individual workers. Reports should indicate the total calls made, the percentage of completion achieved, the number of prospects not yet seen, and the percentage these remaining prospects represent (see Exhibit 3.16). Given the short timetable for each campaign, the committee needs to keep reporting success stories, to maintain everyone's enthusiasm and to keep pressure on those who have not yet made their calls. Embarrassment is a strong motivator for action, and a public form of accountability will motivate some workers to get their calls made after all other methods of persuasion have been unsuccessful.

Accountability also has a plus side for volunteers. Volunteers who have achieved 100 percent success with their calls—both in meeting with everyone assigned to them and in securing the proposed gift from each—deserve to be acknowledged. Competition between teams or against last year's committee performance is a highly positive force for completing, on time, the campaign goal for the number of donors and prospects to be seen.

Reports and accountability include measurement of the cost to raise the funds. Cost per dollar raised using other annual giving methods can be fairly high—$1.25 to $1.50 in direct mail acquisition, and 50 percent net profits from special events and benefits. By comparison, personal solicitation programs are extremely productive because their direct costs are low

EXHIBIT 3.16 Evaluation Form for Annual Giving Campaign Performance by a Volunteer-Led Solicitation Committee

			Prior Gift at $100	Prior Gift at $500
1. Number of qualified prospects and volunteer solicitors available	Prospects Volunteers	= =	250 50	250 50
2. Number and percentage of prospects assigned to volunteers	Number Percent	= =	225 90%	225 90%
3. Number of calls made, number of gifts received, and the ratio (%) of calls made to gifts received	Calls made Gifts made Ratio	= = =	200 175 88%	200 175 88%
4. Average gift size for prior donors and average gift size for renewed donors	Average (old) Average (new)	= =	$105 $110	$525 $580
5. Number of upgraded gifts received, percentage of donors who upgraded, and average size gift for upgrades	Number Percent Average Gift	= = =	35 20% $125	35 20% $650
6. Number of prior donors assigned who did not renew their annual gift, percentage, and value of the lost gifts	Number Percent Value	= = =	50 22% $5,000	50 22% $25,000
7. Number of prior donors who were not assigned but who did make their annual gift after a telephone or mail request, percentage, and average gift size	Number Percent Average Gift	= = =	25 40% $75	25 40% $250
8. Number of prior donors who did not make their annual gift, the percentage, and value of their lost gifts (candidates for follow-up solicitation campaign)	Number Percent Value	= = =	50 20% $5,000	50 20% $25,000

Reprinted with permission from Fund-Raising Cost Effectiveness: A Self-Assessment Workbook *by James M. Greenfield (New York: John Wiley & Sons, Inc., 1996), 120.*

and, even more, because volunteers making personal calls to ask for significant amounts of money will outperform all other solicitation programs every time.

Professional Staff Support

The role of development office personnel is to help volunteers to succeed. A lot of work is required, well before the date the campaign begins, to support annual giving committees. Staff have to recruit and train the leaders and volunteers; prepare the materials for the worker kits; research and prepare summary reports on the prospects; make arrangements for the kickoff, report meetings, and victory celebration; and give guidance and attention to each of the operating areas discussed in the preceding sections. Volunteer committees cannot and probably will not do these tasks, nor are they especially well trained to do them, which reinforces the need for organizations to hire experienced fund-raising staff to guarantee volunteers' success. Too many not-for-profit organizations have yet to learn that their annual giving campaigns struggle to perform at the success rates achieved by other organizations because they lack enough staff help. Either they have incorrectly perceived the value of the annual giving program or they have yet to understand the cost-effectiveness of well-supported volunteer solicitors. Until staffing is adequate, the consequences are inevitable: Volunteers who are neither prepared nor well supported will not be overly successful. The result next year will be not only less money but fewer volunteers. The workers will be elsewhere, where their time will be more productive and better appreciated.

Recognition

When an organization depends on volunteers to raise all the money it needs each year, how valuable is their effort? Proper appreciation of what good people can do and have done should be communicated over and over; they should be told how valuable they are and how grateful the organization is for their many efforts, and never be taken for granted. Recognition of volunteers can take a variety of forms, but, as with donors, it should be sincere, appropriate, and never forgotten.

Summary Report of Annual Giving Campaign Committees

One of the more successful methods of motivating volunteers to solicit their friends for money is to provide them with some competition by comparing their performance with other, prior-year committees. Friendly competition within the volunteer subcommittees also can be healthy as long as everyone is comfortable with it and does not lose sight of the true purpose of the effort—raising friends and funds for the not-for-profit organization. This final analysis will assess the rate of growth in giving over a two-year period; showing this report to all the volunteers involved will demonstrate their success in adding numbers of donors as well as dollars, and achieving improved efficiency at the same time.

The annual giving campaign shown in Exhibit 3.17 has had a steady growth in the number of donors over the past two years (18 percent), which is due partly to increasing the number of volunteers to 50 over the same period, a cumulative growth rate of 29 percent. Overall, net income has increased by 21 percent but budgetary support to a larger number of volunteers also has increased by 14 percent. The slight (2 percent) increase in average gift size suggests volunteers have encouraged donors to give again at the $500 level; some effort to identify candidates within this donor group who could be asked to increase their gift (an upgrade) to the $750 or $1,000 level will yield important new income for the same effort. The key thing to remember about upgrade solicitations is this: Between 10 and 15 percent of donors will upgrade; the remaining 85 percent will likely maintain their current gift level with little erosion in gift size or renewal participation.

OTHER ANNUAL GIVING METHODS

Money can be raised during the year in a host of other ways. None of these "extras" is particularly efficient in building a body of donors and volunteers, but, because they offer some variety and spice, these methods are used from time to time and even planned as annual activities. They raise *some* money; the problems with them are that they are unreliable sources of funds and of faithful donors and their results are inconsistent. Moreover, they may have limited donor and prospect tolerance, or be barely legal, or openly invite less respectable or even fraudulent methods of raising funds.

To be effective as well as efficient, these other methods should follow the prime directive for all annual giving programs, which was mentioned

EXHIBIT 3.17 Summary Report on Rate of Growth in Giving for Volunteer-Led Solicitation Annual Giving Campaign (Prior Gift at $500)

	Two Years Ago	Last Year	Annual Rate of Growth (%)	This Year	Annual Rate of Growth (%)	Cumulative Rate of Growth (%)
Number of donors	125	150	20	175	17	18
Number of volunteers	30	40	33	50	25	29
Number of dollars	$62,500	$77,250	24	$91,875	19	21
Budget	$6,500	$7,500	15	$8,500	13	14
Average gift size	$500	$515	3	$525	2	2
Average cost per gift	$52.00	$50.00	−4	$48.57	−3	−3
Overall fund raising cost (%)	10	10	−7	9	−5	−6

Reprinted with permission from Fund-Raising Cost Effectiveness: A Self-Assessment Workbook *by James M. Greenfield (New York: John Wiley & Sons, Inc., 1996), 122.*

earlier in this chapter: *acquire* donors, *renew* or *retain* donors, and *maximize* donor relationships with the organization, or ARM for short. Each solicitation method used in an annual giving program should be selected not just to produce some amount of net proceeds but also to fulfill most of the following objectives each time it is used:

1. Develop the image linked to the mission
2. Obtain friends to support the mission
3. Identify and acquire new donors
4. Continue to renew most prior donors
5. Build relationships with donors
6. Identify and involve volunteers
7. Develop and train future leaders
8. Raise money in a cost-effective manner
9. Communicate and inform donors
10. Recognize and reward donors
11. Develop major and estate donors for the future
12. Build confidence and trust in the organization.[12]

A short description of the merits, faults, and shortcomings of some popular alternate methods follows. These fund-raising options are available to nearly every not-for-profit organization but are viable alternate opportunities only for those donors who prefer these types of participation and resist traditional methods. These alternatives include:

- Advertising and coupons
- Affinity cards
- Commemorative and tribute giving
- Commercial sales and cause-related marketing
- Door-to-door and on-street solicitation
- Facsimile and Internet solicitation
- Federated campaigns
- Sweepstakes and lotteries
- Gambling (Las Vegas/Monte Carlo Nights) and games of chance
- Multimedia options
- Premiums
- Television and telethon solicitation
- Various other annual giving ideas of merit

[12]James M. Greenfield, *Fund-Raising Fundamentals: A Guide to Annual Giving for Professionals and Volunteers* (New York: John Wiley & Sons, Inc., 1994), 305.

Advertising and Coupons

Paid advertisements and public service announcements (PSAs) published in newspapers or magazines are examples of a method to help build the public image of the organization rather than to raise money. Their impersonal nature is slow to stimulate response. The donor has to cut out a coupon, write a check, address an envelope, add a stamp, and carry the response to a post office or mailbox. Ads can be placed daily, weekly, monthly, or for just a few days in the year, but they cost money and are better used for purposes other than soliciting gifts. These messages are recommended to inform newspaper and magazine readers of a major continuing problem or of how they can alleviate an urgent situation that is currently in the news and needs an immediate response. Nearly everyone in America and many people around the world now learns immediately about the disasters wrought by hurricanes, earthquakes or floods. The American Red Cross promptly receives thousands of gifts because people immediately understand the need when they hear about or see a disaster on their TV screens. They do not need to read an advertisement asking for help in their local paper or latest magazine. The best way to raise money using ads is to coordinate their appearance with direct solicitation by telephone or direct mail, thus capturing some gifts through a "multimedia" communications technique.

Affinity Cards

This idea, popular in the 1990s, involves consumers' using credit cards or making long-distance telephone calls with a portion (a modest percentage) of the total charges being paid to an exempt organization. According to one expert, "In an affinity card program, a charitable or other tax-exempt organization is paid a portion of the revenues derived from the use of the cards by the members or other consumers who make up the affinity group. The IRS position is that these revenues are taxable because they arise from the exploitation of mailing lists and that the special exception for these lists is not available because the lists are provided to noncharitable organizations."[13] The credit card company or utility wants to market and sell its services to new customer candidates. It seeks access to any exempt organization's mailing lists (e.g., alumni, members, donors,

---

[13]Hopkins, *The Law of Fund Raising*, 2d ed., § 6.6 at 478.

volunteers, etc.) as a preferred and prequalified customer pool. The exempt organization's answer to why it agreed to the use of its mailing lists includes offering an extra benefit to its "friends" and to receive some extra cash, based on a percentage rebate, from little or no effort on its part.

Commemorative and Tribute Giving

A commemorative gift marks a special occasion—a birth, an anniversary, a promotion, a graduation, or a death. Tribute is paid to someone by making a gift to a charity in his or her honor or name. The majority of commemorative gifts are made in memory of an individual after his or her death, as an expression of sympathy to the family and of honor to the deceased. The occasion stimulating these gifts is unconnected to the "joy of giving," and commemorative gifts should be handled by recipient organizations in a way that adds respect for each gift made and encourages repeat commemorations. A notice sent to the person honored (in the case of an anniversary, graduation, or the like) or to the family of the deceased should be a worthy representative of the donor and the charitable organization.

Commemorative gifts are usually small (under $25 or less). Donors can use this method repeatedly throughout the year, but will probably not respond when invited to give to an annual giving program. Their first gift was not in response to any appeal, and the charity may have been selected by the person or family involved in the commemoration. Keeping track of this income separately from other annual giving efforts will allow the not-for-profit organization to credit the funds correctly by source, but not to assume similar results in a subsequent year. The stimulus for giving always occurs outside the organization.

Continued use of commemorative gifts can be fostered by providing some aids. Preparation and distribution of commemorative giving information will explain how these gifts are made and their value to the person honored or the family of the deceased and to the organization designated. A supply of easy-to-complete forms with preaddressed reply envelopes should be readily available, to implement the decision to give. Donors should be thanked for each gift and given a blank reply form to use when another commemorative situation occurs.

Commercial Coventures and Cause-Related Marketing

Commercial sales programs, or coventures, are ventures in which a charity and a for-profit organization together use a strategy called *cause-related marketing* to promote a product and a charitable cause. A *commercial coventure* is defined as an arrangement between a for-profit organization and a charitable organization (sometimes more than one), whereby the for-profit entity agrees to make a contribution to the charitable entity, with the amount of the contribution determined by the volume of sales of products or services by the for-profit organization during a particular time period.[14] Cause-related marketing is a fund-raising technique used to generate nongift revenues, involving related and/or unrelated activities; the term usually includes charitable sales promotions and other forms of commercial coventures.[15] When the opportunity for a coventure presents itself, some board members and CEOs of not-for-profit organizations will justify entering into the scheme for the "easy money" plus the opportunity for realizing a level of publicity and marketing value they believe they could neither achieve nor pay for alone. Before embarking on a coventure the board members and CEO of a charitable organization should answer the following questions:

1. What state and local regulations apply to this type of public solicitation?
2. Should a commercial business be allowed to use the name of this not-for-profit organization for the purpose of advertising and selling its products?
3. Does this organization condone the concept of percentage-based or commission fund raising, in conflict with the ethical principles and standards of professional fund-raising practice?
4. Will a written contract citing the complete nature of the sales and marketing promotion, its schedule (start and end dates, frequency, etc.), text or scripts to be used, financial reports due within a stated time period, and so forth be prepared and signed by both parties?
5. What financial records will this organization receive from this business partner to verify the sales volume upon which the gift amount is based?
6. Will this commercial transaction qualify under the IRS Code as "carrying on an unrelated trade or business," for which this organization will be subjected to income tax on the revenue it receives?

In general, can commercial sales and cause-related marketing be used by not-for-profit organizations in their annual giving programs? Yes, perhaps, with lots of "buts," and then only after due diligence and full disclosure by both parties of their dual objectives and their ability to meet

---

[14]Bruce R. Hopkins, *A Legal Guide to Starting and Managing a Nonprofit Organization,* 2d ed (New York: Wiley, 1993), 284.
[15]Ibid., 282.

IRS, state, and local regulations, and without any potential damage to the not-for-profit organization.[16] If a not-for-profit organization wants to build a strong and lasting relationship with any local business, corporation, or firm, it should do so for reasons other than a windfall "easy money" promotional opportunity. This subject will be discussed further in Chapter 4.

Door-to-Door and On-Street Solicitation

Personal solicitation may be the best method of fund raising but it does not work well every time or in every environment. "Cold calls" using door-to-door or on-street solicitation are not successful for acquiring new donors. The public has a strong aversion to both forms of asking; they are too abrupt, too confrontational, too direct for donors' tastes, and they do not permit time to consider the merits of the cause. An unfortunate stigma is attached to them, suggesting that they be avoided by most not-for-profit organizations. Further, most cities and towns have ordinances and regulations to limit these forms of public solicitation. The public has spoken; people do not like being accosted. They may contribute pocket change but will not give a serious or considered gift.

Some organizations and their volunteers have been able to preserve credibility and achieve success using these methods year after year. The Girl Scouts of America conduct cookie sales door to door and their revenues are significant nationwide. But the campaign is closely supervised and most Girl Scouts and Brownies solicit neighbors, friends and relatives, and colleagues of their parents in the workplace—not total strangers. The Santas of the Volunteers of America and the uniformed personnel of the Salvation Army, familiar bell ringers at Christmas, continue to use the chimney box and the red pot hanging from a tripod for Christmas donations. Several national health agencies and other causes maintain open canisters for donations at checkout counters in retail stores. These efforts are designed to keep their image before the public, to gain friends by repeated identification of their purpose, and to help stimulate the giving response. The main drawback of this method is that it prevents the charity from learning who its donors are. No relationship can be built for renewal of these gifts next year.

---

[16] The use of coventures has its proponents too. See discussion in Chapter 4, pages 233–238, and footnote 26 on page 237.

Facsimile and Internet Solicitation

The most recently introduced solicitation methods are the use of facsimile machines and the Internet. Unfortunately, overuse of these technologies in some quarters has already irritated a sensitive public. The issues are unwanted solicitations and invasion of privacy. Fax numbers and e-mail addresses are not protected information and can be bought, rented, or leased in the same manner as mailing lists. The problem with using them for solicitation is that the public reacts the same way it does to excess solicitation by mail and telephone—with distaste. The purpose of these new technologies is to facilitate more instantaneous communications, and their insistent nature often prompts a preconditioned negative response.

Great care and selectivity are needed to solicit via facsimile and the Internet. One advantageous use with less negative impact may be for donor communications. For example, a quick "thank-you" call to a donor the day a gift is received has always been quite positive. Thus, a brief fax or e-mail message to confirm a gift's safe arrival will be equally appreciated. When this first "thank-you" is followed by the traditional receipt and/or gift acknowledgment letter, a second message of appreciation is made. These new messaging techniques help to convey an organization's attitude of attention to its donors and honest gratefulness for their support; plus they allow for two or more occasions to officially acknowledge the same gift.

Federated Campaigns

Selected charities in America conduct their annual giving through federated campaigns. Groups of not-for-profit organizations band together to jointly do their fund raising, marketing, and other forms of public communication. United Way of America is the largest and best-known user of the federated campaign; a few others are trying to compete with United Way in the workplace. These efforts implement a single method of giving and a prearranged time for solicitation. An example is the Combined Federal Campaign, the annual solicitation forum for all federal government employees.

Access to the federation's select audience of millions of people is restricted to only the approved campaign organizations. The normal style of a federated campaign is to conduct one joint appeal each year on behalf of all members of the federation and to share the results among all the participants. This style has a high degree of public acceptance. Each participating organization enjoys a higher visibility and audience than it could achieve by attempting to stand alone, in competition with these and all other fund-raising organizations. Individual costs for fund-raising are shared and thus are lower, which increases each participating organization's net profitability.

Federated campaigns, such as that of the United Way, are usually conducted in the workplace. Employees and employers are solicited and payroll deduction is encouraged as the "painless" method of annual giving. Leadership comes from corporate executives at the highest levels, which adds credibility and legitimacy to the entire effort and promotes acceptance of the appeal within the corporation. Volunteer solicitors are usually coworkers who ask their colleagues for money during work hours. An element of "arm twisting" and pressure to give can enter into these solicitations, stimulated in part by the goals set for both the company and its employees and in part by the enthusiasm of volunteer solicitors. Whether these side effects are real or imagined, there appears to be a residue of resentment among employees for both the method and the place of solicitation. This resentment can be transferred to solicitations performed by other organizations outside the workplace. At present, the public solicitation of employees in the workplace is limited to only a few federated campaigns and no other charities may have direct access to employees in the plant or office during work hours.

As part of this privileged arrangement, member organizations must refrain from any additional or independent solicitation of the general public during the campaign period. Nonmember organizations can solicit the public during the federated campaign period but must realize that competition is keen and they are likely to hear that often used phrase, "I gave at the office." Most charities in areas where federated campaigns are predominant have learned to conduct their appeals at a nonconflicting time or to use alternate methods of solicitation on different audiences.

Sweepstakes and Lotteries

Every state has strict regulations regarding the use of sweepstakes and lotteries as forms of public solicitation. Most states outlaw or limit them, permitting them to operate only under strict state supervision, or specifying how often they can be conducted during the year. They are regulated so strictly because they are forms of gambling and are not easily matched with the mission, purposes, and goals of not-for-profit organizations. Further, their nature suggests some form of possibly illegal behavior by participants. Bingo remains the single exception and largely continues to be permitted and used widely because it is closely supervised by the religious organizations that conduct the games. Bingo also is heavily regulated and supervised by local authorities; it is not a simple program or special event to organize and offer to the public.

Gambling (Las Vegas/Monte Carlo Nights) and Games of Chance

The use of gambling and other games of chance to raise funds gives rise to questions of propriety. Is it philanthropy? Does raising money for charitable purposes remove the stigma associated with gambling? Does this fund-raising technique prey on the motives of participants willing to risk money they cannot afford to lose? Is it against the law or, at best, a test of the legal limits on public gambling activities set by the state, county, or city? In some cases, the answer would be yes to all of the above. Gambling can raise money; however, even though some people may choose to believe the end justifies the means, gambling in any of its many forms is a risky business for a not-for-profit organization to use for fund-raising purposes.

Having said that, charitable gambling is increasing. The best-known activities include auctions, bingo, Las Vegas or Monte Carlo nights, lotteries, raffles, and sweepstakes. Other, lesser-known forms include betting on Calcuttas, horse racing, keno, paddle wheels, punchboards, pull tabs, sports pools, tipboards, and more. The variations are endless, and one result from all this creative enterprise is lawmakers' concerns about overuse, which may lead to outright prohibition. A once-a-year benefit event featuring a Las Vegas or Monte Carlo night is not the problem; too-frequently-held games with poor fiscal controls are. So is the opportunity for abuse by those for whom gambling is a vice.

Multimedia Options

The variety of modern communications methods available to a not-for-profit provides multiple ways to reach the same audience. When these avenues of access are used strategically and in combination, their effectiveness increases significantly. For example, a letter request has five seconds or less to be opened or rejected. The next letter may not fare any better. But when a letter follows a newspaper story or advertisement, or its message is simultaneously reported on the radio and featured in a television "infomercial," or the letter arrives the day after such an infomercial with an audio- or video-tape enclosed, that multimedia combination has impact. Add to this multimedia strategy a telephone call, e-mail, and fax message, all timed to be delivered in a precise order, and the results will be enormous. Managing such a complex communications process is expensive but not impossible, thanks to computers. But managing such a bombardment takes judgment and common sense, considering the variety and level of the additional costs involved, plus the image such activities may convey to the recipients. Results measured in gross proceeds and increased numbers of respondents are likely to exceed the performance of any one of the traditional annual giving solicitation methods or even two techniques used in combination. The true measurement test, however, must include both net income delivered for charity and the renewal and upgrading performance of these donors over three years or more.

Premiums

A premium is a "giveback," an item returned to a donor or new prospect in exchange for an increased gift amount. The item offered is featured in the solicitation request to encourage participation. As such, premiums are offered "for sale" although the material value of the object is well below the asking price of the gift. The theory is that the object is sufficiently desirable to serve as an added enticement, to motivate the donor to "buy" the object by making his or her "gift." Givebacks range from bumper stickers, decals, calendars, and coffee mugs to caps, tote bags, T-shirts, sweatshirts, and umbrellas, all of which may bear the not-for-profit organization's logo and perhaps a key message linked to its mission. Some attention must be given to selecting the premium object to be offered, specifically regarding its unit value (to avoid IRS challenges to the contribution value claimed by donors) and its hoped-for match with the organization and its mission, even if it is just a logo or decal.

Premiums are often distinct from objects used in a recognition program where donors at certain gift levels qualify for defined benefits and privileges. The recognition program offers a menu of benefits and privileges to all donors, no matter which solicitation program invited their gift. These usually include nonmaterial rewards such as names listed in publications and in event programs as sponsors, underwriters, or patrons, and on certificates and plaques. Creative recognition programs may include identification cards, gift shop discounts, valet parking, invitations to and notices of public service programs and other activities linked to the organization's exempt purposes. Although these benefits may be advertised at the time of solicitation, they are not offered as a giveback in the same manner of exchange as are premiums.

Television and Telethon Solicitation

Much of what was said about solicitation via direct mail, telephone, facsimile, and the Internet also applies to television and telethon solicitation. Churches and "televangelists" are frequent users of the television medium, second to public television stations whose annual giving programs depend on their own "on-air" campaigns twice a year. Few other not-for-profit organizations can afford the cost or have the experience and management skill to conduct even infrequent television appeals or a telethon campaign. Examples of those who do are usually groups working in combination with a national campaign or a national organization that uses a telethon as its principal annual campaign method. Two such examples are the Muscular Dystrophy Association's Labor Day telethon and the Children's Miracle Network, a consortium of children's healthcare causes—both are once-a-year telethon efforts. Organizations in considering such a method should, beyond the obvious expense and skill required, be aware of the twin issues of confirming gifts and pledges (usually by telephone and/or mail in a follow-up drive) and collecting the money. This medium has the same problem with confirmations and collections as telephone campaigns, and the expected 20–25 percent default rate is the highest in fund-raising practice.

Various Other Annual Giving Ideas of Merit

It is important to appreciate that annual giving solicitation can be carried out in a variety of ways. And, while creativity and enterprise are valuable and add to the excitement of both volunteers and donors, not all of these ideas perform well even once, much less as a reliable delivery system year after year. Some, perhaps due to their creativity or novelty, may perform well the first time. The harder test to pass is to sustain the enthusiasm of volunteers and donors and to increase public participation levels measured both in numbers of people and in net dollars for charity. All too often, these "new ideas" are not so original after all. They often consist of ideas that have worked at other organizations but are not on the annual giving menu of your organization, such as art shows, sports tournaments that feature celebrities, restaurant openings, or movie premieres. All annual giving ideas can be measured against the following criteria: Does it enhance the image and reputation of the not-for-profit organization? Does it inspire greater public confidence and trust in the organization's mission, vision, and values as well as its purposes, goals, and objectives? Does it promote the not-for-profit's programs and services and stimulate the public to act? Will it attract new volunteers plus new sponsors and underwriters who will commit to helping to grow this new fund-raising program over several years to realize its potential to benefit the organization? If not, why should the organization invest new amounts of time and budget, or, worse yet, divert its resources from already proven annual giving programs to support this new idea?

HOW TO REPORT AND EXPLAIN THE RESULTS OF ANNUAL GIVING

Gift reporting is something of an art form, but whatever creative ways are used to display numbers that reflect results, the reporting must be done faithfully and accurately. Report preparation depends on proper record-keeping and consistent handling of all funds. The value of gift reports to annual giving analysis is that all performance activity within each of the methods in use can be monitored. The organization must gather enough data to know which lists to use and when any segment of prospects should be dropped, or how many events a year can be productive and which ones no longer attract an adequate audience or make enough net profit to justify their continuation. The ultimate objective in developing reports, aside from being able to display the results, is to know how well the annual giving methods are performing this year when compared to last year or measured against the long-range goals and objectives of both the not-for-profit organization and its fund development program.

In a measurement of the overall performance of all the programs in operation, the three prime areas of activity to report on are sources of gifts, purposes or uses of the money raised, and results of each fund-raising program. As shown in Exhibits 3.18, 3.19, and 3.20, both the number of donors (gifts) and the amount of money raised (gift income) in each category are entered on each gift report. The volume of people who participate is as significant to progress and program results as are the dollars they provide; money follows people. When a number of varied annual giving programs are in use during the same year, comparative performance analysis can help to determine which programs to increase or emphasize as the year progresses and to repeat in the following year. Those whose financial re-

EXHIBIT 3.18 Gift Report on Sources of Gifts Received

Sources of Gifts	Number of Gifts	Gift Income	Average Gift Size
Trustees/Directors	15	$25,500	$1,700
Professional staff	21	3,025	144
Employees	65	3,675	57
New donors (acquisition)	285	8,030	28
Prior donors (renewal)	282	18,010	64
Corporations	17	8,500	500
Foundations	12	38,800	3,233
Associations/societies	6	2,850	475
Bequests received	3	31,500	10,500
Unsolicited gifts	42	2,950	70
Other gifts received	12	21,500	1,792
Grand Total	760	$164,340	$216

Reprinted with permission from Fund-Raising Cost Effectiveness: A Self-Assessment Workbook *by James M. Greenfield (New York: John Wiley & Sons, Inc., 1996), 15.*

sults are not outstanding may still have merit because they attract large numbers of faithful donors every time they are offered. Achieving an overall balance of results among annual giving programs is important to long-term growth, which depends on these separate activities' acting in concert.

Several measurement tools were provided earlier in this chapter and in Chapter 2, including those that compare costs with net results for annual giving methods. Equally valuable are comparisons of a category of performance from one year to the next and of one category's results against those of another. Cost comparisons and information on which method happens to raise the most money this year tell only part of the story; the percentage of participants from among those who were solicited and their average gift size tell how the public is responding to what it is being offered. And, because public interests and moods change rapidly regarding charitable causes and issues, the results need to be monitored regularly to detect changing patterns. Each organization needs some flexibility in the way it goes about retaining donor interest and giving levels each year, to allow for a shift in emphasis or a concentration of more budget and volunteer time on those methods that are currently having success. An understanding of the performance of fund-raising methods goes far beyond counting net proceeds.

EXHIBIT 3.19 Gift Report on Purposes or Uses of Gifts Received

Purposes or Uses of Gifts Received	Number of Gifts	Gift Income	Average Gift Size
Unrestricted Funds	225	$34,519	$153
Temporarily Restricted Funds			
Capital/equipment purposes	295	$26,950	$91
Programs/services purposes	138	18,500	134
Education/training purposes	14	22,500	1,607
Research/study purposes	15	26,450	1,763
Staff/employee purposes	58	3,016	52
Other restricted purposes	12	905	75
Subtotal	757	$132,840	$175
Permanently Restricted Funds			
Unrestricted endowment	2	$6,500	$3,250
Restricted endowment	1	25,000	25,000
Subtotal	3	$31,500	$10,500
Grand Total	760	$164,340	$216

Reprinted with permission from Fund-Raising Cost Effectiveness: A Self-Assessment Workbook *by James M. Greenfield (New York: John Wiley & Sons, Inc., 1996), 16.*

It is important to measure several factors in the performance of each method of annual giving, as has been illustrated. Evaluations of the overall annual giving program can focus on other areas to search for improvements to be used next year. For example, one can study results in order to understand the public's response as well as responsiveness, to assess its acceptance of the message as being relevant and urgent as well as valid, and to measure one's own effectiveness as well as efficiency in managing this complex group of programs. Here are a few examples of what an evaluator might seek to discover:

1. Percentage of participation is a clue to how prospects like what is being sent to them. The percentage also can be an early signal of change of interests during the year.
2. Renewal rates and average gift size indicate donors' enthusiasm about an appeal method or a project "for sale." These figures help with forecasts of what these same donors might be expected to do next year.

EXHIBIT 3.20 Gift Report of Solicitation Activities and Results (by Program)

Solicitation Activities	Number of Gifts	Gift Income	Average Gift Size
A. Annual Giving Programs			
Direct mail (acquisition)	285	$8,030	$28
Direct mail (renewal)	282	18,010	64
Membership dues	0	0	0
Donor clubs	0	0	0
Support groups	0	0	0
Telephone gifts	0	0	0
Benefit events	2	12,850	6,425
Volunteer-led solicitations	65	3,675	57
Unsolicited gifts	42	2,950	70
Other gifts received	16	21,500	1,344
Subtotal	692	$67,015	$97
B. Major Giving Programs			
Corporations	17	$8,500	$500
Foundations	12	28,800	2,400
Individuals	36	28,525	792
Special projects	0	0	0
Capital campaigns	0	0	0
Bequests received	3	31,500	10,500
Subtotal	68	$97,325	$1,431
Grand total	760	$164,340	$216

Reprinted with permission from Fund-Raising Cost Effectiveness: A Self-Assessment Workbook *by James M. Greenfield (New York: John Wiley & Sons, Inc., 1996), 17.*

3. Volunteers' personal solicitation performance, in terms of percentage of assigned prospects actually seen and number and size of gifts brought in, is revealed, as are their meetings attendances and contact reports. Those who are ready to be promoted to team captain or assigned to higher leadership roles can be identified.
4. Special event and benefit ticket sales can be studied. Is the same event faring well year after year? Are its sponsorship, underwriting, and in-kind donations holding steady? Is public willingness to continue to attend and support the event still strong? Should ticket prices be adjusted or the event's design or flavor changed? Is a new event needed to keep this audience stimulated and active in its support?

5. Donors' response to the recognition provided, their attendance at recognition events, and their response to invitations to give higher amounts in order to gain more donor recognition privileges should be carefully reviewed. Has the offer of privileged communication altered their behavior from year to year? Any increase in activity may signal some donors' wish to become more involved or give at a higher performance level. They may be expressing a willingness to become more active in some voluntary capacity.

These and other evaluations take time and a little expertise in interpretation. Some professional fund-raising executives believe they must spend all their time raising money, not counting the results or "playing with numbers." Their priority assignment is indeed to conduct fund raising but their understanding will be deficient if it is based on only a report now and then about how much money has been raised. Planning is also part of their job description; the complete facts and an understanding of what they mean permit better planning for the current year and more reliable forecasting for the next year.

One of the best reasons for being able to understand results is the need to prepare (and justify) budget requests. Budgets for fund-raising programs are usually based only on results from the prior fiscal year. To preserve the current level of budget support and produce its corresponding income again next year, there should be ways to demonstrate the direct relationship between dollars spent, program by program, and the individual results. Cost analysis has grown in importance recently; both leaders and volunteers are being questioned about the efficiency of the not-for-profit organization they represent. Donors are becoming more selective in the charities they support. Their choices are based on fund-raising cost; they are supporting charities that have lower costs and that use a high percentage of their funds for public benefit purposes. Annual results should allow an analysis that can suggest overall donor readiness when it is time to begin to prepare for a major capital campaign.

An organization has many opportunities to study the immediate results of any single fund-raising method or new program. These evaluations do not take much time and deserve some honest attention. They are valuable to the decision making required of fund-raising executives. (Methods for measuring them and guides for interpreting them have been given in Chapter 2 and earlier in this chapter.) To convert financial data into budgets requires cost estimates for each fund-raising program to be evaluated later to compare expenses against estimates as well as to measure results. Exhibit 3.21 combines a program-by-program gift report with income received measured against the estimated and actual ex-

EXHIBIT 3.21 Gift Report of Solicitation Activities with Gift Income Measured against Approved Budget and Actual Expenses (by Program)

Activities	Gift Income	Approved Budget	Actual Expenses	Cost per $ Raised
A. Annual Giving Programs				
Direct mail (acquisition)	$8,030	$10,500	$9,855	$1.23
Direct mail (renewal)	18,010	3,750	3,890	0.22
Membership dues	0	0	0	0
Donor clubs	0	0	0	0
Support groups	0	0	0	0
Telephone gifts	0	0	0	0
Benefit events	2,850	1,800	1,350	0.47
Volunteer-led solicitations	3,675	500	485	0.13
Unsolicited gifts	2,950	0	0	0
Other gifts received	21,500	0	0	0
Subtotal	$57,015	$16,550	$15,580	$0.27
B. Major Giving Programs				
Corporations	$8,500	$20,215	$18,250	$2.15
Foundations	38,800	34,525	33,555	0.86
Individuals	28,525	3,210	3,250	0.11
Special projects	0	0	0	0
Capital campaigns	0	0	0	0
Bequests received	31,500	500	550	0.02
Subtotal	$107,325	$58,450	$55,605	$0.52
Grand total	$164,340	$75,000	$71,185	$0.43

Reprinted with permission from Fund-Raising Cost Effectiveness: A Self-Assessment Workbook *by James M. Greenfield (New York: John Wiley & Sons, Inc., 1996), 19.*

penses, plus a bonus—cost per dollar raised for each program. Exhibit 3.22 is a sample budget worksheet for each fund-raising method that uses prior year's indirect costs along with direct expenses to estimate the complete budget required in the next year. With each program budget comes a bonus: the ability to estimate next year's results with greater confidence.

Micromanagement has its limits, especially when applied to fund raising, because of the access to data that is provided by personal computers and their software. There are also limits to the amount of time and money a not-for-profit organization should spend to raise money and to analyze

EXHIBIT 3.22   Budget Worksheet for Fund Development Office

The combination of program expenses (direct costs) with office operations (indirect costs) represents the true and complete budget required for fund raising. Preparation of the annual budget for the fund development office should be based on the analysis of total costs for prior-year activity and productivity measured program by program. These data are to be presented on the following budget worksheet, provided by the business office.

	Estimated Budget	Actual Budget	Next Year's Estimated Budget
A. Salaries and Benefits			
Director of development	$	$	$
Assistant director			
Office support staff			
Part-time employees			
Temporary workers	_____	_____	_____
Subtotal	$	$	$
Fringe benefits (____%)			
Vacation/Holidays (PTO)			
Estimated salary increases	_____	_____	_____
Subtotal	$	$	$
Group A Total	$	$	$
B. Office Operations			
Office supplies	$	$	$
Telephone charges			
Telephone equipment			
Rental equipment			
List fees			
Postage fees			
Printing costs			
Books/Periodicals			
Travel (trips)			
Travel (local)			
Entertainment			
Awards/Plaques			
Dues/Memberships			
Conferences			

(continued)

3

EXHIBIT 3.22 (continued)

Insurance			
Office rental			
New equipment			
Equipment maintenance			
Consultant fees			
Services purchased			
Other expenses			
Group B Total	$	$	$
Grand Total (A+B)	$	$	$

how the money was raised successfully. The primary need is to raise all the money needed, on schedule, and this goal includes the money needed to support all volunteer-led committees. Volunteers must appreciate that their requests (or demands) for staff support represent direct costs to the organization and may reduce the net proceeds to the charity.

If a fund-raising professional's job description includes preservation of donor relationships and production of predictable levels of net revenue, the professional must know how to monitor the ongoing fund raising as well as how to prepare to deliver more dollars.

LEADERSHIP DEVELOPMENT: INVOLVEMENT PLUS PARTICIPATION

As has been stated before in this text, leadership is the single most important ingredient for success in fund raising. Given that they are absolutely essential, how are leaders found and developed? Can they be prepared for such significant work through other than "on-the-job" training experiences? For now, the answer is no. The only training ground for their leadership seems to be in the trenches of the fund-raising activities of today's not-for-profit organizations. Given that reality, who is training volunteers to become the leaders of tomorrow? Several programs are available. The National Center for Nonprofit Boards and local volunteer centers offer classes, workshops, and other training opportunities along with books, articles, videotapes, and more to assist those would seek to improve their service to organizations. Following that, direct experience is the best teacher.

Several layers of leadership are required for not-for-profit organizations. The key leadership roles are chairperson of the annual giving campaign committee, president of the support group, chairperson of the benefit event, and chairperson of the capital campaign committee. Some voluntary roles can be matched closely with professional career fields if volunteers can be found who are professional investment managers (for the investment committee) or attorneys specializing in estate planning (for the planned giving committee). But volunteers, to be successful, do not need to match their professional career field with their not-for-profit assignment. In fact, most would prefer to avoid just this kind of related experience, preferring some relief from the demands of such single focus in their life. Trying something new that uses their skills for other purposes and allows them to enjoy their personal as well as their professional accomplishments can be an attractive reason for accepting a voluntary leadership job.

Volunteers need to be organized and given direction; to be convened as a group and given assignments and deadlines; to feel part of something larger than themselves; to have access to others who are more successful or more widely recognized; to enjoy the camaraderie and pleasure of each other's company; to learn from one another and to grow in experience; and to perform a worthwhile service. In short, they need leaders—people who can provide an organized, productive, rewarding structure for the tasks that volunteers are invited to perform.

Annual giving programs offer a variety of leadership opportunities. Because annual giving programs have one-year terms, performance of the specific tasks assigned can be evaluated readily at the end of the assignment. Accountability for performance is an absolute necessity for any not-for-profit organization's leaders. Good service may be rewarded with another appointment next year, perhaps with expanded areas of work or even greater responsibility. In time, an invitation to serve on the board of directors may materialize. This "career ladder" results from fulfillment of significant positions through voluntary efforts that merit recognition and reward.

Developing Leaders

When annual giving programs are being planned for the following year, an organization must consider whether eligible, qualified, and willing leaders are available for all the required assignments. If not, some programs may be well served by waiting until suitable leaders are trained and ready. There is great merit to developing a program that will identify, recruit, and train people for the voluntary services the organization will require. The alternative is to look for experienced volunteers who are veterans of other not-for-profit organizations' campaigns—a source limited in numbers because people who give service to another organization develop their interest and enthusiasm for its mission, purposes, goals, and objectives. Each charity should grow its own volunteers and worry less about what other organizations are doing. Without enough qualified volunteers present and ready, programs will fail; worse yet, fund-raising methods will lose the confidence of people within and outside the organization and no one will want to work for it.

How important is leadership to success? George Brakeley, Jr.'s reply is

> Able, dedicated leadership has been behind every institution which has prospered and grown; those which have withered and fallen by the wayside invariably failed, for one reason or another, to attract and retain the level and kind of leadership they needed.[17]

A leadership program has five major steps: program design and job descriptions; recruitment and appointment; orientation and training; operations and management; and evaluation and recognition.

Program Design and Job Descriptions

The qualities and talents that must be matched to the volunteer tasks required by a fund-raising program should be carefully defined. A list of all the committees and subgroups needed should include necessary assignments and reporting responsibilities. A simple but complete job description should be prepared for each key position, specifying its exact duties and its working relationship to other levels and to the chairperson.

Recruitment and Appointment

A design may look good on paper but are there any people who can fill the jobs that have been defined? What type of volunteer will be needed? What talents will be compatible with the tasks and timetable? Market research studies can provide insight into how outside people view the organization. These data can be used to deduce where potential volunteers might be found and how to appeal to them. Lists of committee members should be reviewed; some were selected because of their future leadership potential. Present leaders should be polled for their choices, to secure a concurrence on the leadership candidates and the jobs to be offered. How should potential recruits be approached? Being asked by the right

[17]George A. Brakeley, Jr., *Tested Ways to Successful Fund-Raising* (New York: Amacom, 1980), 15.

person may have value to the volunteer and may achieve acceptance. Those who accept should receive an official appointment letter signed by a senior volunteer or the board member responsible for the entire fund-raising effort. Details about the assignment, its importance to the organization, the goal, and the term of office should be stated in the letter.

Orientation and Training

Volunteers need some time to get to know an organization—its goals and objectives, its performance record, the other people involved, its operating rules and procedures, and its style. A thorough orientation program should be conducted, and every key volunteer should attend either a one-on-one session or a group meeting. A key person in the organization should conduct the orientation program. Volunteers will not only be impressed that this person is taking the time to be present but they will appreciate that the role they have been asked to play is recognized as important enough to warrant top-level attention. The verbal and written information provided should take them through each item in the program. The items should be arranged in advance in a logical, step-by-step fashion. Questions and comments should be encouraged; one goal of this meeting is to build some excitement for the work ahead.

The nature of their task should be explained in full—its goals and objectives, their obligations and their responsibility, the reporting relationships to higher authority, and the deadlines. (Some elements of volunteer work are negotiable but these key features are not.) As leaders, they will be able to recruit their own team members to all key positions. They should be given the list of people known to the organization who might be able to help; the leader should make the selection, subject only to top-level review and approval. The leaders chosen should have the ability to bring in new volunteers. Organization charts for the assigned area and for the entire organization (with names filled in below the titles) will inform the new team where everyone is located.

Training sessions for leaders can be conducted individually or for a group. If proper thought is given to preparing these sessions, leadership candidates will develop respect for the organization's consideration of their time and for the efforts invested in making the session maximally effective. If this test is met at the beginning, volunteers who lead will work according to the plan. A brief, succinct agenda, with key institutional leaders present, is recommended. Background information was already covered in orientation. These volunteers should be thanked for their willingness to help out, and then training in performance of their assigned task should begin. Leadership volunteers who had the assignment last

year can be asked to conduct this section of the training session. Their experience will be the best source of verifiable information to the newcomers. A packet of information provided should contain, for example, the
roster of board members, financial information, annual report, case statement, background data on the project for which funds will be raised, roster of fund development staff, and key phone numbers. A preliminary
schedule of required meetings should be developed. Their purpose, the
outcomes required, the meetings' time and place—all can be fitted to each
leader's personal preference and professional schedule, and to the likely
best times for the committee members.

Operations and Management

To conduct meetings, order and discipline, advance notices of agendas,
minutes and handout materials, budgets, and timelines for action are
needed. Professional staff may perform many of these services, but volunteer leaders need to be a part of the preparation for each element
throughout their term of office. Staff are committed to their success, so a
close relationship with leaders is important. Leaders should concentrate
on the issues and decisions required to keep all preparations on schedule,
and on the performance of those whom they have recruited (attendance
at meetings, responses to requests, completion of assignments on time).
Building a well-functioning team out of the committee members is the
leaders' chief assignment and challenge; the professional staff will do
everything they can to assist but they cannot provide leadership.

Management issues need not involve committee members. Budget
preparation and submission according to institutional policy, expense approval procedures, contract and liability requirements, progress reports
to higher authority—all these are the province of committee leaders, who
attend meetings of the steering committee, advisory councils, and board
of directors. They report on their progress, hear reports from other committee chairpersons, and receive additional details from the institution's
leadership. In short, they are "insiders" and receive privileged access to
information about institutional operations and management. Some of
these details they need to report back to their committee; others they do
not need to reveal or discuss.

Evaluation and Recognition

The reporting process permits each chairperson to present the progress
and results of his or her work and that of the committee members. Everyone wants to make a favorable report, not only for the personal satisfaction of providing good news but also to fulfill the mission he or she was

given. Success in voluntary leadership roles can be measured in several ways: how many prospects have been identified, how many have been assigned, and how many contacted; the percentage of contacts made, the number of gifts received, the percentage of donors giving, the average gift size, and the percentage of goal realized (review the committee evaluation form in Exhibit 3.16). These progress statements encourage others to good efforts (or embarrass the giver) and yield vital information for management purposes. Committee chairpersons are alerted to how they will be measured and evaluated; if possible, every committee chairperson should present a parallel progress report. Volunteers will be competitive; they will want to perform as well as if not better than last year's leader of this same assignment. They will want to excel before their peers and to provide a valued and successful service to the not-for-profit organization. As each project comes to its conclusion and they report their final results, the organization has an excellent opportunity to acknowledge their accomplishment with congratulations, appreciation, and recognition.

Not-for-profit organizations should always remember not only to thank volunteers but also to creatively design multiple ways to convey the thanks. Gifts, certificates, and plaques presented during the victory celebration are well-suited for this purpose, even if the volunteer has a closet full of similar types of rewards from other organizations. What is given is not as important as the thought devoted to its choice and its tasteful execution in front of others. The people who were involved with volunteers' recruitment should be present. Recognition must stay within budgetary limits. Consider whether similar or identical methods should be used next year so that prior leaders do not feel "cheated" and future leaders can envision the rewards they can expect to receive.

Added forms of recognition also have value. Thank-you letters from the leadership of the organization offer opportunities for meaningful statements of appreciation and are highly valuable; names and photos of volunteers can appear in the next newsletter; names of chairpersons can be listed on a permanent plaque located prominently in the institution and placed on display during important meetings (kickoff, victory celebration). The updated list should appear in printed materials used each year. All prior chairpersons might serve together as a special group invited to advise and counsel the present chairperson. Most important of all is an invitation, soon after a task is completed, to take on another responsibility, to be "promoted" to a higher position in the organization. Promotion is its own reward for hard work and success; it is as effective in voluntary leadership organizations as it is in the business world.

Leadership in annual giving programs has several other benefits, not the least of which is a pool of talent to draw upon for next year. Individuals who rise to leadership levels enjoy being there and will be willing to serve again. Annual giving programs offer multiple opportunities to exercise and demonstrate leadership. They also permit leadership training and development to be initiated, an equally crucial element in a broad-based and successful fund development program. Present leaders will acknowledge this need and work to identify and recruit future leaders, including their successors. They will want to be sure that all their good work will be continued. Leaders are a community's gift to an organization. Learning to attract and retain the best of them will help to guarantee an organization's fund-raising success in the future.

WHERE DOES ESTATE PLANNING FIT IN ANNUAL GIVING?

Annual giving is not normally the occasion or medium for recruiting future gifts, but annual donors are candidates to make gifts in the future. The pyramid of giving illustrates a natural progression in donors' involvement and enthusiasm, toward an important investment decision—a single large gift or a series of gifts toward an overall major objective. A natural outgrowth of this plan can easily be a final gift made as part of the donor's estate as a bequest.

Because annual giving communications concentrate on this year's needs, they cannot easily mix into their call for urgent action a message about gifts in the future. Or can they? The audiences for annual giving programs represent hundreds, thousands, and even millions of people who are contacted more than once during a year's time. What better opportunity to bring up the subject of other forms of gift support, beyond an annual contribution? Endowment is an outcome of planned gifts; investment earnings will support annual giving priorities in perpetuity.

Development staff, who must manage several programs simultaneously, often do not see annual giving as a lifetime relationship between donors and the institution, and themselves as the temporary custodians of that relationship. Annual giving appeals are only one source of contact, but because they reappear at least once a year, the people involved do not necessarily see each of their gifts as an isolated incident. Annual giving must take the same long-term point of view. Annual giving raises friends as well as funds and easily can promote the gifts needed in the future.

One example of a straightforward approach to soliciting bequests is to add two boxes and these two sentences at the bottom of the direct mail response form:

☐ Yes, I have named your organization in my will.
☐ Yes, I would like information on how to include your organization in
   my will.

When affirmative replies accompany an annual gift (or even when returned without money), the organization must be prepared to respond
properly on planned giving.

A separate letter should formally acknowledge each reply by mail.
This letter should be adapted appropriately, to convey appreciation for
this donor's great respect for the organization, which has resulted in a
commitment to give or an interest in giving some asset or a portion of an
entire estate at death. Without inquiring about the donor's reasons, which
may never be known, the letter should acknowledge that a decision process took place and a choice was made among charities. The letter must
not ask for details on the item or amount involved, nor should it ask for a
copy of the will. These requests can and ought to come later. It can suggest
that, because federal tax law and state estate and probate regulations
change fairly often, a review of the estate plans by an attorney, to be sure
they are up-to-date, may be merited. Names of bequest donors should be
placed on two lists: an "expectancy file" of donors who have named the
institution in their will, and an "estate planning file" of those who have expressed an interest in a bequest. Both lists are sent information, program
offers, or other communications about estate planning or planned gifts.

After the wills information message has been used for a year or so,
new boxes and new information can be introduced:

☐ Yes, I have a established a charitable trust naming your organization
   as a beneficiary.
☐ Yes, I would like information on how to set up a charitable trust naming your organization as the beneficiary.

A new letter should be prepared and sent to each donor who checks either box. A different and more expanded message about the several charitable trust methods available, and their merits to both the donor and the
organization, should be described. After these initial exchanges about
wills or charitable trusts, it is appropriate to follow up and inquire about
the nature and form of this estate gift interest or decision. Two opportunities are to (1) add their donors to a select mailing list to receive other information about estate planning, including workshops, lectures, or seminars,
and (2) invite them to membership in your Codicil Club or Heritage Society
and treat them to all the donor recognition privileges you can. This invitation can be the occasion to ask for a copy of their estate planning document,

the will, living trust, remainder trust, or other form that has been completed.

Annual donors, especially seniors, are valid prospects for information about the estate planning services your organization may offer. Planned giving methods are a complex subject to explain and understand, and information circulated should be prepared or verified by an expert in the field. An organization that promotes a planned giving program can also be providing a valuable service to those who are interested in considering an estate plan for use of these advantaged gift opportunities.

Volunteers can be quite vocal spokespersons for estate planning opportunities. Information circulated to the "estate planning file" should be given to volunteers to share with family, friends, neighbors, and colleagues.

RECOGNITION GUIDELINES FOR ANNUAL DONORS

Each organization has several opportunities to acknowledge donors who participate in one or more annual giving programs each year. Their gifts are valuable, and the donors should be properly thanked and encouraged to give again.

Recognition should be designed at three levels:

1. Overall annual giving, crediting every gift made during a year
2. The annual giving campaign
3. Cumulative gift history

Recognition for Overall Annual Giving

A unique recognition plan can be designed for each method of annual giving—direct mail efforts, visual and audio communications, benefits and special events, support group activities, multilevel donor associations, and the annual giving campaign. Each plan should recognize one year's efforts, whether at the end of the calendar year or on another significant date or anniversary.

An organization's choices are many, but those under consideration should be consistent with its mission and purpose. For example, when a gift of $100 is received by a college or university, the donor might be entitled to preferred seating at campus events and invitations to pre-event receptions, a VIP parking pass, or a library access and privilege card. A hospital might offer a $100 donor tours of new facilities and equipment, health information brochures, invitations to physicians' lectures on new medical advances, or an identification card that provides a discount on purchases in the gift shop. A museum or cultural center might offer a $100 donor invitations to premiere openings, seating preferences, special group sales rates, or an identification card that allows discount privileges on purchases in the museum shop.

The IRS now examines the extent of privileges and benefits given to donors in recognition of their gifts. When these "givebacks" have a material value, the IRS is concerned that the gifts represent an exchange (dollars for products) in such a direct relationship that donors have "purchased" goods or services. Thus, the IRS contends that donors should not be allowed to claim the total amount given as the value of their gift deduction for income tax purposes, but should subtract the market value of the goods and services they received in return. Some alternate methods of recognition should be considered for annual giving programs. (The recognition level is assumed here to begin at $100.)

Direct Mail

Graduated gift levels ($100, $500, $1,000) can be matched to corresponding graduated benefits. All donors of any gift size should receive a thank-you letter, but recognition of larger gifts must go beyond an acknowledgment letter, especially if a renewal gift is expected next year. The solicitation package might announce that donors of $100 or more will receive a quarterly newsletter as well as invitations to public events held by the organization during the coming year. Their name might be added to a roster of "Honored Donors" to be printed in the newsletter and placed on a special recognition plaque to be displayed at the entrance to the organization for one year. A program of graduated benefits will communicate that an organization seeks and welcomes gifts of substantial size and that they will be suitably recognized.

Visual and Audio Media

Appeals on the telephone radio, TV, the Internet, or videotapes are notorious for "premium" benefits for gifts of $100 or more. This particular fundraising method's recognition items—coffee mugs, T-shirts, tote bags, umbrellas, videotapes about the organization—may have sparked the IRS's interest in the value of these givebacks. None of these appeals may want to discontinue the benefit items, but if the IRS has the final word on deductible amounts, the appeal sponsors could alternatively provide the same benefits offered to direct mail donors of $100 or more (newsletter, invitations, publication of their name, and adding them to a published or displayed roster of donors).

Special Events and Benefits

Given the variety of social, cultural, and athletic events available to the public each year, some extra benefits attached to an organization's special event or benefit may be a factor in ticket sales. For a gift of $100 to a $50-per-couple event, the donor might be listed in the program as a "sponsor." Extra benefits to be conferred on these and other donors of higher sums to increase sales and net revenues are the decision of the event committee and its sponsor. However, the amount of the donor's gift deduction is affected by IRS regulations. Most events include some amount of goods and services (food and drink) received by patrons, and they now must be informed in the event's invitation that the value of their food and drink must be subtracted from their original gift amount.

More difficult is the issue of whether donors to the events should receive privileges similar to those of other donors—or any privileges at all. By their nature, special events and benefits are an investment for the sake of a limited percentage of revenue. The full value of gifts received does not flow to the organization as in a mail or media reply. Perhaps the only way to be fair to donors in all other fund-raising methods and still offer similar privileges to event participants is to estimate the total amount of the event's cost (say 50 percent of net revenues) and declare that donors at a higher level, perhaps $200 or more, will be entitled to the privileges of the newsletter, invitations, and plaque list.

Support Group Organizations

These gifts are direct contributions in response to an invitation to become members; donors have made a direct gift to the not-for-profit organization and can be offered the benefits listed above for other donors. In addition, because their support was in the form of a membership in the support group, they are accorded all the rights and privileges of the group, which may include a membership directory, invitations to activities sponsored by the group, and more.

Donor Clubs and Associations

These groups are perfectly suited to $100 donors. The contribution is honored with affiliation in an association of comparable donors, and all the rights and privileges of the association are conferred. What are these benefits? Issues of the newsletter, listing on a roster of donor club participants, invitations to events and activities, and inscription of the donor's name on a plaque honoring all $100 donors that is placed at the entrance to the institution.

Annual Giving Campaign

The annual giving campaign committee normally solicits gifts above $100, perhaps starting at $500 or $1,000. Any donor above the $100 minimum would be eligible for the four benefits mentioned earlier; but the committee is recruiting higher gifts, and the privileges accorded such donors will be the committee's focus.

The design of a *consistent* recognition policy, with guidelines about each form of recognition to be provided to each donor within each program, is important. The consistency must extend across all programs; gifts of the same size must get equivalent benefits. The privileges from giving $100 by mail must be acknowledged in the same manner as those from giving $100 to the annual giving campaign. The privileges and benefits that accompany each gift level must be clearly identified. Some "benefits," such as a complimentary copy of the quarterly newsletter, may be called privileges but are part of a plan to communicate with donors regularly. Making the newsletter a privilege associated with the $100 level of giving gives the newsletter added value to those donors who will now receive it.

Cumulative Gift History

The organization's policy and guidelines should describe how gifts given over the course of a donor's life will be tabulated. Significant recognition should be reserved for donors whose total giving reaches established levels (see Exhibit 3.23). Special methods of recognition should be reserved for these donors—extra privileges not otherwise available. A "donor wall" on permanent display permits donors to watch their progress from one level of giving to the next. Although these levels are currently out of their reach for a single gift, annual giving donors will remember this recognition system, knowing that whenever their cumulative giving achieves a preset level, they too will be honored for their accomplishment. Should their fortunes improve, they will be more inclined to share some of their new wealth with a not-for-profit organization that has treated them as a faithful friend and donor over the years. If this donor recognition system includes planned gifts and gifts by will, these methods can compete favorably for donor attention and use.

Computers have simplified maintenance of donor record files, and a cumulative giving policy offers several valuable advantages:

EXHIBIT 3.23 Policy Statement on Donor Recognition

A. All donors whose cumulative contributions add to $2,500 or more will be recognized on the main Donor Wall as follows:

Friends	$2,500	to	$9,999
Sponsors	10,000	to	24,999
Patrons	25,000	to	99,999
Benefactors	100,000	to	249,000
Meritorious Benefactors	250,000	to	999,000
Honored Benefactors	1,000,000	to	4,999,999
Distinguished Benefactors	$5,000,000	or	More

    1. Included among those recognized will be donors of cash, real estate, pooled income funds, and future interest gifts including irrevocable gifts in trust, life estates, and gift annuities.

    2. Gifts of life insurance will be recognized at cash value until maturity of the policy.

B. The names of those individuals in whose memory $2,500 or more has been given will be listed on the memorial section of the Donor Wall.

C. Appropriate recognition items will also be given to donors at the discretion of the board of directors.

- Donors will be encouraged to maintain and increase their annual gift support.
- Larger gifts are given special attention, but they are attainable by nearly everyone who remains involved.
- Each gift, regardless of its circumstance or point in time, is recorded and credited to the overall gift record of the donor.

ANNUAL GIVING: A PERSPECTIVE

Annual giving is a massive area of fund-raising practice. Anyone can initiate simple ways to raise money; those same methods, when they are part of an annual giving campaign, can have tremendous value—or the potential for serious failure—for a not-for-profit organization. Annual giving raises operating revenues, which are essential funds. Its methods must be constantly reviewed for maximum results and possible improvements.

Nearly every not-for-profit organization in America engages in annual giving using some or all of the means and methods discussed in this chapter, and most of the methods have proven productive and profitable. The challenge is to integrate them better and increase their productivity and profitability as well as reap the numerous other benefits they afford to volunteers and donors alike. Consistent recognition of donors is important to the integration of donor efforts. To amplify the discussion of recognition given here, the full text of an honors and recognition policy appears in Appendix A, section J, at the back of the book.

4 ▼ The Middle Tier: Gifts from Institutions

Fund-raising professionals emerge from the annual gifts tier, the bottom third of the giving pyramid, out of breath and slightly exhausted. Now, they hope and believe, *now* is the time for some "big money." They yearn for one of those few but magnificent gifts that equal or exceed all the dollars raised from the year-long, time-consuming, annual giving programs. They anticipate a little travel and sophistication, some panache in meetings with top executives of America's foundations and corporations, even a touch of appreciation of the mission, purposes, goals, and objectives of their organization. To enter the arena of "big time" fund raising is to enter the middle tier in the pyramid of giving: gifts from institutions. These are not victory garden gifts. The world of foundations and corporations is more akin to groves of trees bearing fruits and nuts—trees that take years of toil, cost, and patience to grow to maturity and productivity.

Where do gifts from institutions fit in an overall program of fund development? When making gift decisions, foundations and corporations think and act quite unlike individuals, and they represent *only* 12 to 15 percent of all the money given away each year. More important, they do not match up well with every cause or issue, nor do they easily fit into every program of fund development.

Institutions are directed by policy and procedure, by guidelines, goals, and objectives that often are expressed as specific restrictions, whether by discipline or geography or available funds. These restrictions tend to limit their interests and their ability to engage the broad spectrum of not-for-profit organizations. Institutions have from 10 to 100 times more applicants than they have money to give away, and 60 percent or more of these applicants never should have requested the funds. Institutions are often accused of being inflexible, mainstream-oriented, ponderous, stagnant, traditional, and out of touch with grassroots issues and rapidly changing societal needs. Because of their reporting responsibilities, they are conservative by nature, unwilling and unlikely to take risks with their money. Not-for-profit organizations cannot hope to effect change in these patterns of behavior, whether by protest or by submission of the most convincing and logical proposals. Unless an organization is an exact match to their priorities, foundations and corporations simply will not give any money. The best approach may be to not even ask them.

Why such harsh words? Because foundations and corporations give away about the same amount of money each year for mostly the same purposes and often to the same organizations. Organizations that have qualified before and receive funds regularly, which takes hard work, look upon foundations and corporations as wonderful donors. For those organizations, they are. However, charities that are not on the contributions list must work very hard to squeeze onto it and must expend considerable unreimbursed time and effort to solicit them. Isn't there a more productive use of the organization's time than to spend it pursuing some of the 12 to 15 percent of all available gifts each year that institutional giving represents? Perhaps, but first let's look at exactly how much institutions give and to whom.

The combined total of institutional gifts was just over $21.5 billion in 1997, an impressive sum. Foundations gave $13.37 billion while corporations gave $8.2 billion. Their total of $21.57 billion amounts to 15 percent of the $143.5 billion given in 1997 by all sources. The level of foundation support is up from the $12 billion given in 1990 due in part to a strong investment performance. The distribution of gifts among recipients since 1990 has also changed, reflecting a shift in givers' priorities as follows:

	1900[1]	1997[2]	Variance
Human services	26%	26%	0%
Education	16	25	+9
Health	21	16	−5
Arts and humanities	14	12	−2
Science and technology	9	4	−5
Social science	10	3	−7
Religion	2	2	0

[1] American Association of Fund-Raising Counsel, *Giving USA* (1989 report) (New York: AAFRC Trust for Philanthropy, 1990), 48.
[2] AAFRC Trust for Philanthropy, *Giving USA 1998* (1997 report) (New York: AAFRC Trust for Philanthropy, 1998), 56.

Nearly all these recipients have been directly involved for years building and maintaining relationships with foundation and corporation staff and directors, and their accomplishments from working together are significant. Those who are "in" stand a good chance of staying. Those who are "out" face a hard time trying to dislodge and replace those who are now in. How many organizations can take on Harvard, Stanford, or Yale and beat them in a grants contest? Any religious organization is unlikely to receive money from foundations and corporations, which is exactly the reverse of the giving practices of individuals.

Foundation gifts and grants are subject to two restraints. First, giving is confined to only those qualified organizations whose programs and projects are matched as closely as possible with the established mission, purposes, goals, and objectives of the foundation. Second, the limit on giving is linked to the foundation's investment performance, which can on occasion experience sudden reversals but yields a more or less steady return of about 5 percent on its portfolio. By law, foundation funds can be distributed only to not-for-profit organizations that are qualified according to strict IRS policy (Code Section 501(c)(3) nonprofit organizations). Because foundations receive hundreds of grant requests they cannot fund, the selection process is intense and competitive. Unfortunately, too many organizations and their fund-raising staff fail to do their homework and they send requests where they should not be applying.

Corporate gifts are even more difficult to achieve. They too are made according to established priorities linked to corporate objectives, which vary greatly from company to company, and to profits, which vary even more. Corporations' priorities can and do change slightly, but only as interests wane or society (stockholders, customers, and the public) pressures companies to alter their focus. Between 1987 and 1993, corporate giving patterns shifted as follows:

	1987	1993[3]	1996[4]
Education	37%	38%	35%
Health and human services	27	27	26
Civic and community	14	11	11
Arts and culture	11	11	10

(continued)

[3] Virginia Ann Hodgkinson and Murray S. Weitzman, *Nonprofit Almanac 1996–1997: Dimensions of the Independent Sector* (San Francisco: Jossey-Bass, 1996), 80.

[4] American Association of Fund-Raising Counsel, *Giving USA* (1996 report) (New York: AAFRC Trust for Philanthropy, 1997), 98.

Religion	0	0	0
Others	11	14	20
	100	100	100

Overall giving performance points out the leaders among major national corporations. The Taft Group collects and publishes corporate giving data and its list of the nation's 10 top corporate givers for 1996 is shown in Exhibit 4.1. Figures include cash from the company and/or corporate foundation plus the value of product donations (companies vary in their method to calculate their product value, using either wholesale, retail, or fair market value).

The corporate profit picture can change rapidly, with the instant result that there is less money to give away. Corporate takeovers appear to cause reduced giving. The truly bad news is that only about one-third of America's corporations had established contributions programs. The other two-thirds can and do give money away but the process of decision making is less institutionalized, being vested in the chairperson, president, principal owners, or partners. The decisions made most often reflect the personal interests of the officers and owners; no committee deliberates and then makes grants based on a written policy and procedure.

Corporate giving policy follows a singular style known as "enlightened self-interest"—a consideration of how each gift made will benefit the corporation. Setting funds aside to be used for altruistic purposes

EXHIBIT 4.1 Top 10 Corporate Givers, 1996

Corporation	Product Value	Total Gifts	Percent of Product Value
Merck & Company	$116,000,000	$140,500,000	82.6
IBM Corporation	62,500,000	100,800,000	62.0
Johnson & Johnson	44,000,000	88,500,000	49.7
Pfizer Inc.	63,900,000	85,473,901	74.7
Hewlett-Packard	56,148,000	71,579,000	78.9
General Motors	17,900,000	66,700,000	26.8
Eli Lilly and Company	40,992,720	66,289,356	61.8
Bristol-Myers Squibb	40,000,000	64,708,575	61.8
Microsoft Corporation	45,164,980	59,166,294	76.4
Intel Corporation	39,104,624	55,613,575	70.3

comes last among the multiple priorities for excess cash use. Corporate giving, as a percentage of pretax income, has declined in the past decade from a high in 1986 of 2.3 percent to 1.1 percent in 1997, as seen in Exhibit 4.2.

Foundations and corporations are not likely to be the sources for new annual gifts to an organization, no matter what its cause or the urgency of its need. They do not welcome such a commitment because it limits their flexibility to change direction. It helps to appreciate that every application they receive has an equally urgent or greater need. They are more likely to be interested in specific projects and programs within well-defined large-scale plans (including long-range, short-range, and strategic plans), *if* these areas match their own priorities closely and can demonstrate some return on investment.

Given that the rules of the game belong to the grantmakers, the time required to secure even one business or foundation grant is extensive. How much time and effort should be spent to solicit gifts from corporations and foundations? Not more than 20 percent, if that much. People, the source of 85 percent of all the money given away, should get the most attention.

The best time to ask foundations or corporations for money is when a special project is planned that is well matched to their current priorities.

EXHIBIT 4.2 Corporate Giving, 1986 to 1997

	Income	Gifts	Percent
1986	$222.6	$5.03	2.3
1987	293.6	5.21	1.8
1988	354.3	5.34	1.5
1989	348.1	5.46	1.6
1990	371.7	5.46	1.5
1991	374.2	5.25	1.4
1992	406.4	5.91	1.5
1993	465.4	6.47	1.4
1994	535.1	9.98	1.3
1995	622.6	7.32	1.2
1996	676.6	7.63	1.1
1997	729.8	8.20	1.1

Reprinted with permission from Giving USA 1997 *(New York: American Association of Fund Raising Counsel Trust for Philanthropy, 1998), 163.*

Only foundations and corporations that can participate in the organization's priorities of need should be solicited. Some not-for-profit organizations will never receive much, if any, corporate money. Even if they do, the money may not arrive for several months or it may be allocated over two years or more. Their efforts to join those on the favored list will take hard work and lots of time, and will always have a high potential for failure. But each victory will be sweet indeed.

FOUNDATIONS' PURPOSE: TO GIVE MONEY AWAY

Foundations have to give away at least 5 percent of their asset value each year. A few give more, but most reinvest their unused earnings in order to increase their asset value and their ability to give more next year and in the future. Most foundations were established to be permanent; their funds are invested as permanent endowment in order to continue their purposes in perpetuity. Foundations are a little like people: Not all of them are alike and even those of the same type do not behave alike. Each is a singular institution with a separate identity and specific purposes for existence. What is uniform about them is that they give money away each year. However, it is that fact that "causes some confusion among fund raisers with little experience in approaching foundations. Naively, they believe that the money is there for the taking. Accordingly, they approach foundations with the idea that they are asking for their share. However, for the most part, it is a foundation's charter that establishes its interest parameters. Trustees and foundation staff observe the guidelines set up in the charter and sometimes additional guidelines specified by the governing board."[5]

Volumes have been written about foundations and their operations—how to research them and how to write successful proposals. The Foundation Center, which has resource centers in New York and Washington, maintains branch offices and data libraries in every state, offering all the information any fund raiser needs. Guidance on how to approach foundations can be found in these sources.

There are four types of foundations in America: general-purpose or public foundations, corporate foundations, community foundations, and, the most numerous, personal or family foundations—approximately

---

[5] Henry A. Rosso, *Rosso on Fund Raising: Lessons from a Master's Lifetime Experience* (San Francisco: Jossey-Bass, 1996), 74.

42,000 in all. "Those with assets of $50 million or more represent less than 2% of all foundations, but they control 65% of all foundation assets and award nearly half the country's foundation grants."[6] Total grants made in 1997 increased by 11.38 percent to a new high of $13.83 billion, thanks to positive investment performance in a continuing bear market.[7]

Grantmakers can and do make major changes in the amount of their grant awards, as the list in Exhibit 4.3 of the 14 largest foundations illustrates.

Private or Public Foundations

Private or public foundations are the largest in terms of assets and the best known. The top 20 U.S. private foundations, ranked by the market

EXHIBIT 4.3 Changes in Giving Patterns for 14 Largest Foundations, 1995 to 1996

	1995 ($ millions)	1996 ($ millions)	Percent Change
Annenberg Foundation	113	89	−22
Ford Foundation	299	348	+17
Heinz Endowments	50	42	−15
Robert Wood Johnson Fdtn	102	255	+150
W. K. Kellogg	234	253	+8
Lilly Endowment	111	167	+50
John D. and Catherine T. MacArthur Fdtn	NA	113	NA
Andrew W. Mellon Fdtn	111	114	+3
David & Lucile Packard Fdtn	93	120	+29
Pew Charitable Trusts	194	174	−10
Rockefeller Foundation	106	89	−17
The Soros Foundation	350	350	0
Joseph B. Whitehead Fdtn	26	90	+246
Robert W. Woodruff Fdtn	73	254	+250

Reprinted with permission from Giving USA 1997 *(New York: American Association of Fund Raising Counsel Trust for Philanthropy, 1998), 84–93.*

[6]Leon Renz, *Foundation Giving 1995* (New York: Foundation Center), 1995.
[7]AAFRC, *Giving USA 1998*, 22.

EXHIBIT 4.4 Top 20 Grantmakers

Foundation	Asset Value
1. Ford Foundation	$8,177,480,000
2. W. K. Kellogg Foundation	7,588,408,314
3. David and Lucile Packard Foundation	7,386,414,000
4. J. Paul Getty Trust	7,160,383,700
5. Lilly Endowment Inc.	6,806,947,975
6. Robert Wood Johnson Foundation	5,595,820,816
7. Pew Charitable Trusts	4,031,999,462
8. John D. and Catherine T. MacArthur Fdtn.	3,423,714,583
9. Robert W. Woodruff Foundation, Inc.	2,957,942,788
10. Rockefeller Foundation	2,738,774,253
11. Andrew W. Mellon Foundation	2,714,725,000
12. Annenberg Foundation	2,584,405,699
13. Kresge Foundation	1,881,619,186
14. Duke Endowment	1,729,067,497
15. Charles Stewart Mott Foundation	1,674,870,543
16. Starr Foundation	1,659,251,095
17. Ewing Marion Kauffman Foundation	1,600,356,000
18. McKnight Foundation	1,501,041,000
19. William and Flora Hewlett Foundation	1,453,340,000
20. New York Community Trust	1,385,229,096

Reprinted from the Foundation Center, The Top 100 U.S. Foundations Ranked by Assets, *World Wide Web page http://www.library@fdncenter.org*

value of their assets are shown in Exhibit 4.4. These foundations are easily recognized by their founders' names, including some newcomers. All of these giants have competent professional staff and make quite deliberate and splendid grants, but only to a select number of not-for-profit organizations, each of which must be a verifiable Code Section 501(c)(3) not-for-profit organization.

Foundations file an annual tax return (IRS Form 990PF) that discloses fiscal details about all their activities. This information is available to the public through the Foundation Center and its affiliate libraries around the country. Foundations are audited by the IRS regularly to verify that each grant is made to a legitimate not-for-profit organization, and other details. Foundations must pay an excise tax of 2 percent on their investment earnings, an idea hatched by the IRS to pay for the number of IRS agents added to conduct audits of foundations. The revenue realized from the excise tax could be better spent for public benefit because "irregularities and illegalities" are seldom discovered.

Private foundations have broad purposes indeed. They make grants to nearly every type of not-for-profit organization, in several disciplines across the spectrum of philanthropic activity, Some, like Ford and Kellogg, define and sponsor their own programs of public benefit and invite selected not-for-profit organizations to apply. All of them require not-for-profit organizations to submit formal (and sometimes formidable) grant requests, which are then carefully reviewed according to strict guidelines. Any formal proposal submitted must be tailored, even revised, to the foundation being applied to and must document in detail how the program plan, in meeting public benefit needs, also fulfills the foundation's stated goals and objectives in the best fashion possible.

Major foundations have full-time professional staff who are experts in their respective foundation's main areas of interest as well as in management of all its operations, and who are available to work with staff from not-for-profit organizations. They aid by explaining the foundation's many qualifications for grant recipients and by guiding request preparations to supply the required information. The level of professionalism on the foundations' side of the table is high.

Formal application to these foundations should be the end result of building an informed relationship. Each request must be well prepared and fully documented in every detail. To help with proper application, these foundations publish and distribute annual reports and application instructions that give details about their purposes and qualifications, priorities and objectives, prior-year grants, trustees and staff, and financial statements. It is a source of continuous amazement to the boards and staff of these foundations that, despite their best efforts with these mass communications, not-for-profit organizations and their fund-raising staff continue to fail to observe their well-publicized guidelines. Their rejection letters often point to a disregard of their application rules. Perhaps it is not as well known that foundations keep complete files on all applicants, whether they receive a grant or not. Failure to follow their rules is not the best way to make friends, especially when the potential friends have such prodigious memories. Most foundation funds are preassigned to already established interest areas that are in concert with current priorities. But foundations are serious when they request proposals for innovative, imaginative, and nontraditional purposes, as long as any new ideas stay within their overall guidelines.

Private foundations are the leaders in institutional grant making. They have set the professional example that many of the others seek to follow.

Corporate Foundations

Corporations that practice an organized program of public support usually set aside revenue from their annual net profits to fund a contributions budget supervised by a contributions committee. Alternately, they may establish a corporate foundation with company cash or assets and empower the board of directors to make all gift decisions and distribute corporate funds through the foundation. Whatever the format (some companies use both), the decisions made are always an extension of the corporation. Yet these are legal foundations with a board of directors made up of corporate officers and board members; they have written policies and procedures, manage their funds as permanent endowment, and use investment earnings along with an infusion of company profits when available. They prepare annual reports, file IRS Form 990PF, and otherwise behave much the same as general-purpose foundations. Their names are identified with household products: Alcoa, ARCO, Eastman Kodak, Exxon, General Electric, IBM, Western Electric, Westinghouse, and others. Their total number may now exceed 800 institutions across America.

The operating style of corporate foundations is different from that of general-purpose foundations. Corporate foundations mirror corporate community relations and self-interest policies and are a conduit to fulfill corporate social objectives. Most make a large number of small gifts each year to numerous organizations across the spectrum of philanthropy, usually concentrated where they have plants or offices. Their occasional major grants to educational institutions are part of a direct exchange between the two: grants for scholarships and fellowships are given to colleges, and their graduates are then hired by the corporation. Corporate foundations make a lot of grants each year, but, like other foundations, they prefer not to be committed to continue this support year after year. Corporations encourage their employees to support not-for-profit organizations and offer to match their gifts with corporate money. This matching gift concept, while laudatory and obviously a positive employee relations program, usually produces only a limited increase in funds for any one not-for-profit organization.

Community Foundations

Community foundations are both grantmakers and fund raisers. They are classified by the IRS as public charities and can both raise gift dollars and give them away. Community foundations have greatly expanded their numbers, assets, and visibility during the past two decades to become the major local resource for organizations of all sizes. Being local gives them unique values: wide representation among board members, breadth in the program areas open for application, flexible policies and procedures, quick decision making, and a positive image in the community as an active partner with not-for-profit organizations in meeting urgent public needs. There were 411 community foundations in operation across America in 1996 with assets of $15.9 billion. That year they made grants of $951 million and received $1.8 million in new contributions.[8] A not-for-profit organization that happens to be located in the same area as a community foundation should study the community foundation and apply for a portion of its funds nearly every year. Community foundations' grants most often are limited by the community's geography.

Personal and Family Foundations

Of the 42,000 foundations in America, about 25,000 are personal or family foundations and are generally known only to those not-for-profit organizations that receive gifts from them. Despite their numbers, their total assets represent less than 15 percent of all foundation funds. Most began as a convenient means to carry out the charitable interests of the individual or family who founded them, or, possibly, to avoid taxes legally. Like all other foundations, they must invest their assets professionally, spend from their investment earnings, file IRS Form 990PF, and fulfill all other regulatory requirements. They are often hard to find and to learn about because they are small and only a few publish guidelines or annual reports. Because most were established to organize their founders' personal giving, they often take a calendar-year approach in their decisions. They can receive annual contributions from each family member who in turn can take a personal income tax deduction for his or her contribution each year. Family members have an easy way to say no to any request they do not wish to consider: "The foundation has spent all its money for this year." Few of these foundations have employees or professional staff. The board of directors is made up of family members along with an attorney and/or an accountant; one person serves as president and another as secretary each year. When their assets grow large enough to qualify, they may be listed in state or local foundation directories. Once listed, they

[8]The Foundation Center, "Trends and Analysis," in *Highlights of Foundation Giving* (New York: Foundation Center, 1998).

begin to receive numerous inquiries and proposals asking for money from fund-raising staff and volunteers who, in their unskilled search for funds, limit their research to copying a name and address from a foundation directory.

Life was simpler for personal foundations prior to the tax reform acts of 1969 and 1976. A few abuses were prominently reported in the press before 1969 and Congress acted to change the foundations' operating rules. All must now file annual tax returns revealing their revenue and expenses, the salaries paid to their directors, and the name, address, amount, and purpose of all grants made each year. (Before the tax reforms, some officers and directors paid themselves salaries and made grants or loans to family members.) Although foundations' conduct is now more professional, an unfortunate result of the reforms has been the decrease in the number of new foundations established annually. Inviting a frequent IRS audit by setting up a personal foundation is the least attractive way to organize personal giving to charity. Some pundits have labeled these tax laws as the "accountants' and attorneys' permanent employment and guaranteed retirement acts" because of the heavy financial reporting and legal regulations imposed.

The best strategy to get a grant from a personal or family foundation is to approach the foundation as though you were asking an individual for a major gift. The internal procedures for review and decision are quite simplified. If John Smith of the John and Mary Smith Family Foundation wants to become a donor, he has only to ask Mary Smith if she agrees and one of them then writes out a check. Either John or Mary Smith can be approached; a request does not necessarily have to be delivered to the John and Mary Smith Family Foundation.

Despite their simplicity, personal and family foundations have a few wrinkles. Some have grown to a large size during the founders' lifetimes and consequently have sophisticated annual operations. Any whose annual grants now exceed $100,000 should be approached as a small general-purpose foundation. If one or more family members is associated with a not-for-profit organization as a board member, volunteer, or annual donor, favorable attention from this foundation might be possible. The person involved should be treated the same as every other important individual donor, to encourage personal intervention for a grant decision. When and if this patron leaves the organization, support is likely to stop unless the active interests of other family members have been cultivated. Some personal foundations limit their giving to only a few not-for-profit organizations, to accomplish a significant purpose or establish a lasting memorial. When the foundation's original founder dies, the priorities may change, but there is more than an equal chance they will continue as before because the family is determined to observe faithfully the traditional interests of the founder as their continuing priority.

Other Institutions

A few other institutions think, act, and look like foundations but are not quite foundations. They are called charitable trusts and most often are managed by bank trust departments or attorneys. They were set up and funded by donors during their lifetimes and after death were activated by a direct bequest from the estate. Many are designed to preserve and continue the lifelong philanthropic interests of the founder (and possibly to escape some estate taxes). The bank or attorney that serves as trustee has full authority to invest the assets and distribute earnings to qualified not-for-profit organizations. These might best be called "hidden foundations" because it is hard to learn much about them. But they are faithful annual donors; they must find qualified not-for-profit organizations that can receive their funds each year.

RESEARCHING FOUNDATIONS

Solicitation of foundations begins with research, and research should start with only those foundations that can reasonably be expected to give an organization money. Research takes time and money and should be professionally carried out in order to be reliable and useful. Most not-for-profit organizations will need to research perhaps only 200 to 300 foundations out of the 42,000 in operation. Major national resource centers, universities, or major medical centers, which have extensive research and educational objectives, will need to research as many as 800 to 1,000 foundations across the country, to identify their eligibility for grant support.

What should an organization look for when it researches a foundation? K. Scott Sheldon replies,

> A major part of the foundation-research function is to be able to understand and interpret foundation guidelines and other written and statistical information. The most important questions that a not-for-profit seeking funding must ask are:
> 1. Does the foundation support other similar "like kind" agencies?
> 2. Does the foundation clearly state that it provides support for the type of project for which the organization is seeking funds?
> 3. Does the foundation make grants in the same geographic area in which the organization is located or conducts its programs?

4. Does the foundation make grants in the same monetary range that the organization is proposing?

   If the agency is able to answer *yes* to all four questions, then the chances for a successful outcome are much higher.[9]

Research about institutions is conducted only to learn what an organization needs to know: the foundation's purposes and priorities, guidelines and deadlines (if any) for application, process for decision and timetable for distribution of funds, board members and staff, and the value of the assets and earnings available for annual grants. Information on prior grants made to comparable organizations is also useful as a guide to qualification and amount to ask for. What amounts, purposes, and projects have been supported? All this information is available in several foundation resource directories and in each foundation's Form 990PF, annual reports, and application instructions.

The key information needed, once a match seems probable, according to the foundation's purposes and priorities, are its guidelines for application. Their current validity should be checked by phone. The challenge in drafting each proposal is that it must present an irrefutably appropriate use of the foundation's funds, which just happens to be matched exactly with the organization's highest planned priorities. The better the fit, the better the chances for a grant. The foundation's instructions on when to apply and what else to send should be followed exactly. All details requested—roster of directors, annual budget, audited financial statement, IRS tax-exempt declaration letter, and more—should be submitted. To withhold any public information from a foundation will delay the application until the relevant document or detail has been delivered.

Fund-raising staff approaching foundations should assume that every not-for-profit organization that might possibly qualify has already applied to this same foundation and that many of these applicants may have already been approved and are only waiting for funds to be available from investment earnings. Whatever the project and whenever a foundation is approached, applying additional pressure for a decision will not help a request. If the idea is a good match and the application is correct, the proposal will be reviewed and placed on the agenda for a decision, perhaps within 90 to 120 days at the earliest. Organizations in urgent need of funds to provide basic services and to make payroll should apply elsewhere because they are not likely to survive until the decision is announced. Foundations' decisions are deliberate and unemotional, and they tend to fund winning proposals and survivors.

[9]K. Scott Sheldon, "Foundations as a Source of Support," in *Achieving Excellence in Fund Raising*, by Henry A. Rosso and Associates (San Francisco: Jossey-Bass, 1991), 247.

Research about the foundation's board members may reveal links that can be put to good use in helping a proposal's chances. But the best service is performed by legitimate qualifications for a grant, the validity of a project, and a demonstration of commitment to its success. Foundation board members will see the roster of the petitioner's board and will not be surprised if someone speaks to them about the organization and its application, to convey personal support. However, these representatives should never ask for any special consideration or for any bending of rules and procedures; to do so is to invite immediate disqualification.

There are limits to what information should be researched and how it should be used. Details about people's lives, professional careers, marital status, children's names, birthdays, and the like are unnecessary. Foundation staff dislike it when an applicant, after being advised against direct contact with board members, attempts an "end run" to reach a board member. Staff can quite easily scuttle a proposal, give it a poor recommendation, or simply block it from further progress. Foundation board and staff place high priority on the faithful observance of their own procedures so that every request is treated fairly and equitably. With the IRS auditing all their procedures and decisions regularly, they cannot tolerate someone who refuses to stay within their rules.

PROPOSALS: PREPARATION AND DELIVERY

Most information written about foundations is about proposal preparation and delivery. The proposal document is crucial. It contains the entire request and must "speak" for the organization at the foundation's board meetings. Any proposal that works can be called a success. If there is a formula, it is this: Have content that meets a foundation's essential criteria (see Exhibit 4.5). Proposals that have been funded contain no secret to success that can be applied to other foundations or proposals. Each story must be told accurately and must reflect an organization's best thinking. No one else can tell that same story. Content is paramount; form and design have a lesser impact. Brevity is appreciated always.

A proposal text from another organization should never be copied. Foundation professionals (and their prodigious memory aids) know best those requests they have approved. There are no shortcuts in writing a winning proposal. If it cannot be done by existing staff, outside help should be enlisted. The text must be presented clearly and in an orderly fashion.

Proposals have to survive a series of tests or hurdles. One of the first things grantmakers look at, according to Susan Golden, is the budget:

EXHIBIT 4.5 Criteria for Measuring Characteristics Essential to Foundation Applications

Characteristic	Score				
	Low				High
Accuracy	1	2	3	4	5
Brevity	1	2	3	4	5
Clarity	1	2	3	4	5
Competence	1	2	3	4	5
Completeness	1	2	3	4	5
Correct English	1	2	3	4	5
Credibility	1	2	3	4	5
Fiscally sound	1	2	3	4	5
Honesty	1	2	3	4	5
Matching priorities	1	2	3	4	5
Public benefit	1	2	3	4	5
Relevancy	1	2	3	4	5
Urgency	1	2	3	4	5
Median Score					

Reprinted with permission from Fund-Raising Cost Effectiveness: A Self-Assessment Workbook *by James M. Greenfield (New York: John Wiley & Sons, Inc., 1996), 168.*

Most grantmakers agree that they look at the budget first and scrutinize it more rigorously than any other part of a proposal. If the grantmaker specifies a format for your budget information, be sure to follow it. If there is no format specified, a template that seems to accommodate most situations is that provided by The Cleveland Foundation. . . . Before you begin to build a budget, be sure to think through all the basic components and parameters of your project:

Its duration
The duration of the period for which you are seeking grant support
The level of resource commitment from your organization
The number and identity of collaborating organizations and the levels of their resource commitments
The number and identity of external funders to whom you are applying
The preferences of specific external funders and any restrictions they will place on the use of funds.[10]

[10]Susan L. Golden, "The Grant-Seeking Process," in Greenfield, *The Nonprofit Handbook: Fund Raising,* 406.

Proposals must demonstrate their own credibility as an integral statement of an organization's current master plan, express true merit in fulfilling a public benefit, be valid in their assumptions, be within the capability of the organization and its staff, and be fiscally sound. They also must be accepted and approved within the organization and signed by the chief executive officer as evidence of formal approval, commitment to do the work if funded, and a high priority of need. The ultimate test is whether the foundation staff and board can agree that the project or idea is within the area of current priority interest and find sufficient funds available to support it. Funding is often delayed after a favorable decision, to await a cash distribution schedule or investment earnings.

Some of the consistently best proposals are based on institutional master plans and drawn from case statements. Others, however, tend to overreach reality and, in their enthusiasm and hyperbole, overstate reasonable capability. For example, no hospital or health-care agency today should suggest that its objective is to cure cancer. Thirty years ago, several organizations did suggest exactly this goal. Now, after three decades of dedicated research around the world, the reality is that cancer is quite possibly the most complex disease yet encountered and is not likely to be "cured" anytime soon, much less within the next decade or two. More correctly, one or another facet of tumor growth and treatment can be better understood or applied with better results in a proposal. An organization must prove that what it is proposing can be done and then prove that it can do it. The proposal is the means to present convincing evidence on both counts.

Proposal documents need a professional appearance and should be presented in orderly fashion; an outline is shown in Exhibit 4.6. They should not be any longer than necessary; foundation staff value brevity as much as clarity. The document should be written in grammatically correct English and can use some illustrations. Foundation staff and boards read hundreds of proposals weekly. Use of jargon, deceptive language, "blarney," misspellings, bad grammar, and a poor appearance will not help any applicant.

Proposals can be delivered in person, in pieces, and by mail. Most are mailed because that is the method most foundations prefer; number of copies and mailing deadlines are usually specified. Delivery in pieces means the foundation first asks for a preliminary letter and a brief description of the program or project. After successful review, the foundation asks for a full presentation (usually by mail) and provides complete details on all requirements to be met in the submission and a deadline. Delivery in person is possible but not common in practice. Visits are usually by invitation only and are restricted to individuals essential to the

---

EXHIBIT 4.6 Outline for Foundation Proposal

Contents
1. Cover letter
2. Introduction and summary
3. History and background
4. Project description and problem statement
5. Goals, objectives, and estimated outcomes
6. Plan of action and project methodology
7. Evaluation plan and reports
8. Budget required and future funding plan
9. Conclusion and summary statement
10. Attachments, appendices, and support materials
    a. Roster of board members
    b. Most recent audited financial statement
    c. Operating budget for current year
    d. Tax-exempt documentation
    e. Curriculum vitae for program director
    f. Charts, drawings, renderings
    g. Remaining essential support documentation

---

meeting (which may not include the fund raiser). These people must be well informed about the foundation and about how to present in succinct and brief form (20 minutes) the content of the proposal text. The foundation will probably conduct the session; time should be allowed for discussion and questions. The organization may also be visited by the foundation and, although a visit is a positive indicator, it should not be misinterpreted as anything more than fact-finding that is required by the foundation. After the visit, a letter should be sent, thanking the visitors for their time and consideration of the project. Any additional information requested should be forwarded promptly. The foundation staff has to complete its review and prepare a recommendation to be included on the agenda for the next meeting of the foundation board. Most foundations will contact applicants after the meeting at which their application was discussed, provided the board had enough time and money left to consider the request; if it did not, the request is postponed until the next meeting. When a request is turned down, the rejection letter should be read carefully. A further explanation can be requested by phone and permission to submit future applications can be clarified. The foundation should be thanked for its consideration and a request prepared for the next foundation.

Nine-Point Performance Analysis of Foundation Solicitations

The approval process can be delayed for months at a time as a proposal passes through the stages of formal submission, foundation staff analysis, board decisions, and, finally, allocation of funds; the entire process can easily extend over two operating years for a not-for-profit organization. Therefore, an analysis of performance is recommended to embrace two to three years or more. The following interpretations are based on the results shown in Exhibit 4.7.

1. The number of proposals prepared and delivered each year was 100, a hefty load to achieve and to maintain. Success in grants received increased from 15 to 28, as did the grant awards.
2. Expenses to support this program began at $68,800, reflecting a full-time staff person and budget support, yielding an average cost of fund raising of 23 percent.
3. Average gift size began high at $19,367 but declined to $13,750 after a larger volume of grants began, for an average of $16,221. At the same

EXHIBIT 4.7 Nine-Point Performance Index Analysis of Foundation Solicitations

	Year 1	Year 2	Year 3	Totals
Participation	15	18	28	61
Income	$290,500	$314,000	$385,000	$989,500
Expenses	$68,800	$76,750	$86,800	$232,350
Percent participation	15%	18%	28%	20%
Average gift size	$19,367	$17,444	$13,750	$16,221
Net income	$221,700	$237,250	$298,200	$757,150
Average cost per gift	$4,587	$4,264	$3,100	$3,809
Cost of fund raising	24%	24%	23%	23%
Return	322%	309%	344%	326%

Reprinted with permission from Fund-Raising Cost Effectiveness: A Self-Assessment Workbook *by James M. Greenfield (New York: John Wiley & Sons, Inc., 1996), 175.*

time, average cost per gift began at $4,587, and then declined to $3,100 by year three, posting an average of $3,809.

4. A first-year net profit of $221,700 was realized with a fund-raising cost of 24 percent and a return of 322 percent. This performance remained virtually constant throughout the three-year period.

5. Overall program performance was stable during the three years while productivity increased as did net income each year. This organization has achieved a success rate of one out of every five proposals submitted for an average grant of $16,221.

6. The balance of performance indicators not in this exhibit will include tracking each grant to meet scheduled progress report deadlines, what levels of recognition the foundation will permit, and other continuing communications to fulfill grant requirements and maintain the interest and confidence of its staff and board members.

7. Maintaining this high level of performance is more dependent on significant programs and services qualifying for foundation support than on fund-raising staff.

Government Grants

Seeking grants from government agencies was not considered within the purposes of this text. Grantsmanship is a skill often shared by those who prepare applications for foundations, corporations, and government agencies, but the means to the same ends are quite different. Government funds are awarded as agreements or contracts for specific services to be performed; public tax-based grant dollars are not charitable contributions. Government funds are an important source of revenue for not-for-profit organizations, and they support many of the same programs and services that individuals, corporations, and foundations are asked to support through contributions. But this text is concerned with fund-raising methods used to build lasting personal relationships between institutional donors and the not-for-profit organizations they freely elect to support. The style and practice of these methods are inappropriate in working with government agencies. Numerous resources are available about methods to search out government sources and to prepare applications for public tax-based dollars. Readers are cautioned, however, that tax-based dollars are quite elusive. Furthermore, some analysts predict a trend toward significantly less reliance on government funding:

> This is an area for deepening government retrenchment. Thus, however significant public sector spending is now in various nonprofit service fields, it is

likely to diminish significantly over time as a proportion of nonprofit organizations' budgets. Thus, it may not seem worthwhile, on the surface, to emphasize the development of government funding for nonprofit services as a dimension for future research.[11]

CORPORATIONS

Foundation fund raising is competitive, but the toughest dollar to raise in America is a corporate contribution. Foundations are the trees that bear expensive but delicious fruit; corporations are the trees that bear nuts—nuts that are tough to crack as well. Many do crack the corporate nut and there is good value inside. However, as in most bags of mixed nuts, a lot of peanuts show up. Corporations exist to make money for their stockholders, not to give it away to charity. Employees in not-for-profit organizations often seem not to comprehend this basic fact, possibly because they know nothing about stockholders.

It has been legal for corporations to give money to charity since the *A. P. Smith* case was tried in the New Jersey courts in 1953, in answer to a stockholder challenge.[12] "Philanthropy thus was not only permissible within a range of corporate enterprise but quite possibly a condition of public responsibility."[13] Over the years since this landmark decision, corporate giving, measured by the number of companies that give money away and the total dollars given, has increased but has yet to exceed a national average of 2 percent of pretax profits (current tax laws allow up to 10 percent). Some corporate leaders and industries have set giving goals for their companies of 1 or 2 percent, with excellent success. The Dayton Hudson Company has the best record in America at 5 percent per year, but the company is a singular example among well-known corporations with a distinguished record. The 1986 tax reform act lowered corporate tax rates from 46 to 34 percent reducing the tax benefit derived from corporate contributions. The net effect was to increase the after-tax cost of giving money away from $0.54 to $0.66 per dollar given, an increase of 22 percent, which is poor encouragement by government indeed.[14]

[11] Dennis R. Young, "Management of Nonprofit Organization Resources," in *Critical Issues in Fund Raising*, ed. Dwight F. Burlingame (New York: Wiley, 1997), 24.

[12] *A. P. Smith Manufacturing Co. v. Barlow*, 98 A.2d 581 (Sup. Ct. N.J. 1953).

[13] Barry D. Kare, "The Evolution of Corporate Grantmaking in America," in *The Corporate Contributions Handbook: Devoting Private Means to Public Needs*, ed. James P. Shannon (San Francisco: Jossey-Bass, 1991), 31.

[14] American Association of Fund-Raising Counsel *Giving USA* (1989 report) (New York: AAFRC Trust for Philanthropy, 1990), 70.

Why do corporations give so little? Their prime directive is to make money. They have a long list of higher priorities that need attention, beginning first with stockholders and moving down to labor relations and employee benefits (including escalating health-care costs), plant maintenance and renovation, capital acquisition, new and replacement equipment, and much more. Giving money to charity has never been a priority of corporate budgeting. In a May 1982 study prepared for the Council on Foundations by Yankelovich, Skelly and White, Inc., the views of CEOs of major American corporations were summarized: "Corporate giving is a relatively underdeveloped, poorly understood function in most companies."[15] More often, the reality is that fiscal conditions and the related decisions change quarterly and do not permit much long-range contributions planning or commitment. The lone exception is the corporate foundation, which has the independent resources to sustain a public giving effort over a brief period of time.

Why do corporations make gifts at all? They give for many motives, most of them linked to investment decisions, which represent some potential return to the corporation. Traditionally referred to as a *quid pro quo* relationship, today's term *enlightened self-interest* is a bit more dignified. The chief reason for most corporate gift decisions is a return on investment, justifiable to owners and stockholders. Exhibit 4.8 offers five reasons why corporations give.

A contribution search should begin with finding a perfect match with business priorities. Corporations are made up of people, but they most often act like institutions. Group decision making is objective, not subjective, by nature; it tends to be conservative and is often defensive. Corporations that have organized programs for public gift support will, like foundations, follow written policies and procedures; have a contributions committee and a staff person, usually part-time, who prepares materials; make recommendations on spending according to established priorities; and meet with volunteers and fund-raising staff. The contributions committee is usually made up of corporate officers and members of the board of directors, who usually divide the available funds in a percentage distribution established by area or type of charity, reserving perhaps 5 to 10 percent for distribution later in the year and another 5 to 10 percent for other projects selected at the discretion of the board. Board members and corporate officers will have the opportunity to direct some funds to their favorite charities, often to those where they have volunteer responsibilities.

[15]Yankelovich, Skelly and White, Inc., "The Views of Chief Executive Officers of Major American Corporations" (New York: Council on Foundations, 1982).

EXHIBIT 4.8 Why Do Corporations Give?

1. *Good corporate citizenship.* Many companies feel that it is important to present a positive image in the communities in which they operate. Such an image can be maintained or heightened through charitable gifts to local not-for-profits that provide community service.
2. *Enlightened self-interest.* Most fund raisers subscribe to the notion that companies make charitable gifts because it is basically in their best interest to do so. Because companies hire local employees, they want to maintain an educated and healthy work force. This often can be accomplished by supporting the work of local charities such as colleges, hospitals, and cultural organizations.
3. *Individual leadership initiative.* Companies are also likely to support not-for-profit organizations simply because of the interest and clout of those in charge. This is often the case in family businesses in which the founder may direct help to a favorite charity without a committee vote. This will also happen in large corporations where the CEO or president uses his or her clout to direct gifts to selected charities.
4. *Location.* Most often a company will restrict its support to not-for-profits in the communities in which the company operates and has an employee base.
5. *Quid pro quo interests.* Many companies use quid pro quo interest (that is, they ask, "What's in it for us?"). Such a company wants to see a tangible return on its charitable investment. Such a direct relationship between making a gift and obtaining something in return (other than general satisfaction) is not always easy to delineate. Some people, however, argue that seeking such a connection diminishes the spirit of philanthropy. Still many companies continue to look for such linkages.

Reprinted with permission from "Foundations as a Source of Support" by K. Scott Sheldon, in Achieving Excellence in Fund Raising *by Henry A. Rosso and Associates (San Francisco: Jossey-Bass, 1991), 247.*

In his column in the April 1990 issue of *IS Update,* Independent Sector President Brian O'Connell collected the following comments regarding the "rationale for corporate philanthropy":

> "The Business of Business is business," observes economist Milton Friedman.
> Irving Kristol, a critic of corporate philanthropy, stated in a 1981 *Business Week* article that companies must be extremely cautious in using company money to "just do good."

Economist John Kenneth Galbraith believes that corporations shouldn't be allowed to make contributions because it gives them too many additional opportunities to exercise influence.

In an Independent Sector survey of CEOs by the Daniel Yankelovich Group, 71 percent of those surveyed said a company has to determine the benefits to its business of each cause it supports. Most are looking for ways to bring charitable giving more directly in line with corporate goals and needs.

In support of the historical lesson that giving is correlated with strong business performance, James Burke, chairman of Johnson & Johnson, asserts that, over the long run, "those companies that organize their business around a broad concept of public service . . . provide superior performance for their stockholders." Burke's own study of companies in existence at least 30 years showed an annual growth of 11 percent in profits compounded over 30 years, better than three times the growth of the gross national product (GNP), which grew at 3.1 percent annually during the same period.[16]

A plan for corporate giving might allow scholarship grants to a select few local or specialized colleges and universities whose graduates represent the predominant source of new employees needed by the company. A scientific or research corporation might invest in a school of engineering or a department of chemistry to attract future graduates and to gain access to faculty and their research work, which could give the company an edge on its competition.

There are several factors that influence corporate gift decisions, including the following criteria for decision on the *size* of the gift:

1. The number of years of previous support
2. The level of involvement by company personnel
3. The degree of benefit to the company
4. The size of gifts being made by other companies
5. Importance of the project to community welfare
6. One-time gifts, or annual support[17]

Corporate social responsibility has been a common theme during the past three decades. "Businessmen for the Arts," an early effort, was followed by development of minority business opportunities, environmental awareness, and other initiatives. Corporations tend to demonstrate their community support where their employee relations motive is strong; grants to local youth programs, day care centers, health facilities, cultural programs, and the like are typical examples. Other employee-related decisions—matching gifts, scholarships for employees' depen-

[16]Brian O'Connell, "Rationale for Corporate Philanthropy," *IS Update* (April 1990): 3.
[17]Sam Sternberg, ed. *National Directory of Corporate Charity* (San Francisco: Regional Youth and Adult Project, 1984) 17.

EXHIBIT 4.9 Sources for Corporate Support to Not-For-Profit Organizations

Source	Description
1. Outright gift	A direct contribution or grant
2. Matching gift	A gift to match an employee's personal gift to a qualified not-for-profit organization
3. Advertising and marketing budgets	A gift for public visibility or for a cause-related marketing campaign
4. Research and personnel budgets	A grant to support company product development or to benefit the employee relations program
5. Corporate partnerships	Joint ventures or contracts where programs and services are arranged for employees or customers
6. Employee volunteers	Time, talent, and expertise shared by employees
7. Equipment and service donations	Use of facilities, equipment, and professional services on a pro bono basis
8. Facilities	Access to buildings, telephones, printing and copying machines
9. In-kind donations	Delivery of products without charge or purchase
10. Corporate foundations	Separate granting vehicle for gifts and pledges

Reprinted with permission from Fund-Raising Cost Effectiveness: A Self-Assessment Workbook *by James M. Greenfield (New York: John Wiley & Sons, Inc., 1996), 150.*

dents, summer job programs for employees' children—are dominated by human resource objectives and are all perfectly logical and to be expected. Please see Exhibit 4.9 for a list of the kinds of support an organization might expect from a corporation.

Corporate giving policies can be subject to public pressure. Planned priorities may be supplanted because of concern about a public image. Advocacy groups "are tearing management apart," says Eugene R. Wilson, former president of the ARCO Foundation. "Many companies like to think they are taking a leadership role in working for positive change. But it has become difficult to find a common definition of what's positive." Public protest, Wilson added, "is forcing a lot of managers to justify to management much more deeply than ever before the outcomes of our grants and to predict public reaction to them. And, if there's a threat that a grant will put the corporation in a box, we'll have a tough time justifying it." On this same point, Peter Goldberg, president of the Prudential Foundation, said, "This opens a Pandora's box of questions for corporate philanthropy. These tactics are on a collision course with the concept that corporations ought to be involved with social issues." Others agreed. "These actions are the nonviolent, domestic equivalent of terrorism," says Robert L. Payton, former director of the Indiana University Center on Philanthropy and former president of the Exxon Education Foundation. "This is going to discourage corporations from strong leadership in their grant making and encourage timidity and ineffectuality. This kind of behavior could cause corporations to gradually withdraw from philanthropy.[18]

A common part of the corporate quid pro quo is a public relations request to accompany a gift announcement. A photo opportunity is sought by the corporation for the check presentation—a picture, for publicity release, of corporate leaders making a community grant. A company's chief reason for the request—and for giving—is to improve its public image and help sell its product. This tactic was used by Sears, Roebuck and Company for many years and was quite effective because Sears has stores in communities all across the land. To get Sears money, arrangements were made to have the charity's top leaders attend a presentation luncheon paid for by the charity, which hired a photographer, wrote a news release, and circulated it with copies of the requested picture—a rather expensive set of prerequisites for a gift of $500 or $1,000.

Corporations, like foundations, look for multiple uses for their gift dollar. The "ripple effect" leverages their money; both the not-for-profit organizations and the company gain an opportunity for improved return. As a consequence, corporate gifts usually come with strings attached. Knowing this fact, not-for-profit organizations should look for opportunities for a mutual benefit contribution package.

Many corporations offer two other valuable resources that may be overlooked by not-for-profit organizations. Only about a third of all corporations reported charitable contributions on their tax returns, but many more made contributions unidentified as gifts or unreported as business expenses. Donations of employee time, use of equipment, printing, low-interest loans, and similar assistance are being stressed much more than offers of dollars. Called "corporate assistance expenditures," they have only begun to be tracked. A 1993 survey by the Conference Board reported that among 98 companies reporting corporate assistance expenditures, "nearly 60 percent of these expenditures were in the form of cash

[18]Anne Lowrey Bailey, "Corporate Giving Under Siege," *Chronicle on Philanthropy* 2, no. 14 (1990): 1.

disbursements (32 percent) or below market-yield loans (27 percent). Other forms of corporate assistance expenditures were donations of property (18 percent); use of corporate facilities (4 percent); and loans of company personnel (6 percent). The estimated amount of these expenditures was $186 million."[19] Another hard-to-measure and hard-to-value area is gifts-in-kind, especially those made by smaller businesses and firms that do not have a formal contributions program or corporate foundation and do not report to the Conference Board. Of high value and immediate use by not-for-profit organizations, gifts-in-kind represent a major area of increased opportunity (see Exhibit 4.10).

Corporate leaders also provide expertise to boards and staff of not-for-profit organizations. Company employees with management skills have a personal interest in community service and probably have more time to give than top executives do. United Way has pioneered the "corporate-loaned executive," who works as part of the campaign team for three to five months at no cost to United Way. Well-trained volunteers have immense future value to the corporation and to any not-for-profit organizations that can solicit their interest.

Dollars from a company's contributions budget are always difficult to get. But there are other budget sources that allow corporate expenditures

---

EXHIBIT 4.10 Opportunities for Corporate Gifts-in-Kind

1. Accounting	13. Office supplies
2. Audiovisual aids	14. Printing
3. Advertising	15. Postage and mailing
4. Computers	16. Products
5. Contacts	17. Repairs and minor construction
6. Contracts	18. Services
7. Co-op purchasing	19. Space
8. Equipment	20. Staff
9. Furniture	21. Transportation
10. Graphics	22. Volunteers
11. Lawyers	23. Copying
12. Loans	

Source: Regional Youth Adult Project in San Francisco 1984 Annual Report.

---

[19]Hodgkinson and Weitzman, *Nonprofit Almanac 1996–1997: Dimensions of the Independent Sector,* 83.

in ways that benefit charities, and these should be actively pursued. A recipient charity is indifferent to whether the funds come from the advertising, public relations, or research budget, as long as a gift is given. Corporate advertising, marketing, and public relations budgets can be the source of sponsorship or underwriting of a special or benefit event, especially when the corporate name will be prominently displayed in all the event promotions and in the printed program for the event. Printing, food, wine, or table favors might be contributed as an in-kind gift. If the company product is usable by the not-for-profit organization, a nice corporate tax deduction is available for making gifts of the company's own merchandise. Apple Computer and IBM have been giving away their hardware and software products to schools and colleges for years, greatly benefiting the institutions and their students. Behind these company decisions is the intent that these young people will remember the brand name when they are in a position to buy future computers.

Corporations can be a reliable source, but the money must be raised every time; it is not going to be given. Corporations can be part of an annual giving plan; they can help special events and benefits with sponsorship and in-kind gifts of their products. They can commit to a multiyear pledge in a major capital campaign; however, they are not estate planning prospects. Not-for-profit organizations that learn how to engage local corporations, to receive regularly a portion of their contribution budget and other available help, will have built the relationship needed to preserve the corporations' frequent support (see Exhibit 4.11 for a list of tips for success in corporate solicitations). There is stiff competition. Other not-for-profit organizations have the same intent, use the same strategies, and are outside the same door, waiting for it to open.

WHAT NOT-FOR-PROFIT ORGANIZATIONS SHOULD KNOW ABOUT CORPORATIONS

As with foundations, some basic research is needed to find corporations with current giving policies that match an organization's objectives. The major difference is that the resource information available on corporations is absent. No corporate-giving directory exists that is on a par with the Foundation Directory, although The Taft Group has assembled data on just about every company that has an established giving program. The obstacle to research is even greater because a vast number of corporations, business organizations, partnerships, and firms in America do not have established contributions programs. As was true with foundations,

EXHIBIT 4.11 "Tips for Success" in Corporate Solicitations

1. Plan ahead when making a corporate solicitation. Consider submitting a proposal on the first day after a deadline has passed to give the prospect ample time to review the request. Proposals received on or near a deadline typically receive less attention.
2. Always read the funding guidelines carefully. Read between the lines to determine what is not being mentioned. Guidelines usually state clearly what is and is not eligible for funding, but some programs or projects may not be specifically excluded or included, thus falling into a "grey" area. Consult with the funding prospect to determine whether a project may be of interest and thus worth a proposal submission.
3. Administrative assistants in a corporate-giving office can provide valuable advice by telephone that sometimes is more comprehensive than what a director will provide on a company's philanthropic program.
4. When approaching a company for the first time, it might be easier to develop a long-term relationship by making an initial request for a small annual gift. A larger grant will be more likely if cultivation is successful and annual support is given each year.
5. Where possible, develop a relationship with corporate-giving consultants who advise corporate funders.
6. Seek out companies with new corporate-giving programs or new personnel. In the early phases to a corporate-giving program, funding guidelines are usually broad and unfocused. It may be easier to obtain support early in the cycle.
7. Utilize corporate employee matching-gift programs where appropriate. A good source for information on matching-gift programs is the Council for the Advancement and Support of Education in Alexandria, Virginia.
8. Determine what professional groups corporate-giving officers belong to and look for ways to become involved with those groups. A not-for-profit may wish to host a meeting for one or more of them.
9. A not-for-profit should invite corporate-giving officers to visit the organization's facilities. Solicitation success rates jump dramatically when funders can see firsthand what not-for-profits seek to accomplish.

Reprinted with permission from "Foundations as a Source of Support" by K. Scott Sheldon, in Achieving Excellence in Fund Raising *by Henry A. Rosso and Associates (San Francisco: Jossey-Bass, 1991), 241–242.*

only a few hundred companies, not thousands, need to be researched. Only those business enterprises whose plants and offices are in the organization's geographic vicinity or service area, and with whom some form of relationship can be established, should be researched. Local companies and major firms are the best candidates for the simple reason that their executives and employees live in the same or nearby community. Companies whose offices, services, and employees are located in another state are not viable prospects. Investigation should focus on the following categories and groups of companies:

1. Those with whom board members are directly or indirectly affiliated
2. Those whose employees and their dependents may use the organization's services or may participate in its programs
3. Those where donors are employed or with whom they are affiliated
4. Those from whom the organization buys products and services
5. Those whose purposes and products match the organization's programs and services to the extent that a legitimate interest in (and possible gain from) investing in the organization's future is justified

What information is needed and in what detail? Research should be kept simple. Learning about the present owner(s) may be the biggest challenge. Other essential data are owners' relationship to controlling interests, roster of officers and directors, most recent revenue and sales figures and dividend details, number of plants and offices in the immediate geographic area, product lines and services, number of total and local employees, and fiscal year-end data. This information can be found at a local library. Unlike foundations, most companies do not publish data on their contributions program, their priorities and procedures for application, the name of the contributions committee staff person, their prior giving history, or the amount, purpose, or project details of grants made. How is this information obtained? Slowly, mostly from direct experience, one company at a time, and usually through leaders or volunteers who have a link to the company, its directors, or its officers. These companies' prior gift history can be researched for details on the date, amount, and purpose of the gift, who solicited it, and from whom. Information on the number of employees and their dependents whom the organization has served and the outcomes of the service may also be productive.

Because corporate giving information is hard to find, alternate, nontraditional sources must be enlisted. Directories published by Dun & Bradstreet, Moody's, Standard & Poor's, and Who's Who are available at any local public library. Corporations can be contacted for their annual report, to verify library data, but it will not contain information about their contributions program. This information comes slowly and changes frequently, which is why the services of The Taft Group are so valuable. Keeping up with corporate changes in profits is only a little bit easier than keeping up with changes in their officers, directors, owners, plant closings, and mergers. Companies with an established foundation are much more likely to receive requests from not-for-profit organizations because of the ready access to their foundation data. Volunteers and donors are one of the best resources for information about their employer and its contributions programs.

One other resource is available: Thorough knowledge and good articulation of the not-for-profit organization's programs and services may simplify their translation into a description that matches a corporation's priorities. How might this plan be of interest to a company and what will they want to know, to discover a matching use or value? Honest but relevant details on present activities and future plans may provide a reason for their gift.

Background details on the officers and directors of any corporation are inconsequential. The avenues opened by the "interlocking corporate directorate" are much more valuable than knowing where corporate executives and directors went to school (except in alumni fund-raising campaigns) or what degrees they hold. Also valuable is realizing that modern-day corporate leaders have a well-developed social conscience that can be appealed to. James A. Joseph writes that

> The new generation of corporate leaders appeals to social as well as economic philosophy in making the case for the importance of corporate public involvement. They usually emphasize one or more of the following themes:
> 1. The idea of stakeholder obligation
> 2. The idea of civic duty
> 3. The idea of enlightened self-interest
> 4. The idea of competitive advantage
> 5. Changing priorities
> 6. Changing leaders in corporate giving
> 7. Few role models
> 8. Slowdown in growth in giving
> 9. Rapidly changing society
> 10. Changing community boundaries
> 11. Continuing barriers to community
> 12. Changing blueprint for community.[20]

[20]James A. Joseph, "The Corporate Stake in Community Involvement: Has Business Lost its Social Conscience," in *The Corporate Contributions Handbook: Devoting Private Means to Public Needs*, ed. James P. Shannon (San Francisco: Jossey-Bass, 1991) 8–16.

Leaders and volunteers can unlock the door for access to many companies. A volunteer annual giving committee chairperson might be a company vice president. That company's board of directors become individual prospects and their companies might make gifts. Access does not mean a gift is automatic, and a volunteer should never be urged to recommend to a company director a proposal that does not match and will fail; embarrassment will be a minor consequence compared to the reluctance of the volunteer ever to work for the organization again. Corporate gifts are important endorsements of a project or an organization from a company's officers and directors. Perhaps these people can be recruited for other service to the organization. Building a corporate relations program begins in this manner, and while a lot of time is required for the "ripple effect" to spread fully, relationships are the key to success in corporate fund raising.

CORPORATE PROPOSALS: PREPARATION AND DELIVERY

Although it is a critical element in corporate fund raising, the actual proposal is the easiest to fulfill because the research and cultivation work that precede it directly affect the decision and because most companies want nothing more than a two-page letter proposal. Crystallizing a project into such limited space is a challenge, but corporate executives are expert at assimilating details and making decisions quickly, and will dismiss a proposal that is not succinct (see Exhibit 4.12 for tips on how to correctly prepare a proposal). The proposal tells them how much the organization wants, why the need is urgent and important, and why this project is a valid use of company money. What's in it for them—the extra values flowing to the company from support of the project—should be emphasized.

Preparations count greatly in corporate fund raising, and success depends as much on others speaking up for a request as on the actual qualifications of the project. As with foundations, doing detailed homework offers the best chance for success. The "shotgun" method of mailing appeal letters to local companies will perform no better than any other direct mail acquisition effort; a 1-in-100 response is all that can be expected.

There are exceptions, of course. Asking a company to buy tickets or be a $1,000 underwriter at a benefit event is quite different from asking for a $10,000 multiyear research grant. But the script is the same; the best approach is through volunteers who have contacts among the decision-

EXHIBIT 4.12 Guidelines for Preparing Corporate Proposals

1. Summarize the request concisely
2. Grab the reader's interest quickly (do not be afraid to use modifiers to make your concepts sparkle; however, avoid using words like *unique*)
3. Link the not-for-profit's request to the company's expressed interests (determine those interests through careful research, reading its published guidelines, telephone and personal contacts, and discussions with others familiar with those funding sources, especially agency board members)
4. Do not ramble on any of the issues addressed in the proposal
5. Confine the request to one page and *never* exceed two
6. Address the request to a person, not to "Dear Friend" or "Dear Corporate Director" (reference sources should be consulted to obtain the names of contacts *and* accuracy should be confirmed by telephone)
7. Reference previous telephone or personal contact with the addressee
8. Cleanly type the proposal on agency letterhead using correct grammar. Proofread for typos. If the agency letterhead does not include a telephone number, it must be included in the cover letter

Reprinted with permission from "The Corporate Support Marketplace" by Lester A. Picker, in The Nonprofit Handbook: Fund Raising, *2d ed., ed. James M. Greenfield (New York: John Wiley & Sons, Inc., 1997), 389–390.*

making officers and directors within the company. When one gift is received, that decision can be used to leverage other companies to join in.

Soliciting routine annual gifts from companies is the method least likely to succeed. Corporations want to use their limited gift dollars in creative ways, to "get a big bang for the buck," to leverage each gift into something else of value to the company, and to receive some tangible return on their investment. All these tests are hard to pass with the casual annual appeal; to make it appear unusual and unique is a test of creative proposal writing. Each request must match company gift priorities, be accurate, and discuss valid projects. It might also be disguised a bit, to look like something special that has timely appeal. In reality, the project can be a routine annual operation; the disguise is only to attract attention to a program or service that matches company interests by dressing it up to make it sound and look special. Is this fair and ethical? Absolutely; the request is the same—to use their money to fulfill the organization's mission, purposes, goals, and objectives. A few lessons can be taken from corporate marketing and sales. A request is a sales promotion designed to achieve the exchange of money. A creative letter offers exciting benefits to a corporate donor who invests in a project: immediate public benefit and donor visibility. The benefits and recognition given to all donors can be offered equally to corporations in exchange for their contributions.

Delivery of a request can be by mail or in person and will be enhanced if handled by a volunteer linked prominently to the corporation. Whatever the means of delivery, applications are given formal review. A key decision is whether the request meets corporate policy. If so, it joins the stack of requests waiting for a future meeting of the contributions committee. If not a match, the request dies here, with or without a rejection letter. Most corporate contributions programs prepare their annual budget before fiscal year end and base it on anticipated company profits, setting aside perhaps 1 percent of net income before taxes as the budget for contributions. Applications should be submitted several months before the fiscal year begins, which is when next year's budget is prepared. If they are received after all the money is committed, they may have to wait until next year.

Corporations' and foundations' limited money for gifts and grants is far too little for all the requests they receive, even those that match perfectly with their areas of preference. Some companies have tried to respond by making small grants to numerous applicants, which is not always the best use of their money even if it reduces community comment and criticism. Given today's competitive environment and the time required for decision, not-for-profit organizations should ask for corporate gifts months ahead of the time they will need to use the money. They should not depend on corporate money for more than one year at a time because these institutions need to spread their money around to help others each year. Institutional gifts arrive on a circuit; they come around with some regularity and are nice extra funds. If a not-for-profit organization has valid answers to why companies should give to them each year, an annual corporate appeal program can be organized, directed at several corporate and business sources in each community. With one or more good contacts, regular opportunities for request submission, and a commitment of the time required to cultivate companies and contacts within them, fairly steady annual income can be realized from companies and firms, even though the actual names of company donors keep changing from year to year.

Follow-Up Activities, Including Rejections

Success in corporate giving does not depend on the receipt of a single gift, but on maintaining a positive exchange between the parties (now partners). This effort must be initiated by the not-for-profit organization in the form of an energetic contact and communications program. Frequently, corporate gifts are major gifts. They deserve the same level of personal attention from board members and senior management staff as does any major gift from an individual or a foundation. The goal of any fund development program is to maintain friend-raising and relationship-building activities, which can be met following an important gift through the donor relations and donor recognition program. The objective of follow up activities is to build on the positive relationship, through all or most of the following suggestions:

1. Personal thank-you letters at board member and CEO levels
2. Donor recognition events and entertainment opportunities
3. Press clippings about programs being supported that report the corporate donor's role in funding these efforts
4. Special reports by program staff on progress, numbers of clients served, and other indications of progress along with financial reports on how the funds are allocated
5. Corporate donor clubs or corporate memberships in existing support groups, with attendant member benefits and privileges
6. Distribution of newsletter, annual reports, and other publications of a general nature from the organization, with personalized notes attached
7. Personal invitations to corporate leadership to become involved, serve on committees or advisory councils, to give of their time and talent, and to encourage their employees also to become involved
8. Personal visits to corporate offices to maintain contact, bring any of the above materials, report on progress, and begin discussion on future plans. As an "investor" in the organization, the corporate donor needs to plan for its future participation based on the same perceived (and enhanced) benefits it currently derives from the relationship

Not every proposal will be approved; in fact, most will not. Rejection is often the result of a variety of factors completely unrelated to the request. The absence of any reply also should not be viewed as a rejection. The corporation may have expended all its money before it could act on your proposal, or the review meeting went too long and your proposal has been put aside until the next meeting. When formal rejection letters do arrive, they first should be acknowledged, thanking the author for his or her consideration of the request. Next, they should studied to understand exactly why the request was turned down, and if it is not clear, the organization's representative will need to make a call or arrange a visit to learn why. The answers to the following questions may not help with this same corporation but will be instructive for the next proposal:

1. Why was the request denied?
2. What suggestions and improvements were recommended?
3. What questions were asked during the meeting?
4. Was the budget realistic? Was the amount requested correct?
5. Were benefits to the corporation clear? Adequate?
6. Is it possible to resubmit an improved proposal? When?
7. What other funding sources are recommended for this project?

Nine-Point Performance Analysis of Corporate Giving

Similar to foundation solicitations, proposals to corporations take time to move through the cycle that begins with the initial deadline and ends with allocation of funds. Therefore, a multiyear analysis of corporate solicitation activity is necessary to gain a clear picture of productivity, efficiency, and effectiveness. The discussion that follows is based on the figures that appear in Exhibit 4.13:

    1. The number of participating companies appears small each year. These figures suggest either a limited number of qualified corporate prospects in the area, an inadequate prospect research effort, few volunteers

EXHIBIT 4.13 Nine-Point Performance Index Analysis of Corporate Solicitations

	Two Years Ago	Last Year	This Year	Totals
Participation	22	28	31	81
Income	$18,500	$25,500	$37,500	$81,500
Expenses	$4,525	$5,850	$6,500	$16,875
Percent participation	18%	29%	30%	26%
Average gift size	$841	$911	$1,210	$1,006
Net income	$13,975	$19,650	$31,000	$64,625
Average cost per gift	$206	$209	$210	$208
Cost of fund raising	24%	23%	17%	21%
Return	309%	336%	477%	383%

Reprinted with permission from Fund-Raising Cost Effectiveness: A Self-Assessment Workbook *by James M. Greenfield (New York: John Wiley & Sons, Inc., 1996), 160.*

with access or willingness to participate, or a lack of programs or services with public visibility with sufficient match to business marketing and promotion objectives.

2. The budget necessary to this program covers only a portion of one staff member's time plus supplies and local travel, which may be the extent of this organization's ability to support this effort. Should other, more promising corporate opportunities arise, added resources will be needed and appear to promise good results.

3. Percent participation suggests one in four requests is successful, a positive clue to the balance of this program's analysis. Attention to research, projects selected for corporate giving, proposal texts, volunteer training, and solicitation methods are logical areas for improvement.

4. The average gift size of $1,006 suggests either this organization is too modest in its requests or the local business community is modest in size and resources. Either way, maintaining this gift level may be a challenge for this program, given these modest amounts.

5. Net proceeds of $65,625 after three years is minimal but adequate for the effort and cost involved. The program is certainly cost-effective enough at 21 percent and a 383 percent return, but it is a fair conclusion that not much effort has been put forth. The question remains whether this organization has any potential for improvement and can increase the number of prospects it has the potential to reach.

6. The balance of criteria not evident in this report is the extent to which staff is maintaining good communications with existing donors. Options include creative means to give the recognition and visibility corporate donors seek that will enable a successful gift renewal in future years.

CAUSE-RELATED MARKETING

Corporations can do many things to benefit not-for-profit organizations, including making direct gifts of cash and products and offering the skills and talents of their employees. These traditional exchanges occur most often where corporations and not-for-profit organizations share common opportunities to enhance public causes and improve the quality of life for local residents, especially company employees and dependents. Cause-related marketing has become a popular alternative to such direct giving. Under this method, a corporation proposes a marketing and advertising campaign that includes a promise to give a certain percentage of the increased revenue from product sales to one or more charitable organizations. The not-for-profit organization, in return, lends its cause, credibility, name, prestige, public trust, and reputation to the company product.

The calculation of the amount due to the charity is based on each unit of product purchased, proofs of purchase submitted, coupons redeemed, credit card or "affinity card" use, or a fixed total based on a percentage of sales realized. A not-for-profit organization that agrees to the use of its name as part of the promotion can expect to receive a cash benefit and a share in the promotional visibility. The great appeal of cause-related marketing to the charitable organization is that the publicity alone has a value greater than most not-for-profit organizations could likely afford and that the organization receives money, a "free gift," with no effort on its part. However, not-for-profit organizations should look this gift horse in the mouth and examine every tooth; several potential cavities are hidden from sight in such an offer. Cavities can be filled and teeth and gums restored but not without some painful experiences in the process.

Fund-raising magazines, newspapers, and journals have been full of debate about cause-related marketing. It was invented by an American Express Company executive in 1981, in connection with the company's support of the Statue of Liberty restoration campaign. The promotion stated that a penny would be given to the renovation project each time an American Express card was used. The results were impressive. A total of $1.7 million was given to the Statue of Liberty campaign; at the same time card use increased by 28 percent and the number of new cards issued rose more than 45 percent. Which was the company's goal, making a gift or increasing card use?

Debate occurs because the amount of money involved in such a campaign can be large and the visibility is enormous. The not-for-profit organizations that may be selected for such a campaign are likely to be only those that have been carefully screened by the company marketing experts; sales will be affected negatively if the cause is controversial, unpopular, or unknown. The primary corporate goal is to increase sales. The company may also believe it will increase its own public respectability by contributing to a recognized name charity. But, "philanthropy is not a purchase. A consumer is not a donor, and a purchase is not a gift."[21]

Cause-related marketing has proven itself not to be just another passing fad, an idea that works for a while and then melts away because the public tires of the "gimmick" and sales fall off. The sponsoring company will discontinue the program quickly if sales drop, regardless of a commitment to a charity, because the project was never a gift program in the first place. Many companies and their not-for-profit partner have benefit-

---

[21] Christopher P. Bryant, "Cause-Related Marketing: Cause Célèbre or Cause for Concern?" (session at the NAHD National Education Conference, Boston, MA, 1987).

ted from their relationship and continued to work together. Any not-for-profit organization that receives an offer to participate in a cause-related marketing campaign should evaluate most carefully several critical factors, beginning with two areas of inquiry suggested by Maurice G. Gurin, that former fund-raising senior statesman, counselor, author, and lecturer:[22]

1. Is this philanthropy?
   —Does the offer qualify as a tax-deductible contribution?
   —Does it represent support with no "strings" attached?
   —Is the offer devoid of any direct financial return to the corporation?
2. Is this an unwise or inadvisable arrangement?
   —Could the offer diminish public approval?
   —Could it weaken an organization's case for philanthropic support?
   —Could it blur the public's ability to distinguish business from philanthropy?

If, after its evaluation, the organization answers yes to the first group of questions but no to the second group, the offer may be valid, but it deserves further investigation. Fund development is a combination of friend raising (relationship building) and money raising designed to meet needs for public benefit this year, next year, and for years into the future. Gifts satisfy donor aspirations; a "quick buck" is never going to be a reliable source of gift income or of donor satisfaction. On the other side, the corporation will argue that the campaign will produce cash for the organization, all with "no effort on your part" (a red flag should go up every time those words are heard!). What is the present relationship between the organization and this company? Has the company been a prior donor and have its executives been assisting as volunteer leaders? What kind of future relationship will exist with the company after the campaign? Are the people recruited by this marketing campaign likely to become future donors? Are those who buy the product likely to give again or are they only onetime customers for the company?

Another consideration is that the not-for-profit organization and its good name are being used for commercial purposes in this venture. The income received may be defined by the IRS as "unrelated business income" subject to income tax to be paid by the not-for-profit organization at the corporate rate of 34 percent. State authorities may consider such

---

[22]Maurice G. Gurin, "Is Marketing Dangerous for Fund-Raising?" *Fund Raising Management* 17, no. 11 (1987): 72.

ventures "commercial sales promotions," which require a written agreement between the company and the not-for-profit organization as well as the exchange of financial reports.[23]

During further evaluation, these five questions may guide in making a decision:

1. Can a corporate giving relationship be established with this company, separate from the marketing program?
2. Are donors or dollars being recruited?
3. Is the organization exploiting its name or is its name being exploited?
4. Will a full accounting summary of all dollars raised in the organization's name be received?
5. Is this method of fund raising regarded as a completely ethical program within the organization?

On its side, the corporation also should review the proposed partnership with care, to be sure the following safeguards are in place:

- Are you thoroughly familiar with the reputation, credibility, and financial management of the charity being considered?
- Do you have a formal agreement with the charity that gives you permission for the use of its name and specifies how the money will be allocated, the duration of the campaign, and the steps that will be taken if problems arise?
- Does the promotion clearly specify how the funds will be raised and allocated and any limitations such as a maximum amount to be contributed?
- Does the promotion meet all applicable state regulations?
- Have you established a separate account to manage the funds?
- Have you planned a financial report that describes the results of the program to the public?[24]

If any question on either of the two prior lists cannot be answered to the satisfaction of both the organization and the corporation, then the organization should reconsider whether the offer has any merit; due diligence is sound advice when entering new territory. All the issues that will come up prior to, during, and after entering into such an arrangement with a

---

[23]The National Association of Attorneys General (NAAG), in December 1986, adopted a Model Law prepared by the National Association of State Charity Officers and the Private Sector Advisory Group, for uniform use by all the states. The full text appeared as "A Model Act Concerning the Solicitation of Funds for Charitable Purposes," *The Philanthropy Monthly* (October 1986). See Section 7, Charitable Sales Promotions.

[24]Cynthia D. Giroud, "Cause-Related Marketing: Potential Dangers and Benefits," in *The Corporate Contributions Handbook: Devoting Private Means to Public Needs*, ed. James P. Shannon (San Francisco: Jossey-Bass, 1991), 151–152.

company should be considered. (Appendix B, "Reality Tests for Cause-Related Marketing," lists 20 additional questions.)

Several cause-related marketing campaigns have now been conducted, most with recognized national not-for-profit organizations. It is too early to measure their effectiveness in stimulating added public support as measured in volunteers and gifts to not-for-profit organizations. Some companies have discontinued the practice; others are improving on the basic concept by acknowledging a financial obligation to the not-for-profit organization's need for promised or anticipated funds. The NFL Charities' continued support of United Way is an example.

The 1984 Olympic Games in Los Angeles demonstrated an additional feature of cause-related marketing—the license to use the name of the cause on the products sold as well as in the advertising. Was there a public benefit? Yes. Was there a licensing agreement with proprietary rights enjoyed by both parties? Yes. Does such marketing mislead the public in promoting philanthropy? Yes, because the exchange was not a gift. This income should *not* be reported by the recipient not-for-profit organization in its financial statements as contributions revenue; it is not gift revenue but "unrelated business income" derived from a sales or promotional exchange. By contrast, the 1996 Olympic Games in Atlanta were criticized for being too commercial, with some damage to the Olympic fund-raising movement.[26] The resolution from debate in Congress to add a tax on unrelated business income (UBIT) provides background on the several related issues of potential taxability to not-for-profit organizations from such a source of revenue, including possible loss of tax-exempt status.

The purposes of a company in seeking a partnership with a not-for-profit organization should be considered, as should the elements it needs to structure an agreement that will protect company interests and help ensure the success of the venture. A typical contract should specify the following: what the company is expected to do: how much money will be given to the not-for-profit organization and when; the time frame of the

[26]The debate among fund-raising professionals about the appropriateness of cause-related marketing continues. See Betsy Hills Bush, "More States Regulate Cause Marketing," *Nonprofit Times* (August 1994): 10–14; Barbara Kushner Ciconte and Jeanne G. Jacob, *Fund Raising Basics* (Gaithersburg, MD: Aspen, 1997) 149–151; Carol L. Cone, "Doing Well by Doing Good," *Association Management* (April 1996): 103–108; John Davidson, "Cancer Sells," in *The Law of Fund Raising*, 2d ed., by Bruce R. Hopkins (New York: Wiley, 1996) § 8.4, 611–620; Giroud, "Cause-Related Marketing: Potential Dangers and Benefits," 139–152; Kathleen S. Kelly, *Effective Fund-Raising Management* (Mahwah, NJ: Lawrence Erlbaum Associates, 1997), 294–298, 596–597; Joseph J. Ptacek and Gina Salazar, "Enlightened Self-Interest: Selling Business on the Benefits of Cause-Related Marketing," *Nonprofit World* (July/August 1997): 9–13; and Lilya Wagner and Robert Thompson, "Cause-Related Marketing: Fund-Raising Tool or Phony Philanthropy," *Nonprofit World* (November/December, 1994): 9–11.

agreement and options for its continuation; an exclusivity clause; auditing procedures; review of all promotion materials and sign-off on rights, logo, and name; liability potential and coverage; and a possible stipulation on "minimum revenue" requirements.

The following questions will be part of the company's evaluations of the results of the campaign:

- Did the initiative meet the sales objective? (They look at the volume and share of sales achieved during the promotion and compare coupon redemption, credit card use, or proofs of purchase against past campaigns.)
- Was it worth it? (They conduct cost/benefit analysis to compare incremental sales against costs.)
- Did the initiative meet trade objectives? (The company examines receptivity to the promotion among retailers and others in the industry.)
- How did the campaign affect the image of the company? (Evaluators look at media responses to the promotion.)[25]

Proponents of this nontraditional partnership between corporations and not-for-profits argue, where's the harm? Is the public harmed? Is the not-for-profit organization harmed? The final question then, is this: Can there be a legitimate use of cause-related marketing? Yes, if an organization is satisfied as to the value of the proposal and recognizes that the arrangement is not fund raising, nor philanthropy, and it probably will not last as a source of corporate income for the future.

MATCHING GIFT PROGRAMS

Corporations continue to support charities through the matching gift program whereby employees' own giving is matched, usually dollar for dollar, by the corporation. The relatively small gifts that result go to a variety of organizations, some of which might not otherwise receive the company's direct contributions. Although the net effect is a combined employee-company gift, the amount may not be larger than the employee's prior gift total as he or she has now arranged for the company to add the rest. Some companies are more generous, matching an employee dollar with two or three of their own. Other are less generous and limit the size of the matching gift to not more than $1,000.

A matching gift plan broadens most corporate giving programs although the corporation usually specifies the not-for-profit organizations

[25]Craig Smith, "Mixing Philanthropy with Marketing," *Corporate Philanthropy Report* 4, no. 2 (1988): 7.

that are eligible for the employees' matching gifts. Companies have been expanding the list of eligible not-for-profit organizations of late. Higher education remains the favorite, due in large part to colleges and universities making considerable efforts to encourage alumni to ask their employer to match their giving. The corporate motive may be improved company-employee relations and increased community visibility (and respect). This increase in giving and public participation also may be the result of a company inducement for employees to become involved with their community along with a response to employee interests. Among the types of normally approved charitable groups, besides educational institutions, are civic organizations, cultural groups, environmental and conservation-minded groups, hospitals, libraries, public television and radio stations, social services, and United Way.

The amount of money generated by a matching gift program can be substantial in total but may not be a large sum for any one organization. The results of a recent survey (see Exhibit 4.14) produced the following data from the United States' top matching gift companies as evidence of a

EXHIBIT 4.14 Matching Gift Trend

Company Giving	Employee Matching Gifts	Percentage of Cash
Microsoft Corporation	$9,500,000	54.9
Nationwide Insurance	4,380,000	40.6
Bankers Trust Corporation	3,500,000	29.2
J. P. Morgan and Company	5,100,000	28.7
Enron Corporation	2,300,000	25.6
Textron	1,500,000	23.1
Prudential Insurance Company	6,550,000	21.9
Chase Manhattan Corporation	7,700,000	18.5
Citicorp	7,000,000	18.4
Lucent Technologies	3,580,966	17.9
American Express Company	4,500,000	17.4
U S West	4,000,000	16.7
Philip Morris Companies	9,500,000	15.8
AlliedSignal	1,550,000	15.5
GTE Corporation	4,200,000	15.3

Reprinted with permission from "Big Business Means Big Philanthropy" by Debra E. Blum and Susan Gray, in The Chronicle of Philanthropy *10, no. 18 (1998):20.*

growing trend toward increased matching gift money as a percentage of cash contributions for employees to direct for charitable purposes.

ASSOCIATIONS, CLUBS, SOCIETIES, AND OTHER ORGANIZATIONS

Perhaps more reliable than cause-related marketing agreements is the relationship between not-for-profit organizations and another group of local institutions—the associations, clubs, societies, and other organizations that abound in every community and are similarly committed to voluntary public and civic service. Many forms of not-for-profit organizations—business or social clubs, neighborhood citizens' groups, and civic improvement coalitions, for example—do not enjoy all the tax-exempt privileges of Code Section 501(c)(3) organizations, but they are nonetheless a public benefit. They are incorporated and registered as public benefit corporations; operate with articles of incorporation, bylaws, elected or appointed boards of directors, and committees; and have a mission and purpose statement and annual goals and objectives that are designed to render community services.

These institutions are a frequent source of institutional gift revenue for not-for-profit organizations. They also can be partners in raising funds for local charitable institutions and agencies and are less driven by the quid pro quo objectives of corporations. Local clubs such as the Rotary, Soroptimists, Lions, Junior League, Elks, and Assistance League often adopt one or more public charities for their annual fund-raising activities and make gifts, grants, and awards to these organizations as well as to individuals (scholarships to local students). Some of these associations have a considerable capacity for fund raising. For example, the Rotary Foundation completed its first international fund-raising campaign in 1988 with over $225 million raised toward the goal of immunizing every child in the world against tuberculosis. Others have adopted a single cause and all their clubs support this same effort. The Lions Clubs support eye research and public eye safety; they give direct funding to the blind and those with impaired vision through clinical support, training of seeing eye dogs, and the issuance of white canes. Most of these associations direct their efforts to the area where their members live and work. Members have reliable knowledge about community needs and can respond to selected projects on a priority basis. While these associations, clubs, and societies usually have only modest funds to share, their value to not-for-profit organizations is also in the awareness of one another's shared objectives for community services.

Civic associations and societies offer volunteer training experience for community leaders who are often local residents. Their influence, personal interests, and involvement are of much greater value than the community grants and awards made by their clubs and societies. These are the people who take an interest in their community, who work together for the common good, and who give these enterprises their time, talent, and treasure; they would (and do) support any number of local not-for-profit organizations. They can become an organization's active supporters, volunteers, and future leaders. Their invitations for membership and for program speakers should be fulfilled, or an organization's own speakers' bureau can be formed. Topic titles can be offered to local clubs and societies for their weekly or monthly programs, not for solicitation purposes but to share information about public benefit programs and services and to join in community projects by working together whenever possible.

Not-for-profit organizations should be active on their own in community relations. Objectives should go beyond having the organization's chief executive officer join the chamber of commerce or inviting local groups to hold their meetings on the premises from time to time. Friend-raising and relationship-building opportunities are available to every not-for-profit organization in several ways; establishing personal friendships and relationships between employees and community residents is only one of them.

Not-for-profit organizations can solicit these associations for gifts each year or may be chosen by them to receive gift support. Working with them to preserve their interest and involvement is valuable even if, in time, they turn to other causes in order to increase and renew their membership and their own fund-raising activities. Their friendship will remain a positive force in the community.

INSTITUTIONAL DONOR RELATIONS

A program should be specially designed to recognize and ensure continued communication with institutional donors. In addition, institutional donors may qualify for other recognition programs offered to individual donors.

A prompt thank-you letter should acknowledge receipt of their gift or grant. Details should be included to indicate a full understanding of all the terms and conditions associated with acceptance of their money, including narrative and fiscal reports required at specified deadlines. A proper accounting procedure should be set up to monitor use of their funds and to demonstrate faithfully that any restricted gifts were used exactly for the purposes intended. Periodic reports on progress, media clippings about activities, and invitations to occasional public events should be sent to them, as to all other important donors.

Most foundation, corporation, and association boards welcome an offer to add the name of their organization to an honor roll of donors or to a plaque that will list the names of those who contributed toward funding of a specific project. They also enjoy print and photo coverage about their grant in both proprietary publications and the public media. If these activities are discussed in advance, their wishes regarding use of their name, any gift details, or prior review of any materials where their name will be used can be clarified.

Donor clubs or semiformal organizations might be designated to help maintain privileged communications with institutional donors. Gift size is most often the qualifying measure. Their board chairperson, chief executive, or senior staff person can be invited to serve on the president's club, advisory council, or citizens' committees. Company officials might be given membership in a Corporate Donors or Corporate Associates Club where the agenda offers additional information about the organization, or they might be offered access to the organization's people and knowledge. These benefits are best assembled by the organization as privileges based on giving history, annual gift size, and relationships with one or more parts of the organization. Such an arrangement permits an opportunity for continued contact toward future gift support.

One concern of foundation and corporate executives is that their separate and independent status will be compromised if they create formal ties to any single not-for-profit organization. Their association as a donor must not impair their impartial consideration of all other not-for-profit organizations. For this reason, they often do not accept appointments to not-for-profit board and committee positions; such a responsibility with any one not-for-profit organization will compromise their objectivity in dealing with all others.

The objectives of institutional donor relations and recognition are to thank them properly for their gift support and to establish the means for continued communication that will help to preserve their interest and attention to the organization. Programs that foster a relationship with these important donors should be defined and implemented. Other not-for-profit organizations will be trying just as hard and as constantly to woo their interest and money. Those who work hard to stay close to their institutional donors will more likely remain on their list of annual and special grant recipients, if they produce results and keep the institution's name visible. Successive gifts may result because the people in this privileged relationship were given the attention they deserved.

5 ▼ The Final Tier: Investment Decisions

Here's a proposition for you: I will give you $1 million, but there are two conditions. First, you have to make a gift of the entire $1 million to one not-for-profit organization within the next year, and second, if you work for or volunteer at a charity, you cannot give the money to that organization. This offer puts you in the shoes of your major gift prospect. How will you decide where to make this gift? What are the steps you will take, the criteria you will follow, the evaluation process you will use in making your decision? As fund-raising professionals, we need to understand something about this decision process before we ask for a big gift.

The best approach to major gift solicitation is to design an individual *strategic action plan* for each major gift prospect. Too often, board members, executive directors, and fund-raising staff in not-for-profit organizations concentrate on the solicitation of their next big, single gift but neglect the ongoing giving potential of their most qualified prospects—their current donors. Major gift cultivation, solicitation, and recognition should all be part of the strategic action plan from the start; most of the effort, however, will be spent in cultivation, whereby each qualified donor and prospect is given the personal attention he or she needs to arrive at a big gift decision. This method, called *moves management*, necessitates that staff give constant attention to the next steps for each major gift donor and prospect as part of their daily work agenda. These benefactors are too important to be only an occasional focus for one large gift solicitation. Cultivation should not be reserved only for capital campaigns that address substantial institutional needs or opportunities. Most major gift donors and prospects have well-developed personal aspirations along with a private agenda for their big gift decisions. They also know they have the freedom to do what they choose, when and how they choose, which is not always matched to the timing, needs, and wishes of not-for-profit organizations. The prime directive for fund development professionals is to adopt a strategy to design a *master gift plan* for each of their best and most generous donors to aid them in fulfilling their individual giving goals— reaching the major gifts tier in the pyramid of giving, that level at which truly significant investment decisions are made.

The master gift plan begins with analysis of all of a donor's prior fund development activities. If the level of personal involvement and interest that he or she has shown over time warrants it, the plan moves on to active discussion of the donor's first investment decision for a major gift. The master gift plan also is designed to assist in completion of several investment objectives during a donor's lifetime and includes estate planning that will provide for family members and friends as well as for the favored not-for-profit organizations named in the donor's final asset distribution. The master gift plan concludes at the time the donor's estate is probated.

Crucial to major gift solicitation is the concept of the *donor-investor*. Two experts offer their view of the relationship between the fund raiser and the donor-investor:

> Encouraging your client to think of herself as an investor/donor might help her to frame the specific questions that must be addressed to make her giving satisfying. The result could significantly increase impact of the gift made as well as the donor's satisfaction with the process. Like investing, good giving requires the self-knowledge that comes from reflecting and articulating on personal goals, values, passions and sense of responsibility to the community. An advisor can encourage that reflection by urging the donor to identify and examine the motivating reasons to create a vehicle for giving. What has impelled the donor or donors to establish a giving program? What are the driving interests and values?[1]

Faithful donors enjoy the knowledge that their individual gift decisions each year are moving them toward the achievement of a higher objective that is consistent with their own master plan. Often, though, the organization is unaware of a donor's master plan for giving. What should be happening is that both parties should be working together to accomplish otherwise unattainable goals of lasting significance and perpetuity. Faithful annual contributors have among them a few more generous donors who will become future benefactors and patrons. Major gifts are the result of years of attention. They almost never happen by accident or without serious, evaluative thinking.

[1]H. Peter Karoff and Melinda Marble, "Strategic Philanthropy: The Concept of the Investor/Donor," *Special Supplement to Trusts and Estates* (June 1998): CG4.

GIFT PLANNING: THE DEVELOPMENT OF BENEFACTORS

A good investor always asks some pertinent questions before deciding to join any enterprise seeking money. Inevitably the first question is "What's the money for?" In answer an organization must be ready to discuss its future plans and directions, both immediate and long-range. As discussed in Chapter 2, institutional readiness combines vision with realistic assessments of programs, services, financial options, and facility requirements. Future plans should address other key questions investors will ask: How will the money be used? What are the specific projects? How does each project fit within the multiyear plan? How will this program address one or more community needs? How much money is required now? How will one gift stimulate other key gifts? How will one giving decision make a difference in the overall plan? How will one gift help to raise all the money that is needed?

Breaking the Annual Giving Pattern

Fund development programs are designed primarily to raise current operating funds, which help to keep an organization fiscally sound and to keep its current programs and services at the required level of quality and quantity. Through repeat annual giving, donors and prospects are most familiar with one-year projects, those funded and implemented within 12 months or less. They are also conditioned to respond to appeals benefiting the most urgent of annual needs. The challenge in the master gift plan is to expand donors' thinking beyond annual giving. First, however, the not-for-profit organization must expand its own thinking, from concentration on annual promotions to more well-rounded, multiyear efforts that offer a range of gift opportunities balanced among all the fundraising methods available for annual, major, and estate giving.

Two Lessons in Reality are needed here. Reality Lesson 1 is that fiscal pressures usually dictate immediate cash results from fund development, which in turn demands that 100 percent of an organization's energy be directed to annual giving for current cash needs. The results may be successful in the short term but a balanced fund development program is not likely to be implemented under these pressures.

Reality Lesson 2 is that concentrating 20 percent of an organization's resources on major gifts each year will yield significantly higher returns (up to four times as much!) than annual giving, from a smaller number of donors. This 20 percent effort can, in fact, produce as much as 80 percent of the total dollars raised in a single year. A comprehensive fund development program allots 80 percent of its time to annual giving priorities and a full 20 percent to major gift opportunities.

Most fund development executives try to build their annual giving programs to a level of efficiency and effectiveness that will allow proper time and attention (20 percent) to be spent on soliciting major gifts. All too often, they are under pressure to meet short-term priority cash needs first, if not exclusively. They must find a way to explain to donors the merits of concentration on major gifts. One approach may be to implement the 80-20 division of attention. Another may be to anticipate several relevant questions donors typically have (Exhibit 5.1). People give of their spendable cash to any number of organizations each year. But they give their time and talent *and* their cash to only a few organizations over their lifetime; they seek to fulfill a need arising from a desire for involvement, visibility, respectability, and other factors. Their major gift decisions (how much and how often) are motivated by the extent of their personal participation and knowledge—elements that should be encouraged by the not-for-profit organizations they have chosen. The biggest gifts will go to only a few organizations with which donors have the best relationship and longest personal association. (Perhaps religious organizations raise the most money each year because religion is a lifetime experience.) These repeated experiences build confidence and reinforce donors' commitment to the organizations they have selected to support. Donors may also withdraw their interest at any time, if insufficient care and attention are given to sustaining their personal involvement and enthusiasm.

Not-for-profit organizations have a responsibility to provide for the personal involvement of as many donors and prospects as possible. Major gifts made as investment decisions arrive as a result of involvement,

---

EXHIBIT 5.1 Relevant Questions Each Organization Must Be Prepared to Answer

Integrity	Is the organization fiscally sound?
Readiness	Does it have adequate plans for the use of the money?
Credibility	Is it trustworthy and can it accomplish what it claims?
Relevance	Does it fulfill serious needs that benefit the public and the community?
Urgency	Does it have an honest need for the money?
Scope	Is the need greater than this major gift can satisfy?

---

which results from an organization's concentrating some of its time and budget on other than annual fund-raising activities. Using the 80-20 approach, an organization has adequate room for both areas of emphasis, with enormous benefits.

Thinking Like an Investor

To develop an appreciation for the people whom you will ask to be major donors, or investors, in a charity, take the $1 million offered at the beginning of this chapter. You are now Ms., Mr., or Mrs. Philanthropist and you have $1 million to give away to *one* not-for-profit organization within the next 12 months. You are not allowed to make a lot of annual gifts to a variety of charities; it all has to be given to one. To justify spending all this money on one charity, your motives for giving must be expanded beyond those used in making annual gift decisions.

You begin to gather some background information on your favorite not-for-profit organizations. You form your own questions, to test the validity of each organization's request. You ask for more details about plans, financial health, and competence in serving as a public benefit corporation. You evaluate carefully the materials each organization sends you, and you listen to how each responds to you. You seek the counsel and advice of others about these answers. You may even use a portion of the immediate investment earnings on your $1 million to hire expert advisers to study each organization. You want an evaluation of the soundness of its mission as well as its performance. You measure the essential qualities of each organization against the criteria shown in Exhibit 5.2.

When the information is complete, what will persuade you in making your final decision? The organizations themselves and their conduct of the actual solicitation, especially if done by people from the organization whom you know and respect, can be the deciding factors (see Exhibit 5.3). A team effort is most effective. When volunteers take time to call on you, you are impressed with the extent of their personal commitment to the organization. Asking for the correct amount is possibly the most difficult part of their solicitation. Do they know you have $1 million and intend to give it all to one charity? Do they ask for too small an amount (disrespectful) or too large (presumptuous)? Have they been articulate, tactful, and confident, or embarrassed and therefore embarrassing? Did their presentation focus on their needs, their use of the money, on how they would use your money to benefit others? Do you get a sense that an organization

5 THE FINAL TIER: INVESTMENT DECISIONS

EXHIBIT 5.2 Critical Questions in Assessing Gift Opportunities

Quality of Leadership and Management
- Is the organization led by competent and visionary individuals? How much leadership depth is there? What would happen if the founder or current executive departed?
- Is there an active board of trustees that understands the mission and purpose of the organization?
- Does the organization have membership, volunteers, or other unpaid constituencies who participate?
- Is there a strategic plan with goals that are shared by board and staff?

Track Record
- Is there a solidly documented record of achievement?
- What is the organization's reputation within its field?
- How do its "consumers" (clients or target population) rate its programs and services?
- Does the organization have a high degree of community support and participation?
- If the organization is new, what is the track record of its founders?

Financial Strength and Stability
- Are accounting and financial recordkeeping systems in place?
- Has there been financial stability over time?
- Is the funding base diverse and stable?
- Does the organization have strong fund development capacity? Does it employ ethical practices in fund raising? How much does it spend on fund raising?
- Is there a cash reserve?

Urgency of Need
- How urgently is the problem or issue addressed by the proposed grant?
- How did the organization identify this need?
- How does their assessment of the need compare with the analysis of others who know the field or community?
- Who will be served by the program, and how much will they benefit?

Efficiency/Cost-Effectiveness
- What is the cost per unit of service?
- How does it compare to similar programs?
- What would the social costs be of not offering this program?

(continued)

EXHIBIT 5.2 (continued)

Potential Impact
- Does the proposed program represent a new model or approach?
- Will it affect large numbers of people?
- Does it have the potential to be a model that is replicable elsewhere?
- Will it sustain or significantly strengthen a critical community resource?
- Does it have the potential to influence public policy?
- Does it have the potential to develop new concepts and contribute significantly to learning in this field?

Degree of Risk
- Are the presented plans well conceived and likely to work out as proposed?
- Is this a tested idea or approach?
- Do outside forces have the potential to hinder implementation of this program?

Strategy/Leverage
- Will our support encourage other donors to give?
- Will it build public support or credibility for this approach?

Potential for Institutionalization and Self-Sufficiency
- Will our support significantly strengthen this program/organization?
- If successful, is this program likely to be replicated elsewhere?
- Is this program likely to affect how other institutions provide services?
- Are there other potential future funding sources for this effort?

determined how much to ask for by using a rating and evaluation methodology based on careful and knowledgeable research?

Rating and Evaluation Methodology

Rating and evaluation procedures are a crucial part of the plan to solicit major gifts. Their purpose is to validate information, especially regarding areas or projects that prospects prefer to support and how much prospects

---

EXHIBIT 5.3 Elements That Influence a Final Decision to Make a Major Gift

---

Complete information
A worthy project
Competence and readiness of the organization
Confidence in the leadership
Public benefit value of the organization
Donors' being part of a larger story
Visible association with a success
Donors' being well asked, for the right amount
Appropriate recognition

---

might be able to give. A select group of key volunteers (accountants, attorneys, bankers, brokers, and investment managers are best qualified) can provide the basic information but they must maintain professional confidence; they can be asked only to verify data and to confirm possible gift ranges. A rating and evaluation committee does not even need to meet to perform this task, but if a meeting is held it should be in a setting that permits complete confidentiality. Members are asked to independently rank (as freely as they feel they can) a list of prospects by identifying a gift range for each:

Group A	or Group B
☐ Under $1,000	☐ Under $50,000
☐ $1,000 to $2,500	☐ $50,000 to $100,000
☐ $2,500 to $5,000	☐ $100,000 to $250,000
☐ $5,000 to $10,000	☐ $250,000 to $500,000
☐ $10,000 to $25,000	☐ $500,000 to $1 million
☐ $25,000 to $50,000	☐ $1 million or more

The only person who will see the combined results is the chief development officer or campaign consultant. The collective judgment provides a reasonable estimate to be used by the solicitation team in discussions with the prospect. The team may add its own judgment, and the end result should be a fairly accurate "best guess" of how much to request.

Major gift candidates are solicited frequently and can be expected to measure the approach of one organization against that of another. They are wise about the use of their money and well coached, and they have access to professional advisers whose collective counsel most often will be to make a business decision first and a gift decision second. An organization's story must be complete, have absolutely solid and credible figures, be well presented by the best people available, and address all the "return on investment" features—management's plans for use of the funds, the expected public benefit, and how donors will be recognized and honored for their gift decision. Donor recognition should be included in the plan when first presented to the donor.

The reasons for a final choice give clues to why people choose to support any not-for-profit organization. Prior knowledge of and personal involvement with an organization is the reason most cited. An organization that can imagine the thought processes of donors who are making major gift decisions can anticipate their questions, appreciate what they need to know, and understand how they feel about asking questions. The organization should prepare well and pay attention to the setting and the comfort level of a meeting with the charity's representatives, even down to the number of participants, the extent of supportive documentation, and similar details. Be careful not to overwhelm the prospect. A general strategic action plan should be custom-tailored to each particular donor. Good preparation yields better results and fewer surprises.

Major Gifts Are Major Opportunities for Donors

Fund development executives must regard all qualified major gift candidates as potential benefactors and patrons; each gift decision demonstrates their level of commitment to the organization. How much they give, the gifts' timing, and how the strategic action plan led to the gift when made are elements to consider when planning the next solicitation.

All donors have aspirations about what they (and their money) can do to make good things happen; these features define the merits of each of their significant gift decisions. They recognize money as a source of power and charitable giving as a means to accomplish significant good. They can be enormously persuasive in any direction they choose. Bold and innovative thinking that realizes maximum benefits from an opportunity to use their money well makes donors see extra value in one organization over another and is conducive to repeat contributions.

Major gift decisions are often made as self-directed and even self-centered decisions because the donor has the power to make things happen. After one or two such gifts, a generous donor may shift emphasis from what he or she can accomplish with his or her money to what the money can accomplish for others.

The Steps Leading to Major Gift Decisions

The solicitation process is easy enough to study, and most fund development executives understand well enough how to coach the people involved. Implementing the process is never easy; the constant demands of annual giving rarely allow time to think about the daily steps needed to move toward solicitation. A significant amount of time is required for major gift donors to progress to the top tier of the giving pyramid. Only through a donor's identification with an organization and access to appropriate information will sincere interest and personal involvement develop, and only when they are confirmed will the investment decision of a major gift be made. Patience and solid planning are required. With the fund-raising professional's (and volunteer's) help, the donor with progress through a series of well-executed situations in the prospect cycle, whereby a pattern of agreement with an organization's requests for involvement, participation, and support is established (see Exhibit 5.4).

The sequence begins at *entry* with a donor's decision to *experiment* with an organization, to share in its *excitement* and the pleasure derived from association with it. Donors enjoy this first spark of *enthusiasm* about the organization's role and reputation in the community. They receive positive feedback when their friends and associates compliment them on their good example in being associated with the good works performed by the organization. Their involvement on committees leads to their turn at leadership and brings them into contact with other leaders. Known and respected individuals add their reputation to that of the organization, with mutual enhancement. The *exhibitionism* factor is created through the personal satisfaction they enjoy from their accomplishments and the visibility of the honors and recognition awarded by the organization. Their *exit* gift decision is the culmination of their giving history and is usually in the form of an estate planned gift.

The "E words" after the first step in Exhibit 5.4 are excitement and experiment. Special opportunities to fund something new that has potential for great significance are of high interest because they are unique, available only through a particular organization, and offered to only the most qualified donors. Donors will take pride in "making it happen" with their money. They will be enthusiastic to see it come to life and to be recognized for the achievement. Being an example to others sets them apart

EXHIBIT 5.4 The Prospect Cycle: Steps to a Major Gift Decision

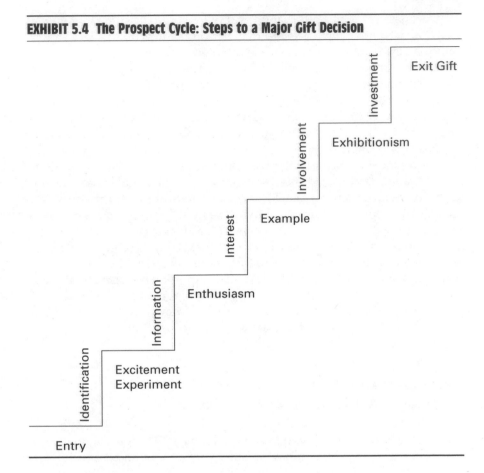

and spotlights their wisdom and resolve. This exhibitionism factor becomes quite real when they are honored and recognized in public for what they have accomplished.

An exit gift usually is not possible until after one or more major gift decisions have proven successful to the donor. The sequence might end as his or her last gift opportunity, or it might lead to another, larger gift, a best-gift-ever, or even an estate gift. Exit gifts can be the most thoughtful and the best-planned gifts of all because they complete what the donor set out to accomplish when he or she gave his or her first gift. Estate planning and planned gifts, the best-known forms of an exit gift, are discussed later in this chapter.

As an example of a gift that is not a planned gift, assume that you, as Ms. Philanthropist, have decided to give your $1 million to a local hospital for a new state-of-the-art cardiac catheterization room and for remodeling of the space where it will be located. Your gift covers the hospital's complete costs to enhance the quality of heart procedures with this state-of-the art technology. As the principal donor, Ms. Philanthropist, you are proud of what you have done; the hospital is excited and pleased, especially because no other financing was available for such an important major improvement.

However, the hospital will need about $100,000 a year to maintain the new "cath lab," including the cost of training cardiac nurses and technicians. Reimbursement for patient services does not pay for training. The hospital has an exit gift opportunity—a request for a *second* $1 million as an endowment to provide the necessary $50,000 a year. With a 10-year pledge to provide $50,000 a year, as your next gift, the equivalent of the investment earnings from a second $1 million gift as an endowment. Your total gifts now will meet all the financial requirements of the new heart procedure room and allow you, as the donor, a continued role in your chosen project. Later, you commit $1 million from your estate to permanently fund the training needed to sustain the program in the future.

Personal Solicitation Techniques: A Strategic Action Plan for Each Donor

How is the major gift solicitation process managed? Where can major gift prospects be found? How much must be known about a prospect before solicitation? The answers are in the design of a strategic action plan, a sequence of cultivation steps required for each prospect. To develop benefactors and patrons, an organization needs qualified donors, qualified solicitors, and a qualified purpose.

Likely candidates to become benefactors and patrons are often right under an organization's nose (see Exhibit 5.5). Trustees and directors whose personal commitment has brought them to high office, present and past donors whose faithful support has already demonstrated their sincere commitment, and volunteers can be the best candidates to become benefactors and patrons. They have the potential and capacity to provide 50 percent of all the major gifts needed at any time.

With few exceptions, newcomers do not begin a relationship by giving the largest gift they can make. People known to have money have a capacity, but are not yet at all informed, interested, or involved enough in

EXHIBIT 5.5 Who Are Likely Prospects?

Candidates
1. Trustees and directors (current and former)
2. Long-time regular donors giving $5,000 or more
3. Multiple-gift givers of $1,000 or more in one year
4. Multiple-year givers of $1,000 or more
5. Newly qualified major gift donors and prospects
6. Volunteers at all levels
7. Benefit event attendees and participants
8. Prior campaign major gift donors and prospects
9. (People known to have money.)

Guiding Principles for Major Gift Solicitation
The challenge is not to find prospects; The challenge is to qualify them.
The next challenge is to find and train qualified solicitors.
The final challenge is to have a qualified use for each qualified prospect's money.

your organization to make an investment decision. Research will qualify major gift prospects by potential size of gift only. An organization should beware of any solicitation plan that relies too much on newcomers' making major gifts.

Donor records are another source of prospects. Which donors have made multiple gifts in any one year? Their total participation and support quietly signal their enthusiasm. Which donors have given $1,000 at any one time? If given personal attention, they may have the potential to do much more.

Where else can future benefactors and patrons be found? The odds are slimmer once the board, long-time faithful donors, and volunteers have been solicited, but faithful attendees and participants in activities and fund-raising events have shown that they care and may have the capacity to give a significant amount of money. Other reliable sources of annual support may not be prospects now, but should be kept in mind for estate planning and planned giving programs later on.

While appearing on the surface to be natural candidates, the known wealthy, if they lack involvement and participation with an organization, are unlikely to begin giving just because they are asked for a big gift. Although fully qualified because of their capacity to give, they will need to become participants in the organization before they will make any serious investment. They can be cultivated in the expectation that a major gift decision will eventually result.

Several critical factors must come together for the donor and the solicitor when a major gift decision is requested (see Exhibit 5.6). Wealthy people appreciate the value of money and the influence it can exert. Thus, they tend to rely on their instincts in making decisions. Influenced by success in fulfilling their *desires,* they *dedicate* themselves to each project with the *determination,* the *discipline,* and the attention to *detail* to see it to completion. These donors will likely show some possessiveness as the project becomes their *dominion.* In the end, they most seriously want to make a *difference.* In a parallel process, major gift solicitors must prepared themselves, accessing information and using *research.* They also must be willing to engage in a planned sequence of cultivation events, not unlike engaging in a *romance,* the object of which is to bring circumstances to a state of *readiness* for actual solicitation. The nature, form, timing, and manner of the actual *request* are worthy of care and attention, to be followed with *recognition* after the donor's gift decision. Finally, solicitors must *retain* the donor's interest, enthusiasm, and generosity.

When several prospects have been identified, research on each should begin. The information gathered is a tool to help in solicitation, not an end in itself. An organization should not be dependent on data collection and its completion before it can act. How much does the solicitation team need to know about prospects? Basic details (address, education, professional career, public interests, civic service) are readily available

---

EXHIBIT 5.6 Guiding Principles in Major Gift Decisions

Major Gift Donor	Major Gift Solicitor
Desire	Research
Dedication	Romance
Discipline	Readiness
Detail	Request
Determination	Recognition
Dominion	Retention
Difference	

Reprinted with permission from "Profiling Major Gift Fundraisers: What Qualifies Them for Success" by Ernest W. Wood, in Developing Major Gifts, ed. Dwight F. Burlingame and James M. Hodge, New Directions in Philanthropic Fundraising, no. 16 (San Francisco: Jossey-Bass, 1997).

from standard reference sources. More helpful data can come from information accumulated during the association with each donor and prospect: gift history, interest areas, volunteer contacts, and results of the rating and evaluation process. A step-by-step strategic action plan with a flexible timetable is the best use of research information. The intent is to use all research data to prepare a sound cultivation plan and conduct a solicitation that keeps the donors' best interests in mind and that can be matched to the organization's priorities.

Solicitation Strategy: The Steps to Success

Solicitation is neither simple nor predictable, but observing the action steps in Exhibit 5.7 will help. Every solicitation will be unique and will require flexibility, but those characteristics make major gift fund-raising fascinating and rewarding. To simplify the action steps, a few fictitious people are presented in the following illustrative example. The example demonstrates that the key role of the fund development professional is to counsel and advise, not necessarily to perform all the steps involved. The fund-raising project in the example is a major gift of $250,000 to remodel space for a new science laboratory. A candidate and solicitation team have been identified and the fund development staff has prepared the strategic cultivation plan. The paragraphs of the example are numbered to match the relevant steps in Exhibit 5.7.

EXHIBIT 5.7 Solicitation Strategy

1. Identify qualified prospect and match with qualified solicitor.
2. Meet with qualified solicitor to review action plan; identify spokesperson to assist if needed.
3. Seek first appointment of solicitor team with prospect.
4. Conduct first meeting with prospect; plan follow-up.
5. Arrange second meeting (site visit); ask to make formal presentation.
6. Prepare full presentation; brief the team; prepare them to ask for gift if right to do so.
7. Make full presentation; include the solicitation if prudent to do so.
8. Mark the formal solicitation request during a solicitor follow-up.
9. Receive a gift decision and closure.
10. Send a thank-you. Begin donor relations program and perform recognition. Prepare plan leading to next gift.

---

1. Research of present annual donors identifies Mrs. Mega Bucks as a qualified candidate. She has made three gifts (one at $25,000 and two at $50,000) within the past three years; her most recent gift was directed to a similar laboratory program. She has a good relationship with a board member, Mr. Trust Worthy.

2. The information and a draft of a strategic cultivation plan are presented to the rating and evaluation committee and development committee chairperson. They suggest that a gift of $100,000 is possible and agree with the plan. The chairperson asks Mr. Worthy to accept the assignment. The fund development professional meets with Mr. Worthy to review Mrs. Bucks's gift history and other data along with the draft of the strategic cultivation plan, to determine the likely sequence of steps to be taken. The professional knows that Mrs. Bucks has a more-than-adequate knowledge of laboratory work (her husband built and ran a chemical company). Mr. Worthy describes himself as not well informed or comfortable in discussing any technical details. The fund raiser suggests that the laboratory director, Dr. Bright, join the team as technical spokesperson for the project. Dr. Bright has met Mrs. Bucks twice in the past year and she has shown some confidence in his direction of the laboratory. Dr. Bright, Mr. Worthy, and the fund raiser meet, review the plan, and agree to go forward.

3. Mr. Worthy agrees to call Mrs. Mega Bucks to report his conversation with Dr. Bright about progress in the laboratory and the board's decision to expand his science project into space for a new laboratory, which he believes Mrs. Bucks might like to hear about. He offers to arrange for Dr. Bright to join him in a meeting with her to provide this information. She agrees to the meeting and the date is set. (This call for the first appointment is crucial; thought, preparation, and maybe a rehearsal are needed. If this step is not successful, all else may be lost.)

4. Before the first meeting, the fund raiser reviews the action plan with both Mr. Worthy and Dr. Bright. It is agreed that Mr. Worthy should conduct the first meeting. The objectives of the first meeting—to report information (with enthusiasm) and to learn the extent of Mrs. Bucks's interest in the new project—are reviewed carefully. The meeting is held and all goes well. Mrs. Bucks states that this new laboratory has long been needed and she thinks the organization should proceed without delay. She asks a lot of questions about choice of equipment manufacturers, prices, installation costs and timetable, staffing requirements, annual operating costs, and maintenance expenses. Dr. Bright provides some of these details and promises to get the balance of information as soon as he can. He suggests that they meet again, perhaps at his office, to review this information. Mrs. Bucks agrees to the next meeting.

5. The fund raiser and Dr. Bright prepare all the information; they meet with Mr. Worthy to review the data, action plan, and meeting objectives. Mr. Worthy sets the date for the second meeting and offers to give Mrs. Bucks a ride to Dr. Bright's office. The purposes of the meeting, he states, are to provide the information she requested, show her the site and design drawings, and give her a tour of the laboratory area that her prior gift supported. Dr. Bright is to conduct this meeting. He arranges the meeting agenda and laboratory tour and organizes all the information she requested in a notebook to be given to her. The fund raiser instructs Mr. Worthy to observe Mrs. Bucks's reactions throughout, to determine whether to ask her if she would like to consider personal support of the project. Mr. Worthy knows she has to talk with her financial advisers before any such decisions are made; he has been unable to learn whether she has done so. Mrs. Bucks enjoys the tour and appears quite comfortable talking with Dr. Bright, who offers to prepare a project summary for her. On the way home, she suggests to Mr. Worthy that he call her in a week to make an appointment for a discussion of how she might be able to help. The "ask" might have been made, but the moment was too early. Having a proposal ready at this point would have been presumptuous. The object until now has been only to provide Mrs. Bucks with information; no one has suggested she make another gift. But she has now suggested that she may be able to help. She is fully aware she is being recruited to support this project. Her concern is whether she can afford the contribution right now. Timing of the ask is critical; the team decides that she is more likely to be ready after she confers with her financial advisers.

6. The proposal is now prepared. It describes and illustrates the new lab, the research program, and its benefits; details that are of keen interest to Mrs. Bucks are included. The plan now includes a request for $100,000 and adds as recognition a proposal that the new laboratory space be created in her late husband's name. The fund raiser works closely with Mr. Worthy and Dr. Bright to prepare the proposal and rehearse the presentation that will lead up to the solicitation. The trio evaluates whether Mr. Worthy and Dr. Bright remain the right people to meet with her and conclude that bringing in an outsider will not help. Mr. Worthy calls Mrs. Bucks to report that the information is assembled, and an appointment with her is set up.

7. Mr. Worthy and Dr. Bright present the entire program plan, referring to the illustrations in the notebook given to her at their prior meeting. Mrs. Bucks has many questions about the direction of Dr. Bright's research work and the cost of annual operations. Dr. Bright answers these well; such questions were anticipated and these data were included in the

full proposal. Mr. Worthy announces he is authorized by the board of directors to offer the special recognition of naming the laboratory after Mr. Bucks, and he discusses the board's wish to conduct a formal dedication and reception when the laboratory is finished. The ask may or may not happen here, but all the details have now been presented. Dr. Bright gives Mrs. Bucks the formal proposal. Mr. Worthy offers: "We will be pleased if you can consider a gift of $100,000 for this purpose, in honor of your late husband, perhaps payable over two years." Much depends on Mr. Worthy's sense of the correctness of asking at this point, leaving the proposal, and promising to call her in a few days. (If he judges the time is right to ask for her decision, he must be prepared to do so and be able to respond to any special requests that she may have, including language, location and size of the plaque, date of the dedication and reception, and size of the invitation list.)

8. Mr. Worthy judges this meeting is not the time to ask for her decision. The recognition proposal has surprised and caused some emotion for Mrs. Bucks. Mr. Worthy calls in three days to ask for her reaction. She asks for a few more days, to talk with her financial advisers. All the facts have been communicated and the gift decision is in her hands.

9. She calls Mr. Worthy after five days to report her decision is to make a gift. She then announces her gift will be $250,000 to fund the entire project, all of which will be made in 60 days! She tells him she wants to see this laboratory program begin and believes any delay is a waste of Dr. Bright's time. She also describes this laboratory as a proper memorial to her husband and thanks Mr. Worthy for offering such a thoughtful idea. Mr. Worthy is prepared to discuss when the gift will be made and how she will make it. He asks for her thoughts about language on the plaque; she says it is perfect as it is and adds that she wants only a few close friends invited to the ceremony.

10. Thank-you letters are sent from Mr. Worthy, Dr. Bright, and the chairperson of the development committee, although the money has not yet been received. Additional acknowledgments are sent from the board chair and the president/CEO when the securities arrive within 60 days. Work begins immediately; completion is estimated to require nine months. The recognition plan and dedication ceremonies are reviewed with Mrs. Bucks, and Mr. Worthy calls on her in three months to review preliminary plans for the dedication ceremony. He brings along the draft of a short news article about her gift, prepared for release to local papers and for use in the organization's newsletter. Dr. Bright reports on progress by phone and in writing every 60 days. The project is completed and the small reception arranged as Mrs. Bucks wanted. Mr. Worthy provides transportation for her. The festivities are conducted by Mr. Worthy

with Dr. Bright and include a tour of the laboratory and the unveiling of the memorial plaque. A small replica of the plaque is given to Mrs. Bucks as a memento of the occasion, a gesture that delights her. Details of how Mrs. Bucks will continue to hear about the laboratory and its progress have been prepared with Dr. Bright, who fully appreciates that donor relations requires continued communications. Mr. Worthy and Dr. Bright are aware that annual operating costs will run about $50,000 per year. Mrs. Bucks is the lead candidate for this annual gift next year. She is also being considered for gifts needed to establish an endowment of $2.5 million for permanent support. They agree on a plan to visit with her in six months to tell her of this long-range plan and to ask her to join with them to solicit any of her friends or her husband's colleagues who might help finish this project's master plan with a permanent endowment fund.

The key contribution made by the fund raiser was to prepare and guide the solicitation team. The actual ask was perhaps the most critical part of the entire cultivation strategy, but Dr. Bright and Mr. Worthy were well coached on this, "the moment of truth." Exhibit 5.8 offers a summary of helpful hints collected from successful major gift volunteers, a study of which can add to the confidence of volunteers willing to undertake this assignment. Solid preparation and patience will bring the best chance for success.

The Essential Role of the Volunteer Solicitor

As has been stated, nothing important happens until someone takes charge. Volunteer leadership in the prior example began when Mr. Worthy accepted responsibility for contacting Mrs. Bucks about a major gift opportunity. His commitment made it possible for Dr. Bright to do his part, and the ask was eventually made when Mr. Worthy felt the right moment had arrived. This example can be shared with volunteers who are willing to ask for money. Without such an example, you risk wasting your volunteers, for they may do only the minimum asked of them or nothing at all. To be successful, volunteers must be trained for this task; such training provides the assurance and confidence they need to do it well. Training also counters their fear of failure—many are afraid of failing in front of their peers as well as with their assigned prospects. To prepare your volunteers for success, encourage them to follow the tips in Exhibit 5.8 as well as the following guidelines:

- Believe in the institution.
- Understand something of the prospect's background, interests, and capabilities.

EXHIBIT 5.8 Tips from Successful Volunteer Solicitors

- Preparation is 90 percent of the process.
- Know as much as you can about the prospect.
- Put yourself in the prospect's shoes; figure out what will capture his or her interest.
- Know the case well enough to internalize it; make the case your own statement.
- Tell why the project is important to you and to the prospect. Stress the specifics you feel strongly about.
- Tailor the request to the prospect.
- Determine what is special to the prospect.
- Know what you are going to do before the meeting.
- Recognize the prospect's mental attitude.
- Concentrate on reading the prospect.
- Present the case; tell it like a story. Put the case in your own words.
- Make the request specific.
- Mention your own commitment; speak of it with enthusiasm and passion.
- Once you make the ask, stop talking and listen.
- After the ask, confirm the agreement, clarify the terms and the pledge period.
- Keep in mind that you are giving the prospect an opportunity to do something rewarding for him- or herself.
- Be confident; nothing is impossible.
- Be ready for a "no" and for objections.
- Convince the prospect that the investment is worthwhile.
- Show the prospect that you have a personal interest in him or her.
- Recognize the competition; go out and beat it.
- Ask for an investment.
- Set aside sufficient time to be effective as a solicitor.
- Most people do not give because they have not been asked.
- Talk about the benefits of giving.
- People give because they want to.
- Most people respond positively.
- Bring the cause to life.
- Make your case, then listen!

Reprinted with permission from "Overview of Major Giving" by M. Jane Williams, in The Nonprofit Handbook: Fund Raising, *2d ed., ed. James M. Greenfield (New York: John Wiley & Sons, Inc., 1997), 366.*

- Bring your own personality to the solicitation.
- Don't be afraid to ask.
- Know how to listen and adapt.
- Prove, by your own example of generosity, that the campaign is worthy of support.[2]

In many organizations, the "culture" for volunteer-led personal solicitation has not yet been introduced, or perhaps it has been introduced but has yet to flower into a reliable workforce that can attain the level of direct contact essential to a major gift program. In some instances, a decision may have been made to forgo the extensive efforts to identify, recruit, train, supervise, and reward volunteer solicitors, preferring to hire fund-raising staff and require them to conduct most of the direct contact with major gift prospects. The performance level of each option should be measured, either in a combination trial of both at the same time or by measuring reliance on one over the other. In the end the strategic choice of one as the other depends more often on the realities of major gift solicitation facing the particular organization. Evaluation of the following factors will aid in this decision:

- Is there board-level leadership to this effort?
- How many current volunteers have access to the wealthy?
- Is there an available volunteer pool who will have access?
- Are there any experienced fund-raising leaders in this pool?
- How much time will be required to recruit and train a volunteer-led solicitation team?
- How long before their effectiveness can be demonstrated?
- Is staff capable of support for a volunteer-led program?
- What is the budget to support a volunteer-led program?
- What is the cost-benefit analysis of a volunteer-led program?
- What is the likely donor and prospect response to staff solicitors?
- How long before the effectiveness of a staff solicitation model can be demonstrated?
- Is there a reasonable expectation that staff can succeed in raising as much money as a volunteer-led program?
- What salary package and office support is required for the staff option?
- What is the cost-benefit analysis of a staff solicitation program?

---

[2]Charles E. Lawson, "Capital Fund Appeals," in *The Nonprofit Handbook: Fund Raising*, 2d ed., ed. James M. Greenfield (New York: John Wiley & Sons, Inc., 1997), 454–455.

In summary, many smaller not-for-profit organizations depend on volunteers for personal solicitation because they lack the budget to hire and support fund-raising staff. Also, such organizations' priority is cash for operating expenses, which limits time and attention to development of major gift prospects. Larger, well-established entities with a history of annual giving success may have already used volunteer-led personal solicitation for their larger annual donors, an advantage that can easily be applied to major gift work. Such a volunteer corps offers the advantage of becoming effective more quickly and with more potential for early success than new personnel, which allows the organization to consider a large goal and a possible capital campaign (see Exhibit 5.9 for a list of other advantages of volunteer-led personal solicitation).

The Master Gift Plan

The master gift plan is a method to be offered to each major gift donor, to accomplish significant giving objectives and provide purpose and direc-

---

EXHIBIT 5.9 Advantages and Attributes of Volunteer-Led Personal Solicitation

1. Provides opportunities for volunteers to play an active role in support of their favorite not-for-profit organization
2. Identifies and recruits volunteers willing to ask their friends for money
3. Identifies and recruits leaders able to direct others to perform a special assignment by a deadline
4. Tells current donors and qualified prospects they are appreciated for who they are and what they can do for others
5. Asks current donors to increase their level of support above their annual giving commitment
6. Invites qualified prospects to begin at a gift level that commands respect for their decision
7. Invites current donors to become volunteers and actively help their favorite not-for-profit organization
8. Identifies planned gift prospects for future gifts
9. Succeeds because personal solicitation is 16 times more effective than direct mail and 8 times more effective than the telephone
10. Succeeds because personal solicitation, at $0.10 to $0.20 to raise $1.00 (or less), is the most cost-effective method of solicitation available
11. Results in increased commitment and enthusiasm, which is infectious; spread it far and wide.

---

tion to all of his or her contributions. Using Mrs. Mega Bucks as an example, her three annual gifts of $25,000, $50,000, and $50,000 and a one-time gift of $250,000 suggest that the $375,000 in gifts might be assembled together for special recognition. Further, all future gifts might be directed toward the objective of funding a $2.5 million endowment of the new laboratory in her husband's name. The master gift plan next shared with her would offer this new goal. This new objective has been created as a result of her individual gifts, although that was not her design from the start. A donor who has resources, clearly identified interests, a strong motive, and a demonstrated level of commitment merits the best attention an organization can possibly provide. What was lacking at the beginning was a plan that would assist her in fulfilling perhaps her highest aspiration, to honor her husband. The master gift plan designed for Mrs. Mega Bucks becomes a series of "next gift" decisions toward a single purpose rather than a series of unconnected requests toward unrelated purposes.

A master gift plan is a method that should be offered to each major donor. The plan must include recognition details—how each donor will be treated and what privileges and benefits will be offered in response to donors' generosity. Recognition details are worthy of an organization's best thinking, time, and attention. They define a privileged association with the organization and its present and future plans and may state how donors earn the right to be considered for election to the board of trustees.

The worksheet for a master gift plan (see Exhibit 5.10) distinguishes three levels or phases of gift decision. The first level concentrates on gifts for current purposes and combines annual giving opportunities and occasional major gifts with extra gifts required in capital campaigns. The second level introduces endowment giving. Donors can restrict cash gifts for endowment purposes to perpetuate their annual support. Using planned giving options, they can still retain their current income by committing an asset to irrevocable future support of the organization. The third level is an estate plan. A donor's will defines final gift decisions that complete their ultimate objective.

Each level represents more than one gift opportunity and each opportunity requires a significant gift decision. Assembled together, the master gift plan shows major gift donors how much their funds can accomplish.

Every major donor is a likely candidate for a master gift plan. The challenge is to design a plan in which the donor's objectives mesh harmoniously with the organization's own long-range plans so that the objectives of both are fulfilled.

The master gift plan is not so much a new idea as it is a disciplined process. An organization's management and volunteers may not immediately appreciate its value. In their concern about losses to annual in-

EXHIBIT 5.10 Worksheet for the Master Gift Plan

Group A *Major Gifts for Current Purposes*		*Gift Value*
Annual giving opportunities		$25,000
Cash or "cashed in" asset gifts		75,000
Campaign gifts (multiyear pledges)		250,000
	Subtotal	$350,000
Group B *Gifts for Endowment Purposes*		
(payable from current assets)		
Cash or "cashed in" asset		$150,000
Pooled income fund gift		50,000
Charitable life insurance gift (net present value)		100,000
Charitable remainder trust or gift annuity		300,000
	Subtotal	$600,000
Group C *Gifts by Will (payable from donor's estate)*		
Transfer of cash or assets		$400,000
Charitable trust or living trust		200,000
Transfer to personal foundation/trust		2,000,000
	Subtotal	$2,600,000
	Master Gift Plan Total	$3,550,000

Reprinted with permission from Fund-Raising Cost Effectiveness: A Self-Assessment Workbook *by James M. Greenfield (New York: John Wiley & Sons, Inc., 1996), 187.*

come, resolution of changes in institutional plans, and donors' flexibility to meet unforeseen future needs, they may need to be reminded that the first goal is to meet the donors' objectives. Major gift donors are any organization's best friends; they want to be flexible, to help meet the changing needs of the organization. Benefactors and patrons have established an extensive personal involvement; the organization should meet with them to keep them informed of any changes it anticipates. The design of a master gift plan is not a concept written in stone but a continuous series of communications and actions that link institutional priorities with donor desires and flexibility. Such a plan should not be denied to donors because of institutional uncertainties or a concern over the organization's ability to control its best donors' future gift decisions!

The Moment of Truth

With a master gift plan, each gift decision becomes part of a larger whole. Still, each solicitation's moment of truth, a final closure, can elude or discourage a solicitor and justify some fear and trepidation. Success in actual solicitation of major gifts often results from combining a good strategic action plan and the four CARE ingredients: comfort, anticipation, readiness, and enjoyment.

Comfort

The solicitation plan must include attention to how the donor and the solicitation team are getting along as well as to whether the donor is comfortable with the ideas being presented. The solicitation team must be able to determine whether a prospective donor likes the program or project being discussed, respects the solicitation team, and enjoys the progress of discussions. They need to observe whether the prospect is agreeable to a project's cost or at least thinks the cost allows consideration of an active partnership in the funding. The team must be alert to the timing of all phases of the solicitation plan and must know when to move on to the next step.

Anticipation

Discussions must be designed to bring the prospective donor toward a favorable decision. The solicitor's big question is how much to ask for and when. Enthusiasm and excitement build during this process, as does the donor's appreciation of his or her ability to make something worthwhile happen individually or jointly with one or two other donors. The donor's big question is whether it is affordable. He or she can be encouraged to feel some pride of potential accomplishment: "I can do this!"

Readiness

A plan offered for donors' involvement and investment is larger than the project itself because of its value to benefit others. Donors who are offered such a unique opportunity must see it as originating in a careful plan that demonstrates respect for them and confidence in their understanding of both the process, the need, and the value of the outcome. The approach of the solicitation team must reflect the entire thoughtful process leading to the point of decision.

Enjoyment

Both sides should feel satisfied about what will be accomplished by a gift decision. The true merits of a project direct discussions of details toward a higher purpose. Treatment and recognition of donors and volunteers must reflect the mutual enrichment made possible by sharing in a successful experience. Their association may continue to accomplish other major gifts in the future.

Philanthropy is performed on behalf of others and benefits someone other than the donor. Anyone who makes a large gift cares about a cause and its public benefit; the amount of the gift may be a measure of a donor's degree of commitment. However, not-for-profit organizations must remember that donors also care about what happens to the money, how it is used to benefit others, and their own sense of worth and pride in being able to make such a gift.

Necessary Details

Any strategic cultivation plan must make provisions for recognition, for managing the intensity of the process leading to solicitation, and for subsequent relations with the major gift donor.

Donor Recognition

When planned from the beginning, donor recognition will help to bring other parts of the solicitation plan together. The donor must make the decision of what the money is for. The organization should define exactly how the funds will be used from the day received (interim investment, discount price negotiations due to tax-exempt status, leveraging other gift decisions, important project enhancements from other gifts), to demonstrate its ability to make maximum use of all contributions. If the project is not easily seen by the public or is located in areas restricted from public access, the visible location for recognition of the gift must be part of the recognition proposal. Individual taste can be hard to manage, especially when a desire to show appreciation has been enthusiastically expressed but a particular preference for the location and presentation of their recognition is known to be a key motive in the donor's decision to give. A standing recognition policy such as provided in Section J of Appendix A defines how all donors will be treated fairly and equitably.

The advantage retained by the organization is that recognition is a privilege bestowed on the donor; it can be given as the organization chooses. A cumulative gift policy that adds rewards to donors for their total gifts made over time is an option of the organization's own choosing. The policy enhances each gift decision by qualifying donors for higher levels of recognition that carry extra privileges, such as more visibility through displays in a variety of locations (see Exhibit 5.11). However, the policy is not mandatory for any organization and should remain identified as a privileged treatment of donors.

Maintaining Intensity

A major gift solicitation is a management skill that both fund-raising staff and volunteers need to appreciate and cultivate. The greatest value of the strategic cultivation plan is that it defines a series of steps and can be used to keep all participants on track and in synch with its timetable. Timing and flexibility are always the judgment call of the solicitation team and their decisions must be respected unless "It's not the right time" is being used as an excuse for inaction. Deadlines on paper are important but mean less than keeping to a right order of action based on the donor's response to each step. Flexibility is essential; the action plan will be adjusted as needed.

Here are four suggestions to maintain intensity:

1. Regular committee meetings, requiring updates and activity reports, frequently serve as gentle reminders to keep things moving as agreed to in the last session.

EXHIBIT 5.11 Donor Recognition Plan—Basic Ingredients

Basic Plan
Honors and recognition policy
Cost-effective analysis
Donor relations program plan

Enhancements
Cumulative giving ladder
Naming of individual area
Plaques and portraits
Master plaque system (donor wall)

Perpetuity
Name on major wing, building, or whole organization
Name on fund or project
Name on endowment fund

---

2. Fund raisers must keep major gift solicitation high on their priority list for daily attention. Frequent contact with team members will keep up their interest and attention to the next step's actions.
3. Everything else that is going on with the organization and its other fund-raising programs may offer added opportunities that can be used to advantage; for example, the team might invite a prospect as their special guest at special events or public occasions.
4. Notices in regular publications allow for "special handling" of donors. Delivery by first-class mail with a personal note enclosed will be seen as a thoughtful gesture. Any publication or media coverage that talks about the project or program under consideration is an opportunity to send a copy along in some special fashion.

Donor Relations

This never-ending action program, especially for major gift donors, has been the greatest sin of omission among development staff. Donor relations is a continuous communication with major gift donors that begins the day a donor makes his or her gift decision. To be brought together in the solicitation experience can be an invigorating, intense experience for both donors and solicitors. Too often, the "wooing" and attention cease abruptly after the gift decision. Contact during the after-gift phase is not as intense as during solicitation, but to appear to drop all the former attention given is poor manners indeed. Keeping in touch is not difficult and is appreciated by donors. A plan for donor relations (see Exhibit 5.12) should be prepared and followed as part of the strategic cultivation plan.

Volunteers can be asked to continue to contact their donors, perhaps every three or four months if they do not have occasion to see them in any of their regular business or social routines. A personal visit once every six months is advisable. Volunteers are the best candidates to escort donors to events, an easy way to maintain the positive relationship developed among donors, volunteers, and the organization.

Project and professional staff who were involved in the solicitation or who benefit from the funds received can communicate easily by sending reports on their progress or related activities. Staff can be placed with donors when arranging the table seating at events. If professional activities (conferences, special visitors, or lectures) are held in or by the recipient department or facility, its staff can invite their donors to attend. These actions are necessary regardless of whether the donor can attend; the point is that an invitation was sent.

Fund raisers must take the lead to stimulate both volunteers and staff to stay in touch with donors. The volunteer solicitation team should re-

EXHIBIT 5.12 Donor Relations Program

The volunteer solicitation team can:
Call the donor every three months
Visit the donor every six months
Escort the donor to special events

The project/professional staff can:
Call the donor every three to six months
Visit the donor once a year
Send activity reports at least annually
Send copies of other items at any time
Join the donor at events
Invite the donor to project activities

The fund development staff can:
See that volunteers and staff keep in touch with donors without fail
Keep the solicitation team informed of communications and any feedback
Place stories in organization publications and show donors drafts, creating
    a reason to write or visit
Conduct a dedication or reception event
Prepare a photo album, to be delivered later by a solicitation team member,
    of the dedication or reception
Conduct a six-month review of the entire donor relations program

---

ceive a report on any activities by their donor—other charitable gifts, elections, appointments, honors awarded, media coverage, and the like. The fund raiser should ensure that items about both donors and volunteers are included in the organization's publications when and where appropriate. Review of a draft story about the donor and the gift can be an occasion for another volunteer visit or contact. The critical role for the fund raiser is as monitor of each donor's recognition plan; he or she should review its progress every six months.

Every not-for-profit organization should consciously manage a major gift solicitation program. Every fund development office can define a strategic action plan for a select few benefactors and patrons, to assist them in their major gift decisions. The responsibility for managing a major gift program rests with volunteer leadership and fund-raising executives. Donors are unlikely to put a plan together to solicit themselves, and volunteers are unlikely to design a strategic action plan and supervise it alone. The fund raiser must define the course of action and guide it from start to finish. Except in rare cases, fund raisers cannot perform major gift solicitations by themselves. If their personal relationship with a donor allows, the staff might become active participants in the solicitation. However, the help of volunteers is the proven means to success.

Nine-Point Performance Analysis of Major Giving

The results of an organization's major gift solicitations should be tracked and analyzed over the course of several years. A sample analysis of three years' worth of results is given in Exhibit 5.13. This review provides a solid evaluation of productivity and profitability plus suggested steps for future action, as follows:

1. The number of major gift donors is small but growing, as is the percent participation, or response rate, from current major gift solicitations (45 percent resulted in gift decisions in this three-year period). The average gift is nearly $15,000. If this level of progress is maintained for another three years, it can be anticipated that some 100 qualified prospects and past donors will have been involved in major gift decisions—excellent preparation for a large special project or capital campaign that may be on the horizon.

2. The budget allocated suggests a part-time effort led by a fund-raising staff member aided by volunteer solicitors, which accounts for the

EXHIBIT 5.13 Nine-Point Performance Analysis of Major Giving

	Two Years Ago	Last Year	This Year	Totals
Participation	12	18	23	53
Income	$172,500	$215,000	$358,000	$745,500
Expenses	$16,850	$18,200	$18,900	$53,950
Percent participation	33%	46%	53%	45%
Average gift size	$14,375	$11,944	$15,565	$14,066
Net income	$155,650	$196,800	$339,100	$691,550
Average cost per gift	$1,404	$1,011	$822	$1,018
Cost of fund raising	10%	8%	5%	7%
Return	924%	1,081%	1,794%	1,282%

Reprinted with permission from Fund-Raising Cost Effectiveness: A Self-Assessment Workbook *By James M. Greenfield (New York: John Wiley & Sons, Inc., 1996), 193.*

average cost per gift of just over $1,000. It is not yet clear whether adding staff and budget will be able to improve this performance outside the unique gift opportunities to be offered in a new special project or capital campaign.

3. The cost-of-fund-raising and return percentages are well within reasonable guidelines, even commendable for a program of this size and part-time effort. Certainly, such efficiency and profitability should be encouraging to the board of trustees and management; this performance indicates that the organization's future plans have a proven potential for successful funding. What will be required is an increased investment in a larger major gift program but with the expectation of increased public participation and net income.

4. If not in place yet, a new patron or benefactor donor recognition level might be initiated for donors of $10,000 or more, to include a selection of new, higher categories at $25,000, $50,000, and $100,000 and more, with appropriate benefits and privileges, to recognize cumulative as well as single gifts, and let everyone know that gifts of such size are welcome.

THE ROLE OF THE SPECIAL PROJECTS CAMPAIGN

One way to keep the attention of a few major gift prospects is with a special projects campaign, something of a lost art in fund raising. Special projects are not a part of annual giving (they may not happen every year), nor are they a major capital campaign. Only a few donors and volunteers are needed for a special project, which can be defined as any institutional priority that fits the long-range plan. The project must be exciting enough to command attention, have a total cost or goal of from $50,000 to $2 million, and qualify as a major gift opportunity suitable for funding by a single donor or a small group of donors. It may be just the right opportunity for a major gift prospect who is anxious to do something alone or with 5 or 10 close associates, some of whom may be new prospects for future contributions. The ingredients for success are a good idea, a respectable goal, an urgent need for the money linked to a relevant public benefit, and a project that can proceed as soon as the money is raised.

Concentration on annual giving methods often limits the attention volunteers and staff can give to major gift prospects. A corollary possibility is that these large-stakes players are denied any stimulation, excitement, or challenge. They will find all three in a special project!

Special projects campaigns can be conducted outside of or between annual giving appeals, mailings, special events, or benefits, and they can involve some of the same donors. The enthusiasm of some of an organization's biggest annual donors can be "tested" on a special project. Annual donors who resist "group giving" or being herded into support of projects in which they have a less-than-keen personal interest can be motivated to participate in special projects. Volunteers who are ready for something larger than repeat annual gifts might be teamed with a small group of prospects and assigned one or two special projects. Special projects serve as superb training opportunities for volunteers who need experience at major gift solicitation and who would like to work with one or two major donors to demonstrate their maturing skills.

Any number of special projects can be identified each year within the annual fund, without competing with operating priorities. Packaging these annual needs as special projects may give them some appeal for foundations or corporations, which shun annual giving appeals and are usually not interested in annual operating needs. Refining one or more routine annual needs into "special projects" creates a unique gift situation that may capture the attention of a few major gift prospects. For example, routine renovation and equipment replacement needs lack any spark to increase annual giving results. However, when identified with the program or service this space or equipment supports, the story of the need is presented as a special project—that is, to increase the space so that more clients can be served, to repair and modernize a building, or to markedly improve the quality of results from the use of new, state-of-the-art equipment. Some research can identify likely prospects, and a strategic cultivation plan can be developed to solicit them.

Special projects campaigns do not require an all-out organizational commitment or multiyear pledges and other traditional capital campaign paraphernalia. A few qualified and eager volunteers and a large project or two that can stand alone are all that is needed. When they do *not* conflict with a major capital campaign, special projects offer to the best donors a few exciting opportunities each year to retain their keen attention and high level of support.

Special projects campaigns produce a cadre of willing donors and experienced solicitors, and they breed some confidence that a multiyear, multimillion-dollar campaign effort could be sustained. These smaller "test" campaigns build a bridge for donors between routine annual gift decisions and major campaign commitments. Once the master gift plan is introduced to major gift donors and prospects, a continuous menu of exciting and significant projects must be served, to allow them to continue, without interruption, their overall, lifetime objective.

Implementation of a special projects campaign is fairly simple: A willing volunteer or two, a handful of qualified prospects, and a special project are all that is needed. The project is the featured attraction because of its ability to "make something good happen." As an example of a special projects campaign, the gymnasium of a small private school burned down in October. The school's annual fall appeal for funds to meet annual operating expenses was in progress. Replacement of the gymnasium as soon as possible was essential but would cost $1 million. Two board members took up the challenge. They wrote and called 250 key alumni who were current annual givers at $500 or more and who had participated in athletics during their school years. They asked each prospect for a gift of $5,000 *over and above his or her annual gift*. In three weeks' time, they received firm commitments for over $1 million. The gymnasium was rebuilt and opened before the school year ended and no annual giving revenues were lost.

Nine-Point Performance Analysis of Special Projects Campaigns

Exhibit 5.14 illustrates the results of three separate special projects campaigns. Each has progressed differently and the analysis offers some insight into the range of activity and effort required for different types of

EXHIBIT 5.14 Nine-Point Performance Index Analysis of Special Projects Campaigns

	Special Project 1	Special Project 2	Special Project 3	Totals
Participation	5	185	11	201
Income	$25,500	$1,025,000	$60,500	$1,111,000
Expenses	$1,450	$41,550	$1,500	$44,500
Percent participation	83%	74%	61%	73%
Average gift size	$5,100	$5,541	$5,500	$5,527
Net income	$24,050	$983,450	$59,000	$1,066,500
Average cost per gift	$290	$225	$136	$221
Cost of fund raising	6%	4%	2%	4%
Return	1,659%	2,367%	3,933%	2,397%

Reprinted with permission from Fund-Raising Cost Effectiveness: A Self-Assessment Workbook *by James M. Greenfield (New York: John Wiley & Sons, Inc., 1996), 204.*

campaigns to be successful. Every special projects campaign has unique goals, objectives, timing, and gift opportunities. Using a nine-point performance index for evaluation can help demonstrate the merits of this effective and efficient method of major gift solicitation.

Some background for these three examples follows: Special project 1 is a family's joint gift plan for $25,000 to replace a major piece of equipment given in honor of its parents. Special project 2 is the $1 million gymnasium campaign mentioned earlier, during which 250 former athletes were solicited. Special project 3 is a challenge gift of $25,000 offered by one major gift donor who believed in the project and chose the challenge gift strategy to stimulate other donors to participate in the $50,000 goal. All three campaigns asked for minimum gifts of $5,000 from each donor. The following observations are made:

1. The $25,000 family joint-funding project (campaign 1) invited all five family members to make a gift of $5,000 each. Their average gift of $4,250 suggests one or more was unable to give this much but one gave more to achieve their common goal. Net income after modest expenses of $1,450, mostly for recognition purposes, was $24,050, a bit shy of the true goal, but the total income exceeded the goal by $500 and all five family members participated. The cost to conduct this special projects campaign averaged $290 per gift, which is the highest average cost per gift among these three examples.

2. The gymnasium project (campaign 2) also reached its goal at a cost of $41,550 (mailings are expensive!) and provided net income of $983,450 for the gymnasium. Of those solicited, 74 percent responded with gifts at an average of $5,541—quite positive. Overall cost of fund raising for this emergency campaign was $0.04 with a return on expenses of 2,367 percent. Emotional appeals are a strong motive, indeed!

3. The challenge gift campaign (project 3) also met its goal with an average gift of $5,500. Because volunteers performed all the solicitations, costs were modest (the average cost per gift was $136, the lowest in these three campaigns). Also lowest was the cost of fund raising at $0.02 with a corresponding 3,933 percent return. Volunteer solicitation is the most cost-efficient strategy.

4. All three campaigns met their gross revenue goal but each also fell slightly short of estimated total dollars required after fund-raising expenses. A reality in fund raising is that "it costs money to raise money." Every solicitation project should include in its goal an estimate of the costs involved, so that the net income will be sufficient to fully fund the project.

5. Special projects campaigns are unusually successful for several reasons: their unique, one-time-only nature; a sharp focus and defined goal; a limited prospect pool; a rational deadline; modest costs; and the effective use of volunteer solicitors. In all three examples, the average gift size of about $5,000 also was modest. For the organizations involved, these important new projects were funded enough to be implemented quickly, thanks to a successful fund-raising strategy for each campaign.

THE MAJOR CAPITAL CAMPAIGN

Capital campaigns are one of the most productive, efficient, and cost-effective methods of raising large sums of money yet invented. They work well because they demand a total effort throughout the organization, which forces everyone to concentrate on campaign objectives and on major gifts. Major capital campaigns used to be held as needed; volunteers and donors had a break between campaigns, to "rest up." Not any more! They used to be centered on a big project, such as a new building or several new buildings, and on endowment funds that would later support their routine operations. Not any more! The large capital campaigns in America were first launched in the late 1980s by Stanford University who raised $1.1 billion by the end of 1991. Stanford's goals have included buildings and endowment, but the campaign was in fact the ultimate annual fund campaign: The real objective was to increase annual income from all sources to new heights of reliable revenue each year. Other organizations are following this pattern, which may explain the "unending campaign" style for many institutions and agencies seen today.

Most not-for-profit organizations lack the extensive "critical mass" required for an unending campaign. They can and will continue to plan and conduct periodic capital drives with a high degree of success—if they can pass the "CRUP Test" by having achieved *c*redibility, *r*elevance, *u*rgency, and *p*ragmatism.

One of the first questions to ask about a capital campaign is whether it is truly needed. This question deserves a deliberate answer. Capital campaigns are not for raising significant numbers of gifts or significant numbers of large gifts, and they are not for achieving prestigious gifts or important objectives. A capital campaign is one means to financial security, but it should and, in most cases, it must represent the studied conclusion that all traditional funding options have been exhausted and a capital fund drive is now required to raise most or all of the money needed by a certain date.

The decision to conduct a major capital campaign should be the best decision possible for all the right reasons.[3] Credibility, relevance, urgency, and pragmatism are essential because without them an organization cannot defend its fundamental arguments for constructing more buildings, expanding its services, improving its quality, and financing its future. The first of all questions, "What's the money for?" must be answered exceptionally well. The case for support must be so convincing that people hearing it will agree with its conclusions, not because of what the money is for but because what the money allows to happen is so necessary.

Is there another way or combination of ways to raise the money needed without a capital campaign, perhaps using a major gift program? An organization should use a fully developed annual giving program and corporation and foundation grant opportunities to their fullest potential before leaping into a capital campaign. One of the important points made earlier in this chapter is that major gift solicitations can be made without being in a capital campaign; planned giving and estate planning can also be carried out without a capital drive. Not-for-profit organizations and their fund-raising staff tend to conclude too quickly that a capital campaign is all that should be recommended. They do so for all the wrong reasons: a quick fix, an easy solution to major funding needs, a path to glory and their own reputation for success (volunteers and staff can be equally guilty). So many good reasons are built into a good capital campaign that these unnecessary and irrelevant reasons have no place in the decision.

Readiness Is Everything

The decision to conduct a capital campaign must be made months ahead of starting any campaign solicitation. The CRUP Test is only the first evaluation needed to demonstrate whether an organization is ready. Readiness begins with leadership. Volunteer training and experience, prospect identification and research, adequate staff, budget, space, and office systems are all part of a cycle that restarts again with leadership. Readiness includes complete analysis of institutional stability, especially in annual financial operations; a realistic schedule of projects linked to the master or strategic plan; and sound decisions (unflavored by any personal ambitions) leading to the choice of the capital campaign as the best method available. A professional market research study, a precampaign develop-

---

[3]For several key pros and cons for conducting campaigns, see also Kent Dove, *Conducting a Successful Capital Campaign* (San Francisco: Jossey-Bass, 1988), 167–169.

ment planning analysis (also called a feasibility study), and an audit of the development office and current programs all should be conducted by outside professional firms before the campaign decision is made. These studies will evaluate potential prospects and the impact of the campaign on all other marketing and public relations priorities and on fund-raising programs now in place. A campaign will take money and volunteers away from all of them; the studies can estimate the numbers involved.

A feasibility study should always be conducted prior to a campaign, as there is a wealth of information needed to make precampaign decisions. "If a feasibility study is to result in an adequate test of philanthropic potential and that test be followed by a systematic, progressive plan of action, then the organization:

1. must have a studied plan for, say, at least five years anticipating services and programs to be budgeted and/or funded;
2. must have a financial plan of costs and contingencies for the approved plans and programs;
3. must have represented on its board the kind of leadership who can serve as authenticators and leaders not only in advocacy but also in personal gift commitments;
4. must have a sales-oriented, production-oriented, creative development staff;
5. must have a comprehensive financial development program for annual support, capital fund and planned gift policies and opportunities; merchandising—putting ideas on the shelf for people to buy; and to endow budget relief items;
6. must have identified, researched, and cultivated prospects *capable* of providing the kind and level of gift support expected, estimating capacity not proclivity; and
7. must have a motivational sales case or prospectus for substantial philanthropic support meager on history, dynamic on services, and competent on projections for the future."[4]

Readiness, while essential to measure, is an elusive ingredient. "It does not just happen. To gear up for a major campaign often takes several years," reports Gene A. Budig, chancellor of the University of Kansas. "In establishing goals, [an organization] must assess its strengths and weaknesses, know its true needs, weigh its record in fund raising and take into consideration the position of its state and regional economy."[5]

[4] Arthur C. Frantzreb, *Not on This Board You Don't: Making Your Trustees More Effective* (Chicago: Bonus Books, 1997), 138–139.
[5] Gene A. Budig, "Driving Past the Goal," *Fund Raising Management* 21, no. 5 (1990): 39.

Donors must be prepared as well. Seymour[6] defines fund raising as "the planned promotion of understanding, participation and support" but says that it needs a good case (one that "covers the ground, aims high, catches the eye and ear, warms the heart, stirs the mind") that creates the right mood ("relevance, importance and urgency, supported by faith and confidence"). This combination is especially relevant for capital campaigns. The donors must be prepared to welcome the invitation to give.

Conducting a Successful Capital Campaign

A capital campaign is a massive planning challenge. It must be thought through in complete detail from beginning to end. Exhibit 5.15 lists the steps needed. Their order is not absolute and they are not suited to every organization. The following sections amplify their meaning.

1. Institutional Plan

The master plan for the next five years, or the next decade or two, describes the vision for the future of the organization. It answers "What's the money for?" with a panoramic view. Without it, the case for support is weak. It should always be written down.

2. Strategic Plan

Specific projects from the long-range (three to five years) master plan should be arranged in the order of their proposed completion. Estimated costs, timetables, and other details should be reported. A realistic strategic plan includes a list of actual campaign projects and their individual costs.

EXHIBIT 5.15 The Steps to a Successful Capital Campaign

1. Institutional plan	7. Discipline/momentum/hustle
2. Strategic plan	8. Midpoint rally
3. Assessment/analysis/answers	9. Feedback on progress
4. Preparations and readiness	10. Finishing the capital campaign
5. Advance gifts	11. Post-campaign activities
6. The kickoff	12. Overcoming mistakes

---

[6]Harold J. Seymour, *Designs for Fund Raising*. (New York: McGraw-Hill, 1966), 57, 95, and 115. (2d ed. paperback: The Fund-Raising Institute, 1988.)

At the top of the list put the projects that must be completed on schedule before the balance of the strategic plan can be begun.

3. Assessment/Analysis/Answers

The results of a precampaign planning or feasibility study, market research, development office audit and other analyses will help to validate campaign goals and objectives, leadership potential and volunteer pool, campaign organization and timetable, budget and staff required, and similar factors including a realistic assessment of external conditions that can affect results (review Exhibit 2.5, page 65). Reality must be separated from myth. Exhibit 5.16 shows the information that can be revealed by market research and feasibility studies. Its value is inestimable. A professional firm with direct experience conducting research projects for not-for-profit organizations should be employed and its findings should be believed, even when it recommends raising or lowering a goal, waiting to begin, or remedying factors such as lack of leadership, absence of a lead gift, inadequate staff, and outmoded office systems. The research firm's assessments focus everyone on how/what/when/where/whom/how much issues and serve as backup to the campaign decisions required: when to begin; how much to seek from each source; what organization and structure to implement; how many leaders, volunteers, and committees are required; and how much budget is necessary. These data are the intelligence necessary to create a plan that will result in a successful capital campaign.

EXHIBIT 5.16 What a Feasibility Study Can Reveal

1. The response for campaign giving
2. How much each audience might give
3. The identity of major gift prospects
4. The identity of leadership candidates
5. Problem areas (case, timing, image, leadership, staff, systems, others)
6. An overall campaign objective
7. Specific goals for each giving audience available
8. A timetable and sequence for solicitation
9. Elements of the case statement and all support documentation required
10. Staffing and budget required
11. Public relations support plan
12. Where and how campaign counsel will be needed

---

4. Preparations and Readiness

Success begins with the identification, recruitment, and training of leaders; little will happen until key people are in place. They must lead, gain the respect of others, give, and be well-organized, resourceful, aggressive or even fearless, and committed to the success of the campaign. Proven leaders from annual giving programs are recommended candidates. The overall campaign chairperson should be chosen first. Once in place, the chairperson can help to select the key leadership team, and each person joining the team can participate in selection of the balance of the volunteers needed. There is great value in the chairperson's opportunity to design the team and to form the campaign executive committee. This small unit will be working closely throughout the entire campaign period, establishing policy and exercising overall control. The synergism of the chairperson and the executive committee will invigorate and infuse the campaign with the energy and enthusiasm required for its successful conclusion.

Other elements of readiness include the printed materials: case statement, brochures, pledge forms, volunteer kits, training programs, meeting notices, plus donor and volunteer recognition plans. Other support items, such as slide shows, videos, and computer-generated presentations also may be necessary. Once the campaign begins, little time will be available to prepare these support items.

5. Advance Gifts

A delightful time in any campaign is when the first prospects are invited in and offered the opportunity to make the lead gifts. Their actions can stimulate the entire campaign effort and ensure its success. The second category of advance gifts are those required of the campaign leadership and the board of the organization. Full participation (100 percent) is as important as how much money is given. The true value of early gift decisions by key donors and campaign leaders, even if they represent only a small percentage of the goal, is to establish an immediate legitimacy to the campaign and to create momentum. Their commitments bring the campaign to the launch point and signal its readiness.

6. The Kickoff

A wise campaign manager makes the most of this event. Banners, balloons, and buttons can create a backdrop for an exciting message, communicated to the best group of prospects that can be assembled. The organization is now committed and the community must be enlisted in this future plan. Results should be emphasized, not how they will be achieved.

7. Discipline/Momentum/Hustle

Once begun, the campaign must stick to the process outlined in the plan. Its structure should serve the manager and the executive committee. The schedule should be monitored but kept flexible enough to be moved forward and back as the situation demands. The executive committee should resolve early in a written policy what will count toward campaign goals and what will receive campaign credit. No exceptions should be made.

Momentum cannot be maintained at a fever pitch every day of the campaign. But by staggering the several campaign elements (board giving, followed by staff, and then employees), the success of each group can be leveraged to stimulate others who are getting ready to begin or who may be struggling (see Exhibit 5.17 for helpful hints to maintain momentum). Gift reports help others believe that they can be successful if they follow the plan and do what is asked of them. The work required should be done with enthusiasm and always with a positive attitude; the manager's attitude especially, can be infectious.

8. Midpoint Rally

Slowdowns can occur anytime from 6 to 10 months after the kickoff or when 45 to 50 percent of the goal is in hand. People take vacations in August or during the December holidays and the campaign momentum is slowed. It must be restarted as soon as possible because optimism and confidence in the campaign plan are being tested. A big gift can be the spark to reignite the team, as can a midpoint rally at which the volunteers report their progress. The deadline of the rally will spur volunteers to action so they can report positive results. Embarrassment and guilt are wonderful motivators for volunteers and donors, but should be used selectively.

9. Feedback on Progress

As each segment completes its work and meets (and exceeds) goals, focus shifts to the remaining team members and their prospects to reach their goal and help "put us over the top." Among the major gift candidates who have yet to make their commitment will be people who will watch progress and want to be sure the effort will be a success before they join in. Preplanning for this phase includes having some reserves who can step forward now with their decisions. They may come from the bottom tier of giving and may contribute less than 10 percent of the rest of the

EXHIBIT 5.17 Maintaining Campaign Momentum

1. Keep doing what you are doing, especially where it is effective and efficient; these strategies have worked well.
2. Study all performance data (research, contact reports, gift and pledge levels, volunteer action, etc.) to learn where improvements may lie and what modifications are needed.
3. Report results to campaign leadership; explain your interpretations.
4. Define options for change and be willing to risk investing time, people, and money in them.
5. Review cultivation strategies and solicitation plans for each qualified prospect; be flexible as each situation may have changed. Be sure all the data confirm a major gift remains possible.
6. Keep in regular contact with all volunteers and volunteer leaders.
7. Seek opportunities to utilize other organizational activities and events to advantage (e.g., bring major gift prospects as special guests).
8. Propose changes to current strategies and plans based on overall campaign success to date.
9. Document improvements possible; define the strategy that will produce the most likely results to rekindle confidence in the plan.
10. Review the recognition proposed in each solicitation strategy.
11. Implement a new activity for donors and prospects, such as hard-hat tours of the building or wing under construction or advance briefings on new program plans, to maintain positive contact.
12. Ask board members and campaign volunteers for assistance.
13. Ask for more budget if needed, to implement each new strategy or activity based on your analysis of improvements and success to date.
14. Make it happen.

money needed to reach the campaign goal. But the timing of these contributions and the feedback to other team members and prospects will help the campaign regain momentum and shore up any waning enthusiasm. Soliciting in the bottom tier for the campaign may cancel some annual gifts from the same donors. The organization may have to be flexible in its priorities and seek other sources for these replacement contributions.

10. Finishing the Capital Campaign

The commitment of leaders and volunteers will be tested to finish the campaign in the final weeks. The resolve of the chairperson and executive committee to stay on course until the goal has been achieved will stimulate others to complete their work. Some volunteers will be reluctant to see difficult prospects. Successful volunteers can be teamed together to conclude the solicitation of every qualified prospect. Some donors may give a second gift; those who gave early may wish to improve their gift to meet or exceed the gifts of others. Annual giving donors will appreciate being invited to join too, provided their cash can be diverted without harm to the operating budget.

11. Post-Campaign Activities

A victory celebration can be appropriately staged at the site of the kickoff or at the location of the new project. The celebration is held to thank donors, campaign leaders, and volunteers for their outstanding effort. The campaign could not have been conducted without them, all of them, even those who failed. Their hour of victory has been earned.

Wrap-up details include implementing the recognition program, which may take months to conclude. If the campaign goal is a building, it must first be finished; dedication ceremonies, receptions, and the unveiling of plaques and donor walls can then be scheduled. Hard-hat tours during the final months of construction can retain donor interest and excite others. Pledge records are verified; billing is begun and pursued. Campaign statistics are verified; donor records and files are posted with activity reports and results; progress reports on the project are initiated and communicated to donors and volunteers. Unfinished solicitations of campaign donors can be concluded. "Normal" fund-raising operations can be resumed, with renewed attention to annual giving.

12. Overcoming Mistakes

Of course, not everything in the campaign will work as it should. Some volunteers will not see their prospects or will bring back gifts well below the donors' potential. Some groups will get behind schedule and delay those that follow and rely on their success. Deadlines will be missed and mistakes will be made. Murphy, that world-famous imp, appears all too often during any campaign to undo the best of plans. The highly successful campaign by Stanford University in the late 1980s, the first to set a goal of $1 billion, could have been derailed by a major earthquake that hit right in the middle of its drive. But Stanford revised its case, redefined its goals, and raised $1.1 billion in the end. Because unplanned and unforeseen events will occur, try to be prepared. It may help to remember that in 1991 plans for Desert Storm, perhaps the best operations strategy created since the invasion of France on D day in World War II, did not work exactly as anticipated every day, but victory was achieved by sticking to the

---

EXHIBIT 5.18 The Worst Mistakes in Capital Campaigns

Changing needs in the midst of the campaign.

Not asking for a gift.

Asking for too small a gift.

Poor campaign leadership.

Expecting the board to do more than it is capable of doing.

Using the wrong case.

Conducting a campaign without a study.

Having inexperienced development staff and/or professional counsel.

Using the wrong public relations message.

Not telling the story of the organization's achievements and potential for the
community.

Overlooking the organization's heritage, previous donors, and past
leadership.

Setting too low a goal.

Not knowing the membership or the potential for leadership and key gifts.

Wrong timing from one of two standpoints: either running into a
competitive campaign or not allowing enough time to conduct the
campaign.

Having a board that is not involved.

Concentrating only on corporations and foundations and not developing
affluent individuals as prospects.

Presenting needs in terms of the organization rather than in light of needs
and benefits to the community.

Reprinted with permission from "Capital Fund Appeals" by Charles E. Lawson, in The
Nonprofit Handbook: Fund Raising, *2nd ed., ed. James M. Greenfield (New York:
John Wiley & Sons, Inc., 1997), 459.*

plan and being flexible when necessary. Some issues cannot be avoided.
To help preserve sanity and perspective, review a list of the most common
mistakes to be avoided (see Exhibit 5.18).

Special Opportunities Unlocked by Campaigns

Capital campaigns serve many more purposes than just raising money.
They help an organization appreciate its ability to add revenue through
its investment in a viable fund-raising program. A campaign can improve
overall public image. Community awareness about an organization's current plans and progress will be heightened by the publicity resulting from

a capital campaign. Few other occasions for maximum visibility last over such an extended period of time. Several marketing and promotional additions can be "hooked" onto this campaign visibility and used to assist current operational objectives as well.

Several other fund development opportunities are unlocked by a capital campaign, as described in the following sections.

Leadership Gifts

The first major gift in the campaign, usually announced early, in the advance gifts phase, needs to be the biggest gift possible at that moment. Leadership gifts set an example, create attention, and raise everyone's sights. Most often, every gift that follows the lead gift will be below its sum. Smaller leadership gifts are needed in each segment of the campaign and can be used just as effectively with each audience being solicited.

Thoughtful Gifts

These are rare. They may come from a major gift prospect who asks how his or her gift can most effectively be used to stimulate others. Some committed donors will select a hard-to-sell or less-than-visible project on the list—the cost of mechanical equipment for a new building, for example. They commit their funds to this project because they feel it will not be attractive to other donors. Their example will encourage others.

Rare Gifts

A donor may choose to add a little mystery and intrigue by coming forward early with a gift but asking that it be announced as anonymous. Or, donors may ask if they can pay for enhancing features that are not included on the campaign list—extra landscaping, or art works to decorate the interior of the new building.

Creative Gifts

Some donors display an understanding of what the project will provide or how the campaign's goal will benefit the community by using their funds to extend the results of the finished product. For example, during a hospital campaign for a cancer center, a few donors may fund an endowment to pay for the care of indigent cancer patients.

Challenge Gifts

Competition can be a positive feature between groups—college reunion classes, employee departments, or foundation/corporation versus foundation/corporation. Many campaigns have success with a major donor's offer to "match" the gifts of others with an announced percentage, or dollar-for-dollar, or two-to-one, to encourage reaching certain goals as a group or increasing average gift size to qualify for the matching gift.

Anonymous Gifts

Some donors' giving style is to be unseen. They trust an organization's ability to keep their identity secret. For some donors, anonymity is necessary to avoid criticism from other institutions where they are also involved. Others may wish to prevent the abundance of follow-up solicitations that could come from other organizations if the donors' ability to make significant gifts became public.

Family Gifts

Family members may collaborate on a joint gift to honor one of their own. Their collective contribution may be more than might have been achieved if each family member had given independently. This opportunity should be proposed to families whose interest may match one of the organization's goals or who have a family member closely associated with the organization.

Leveraged Gifts

Some gifts influence another gift decision or series of gifts by a related individual, a group of people, or a corporation or foundation. One person or group may make a major gift and then solicit or challenge other persons or groups to match their total. Perhaps one entire project within the campaign goals list can be packaged as a special projects campaign and offered to a group of people as their fund-raising goal, with the option to name the area in honor of someone of their own choice.

Necessary Gifts

There are key people whose commitment is important in any campaign. These donors, known as "players," are usually quite visible, and their early gift decision sets the tone for the entire campaign. Examples might be the board chairperson whose personal gift illustrates to other board members the gift that is expected of them, or a well-known local philanthropist whose gift early in the campaign will influence others in the community to give. A "package" can be developed for board members that allows them one extra year to pay their pledge in order to increase their overall total and make their total giving look better.

Visible Gifts

Packaging the list of giving opportunities is something of an art because it requires making every piece of the campaign sound enticing and appear to be a naming opportunity. Only so many main entrances and lobbies can be sold and named. Pricing of the list is worth careful thinking. What amount is not too high (unrealistic) but not too low (underselling a good feature)? Pricing of gift opportunities for recognition purposes does not have to use the actual estimated cost, but the cost should be close to reality. The total of all items on the list should approximate or exceed the campaign goal. The figures can add to a higher sum than the goal because many of the projects are priced to be sold at half-price; the campaign recognition policy allows a donor to name an area if his or her gift is at least 50 percent of the cost. The recognition plan linked to major gifts should be prepared before the campaign begins so that everyone can see how and where their own recognition will be carried out.

The Gift Range Chart

Most capital campaigns draft a gift range chart, to illustrate how many gifts of various sizes will be required for success. The principle is quite simple: Campaigns must concentrate most of their energy on major gifts, not a multitude of minor ones. The chart, an effective tool in capital campaign design, follows a guideline called the "rule of thirds," which was never mathematically accurate although the concept is valid. The rule of thirds suggests that the top third of campaign gifts will come from a small number of people, the second third from a number ten times the first group, and the remaining third from everyone else (see Exhibit 5.19). No two gift range charts will be the same and none will be divided this neatly.[7] In fact, they will be alike only in illustrating the key principle: Secure the largest gifts first, and for good reason—everyone else is likely to give less. With two-thirds of the money coming from the smallest number of donors, concentration must remain on major gifts throughout the campaign. The firm of Brakeley, John Price Jones has used a guiding principle

---

[7]For more examples of gift range charts, see Lawson, "Capital Fund Appeals," 444–445 and 447.

EXHIBIT 5.19 The Gift Range Chart (the Rule of Thirds)

Campaign Goal: $9,000,000

Number of Gifts	Dollar Amount	Goal	Comments	
1	$1,000,000			
2	500,000	$3,000,000	Top 8 gifts	(0.5%)
5	200,000			
10	100,000			
20	50,000	$3,000,000	Next 70 gifts	(4.8%)
40	25,000			
60	15,000			
100	10,000			
125	5,000			
		$3,000,000	All other gifts (1,385)	
250	1,000			(94.7%)
350	500			
500	100			
Total 1,463		$9,000,000	1,463 gifts	(100%)

known as sequential solicitation, or "Top down; inside out." The biggest gift—10 percent of the campaign goal—should be secured first, then the next largest, and so on down the prospect list. To conduct a campaign from the inside out, commitments are secured from the "family" of board members, staff, and employees before going outside to the public for the rest of the money.

The Role of Research

Capital campaigns make the best use of research because of their intensity and their need for a volume of qualified prospects. Staff should report new prospects to volunteers for immediate attention. More prospects than you think you'll need should be identified, and Level I research (see Exhibit 5.20) should be conducted on all of them. Prospect research is both an art and a science. The art is in knowing how to do it today using electronic data sources. The science is in knowing how to use it to assist

EXHIBIT 5.20 Research Requirements

Level I

Basic data	Name, address, telephone, business name, address, telephone, date of birth
Contacts	Those in the organization who know and can talk to the prospect
Involvement	Affiliation (where this prospect is already involved)
Gift history	Last gift (date, amount, purpose); largest gift (date, amount, purpose); cumulative total gifts

Level II

	All of the above
Basic data	Spouse information; educational degrees, field; professional position, career; family and marital status; hobbies and outside interests; religion and politics
Contacts	Possible contact people; known interest areas within the organization
Involvement	Current for-profit board positions; current not-for-profit board positions; current voluntary positions; known major gifts to other organizations
Gift history	Detailed gift history; employer gift history
Rating and evaluation data	Estimated salary, annual income, bonus plan; estimated securities holdings and value; inherited wealth; other known assets and value; name of attorney, accountant, or other financial advisor; name of bank, investment broker

volunteers and staff in major gift cultivation and solicitation.[8] Research often is underutilized; information on qualified prospects must be kept current and accessible. Once a prospect is qualified or a prior donor is elevated to major gift status, additional research work (Level II) assists with preparation of the strategic action plan. After the campaign is over, those remaining prospects who were qualified but not solicited represent a pool available for continuation of the major gifts program.

---

[8]For a solid introduction to prospect research, see "Prospect Development—An Art" by Bobbi Strand in Greenfield, *The Nonprofit Handbook: Fund Raising*, 2d ed., 177–195.

Campaign Gift Reports

In reporting campaign results, organizations must be especially accurate and follow strict accounting procedures. Among other things, the organization must separate contributions made for other purposes from those restricted to campaign objectives; tally and track multiyear pledges and their collections; fix the value of in-kind and property contributions; factor in gross-to-net proceeds from benefit events; estimate cash flow to meet construction costs, distinguishing between contracts and contributions; and segregate planned gifts made for campaign endowment objectives whose receipt is in the future. All those tasks have to do with counting income, which is quite important because of the large sums involved over many years. Accounting for campaign costs is another subject that requires exacting attention to detail, but which remains a special problem area due to a lack of industry-wide accounting guidance. There is also the necessity to reconcile campaign finances with the not-for-profit organization's own financial statements. Together, these financial details represent accountability for campaign performance essential for public reports to donors and volunteers, board members and management, campaign staff, and other interested parties. These data are also used to forecast likely campaign outcomes and to compare with the results of the next campaign. Despite their importance, uniform campaign reporting procedures are not yet at hand. The best resource today is the *CASE Management Reporting Standards*, which are used by educational institutions and have gained wide acceptance at all levels of academia.[9]

The Role of Professional Consultants

Only the most experienced chief development officer (with more than one campaign under his or her belt) would risk not using professional consultants in an upcoming campaign. Consultanting firms bring to bear people with expertise based on multiple campaign experiences in a variety of settings and circumstances. A consulting firm should be invited to assist early, when the organization begins its long-range planning process, to conduct public opinion surveys to gauge the public's knowledge and per-

[9]Council for Advancement and Support of Education, *CASE Management Reporting Standards: Standards for Annual Giving and Campaigns in Educational Fund Raising* (Washington, DC: Council for Advancement and Support of Education, 1996).

ception of the organization. Consultants also can be put to work immediately in the development office evaluating current staffing and systems along with results, plus assessing strengths and weaknesses to determine readiness to begin and sustain a capital campaign. Prospect research can begin immediately, if the capability is present; if not, the firm can provide guidance on how to begin. Once the organization's future plans are resolved and details about the new programs, facilities, and equipment are available, including estimated costs, a precampaign development planning study, or feasibility study, on likely fund-raising priorities can be conducted by the consultant. This special market research tool is a detailed, objective analysis required as the first step in campaign preparation. Its purpose is to provide internal and external assessments that lead to accurate campaign plans for goal setting, leadership requirements, identification of major gift donors, and more (review Exhibit 5.16 for a list of the benefits of a feasibility study). The firm will prepare a draft of the proposed campaign "case statement" to describe the priority projects that need funding. The case statement, along with a questionnaire, will be used to test the likelihood of the public funding proposed campaign goals and objectives, and to test public perceptions of current programs and services, including opinions of existing fund-raising activities. The organization must help by identifying the individuals, corporations, and foundations, along with current donors (those most likely to be early major gift prospects) and volunteer, leaders, to be interviewed (between 40 and 60 names are usually required). All of this preliminary work must be directed by the senior development officer or, lacking someone with that experience, by the professional consultant.

Professional consultants are available to provide assistance in nearly every area of not-for-profit management and operations including all the fund-raising programs. "Among the most important decisions a not-for-profit makes", writes Henry Goldstein, "is whether to work with a fund-raising consultant." Goldstein cites the following reasons for an organization to employ a consulting firm or individual:

1. The nature of the fund-raising project is beyond the organization's experience. Example: A human services agency wants to expand into its own building and will have to raise $3 million in a capital campaign. No one on the board or staff has ever been involved in this type of campaign.
2. The staff is technically inexperienced or cannot undertake additional work. Example: One member of the development staff has conducted a capital campaign previously but feels her effort should be devoted to annual giving and government grants, which produce the bulk of the organization's annual income. She does not think it wise to be diverted from this top priority.

3. The feasibility and prospects of fund-raising success are uncertain or un-determined; an objective analysis is desired. Example: The board is not convinced a capital campaign can produce $3 million. Having never been involved in a capital campaign, the development committee feels an objective study of community attitudes, the case for philanthrophic support, likely campaign leadership, and potential major gifts should be undertaken to ascertain the prospects for success.
4. A specific fund-raising task is to be accomplished. Example: Having determined to run a capital campaign in-house, the development director has decided to use a consultant to prepare the case statement, train the solicitors, and provide strategic advice.[10]

Retaining of specialists or consultants for the campaign itself may be discussed during the feasibility study period and, although it is expected that the firm will recommend its services to assist the campaign, several options are available as to how these professionals can best be utilized. The decision as to whether or how to use consultants originates from the board of directors, development committee and the fund raiser. The decision depends on the campaign experience of the fund development office staff, who will be asked to add campaign duties to their present assignments. The options in using consultants are as follows:

- A consultant can serve as full-time campaign director, responsible for most of the day-to-day decisions and operational management.
- Personnel from the firm can be hired to serve as campaign staff reporting to the organization's own fund-raising professional, who retains the responsibility of campaign director.
- Consultants can be retained to advise directly how to conduct the campaign.

Outside firms should be retained for as long as they are able to assist in materially moving the campaign forward. Their greatest contributions are their early work to get the campaign off the ground and their single focus during the campaign; they are not distracted by management meetings or other administrative functions performed within the organization. When their services are over or their assistance is no longer needed, the agreement concludes and the contract is terminated. If this decision occurs prior to the campaign's completion, which is normal, the benefits of their training of volunteers and the momentum they have established will carry the campaign through to the end.

[10]Henry Goldstein, "Fund-Raising Consultants" in Greenfield, *The Nonprofit Handbook: Fund Raising*, 2d ed., 608–609.

Final Considerations

Capital campaigns remain among the most intensive, successful, and cost-effective methods to raise major gifts. Among the campaigns' benefits are the following:

- The organization will not be the same afterward; it will have grown and been enriched by the intensity required by the campaign.
- The campaign's success generates among team members a conviction that they can do it again.
- The campaign causes an increased awareness of the need for and value of continued attention to major gifts and gives volunteers experience in soliciting them.
- The campaign enhances the image of the organization in the community, especially in the eyes of all those who made gifts to the campaign.

Some organizations have adopted the practice of a continuous capital campaign as their fund-raising style, perhaps because of its ability to succeed with major gifts. Does any organization have the ability to find and continually recruit the additional numbers of qualified major gift prospects needed to match the intensity of a continuous capital campaign? The organization may be pressing its constituency too hard and building resistance rather than a willingness to support. Will organizations that rely almost exclusively on philanthropic dollars be able to meet their present and future needs? They should develop alternative sources of revenue. Endowment goals should be included wherever possible; their annual earnings will help to meet the demands of future annual requirements. Excessive demands lead to donor and volunteer burn-out, disenchantment, and resignation—all undesirable outcomes. Does the community have the capacity to support all not-for-profit organizations evenly? There may be merit to the practice of some rotation of campaigns, at least among leading local charitable institutions and agencies, to preserve the willingness of volunteers and donors to serve the needs of each in turn.

Nine-Point Performance Analysis of Capital Campaigns

Comparative analysis of capital campaigns, as is the case with all other fund-raising results, is difficult to perform. Campaigns are seldom enough alike in performance, even those conducted by the same organization, because so many conditions change between campaign periods.

Volunteer leaders and donors are not the same, nor is the external economic environment or the public's perception of priority projects to be funded. To further complicate matters, analysis must wait for the books to be closed, including pledge collections. Several campaign areas can, however, be evaluated for their relationship to other major gift programs and for future reference. For example, the performance of campaign leaders and volunteer workers is valuable to record, and an analysis of campaign systems will help improve future major gift efforts. More specific details, such as how the campaign start-up strategy performed, accuracy of market research and feasibility study reports, problems encountered and resolutions, and other incidents are worth study.

The results of three capital campaigns are shown in Exhibit 5.21 to illustrate a few performance characteristics. It is useful here to compare the results of several campaigns conducted by the same organization rather than pin too many conclusions on just one campaign although the caveat just mentioned about comparisons should be kept in mind. The capital campaigns shown in Exhibit 5.21 were conducted within 12 years by the same organization. The following observations are made:

1. The number of participants in each reveals how very dependent a capital campaign is on very large gifts. Campaign 2 needed many more donors to reach its goal because of smaller gifts, which increased costs, but involved more participants. By the time it conducted campaign 3, clearly a major step up, the organization had succeeded in overcoming

EXHIBIT 5.21 Nine-Point Performance Index Analysis of Capital Campaigns

	Campaign 1	Campaign 2	Campaign 3
Participation	1,422	6,075	11,829
Income	$880,000	$1,089,450	$23,450,000
Expenses	$107,550	$259,650	$1,875,750
Percent participation	59%	48%	77%
Average gift size	$619	$179	$1,982
Net income	$772,450	$829,800	$21,574,250
Average cost per gift	$76	$43	$159
Cost of fund raising	12%	24%	8%
Return	718%	320%	1,150%

Reprinted with permission from Fund-Raising Cost Effectiveness: A Self-Assessment Workbook *by James M. Greenfield (New York: John Wiley & Sons, Inc., 1996), 219.*

the public issues evident in campaign 2 and had developed widespread confidence and support.

2. Cost of fund raising for capital campaigns should be in the 10 to 20 percent range. Smaller goals are more likely to result in higher costs. Campaign 2 was the least effective because of lower participation and lower average gifts.

3. Percent participation provides insight into how important these constituents believed the priority projects were. To be successful with any major gift activity, the organization must have the confidence and trust of its community of constituents. Campaigns 1 and 3 enjoyed a 59 percent and 77 percent response respectively from those invited to participate. Campaign 3 needed a large volume of donors because of its high goal, but 11,829 gifts is indicative of strong community support for the organization as well as the campaign objectives.

4. Average cost per gift was highest for campaign 3 ($159) due to its 11,829 donors, but their average gift was $1,982. Campaigns should be major gift programs to be successful; number of participants is important but this is not a popularity contest. Stretch giving is essential, which campaign 2 lacked; because of its average gift of only $179 it required more than 6,000 gifts to reach $1 million. Campaign 1 raised $880,000 with an average gift of $619 at a cost of $76 per gift. Size of goal does not matter as much as average gift size.

5. All three campaigns may or may not have provided enough *net income* to fully fund their priority projects. Fund raisers must calculate campaign costs and include them as part of the campaign goal to be sure to deliver adequate net income to fully fund the project. Donors and volunteers will expect reasonable campaign costs but want to be certain their goal of enough money for the project will be delivered.

EXIT GIFTS: ESTATE PLANNING AND PLANNED GIVING

Exit gifts are gifts that can be made now with income retained by the donor and the asset transferred to a charity later or upon the death of the donor. Exit gifts are often major gifts because they are a portion of the accumulated assets of the donor, divided according to an estate plan. Exit gifts to not-for-profit organizations help to assure their future. They make maximum use of charitable deductions allowed by both federal and state tax law. They are the chief means to build an endowment; some studies have estimated that as much as 50 percent of the future contributions to not-for-profit organizations will come from gifts planned years before. Lastly, exit gifts are the most creative form of giving, a splendid means for donors to accomplish many of their aspirations and benefit their favorite not-for-profit organizations at the same time.

Estate planning has increased in popularity and understanding among the American public, perhaps as an effect of personal asset growth due to the 1990s bear market and a growing awareness of retirement planning. More people have been able to amass assets and therefore require estate planning. An aging population indirectly benefits not-for-profit organizations by requiring better planning to preserve lifelong assets and ensure financial security for the rest of their life. Both commercial and not-for-profit organizations have conducted marketing and communications efforts that actively recommend estate planning to their constituencies. Whatever the impetus, use of estate planning will continue to grow; significant benefit can be realized by not-for-profit organizations that engage in planned giving programs.

This trend has been matched with the development of a sizable amount of literature in the field. Although many of these resources are technical in nature, they can assist prospects, fund raisers, and volunteers in many ways. Attorneys, accountants, stock brokers, life insurance agents, bank trust officers, real estate agents, and certified (and uncertified) financial planners promote their services and hold frequent seminars and workshops to introduce the public to the many advantages of planning for the future. These same advisers have become involved in not-for-profit organizations' expansion of their development programs to include planned giving. Along with full-time employees trained in promoting and managing estate giving, they work directly with donors to make planned gifts. Despite all these efforts to assist the public, too much confusion and even mystery are associated with this form of giving; it still intimidates many people. Estate planning needs to be made simpler to understand. Isolated incidents of illicit or unscrupulous behavior in which the elderly were bilked of their life savings or were persuaded that planned gifts were "tax shelters" have not helped general response. Fund-raising professionals must proceed with great care to preserve these valuable gifts as creative options for donors, to benefit the long-term financial stability of not-for-profit organizations. Fund raisers, as Douglas E. White has noted, should also understand that planned giving is not a substitute for an organization's annual and capital giving programs: "Planned giving, like dessert, should be employed only as an addition. It can never replace the need for an annual giving program or currently needed capital gifts. Nor can the process of cultivation, a requisite for securing any large gift, current or deferred, be hastened beyond the limits of the relationship between prospect and charity."[11]

Most people have a fair knowledge of income tax law and their annual obligation to file tax returns but few know much at all about gift tax and estate tax law, which come to bear early in estate planning. These tax matters are always complicated, but donors must be made to understand the implications of failing to plan their estate. Most Americans are tax-paying citizens who appreciate their government's endorsement of legal tax avoidance through charitable contributions and their freedom to use it to their best advantage by planning their estate with their favorite not-for-profit organizations in mind.

The federal individual income tax is the largest single item in the budgets of many taxpayers. Minimizing the income tax burden is, therefore, a legitimate part of personal and family financial planning. Taxpayers should not make important financial decisions, including those dealing with significant charitable contributions, without considering their income tax consequences.[12]

Exit Gifts and Major Giving Programs

We have seen in this chapter that major gifts can and should be an active program carried out by not-for-profit organizations. We have seen that special project campaigns can be a means to focus attention on unique needs and to meet the specific objectives of a single donor or small group. We also have seen that capital campaigns rally everyone around a large group of funding objectives of highest priority to the organization. Such major gift situations offer opportunities for estate gifts and planned giving. The incentive to avoid capital gains tax by making a gift of an appreciated asset can be compelling; when matched with a favorite organization's request for support, the gift can become truly magnificent. Some donors' and prospects' present financial situation will not permit release of a major asset, or their asset will not be properly positioned to be useful in a gift transfer. For them, the option of a planned gift may be the best advice. One strategy of tax planning is to place deductions in the year they will yield the greatest tax benefit. Charitable contributions offer the best possible opportunity for such planning because they generally can be made at a time in life that best suits the

---

[11] Douglas E. White, *The Art of Planned Giving: Understanding Donors and the Culture of Giving* (New York: Wiley, 1995), 249.

[12] Arthur Anderson, *Tax Economics of Charitable Giving*, 12th ed (Chicago: Arthur Anderson, 1995), 1.

needs of the donor. Each donor who wishes to can then make a meaningful gift of great value and benefit to his or her favorite organization.

The methods to accomplish planned gifts are varied, as shown in Exhibit 5.22. Each method has its special features, benefits, and value to the donor and the recipient organization, and each has different "bottom-line" answers to the tax deduction and retained income questions. The great flexibility among these methods helps them to meet donors' individual financial needs, which vary because of their age, their dependents and heirs, and the amount required to meet their annual income needs. Planned gifts take the long view, but they must be decided now on the basis of how they can assist both the donor and the organization over time and continue gift support after the donor's death. They are permanent investment decisions.

Preparations to initiate a planned giving program should be done with the understanding that, once begun, it does not end. Organizations that make life-income agreements are obligated by contract to continue each gift form for the life of the donor and to use the funds received at maturity as the donor directed. Starting a planned giving program also requires that a portion of the fund development budget be invested without the expectation of immediate returns. Here is one expert's list of items necessary to initiate a new planned giving program (marketing the program has its own considerations, and a list of suggested marketing activities is given in Exhibit 5.23):

1. A definition of a deferred gift as it applies to the institution
2. The rationale for establishing the program
3. An explanation of the various forms of deferred gifts that will be acceptable to the institution (for example, the decision whether or not to established a pooled-income fund should be a board, not a business office decision)
4. Suggested drafts of deferred-gift forms to be used by the institution
5. Recommendations on investment procedures, including objectives for funds, fiduciary responsibilities, and so on
6. A suggested statement of policy governing the institution's program, including advertising, conflicts of interest, staff solicitation, and protection of donors and the institution
7. A list of recommended institutional representatives authorized to negotiate deferred gifts (I suggest the chief executive officer and the senior development officer)
8. A request for permission to establish a deferred-gifts advisory committee, and a list of suggested members
9. A suggested legal counsel to be retained by the institution[13]

---

[13]Thomas E. Broce, *Fund Raising: The Guide to Raising Money from Private Sources*, 2d ed. (Norman, OK: University of Oklahoma Press, 1986), 168–169.

EXHIBIT 5.22 Methods Available to Make Estate and Planned Gifts

Gifts by Will or Living Trust	Simple language will add a charity to a will or living trust for a dollar amount or percentage of an estate. The value of the gift at death is deductible from estate taxes.
Pooled Income Funds	In this charitable "mutual fund," a donor makes a gift of cash or appreciated property and joins a trust "pool" with other donors; annual income is received based on units of participation determined at the time of the gift. Gift deduction is for the present value of the future gift. Income is subject to income tax.
Charitable Remainder Trust	A donor transfers cash or appreciated property in trust and receives annual income based on trust assets as revalued annually. A minimum payout of 5 percent is required. The gift deduction is equal to the present value of remainder interest. Income is taxable.
Charitable Remainder Annuity Trust	A donor transfers cash or appreciated property in trust and receives fixed annual income based on the fair market value of the assets placed in trust (minimum of 5 percent). The donor's deduction is equal to the present value of the remainder interest. Income is taxable.
Charitable Gift Annuity	A donor transfers cash or appreciated property in exchange for an annuity. The donor's deduction is equal to the excess of value of contribution over value of annuity. Life-income payments consist of tax-free, ordinary, and capital gain income, depending on the nature of the asset given. Annuity payout rate is related to number of annuitants, ages, and starting date for payments.
Charitable Lead Trust	A donor creates a trust funded with cash or securities. A fixed annuity amount, a unitrust percentage or all of the trust income, goes to the charity for a term of years (usually 10) after which the original gift returns to the donor or passes to another person when the term expires. There is no charitable deduction, but the trust allows the grantor to pass assets to heirs with gift and estate tax benefits and a onetime generation-skipping tax benefit.

(continued)

EXHIBIT 5.22 (continued)

Life Estate Agreement	A donor transfers ownership of a residence to a charity and retains the right to occupy the property for life. Usually the donor continues to maintain the property and pays taxes. Donor's deduction is fair market value of interest transferred. Upon the donor's demise or gift of the retained interest, the charity may take possession and hold the property or sell it for cash.
Life Insurance	A donor transfers ownership of an existing policy designating a charity as the beneficiary. A limited reserve value and subsequent premium payments are deductible. Or, a donor transfers a fully paid-up policy designating a charity as the beneficiary. The donor takes a tax deduction for the cash surrender value of the policy. The charity can cash out the policy or hold it to receive full death benefits. If a new policy is donated to charity there is no deduction for the donor, but future premiums are deductible.

This text addresses the management of fund raising rather than how to raise funds. Tax laws and regulations change frequently, which quickly outdates any attempt to explain planned giving with accuracy. Several areas of management that are useful to the design of an exit gifts program are described here.

Role of the Board

For planned giving to succeed the board must understand at the outset what an estate planning program entails and what its own obligations will be. In general, the program will need policy guidelines on each planned giving technique to be offered, a technical advisory committee, professional staff and budget, expert consultants, competent investment management and administrative services, a marketing plan, donor recognition, and more, as explained in the sections that follow. "The board," write Linda Moerschbaecher and Erik Dryburgh, "has to be willing to participate in several policy decisions, among them a policy regarding the confidentiality of donor information, a decision to accept the fiduciary role that planned giving requires (not trusteeship), a policy concerning ethics in planned giving, policies and procedures for the acceptance of

EXHIBIT 5.23 Elements of a Planned Giving Marketing Plan

1. Understanding who the organization is in relation to the marketplace. This involves demographic and psychographic studies of the potential donor base, to determine what groups of people might realistically give to the planned giving program. Not every organization is willing to pay the cost of such a study, but those who have taken the extra step have found the study to be invaluable both for delivery of services and for fund raising.
2. Segmenting the marketplace into target markets based on identities of wants and needs of the potential donors in each of the market segments.
3. Designing planned gift strategies that may be appealing to each target market and that meet the perceived wants and needs of that target market.
4. Checking similarly situated organizations to see what the competition is doing and what outreach programs they are planning that may overlap or conflict.
5. Developing effective outreach efforts based on the market studies done in accordance with the preceding steps. These will no doubt include donor and professional seminars, bequest mailings, newsletters, advertisements (perhaps), and other means of reaching people who may be willing to commit to the planned giving program.
6. Creating effective private communications, once an individual prospect is identified.

Reprinted with permission from Linda S. Moerschbaecher and Erik D. Dryburgh, "Planned Giving: Gift Vehicles," in James M. Greenfield, The Nonprofit Handbook: Fund Raising, *2d ed. (New York: John Wiley & Sons, Inc., 1997), 493.*

real estate in light of environmental liability, and others as they come up in the administration of the program."[14]

Policy and Procedure

The organization's board of directors must understand its obligations and those of the organization when they accept any planned gifts. A written policy and procedure is necessary, to explain what is being offered and to describe any specific features (types of planned gift offered, minimum gift amount, range for percentage payout, assignment as trustee,

[14]Linda S. Moerschbaecher and Erik D. Dryburgh, "Planned Giving: Gift Vehicles" in Greenfield, *The Nonprofit Handbook: Fund Raising*, 2d ed., 483.

service of annual tax reports, and more). The policy and procedure document should explain what types of planned gifts the organization will entertain and all procedures for preparation and review (see Section K, Appendix A). The guidelines should be shared with professionals who support clients with these potential interests.

Planned Giving Committee and Endowment Council

The cultivation and solicitation of planned gifts, just as any other fund development program offered by an organization, require a committee of trained volunteers and identification of prospects. This committee requires members whose professional areas of expertise include estate planning. Their roles are to define policy and procedure and to supervise the application of the program through the endowment council, which is managed by the planned giving officer or other fund development professional. They also provide technical support and professional consultation when donors and their advisers need assistance in making a planned gift. The committee should select and appoint the members of the endowment council, who act as the "arms and legs" of the program. Endowment council members can actively promote and market the various estate-planning opportunities to their clients and can take turns with the planned giving officer in conducting seminars and workshops for donors and prospects.

Professional Staff

Like other programs to raise funds, the program to recruit planned gifts requires a well-trained staff for leadership and direction. Several areas serve as appropriate background experience for this work: legal or paralegal training, accounting, trust management, life insurance, real estate, or financial planning. Some experience with fund development is also recommended because this work is designed to raise funds, not to engage in commercial sales.

Investment Management

Once the program is begun, the organization must accept full responsibility for fiduciary stewardship of all funds received. This serious obligation requires expert help and will incur management costs. Employees in the business office can provide many of the services required, including federal and state annual tax reports, but most not-for-profit organizations elect to retain the professional services of qualified trust managers. "[T]he trust management (agreement maintenance) function . . . is the key to financial success."[15] Supervision of trust performance is a duty of the board of directors usually in concert with the finance committee or the investment management committee. One of those committees sets guidelines for performance, evaluates investment decisions and outcomes, selects professional managers, negotiates fees for services, and acts as fiduciary for funds held in the name of the donor for the life of the agreement.

Marketing and Communications

Planned giving is, by definition, a complex and technical subject and not easy for donors and volunteers to understand. Fund raisers should use brochures to help them describe each vehicle of giving, to illustrate how each can serve the donor's and organization's interests, and to address income and estate tax consequences. Not an easy task. But a systematic approach is helpful: "Continuity, repetition, and perseverance are key qualities. Planned giving materials must appear continually over a long period to educate donors and prospects. Each marketing piece, whether a newsletter, advertisement, or other publication, should be produced in a consistent style and placed in approximately the same location in a publication each time it appears. Remember that planned gifts do not usually close immediately, and it is the cumulative impact of marketing over time, along with follow-up, that results in a donor making a planned gift."[16]

Records and Files

Complete documentation is required to support each donor's gift. These data are sensitive and should be placed in safe deposit boxes or locked file cabinets; access should be reserved to planned giving staff and financial officers. Donor records will include documents that verify the value of the assets transferred, original agreements and contracts, management reports, tax returns, accounting reports, annual audits, and similar evidence. Planned gifts take time to prepare and correspondence files should record details on progress, updates on the status of negotiations, document drafts, and minutes of discussions and meetings. On occasion, family members, partners, or other not-for-profit organizations may challenge these gift decisions, claiming that they have been promised a por-

[15]Norman S. Fink and Harold C. Metzler, *The Costs and Benefits of Deferred Giving* (New York: Columbia University Press, 1982), 88.

[16]Ronald R. Jordan and Katelyn L. Quynn, "Planned Giving: Management and Marketing," in Greenfield, *The Nonprofit Handbook: Fund Raising,* 2d ed., 510.

tion of the estate. Complete records will protect the donors original intentions and preserve the gift. A record of discussions about the use of the funds when they become the property of the not-for-profit organization will ensure that any restrictions are known in advance. If the official documents do not specify any restrictions, the organization will rely on discussion notes to verify any wishes it may be obligated to observe.

Budgets for Planned Giving

Given the nature of the deferred methods involved, investing budget in advance of any returns should be considered. The cost-benefit ratio is excellent because major assets are involved,[17] although patience is needed to allow these important gifts to mature. Some organizations have decided against a planned giving program because their financial analysts have suggested they would have too long a wait to get their money back. Such short-term thinking does not reflect an adequate understanding of the concepts of asset development (endowment) or of estate and planned giving programs.

Donor Recognition

Planned gifts donors are fully entitled to the recognition offered to cash donors. As appropriate acknowledgment of their irrevocable gift, rights and privileges in a donor club or recognition society based on size of gift, net present value, or cumulative giving total should be awarded. Enjoyment of the same benefits as all other donors will help stimulate planned giving donors' decision to give. A separate "Heritage Club" can be designed for donors who use estate planning and planned giving methods, to treat these donors in a manner that reflects how much their gift decision is valued and appreciated. Exit gifts are more than worth the special attention.

Nine-Point Performance Analysis of Planned Giving

To begin with, measuring performance in planned giving is complicated by several factors. First, funds spent in one year may not result in a gift

---

[17] Ibid., 54. The study of the cost-benefit performance of planned giving programs at Pomona College after 40 years concludes that "20% to 30% is a reasonable estimate of the annual internal rate of return for the Pomona Plan without including bequests." This rate of return is convincing as a more profitable investment than benefit events (50 percent net proceeds) and direct mail acquisition ($1.25 to $1.50 per $1.00 return).

decision until the next year or even years later. Second, continued communications with the donor will require time and some expense. Third, the value of a new planned gift, when executed, cannot be reported as revenue by the not-for-profit organization until the gift matures at the death of the donor. Fourth, there are three values to establish: fair market value, charitable contribution deduction value, and an estimate of net present value at the point of maturity. And fifth, the actual monetary value upon eventual receipt (which may not occur for another 10 or 20 years) may be quite different than any of these figures because of the unpredictable performance of the investment.

How does an organization determine the success of its planned giving program? By counting the number of executed irrevocable gifts, calculating the gifts' fair market value, tallying the number of gifts in progress, estimating bequest income from confirmed expectancies, noting how many donors attend workshops and seminars, measuring mail responses, and more—all of which represent time and money spent in support of planned giving. Calculations of expenses should take into consideration that the costs to recruit and manage a few donors who choose charitable trusts will appear more efficient and profitable than the costs of recruiting numbers of donors who choose to join the pooled income fund or execute gift annuities, because the gift sizes will be markedly different. Gift reports should contain three separate accounting summaries: (1) bequests received and the value of planned gifts at maturity, (2) fair market value and net present value of irrevocable planned gifts in force for which the organization is trustee, and (3) the same two values for irrevocable planned gifts for which the organization is not trustee. Other details of value that may be included are the type of planned gift, initial contribution value, date executed, age of the donor, percentage payout, and income distribution schedule.

A three-year summary of a new planned giving program is shown in Exhibit 5.24. The nine-point performance analysis illustrates a high level of productivity and profitability, based on the following interpretations:

1. The number of bequests received, while always unpredictable, has been steady. Bequest income, equally unpredictable, illustrates how a single large bequest in year 2 can distort that year's results. A casual reader might think that something was wrong the following year because it appears that "bequests are off!"

2. The main effort in this program is clearly directed toward the preparation and completion of new irrevocable planned gifts—the correct course of action. A full-service planned giving program will offer

EXHIBIT 5.24 Nine-Point Performance Index Analysis of a Planned Giving

	Year 1	Year 2	Year 3	Total
Bequests received	8	9	12	29
Bequest income received	$55,000	$870,000	$39,500	$964,500
New planned gifts written (irrevocable)	5	13	9	27
Value of new irrevocable planned gifts written	$110,000	$425,000	$375,000	$910,000
Total number of gifts	13	22	21	56
Total value of gifts	$165,000	$1,295,000	$414,500	$1,874,500
Expenses	$129,550	$165,000	$142,250	$436,800
Percent participation	38%	61%	42%	47%
Average gift size	$12,692	$58,864	$19,738	$33,473
Net income	$35,450	$1,130,000	$272,250	$1,437,700
Average cost per gift	$9,965	$7,500	$6,774	$7,800
Cost of fund raising	79%	13%	34%	23%
Return	27%	685%	191%	329%

Reprinted with permission from Fund-Raising Cost Effectiveness: A Self-Assessment Workbook *by James M. Greenfield (New York: John Wiley & Sons, Inc., 1996), 239.*

several vehicles or instruments including pooled funds, gift annuities, and life insurance along with the array of more complex charitable remainder trusts.

3. Ten percent of expenses for a planned giving program often are spent on processing bequests and 90 percent to develop new gifts. This budget increased each year, reflecting an increase in activity related to staff time and expense plus the accounting, appraisal, investment, legal, and brokerage fees required to execute and manage new planned gifts.

4. The average gift appears to require almost $8,000 to procure. However, the gifts themselves have an average value of $33,473, so the cost of fund raising at 23 percent is reasonable and likely to decrease as the number of new planned gifts continues to grow.

5. The conclusion to be drawn from this illustration is twofold. First, $964,500 in bequest income has been received. These valuable gifts should be set aside as endowment if possible; they will never occur again. Second, irrevocable future gifts with an estimated fair market (present-day) value of $910,000 have been completed. If added to endowment

when they mature, nearly $2 million in present and future assets have been secured in just three years of planned giving operations.

6. This new planned giving program is well launched and should expect continued success. Continued marketing and communications are necessary to stimulate new inquiries leading to new estate-planning sessions with donors. Testimonials from the new donors can be added to the marketing strategy. The organization's newsletters and brochures can feature their stories about why they made their gifts, the peace of mind it has given them, and the future value they have delivered to their favorite not-for-profit organization.

DONOR RECOGNITION: THE ENHANCED VERSION

Donor recognition is the start of a long-lasting relationship between donors and the organizations in which they invest. "[D]onor recognition should be thought of not as the end of the fund-raising process, but as the *beginning*: donor recognition should be treated as the preamble, not the postmortem. Done well, and done often, it should be the *beginning* of the next ask."[18] Recognition should be discussed with donors as a part of each master gift plan, each capital campaign decision, each planned gift negotiation. Make it stand out for donors early, whether or not they seek it, because it conveys the organization's honest appreciation for every major gift decision.

"Names that live forever" may be the strongest form of donor recognition possible. Perpetuity has a magnetism all its own. An organization can offer its most generous donors various forms and options, but they should be reserved for a required size of gift. If similar opportunities are offered for low levels of giving, the impact for major donors is lost. Buildings, wings, walkways, special-purpose areas, gardens, endowment funds, and commemorative named funds have the appearance, if not the ability, to live on after the donors are deceased. They should be saved for the best donors.

As in other human relationships, the thought—in this case, how the organization responds to a donor for a major gift decision—counts the most. Truly personal thank-you letters that come from the highest officers in the organization are a good first step, especially if these executives have been directly involved in the solicitation. Benefits and privileges ac-

---

[18]Lawson, "Capital Fund Appeals," 465.

corded to donors are opportunities for personal contact; they should not be impersonal mailings, invitations, or hardware. If the donor relations program includes small gifts as tokens of appreciation, these should be personally delivered—and not always by paid fund-raising staff.

Dedications can be suggested for any major gift even when no building or room is involved. A ceremony to initiate a new endowment fund can feature announcements about the first beneficiaries. Colleges and universities and symphony orchestras are especially good at bringing together donors of endowment funds and the recipient. Dedications are social affairs that permit donors to invite their friends and colleagues to join in celebrating their munificence. Much thought should be given to the how, when, and where of staging recognition events, because they are an opportunity for donor interaction. Bands playing and crowds cheering might not be possible every time, but the party should be made a fun experience for everyone. Other donors watching how the situation is handled will judge how they might be treated if they were to make such a gift someday. Small touches, like having a photographer present to create an album that is presented to the donor later as a keepsake, will have special meaning to donors. A small replica of the plaque or portrait hung at the site of the named facility should be given to the donor to take home.

Some dedication ceremonies approach press conference status, which may in fact be justified by the significance of the gift. However, media attention is not always welcomed by the very wealthy, who may prefer less conspicuous recognition. They will not usually resist release of the information to the press or use of it in the organization's own publications, especially if a draft is shown to them in advance and if it portrays them as exemplary for other donors.

What is the proper level of enthusiasm and good taste for each donor's major gift recognition plan? Some people expect more than is reasonable. Some donors hold up their gift decision until the level of recognition offered meets their expectations. Each situation must be resolved as fairly as possible, and always with an eye to precedent. The appropriate forms of recognition for substantial gifts should be described in the organization's written policy on honors and recognition (see Section J in Appendix A). The fund development office should follow the six basic guidelines shown in Exhibit 5.25 to create organizational policy for recognition of gifts to the major and planned gifts programs.

Extensive "wooing" precedes major gift decisions. Donors who enjoyed all this attention during their gift giving will miss it immediately when the organization turns its attention to other potential donors. The best design is a management plan for senior donors, a plan that is per-

EXHIBIT 5.25 Criteria for Donor Recognition

- *Gift acknowledgments.* Describe the kinds of letters to be sent, who signs, and whether or not the letter should be handwritten or computer generated.
- *Memorial giving program.* Describe the kinds of acknowledgments and memorial cards and incorporate a message of sympathy from the institution. If applicable, describe the use of plaques or whatever is appropriate for a "memorial" area of the organization.
- *Donor recognition.* Describe policies for named gifts, gifts of buildings or floors, levels of giving, and gift opportunities for equipment or special programs.
- *Recognition wall design.* Describe wall displays and/or donor recognition areas within the facility. Incorporate photographs indicating levels of giving and recognition.
- *Giving clubs.* Describe the various kinds of giving clubs—accumulative, annual, or planned gift programs. Incorporate gift amounts, benefits, and the case for each giving club.
- *What constitutes a gift.* Describe what the organization deems to be a recognition gift: gifts of cash, gifts-in-kind, life insurance, other nonrevocable planned gifts, bequests, and pledges.

Reprinted from "Donor Recognition and Relations" by Jerry A. Linzy, in The Nonprofit Handbook: Fund Raising, *2d ed., ed. James M. Greenfield (New York: John Wiley & Sons, Inc., 1997), 619.*

sonalized, planned from the gift decision, budgeted, tracked, evaluated, scheduled six months ahead, and open-ended for what else can be done.

Major gifts represent the culmination of the entire fund development program. They allow donors to reach the top of an organization's pyramid through the use of their master gift plan. Their value to the organization is greater than the money involved, especially if the gifts are endowments. Their example is infectious. They command the attention of top leadership and often identify candidates for future leadership. No other fund development program can deliver equal value to an organization.

6 ▼ Management of the Fund Development Process

This final chapter reviews several of the factors inside and outside not-for-profit organizations that can affect how fund development is managed. Not-for-profit organizations have a huge thirst for fuel as did the vegetable garden and fruit trees cited in earlier chapters. Their fuel is *money.* Money in multiple forms, as government grants or reimbursement payments, investment earnings and loans, an excess of income over expenses in the budget, and contributions of all kinds. By priority, these funds are committed to programs and services, which limits budget money for fund raising, despite its profitability. Fund raising is not in the same business as the rest of the organization.

Fund raising should be looked upon as an investment strategy with the expectation of a high rate of return. Three factors are critical to managing a fund-raising program for a profit: (1) complete your organization's long-range planning process so its mission and vision are current and its need for funds are fully documented; (2) analyze the internal and external factors that influence fund-raising success (see "The Fund-Raising Environmental Audit" in Chapter 2, pages 63–76; and (3) get to know your fund-raising professionals and support staff, their strengths and weaknesses, their experience and knowledge, their space and systems, and support them.

Fund-raising professionals are embarked (or should be) on a career path that leads to personal competence, service, and leadership of their organizations. They cannot achieve these goals alone and few outside the profession understand how to evaluate their success. There is much more to fund raising than asking for money. The entire effort must operate at a high level of efficiency because so many features are in action at the same time—planning and preparing, perception and positioning, promoting and petitioning. The fund-raising professional must give his or her time and attention to volunteers and donors, board members and other management staff, professional and support staff, gift acknowledgment and donor records, and the daily challenge of running an office trying to satisfy a variety of people's needs, wants, and desires. All these operations must be well managed and run smoothly throughout the year. Add to these basic but essential requirements the expectation of increased net proceeds at a low cost-to-benefit ratio and accurate accounting and audit trail procedures—always with a smile for everyone. All the above is ample measurable evidence of a fund raiser's performance.

Special issues arise when fund development staff are assigned additional, related duties, such as marketing, public information, publications, and more. These are distinct functions, each requiring its own skills and coming with daily demands for the fund raiser's instant attention and response. The staff must be flexible and design its programs to meet current and future needs according to the organization's annual, capital, and endowment priorities. Some fund-raising departments are set up as subsidiary operations, either in a centralized or decentralized style. Others administer semiautonomous related organizations such as guilds or support groups, or direct the entire program through a separately incorporated foundation. Fund-raising departments face both legislative and administrative changes, such as new tax laws, and accounting standards that affect day-to-day operations and increase reporting and audit requirements, not to mention the time required to educate the public about their ramifications.

Boards of directors and professional staff must be alert to these problems and changes and understand how they affect routine operations and future plans. Long-range planning, marketing, market and prospect research, and other support areas are growing in importance and expertise; improved methods of performance evaluation and productivity analysis, including cost-effectiveness, are being requested. Staff professionals are being asked more often by volunteers to perform direct solicitations, which places them in conflict with traditional volunteer roles and weakens volunteer commitment, especially when major gifts are involved. Government at all levels is adding legislative and regulatory requirements to fund-raising practice and is persistently whittling away at the four legs holding up the table of tax exemption. Acquisitions, mergers, and corporate restructuring present unique problems. How can donor commitment be preserved when locally recognizable organizations now have new names and owners? Not-for-profit organizations are facing challenges that have the capacity to change present practices, to hinder performance, and to reduce the amount of money raised.

Fund raising is first and last about raising friends and building relationships; friends need to be kept well informed about changes to "their" organization. Everyone involved must have a high degree of confidence and trust in the organization and its programs and services, including its fund-raising practices. Donors and volunteers as well as prospects and suspects are *the most* essential factor for the present welfare and future success of the organization; they deserve a continued investment in the form of attention, respect, recognition, and reward for their commitment and generosity. Preservation and enhancement of this relationship between not-for-profit organizations and their constituents is the duty of the fund-raising professional. This responsibility cannot be carried out by any fund raiser alone; the commitment and support of those within the organization whose duty is to fulfill its mission must also be present and include some appreciation for the difficulty of this assignment. "The men and women who have been charged with the responsibility of managing the advancement function in nonprofit, public service organizations and institutions have good reason to take pride in what they do. Theirs is the critical task of ensuring that their organizations develop, with their publics, the psychic and financial support necessary to ensure that those organizations are able to accomplish their several missions. To a remarkable degree they are accomplishing that task."[1]

WHY DO PEOPLE BECOME FUND RAISERS?

> The development officer, as the pivotal person in the total development process, is primarily a teacher and a manager; thus, she or he is a leader, a planner, an advocate for the cause, a communicator, a negotiator, an analyst, a cheerleader, an activist, a boundary spanner, and a bouncer of multiple balls to keep the fund raising action synchronized, spirited, and moving forward. This person is the staff professional whose job it is to manage all aspects of the ongoing fund raising program.[2]
>
> HENRY A. ROSSO

---

[1] Duane L. Day, *The Effective Advancement Professional: Management Principles and Practices* (Gaithersburg, MD: Aspen Publishers, 1998), 1.

[2] Henry A. Rosso, *Rosso on Fund Raising: Lessons from a Master's Lifetime Experience* (San Francisco: Jossey-Bass, 1996), 37–38.

Many fund development professionals began their career by backing into this field. Degree programs in the specialty are only now being defined; a few graduate courses in not-for-profit management are available in schools of business education, or the social sciences. Why do professionals work in a field that has so little public acceptance?

Service

Fund raising is the business of enabling a charitable cause to help others, many of whom are living in substandard circumstances. The hungry and the poor, the homeless and the hurt, the curable and the incurable, the indigent and the illiterate, the uneducated, unwashed, and unaware—all these are fund raising's clients. Money is raised from those who can spare it to help address basic human needs, to improve the quality of life, to even out the differences, or to permit access to improvements of the mind and a lifting of the spirit. Fund raising is also helping donors to realize their aspirations by doing something worthwhile and praiseworthy with their money. Fund raisers are advocates of charity who actively encourage donors and volunteers to give something of themselves—time, talent, or treasure—to benefit others. Their rewards are "warm feelings" about the experience, and they are likely to provide help for good works again. Fund-raisers' rewards are knowing that they played a part in donors' satisfaction and that their work enables funds to be channeled into useful and beneficial purposes. The job does not stop there. Every fund raiser should aspire to two additional objectives, described by Paul Pribbenow as follows: "(1) the need for all who are involved in philanthropic fund raising to seize the crucial role as teachers whose chief aim is to 'form' professionals as persons who are reflective, responsible, skilled, and imaginative practitioners; and (2) our obligation as teachers and rhetors to position all professional work in the service of the public good; indeed, we have the responsibility to 'form' professionals to be public servants, to be accountable to the needs, the goods, the processes that define a genuine and healthy participative democracy."[3]

---

[3]Paul Pribbenow, "And We Will Teach Them How: Professional Formation and Public Accountability," in *Critical Issues in Fund Raising*, ed. Dwight F. Burlingame (New York Wiley, 1997), 4.

Walking a Fine Line

Matching the desires of donors and volunteers with the needs of not-for-profit organization is an art. The science is in matching an organization's priorities with the needs of donors and volunteers. Both require thought, planning, management, judgment, and time. Without exhortation or preaching, fund raisers must motivate and inspire. If people respond positively, it is because they believe their time will be well spent and the plan will be successful, or because they cannot turn down the leaders who ask them to help. In years past, anonymity was considered the proper form of conduct for fund development officers. Today's professionals are more directly involved both in solicitation and in leadership, but they must pass the glory on to others so that they will remain motivated and continue to participate. All of these qualities require no small amount of skill and tact.

Satisfaction

Creativity has its own reward; seeing ideas and plans come to life is fulfilling. Fund-raising goals change from year to year, but the basic plan for fund development remains—providing a return on investments for an organization long after its original dollars were spent on implementation. Satisfaction also comes from being part of an institution when it initiates an important new program or adds a service that benefits the people in the community. "There is something about fund raising that never loses its hold on fund raisers," writes Maurice G. Gurin, "I think that's because it gives them a sense of satisfaction, of accomplishment in a worthwhile cause. I experience that satisfaction today when I pass a museum or school that was built through a campaign I counseled, or when I read about a program or service that I had some hand in making possible."[4]

PLANNING A CAREER BY CHANGING JOBS

Is the nomadic lifestyle of fund development people a weakness inherent in the profession? Employers worry about how long the person hired today will remain and how soon they will have to recruit another replace-

---

[4]Maurice G. Gurin, *Confessions of a Fund Raiser: Lessons of an Instructive Career* (Washington, DC: Taft Group, 1985), 93.

ment. A few well-traveled people who appear to begin their next job search the day after arrival reinforce this image. Employees are not entirely to blame, however. Organizations and their volunteer boards have high expectations, sometimes too high for the individual charged with meeting them, or fail to support an effort themselves, or are impatient with the time required for results. "Conventional wisdom maintains that long tenure and continuity of staff is a major factor in long-term fundraising success, a corollary of the premise that long-term fund-raising success is a developmental process built on long-term relationships."[5] The reality, however, is that job changes are a necessity for most professionals, in order to achieve personal growth and career enhancement. Competence comes from varying experiences in different settings and at progressively higher levels of responsibility. The methods used in fund development do not perform the same everywhere. Employers may not relish recruiting, but each change can be an opportunity to move their fund development program into new areas and to realize higher efficiency through the competencies and prior experiences of the next employee hired. Fund development is an experience-driven model that benefits employers and employees equally. Employees can exploit all they have learned and apply it fully in their new setting, thereby enriching the next employer organization.

The skills refined through on-the-job training declare immediate dividends. Every organization profits from the experiences gained by present and future employees, and the growth of fund development professionals results from employers' investments in staff training, a common contribution of all not-for-profit organizations.

Although still a reasonably new career field, fund raising has achieved significant growth if measured by the National Society of Fund Raising Executives (NSFRE) membership, with its 150 chapters and 20,000 members. Who are these people and what is their profile? "The typical respondent to the 1995 career survey is a 45-year-old who entered the fundraising field at age 32, has 17+ years of education, has held two jobs in fund raising, and has an annual salary of $46,100. The trend toward an increasing ratio of females to males in the field continues, as does the trend toward a younger age of entry to the field. Although the number of females in higher salary ranges (greater than $50,000) is increasing, women continue to earn less than men overall. Fund raisers who work for hospital and medical centers earn the highest salaries, followed by fund raisers

[5]Margaret A. Duronio and Eugene R. Tempel, *Fund Raisers: Their Careers, Stories, Concerns, and Accomplishments* (San Francisco: Jossey-Bass, 1997), 58.

who work for universities and consulting firms. Overall, fund raisers express a strong level of satisfaction with their careers."[6]

The Career Ladder: Climbing to Competency

Fund development's status as a profession may be of limited concern to most people working in the field. Their career's progress is being defined, refined, and expanded daily. Each step they take up the career ladder demands more competence and expertise. Specialization in a single fundraising method—annual giving, grantsmanship, benefit events, capital campaigns, or planned giving—is one career option. Specialists can progress to a comprehensive knowledge of several select methods over the years; their extensive experience in various settings may lead them to choose consultancy. Another option is to stay with the same type of organization, although with different employers—a college, hospital, or arts organization; a nationally recognized charity such as United Way, American Cancer Society or American Heart Association, YMCA or YWCA, Girl Scouts or Boy Scouts of America. Higher levels of responsibility can be achieved within the same organization, perhaps in several of its locations. Other fund raisers aspire to a combination of experiences, an overall competency as generalists. These people are of great value to any employer because they have prepared well to manage nearly every program. The final option is to remain with the same employer for an entire career, gaining in-depth experience from that organization's breadth of fund development programs and growing with the involvement and participation of volunteers and donors who progress to higher positions of responsibility within the organization. All these options are equally valuable for gaining the experience necessary for professional competency. Fund raising is not yet a full profession. "In particular," writes Kathleen Kelly, "fund raising lacks a theoretical body of knowledge and a program of formal education."[7] That day may come. In the meantime, aspiring fund raising professionals can use the following seven-step guide to grow themselves into much needed, competent practitioners: "*first*, by self-evaluation of personal traits, talents and skills required; *second*, by step-by-step growth in the process of applied experience; *third*, by careful observation and listening to policies, procedures, practice and results;

[6]George J. Mongon, Jr., "Profile," in *National Society of Fund Raising Executives Membership Survey* (Alexandria, VA: NSFRE, 1995), 17.

[7]Kathleen S. Kelly, *Effective Fund-Raising Management* (Mahwah, NJ: Lawrence Erlbaum Associates, 1998), 103.

fourth, by personal interpretation of those observations; *fifth,* by observing others in their implementation of related functions at peer and competing institutions; *sixth,* by becoming students dedicated to developing the art of the advancement process; and *seventh,* by becoming students of the philosophy, psychology, and spiritual essence of philanthropy, including the motivations of people who share their time, talents, and treasure."[8] Exhibit 6.1 projects a general timetable for progress toward chosen career objectives.

Thomas E. Broce has enumerated the key characteristics of a successful fund development officer as follows:

1. Is genuinely concerned for the well-being of the institution or organization
2. Accepts responsibility, establishes standards, originates action, sustains a mood, and keeps things going
3. Understands people and knows how to organize, direct, and motivate them
4. Is not afraid of hard work, long hours, disappointments along the way— or a few words of appreciation
5. Has the capability to coordinate special events to take maximum advantage of such occasions

---

EXHIBIT 6.1 General Timetable for a Fund Development Professional's Career

---

0 to 8 Years
Entry level assignments
Mastery of the methods
Specialty concentration

5 to 10 Years
Manager of fund development programs
Specialty assignments and competency

8 to 15 Years
Executive for resource development

10-plus Years
Senior management executive
Institutional leadership

---

[8]Arthur C. Frantzreb, *Not on This Board You Don't: Making Your Trustees More Effective* (Chicago: Bonus Books, 1997), 163.

6. Communicates honestly and effectively the goals of the institution and describes accurately the ways in which these goals will be met
7. Is versatile, able to assist the chief executive officer and volunteer workers in a wide range of duties
8. Has the skills (or is acquiring them) to provide the mechanical and professional support necessary in all phases of the development process
9. Continues to grow professionally
10. Is a person of integrity who respects the integrity and dignity of others[9]

The following sections describe the rungs of the career ladder for fund development professionals (see Exhibit 6.2).

Mastery of the Methods

Most newcomers enter the field without prior experience or academic preparation. Volunteerism is closely related and "how-to" training programs help, but there is no substitute for beginning with direct responsibility for one or two assigned methods of fund raising. Most begin with annual giving methods because these are present in almost every fund development program. They may direct an annual giving committee of volunteer solicitors, supervise a direct mail acquisition and renewal program, or prepare one or more special or benefit events. They have no choice but to be swept into the "learning-by-doing" training method where experience teaches the required fundamentals. Given some guidance, new professionals can be allowed to make the mistakes that teach basic tenets, respect for planning, attention to detail, and flexibility. Without such help, they may be sacrificed on the altar of performance before they have had the opportunity to learn how to succeed. One type of guidance that will surely help newcomers is the training class, or workshop:

> The value of participation in classes and workshops designed to hone the skills of the advancement staff member goes well beyond the formal content. The participants get to know and exchange ideas with peers charged with similar responsibilities and, thus, to create networks of similarly tasked individuals who are available to render advice, counsel, and emotional support as needs arise. The staffer sent to a training session comes to understand that he or she is worth an investment by his or her employer of time and money for future effectiveness. The sending organization (the employing institution) is valued for willingness to invest in staff potential. Voluntary sector organizations, of whatever size, find that the commitment for training of a sum of 3 percent to 5 percent of budgeted professional salaries will have a pay-off in

[9]Thomas E. Broce, *Fund Raising: The Guide to Raising Money from Private Sources*, 2d ed. (Norman: University of Oklahoma Press, 1986), 42.

EXHIBIT 6.2 The Career Ladder to Professionalism

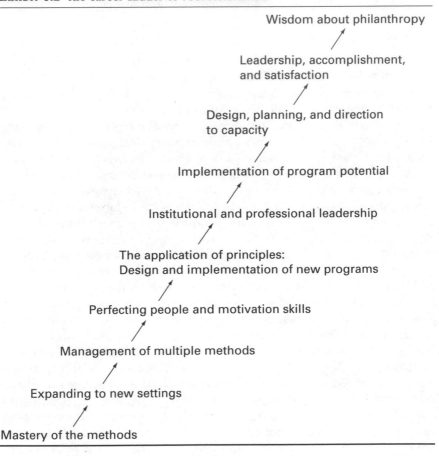

Wisdom about philanthropy

Leadership, accomplishment, and satisfaction

Design, planning, and direction to capacity

Implementation of program potential

Institutional and professional leadership

The application of principles: Design and implementation of new programs

Perfecting people and motivation skills

Management of multiple methods

Expanding to new settings

Mastery of the methods

advancement effectiveness equal to several times the actual dollars expended.[10]

The seven annual giving methods described in Chapter 3 are excellent teachers that will, with a bit of guidance, ensure a basic understanding of principles and will lead to a beginning of mastery of each of the methods. Yogi Berra's second most famous quote is "We lost the game because we

[10]Day, *The Effective Advancement Professional*, 25.

made all the wrong mistakes." In the right kind of environment, young professionals are nurtured and instructed by their errors.

Expanding to New Settings

Some professionals spend their careers at one organization, rising to the most senior levels because of their comprehensive knowledge and extensive internal job training. Among the many reasons for their great value is a complete knowledge of all the donors and volunteers and of how everyone and everything works. Their greatest contribution may be continuity, a rarity among fund development professionals. The opportunity to enjoy such a long-lived career is also likely to be rare in the future. The enormous needs of our society demand bigger and better fund-raising results—a volatile atmosphere that continuously creates new job opportunities. Burnout has become a reality too. Working in larger organizations allows the unique opportunity to "go through the chairs" and to learn every method of fund development in use by that employer. Most not-for-profit organizations are small, however, and cannot offer the breadth of exposure that would teach newcomers—access to senior mentors, established programs, smooth office systems, and the like. Career development for most professionals has been achieved by changing jobs. The factors in the environmental audit, described in Chapter 2, require fund raisers to apply basic skills differently in order to be successful in each new setting, which will have its own unique set of challenges. The greatest lesson learned from moving between institutions is that different decisions may be required to achieve fund development success each time, even though other methods were successful at another organization of the same type—another college, hospital, or museum. Whatever each program has achieved, it probably has room for new ideas, refinements of present methods, or better management that will yield greater results. Consultants can speed understanding of what's possible and can accelerate program performance. Selecting and working with professional consultants can offer timely instruction.

Management of Multiple Methods

It is one thing to become competent in one or more fund development methods. It is quite another to use those skills with greater efficiency, productivity, and benefit to each organization served and to progress to simultaneous management of multiple methods and successful direction of their combined application. Competition for volunteers, donors, and prospects tugs at the efficiency of each method. When larger donors demand more attention, they are moved from a broad-based effort to a more personal program and their revenue is lost to the original effort's results. Similarly, when proven volunteers move up to new responsibilities, their services and the gifts they brought in are taken away from a program's performance. Nevertheless, people's upward movement will be of greater benefit to the organization. Successful management of all the methods of annual giving, year after year, requires considerable skills. Chief among these is the ability to effect a high level of communication, coordination, and cooperation among the separate programs while still increasing the number of donors and volunteers and the net gift revenues each year.

Somewhere along the way, this same manager must acquire knowledge and understanding of basic management skills: hiring and performance evaluation of staff; recruitment and training of volunteers; budget preparation and supervision; in-office computer systems design; equipment selection, installation, and operation; and performance measurement of all gift results, to evaluate cost-effectiveness and productivity.

To reach the managerial level may take five years or more, depending on circumstances, opportunities, and personal desire. New professionals should enter the joint certification program founded by the NSFRE and the Association for Healthcare Philanthropy (AHP), and prepare to meet the requirements for first-level certification, the Certified Fund Raising Executive (CFRE).

Perfecting People and Motivation Skills

Supervisors, managers, employees, board members, committee chairpersons, volunteers (new and old), donors, and prospects are among those with whom a manager interacts daily. People skills are essential, and each individual requires different application of those skills and flexibility in interpersonal relations. Some people inspire awe because of their position or the amount of their contributions. Others, less important purely in terms of dollars, require equal attention and respect. Despite hard work every day to facilitate everyone's wishes, desires, needs, and aspirations, not everyone will be appreciative or pleased. Conflict with people in authority and with major donors should be avoided. This is never easy because donors, volunteers, and others often do not understand that development professionals are proactive; they push, prod, and "bug" people to act. Their sins are all from trying harder. However, many a budding career has been curtailed or ruined by an innocent error or an offense taken by important people or their spouses in the process of encouraging them to fulfill the task they volunteered to perform.

To gain mastery of fund development requires the ability to mix knowledge about the organization and its needs with the willingness and enthusiasm of many people, both inside and outside, who agree to support its mission, purpose, goals, and objectives. Whether this enlists motivation or salesmanship, it is not an easy assignment. Confidence, reliability, and trust must be transmitted to *everyone* with whom the manager and the institution have contact, no matter what their means of communication, their solicitation method, their position, or the potential size of their gift.

How can people be engaged to support whatever plan is offered them? The art is motivation; the science is stimulation of the needed responses. A fine line separates success and failure when working with people. Experience teaches that the line is drawn by an ability to respond personally to each relationship. Fund development executives pray for more people who are understanding, cooperative, and willing to join in and who appreciate the efforts of staff and volunteers alike. They also pray for fewer people whose sensitive egos demand constant massage and drain energy away from more deserving prospects. These egoists can, in fact, ruin a career. Many personalities must be balanced, to fulfill the multiple needs of the organization.

The ideal fund development manager possesses the ability and desire to assess, motivate, lead, and listen to people. An extensive inventory of management skills and qualities fund development managers should aspire to is presented in Exhibit 6.3.

The Application of Principles: Design and Implementation of New Programs

To add new fund-raising methods to existing programs or to expand existing programs to new levels of performance is the next rung on the ladder. Opportunities to design and launch a new fund development office are becoming rare because just about every not-for-profit organization has begun its program. Expectations are for instant results, but, given no prior activity, any positive results will be an improvement. More challenging and more enjoyable than inheriting a program and trying to maintain and/or fix it is the task of education that goes with the start-up of new fund development activities. Defining what methods to add, what design to implement, and in what order is a tough decision. Beginnings are exciting and can be rewarding, but they also can spell disaster if the total program has not been thought through and will planned from start to finish.

Talking to people inside the organization about the arts and sciences of fund development and how they work can never be started too early.

EXHIBIT 6.3 Fund-Raising Manager's Fundamental Competencies

- *Knowledge of the local and larger community's* issues, needs and events that could impact the organization or to which the organization could contribute in a mutually beneficial way.
- *Conceptual thinking* that allows the manager to identify underlying issues or connections between situations that are not obviously related. This ability helps the advancement manager to "put a face" on a campaign in such a manner that it has widespread appeal and is perceived as a valuable cause by potential contributors.
- *Skill in organizational influence* that enables the manager to understand the formal and informal ways in which the organization can change, and how he or she can effect that change.
- *Skill in the assessment of people,* which is required for the manager to select competent staff members and to match their competencies with specific job assignments.
- *Leadership,* demonstrated by the advancement manager, creates group cohesion, commitment, and motivation to work beyond the call of duty. It is the capacity to demonstrate "360-degree leadership," providing insights and direction to the larger organization, influencing the community, and communicating the institution's vision in such a way that others understand where the organization is headed, what their role is, and how they can contribute.
- *Impact and influence* that requires the manager to know how to persuade, convince, or influence others to support the organization's agenda.
- *A need to achieve,* which is demonstrated by high motivation for the individual, the advancement function, and the organization to succeed.
- *Self-confidence,* which is essentially the courage of conviction, despite rapidly changing landscapes, uncertain directions, and ambiguities so characteristic of growing institutions.
- *A sense of social responsibility* that enables the advancement manager to keep focused on the reality of the organization's mission and to use his or her power and influence to enable that mission to be achieved.
- *Curiosity and information seeking.* Successful advancement managers exhibit a curiosity that drives them to know more about people, things, and issues. Combined with their analytic and conceptual thinking, they are able to gain and communicate insights about future developments that could create opportunities or avoid problems for the institution they represent.

(continued)

EXHIBIT 6.3 (continued)

- *Developing and empowering.* The best advancement managers are those who can develop others. They manage with a coaching style that emphasizes shared responsibility and empowered staff. They make expectations clear and then give their capable staff the room to develop their own solutions and take action.
- *Listening and responding.* The advancement manager must be responsive to a number of stakeholders: the CEO, board of directors, the institution's other managers, community organizations, the advancement staff. The successful manager hears and understands the concerns and perspectives of each of these constituencies.
- *Initiating action.* The successful advancement manager is not satisfied with great ideas or even quick responses. He or she is able to take action to either prevent problems from ever occurring or create opportunities for the organization's future.

Reprinted with permission from The Effective Advancement Professional: Management Principles and Practices *by Duane L. Day (Gaithersburg, MD: Aspen, 1998), 269–270. © 1998 Aspen Publishers, Inc.*

Before initiating a new program, the professional should explain to staff and volunteers how the new effort will be designed and offered to the public, and what results can be expected. Early failures happen to new professionals because, while determined to raise some money as soon as possible, they neglect to inform their employer what they are doing, how it works, and what results can be expected. Professionals at this point on the career ladder are assumed to have acquired a good understanding and appreciation of how everything works. But they also need the ability to explain to others, clearly and convincingly, exactly what they are doing. The ability to apply basic principles in new settings and to design and implement new programs is a level of competency that should be in place at this halfway point up the ladder.

Institutional and Professional Leadership

Opportunities for expanded management experience through other assigned duties and responsibilities may be offered by the not-for-profit organization itself. Many fund development executives have at some time been responsible for such related management areas as communications, community relations, public relations, publications, marketing, planning, volunteer relations, and government affairs. These skill areas require added professional training and experience, and their reward is a healthy breadth of exposure, personal development, and access to executive skill areas.

A second opportunity for professional growth is to volunteer in another not-for-profit organization. This is excellent exposure to and education in the separation of staff and volunteer roles and the proper behavior in both. Well-established organizations, especially those that have well-defined operating policies and procedures for their fund-raising activities, offer a model for learning. Their management procedures can be studied and possibly applied to present and future employers where and when appropriate. Charitable organizations are not the same in how they perform fund raising, nor does fund raising perform the same for every organization.

Learning more about the organization's professional programs and services, whether by volunteering or by being more a part of the management team, creates another area for growth. Involvement in the program and service areas brings contact with other professional staff who are likely to be interested in learning about fund development. A mutual understanding of activities and responsibilities will result. "One of the chief fund raising officer's roles is that of a teacher. As such, she or he must always take advantage of an opportunity to explain fund raising to others and to persuade, cajole, and induce them to take fund raising seriously, according it the respect that it merits."[11]

Joining professional societies is a fourth area for growth. Depending on the type of employer/organization, one or more local chapters of national societies may provide training programs in fund development as well as other services to members. Among the leading organizations that provide support to fund development professionals are the AHP, the Council for the Advancement and Support of Education (CASE), and the NSFRE. Active participation through attendance at meetings, workshops, and conferences, and service on committees and on the board of directors are important for self-education. Eventually, giving a conference session can provide an excellent opportunity to organize ideas and to share experiences and knowledge with others. Articles on relevant topics can be contributed to professional journals. All these activities are recommended as part of the certification programs offered by AHP and NSFRE. No other demonstration of commitment to the profession is as visible as having met these requirements.

[11] Rosso, *Rosso on Fund Raising*, 125.

Implementation of Program Potential

Fund raisers are all accustomed to answering the question, "How much money have you raised?" A more important question is, "Are you raising as much money as you can?" The next question is, "How much did it cost?" As this book has illustrated, fund raising is much more than raising money. Friend raising, relationship building, and donor relations are never-ending assignments. Another elusive but important factor is the "pursuit of potential." This is not a magic figure or a sum of money that can be raised in any year; it is a measure of how successful each fund-raising method can become. Once implemented and running smoothly, fund-raising methods take on patterns of behavior and performance that, because they become reliable, are left alone. Little attention may be paid to their original design after years of successful operation, but are they operating above or below true potential? Every method, every technique, every component of the fund development program can stand scrutiny and evaluation at least annually. Senior professionals should be fully comfortable with performance measurement and accountability. They are responsible for everything's working well on its own and they must contribute to the total effort with high efficiency and maximum profitability. Comparing results against prior years is necessary, but comparing results against changing institutional needs is more important. The senior development professional must study performance, evaluate how each program is working on its own, and observe how its success is lifting up other areas, enabling them to thrive as well. This type of analysis requires a comprehensive knowledge of each method in use and of how to evaluate and report results. Senior professionals should continue to attend conferences and workshops, to expand their own understanding. They should consider the use of outside consultants to help already effective programs reach their full potential and then move toward their capacity.

Design, Planning, and Direction to Capacity

Potential and capacity are not the same. Potential is a current estimate of what is possible; capacity is a realization of the sum total of everything possible by raising as much as you can. Fund development programs may never achieve their capacity but should be well aware of what and where it is as they work to maximize their current potential. Stanford University reached its $1.1 billion goal ahead of schedule. Was this sum Stanford's capacity? No. The pursuit of more dollars began the day after the goal was reached. Did Stanford raise all the money that could have been raised during the campaign? Not at all.

For a fund development program to achieve potential and reach for capacity requires maturity in the program in all respects, in the leadership, volunteers and staff. The organization should have begun to achieve full potential for each of its fund-raising methods and its management should be a unified force within the organization (no small accomplishment). There is always room for growth, for improvement, for excellence. Fund development professionals are both opportunists and optimists; they strive to work harder and smarter, especially where such enterprise is encouraged and rewarded.

Leadership, Accomplishment, and Satisfaction

There are rewards for long and faithful service—director of development, vice president for institutional advancement, executive director, and even president and chief executive officer. Along the way, the professional may have been the supervisor for fund development, communications, community relations, public relations, publications, marketing, planning, volunteer relations, or government affairs. Senior professionals who, by reaching their own capacity, have mastered the skills of managing multiple areas have also risen to an executive position of responsibility within their organization, often senior executive in charge of all fund development activities. They may also be providing active leadership to their professional associations and to civic groups in their community. Henry A. Rosso's description of a CDO illustrates the role this executive plays in facilitating communication with the organization's constituency: "If the chief development officer is functioning in accordance with the requirements of this leadership position, she or he is performing as a boundary scanner, as a communication conduit to the extremities of the nonprofit's constituency environment. In this role, the development chief is fulfilling a precious function, maintaining a positive communication link with constituents far and near. It is essential for this person to be sensitive to and knowledgeable about every aspect of the nonprofit's governance, management, and program policies and procedures in order to maintain communication integrity between the nonprofit and its broad-flung constituency."[12]

Wisdom about Philanthropy

It takes a lot of years, a lot of experiences, a lot of scars to achieve even the beginnings of wisdom about any craft or profession. Senior professionals have much to share. They have learned much, they have survived, they

[12]Ibid., 40.

know a lot about the management of not-for-profit organizations, and they have profited from each experience. They are masters in the arts of motivation and interpersonal relations. They also understand philanthropy and professional practice. They have achieved respect within their institution, their profession, and their community. Their minds remain open to new ideas and, although tempered by all that they have learned and by their intuition, they still are able to see the positive attributes of any idea, of any good person, of any occasion where their organization may benefit in some fashion. They are an institutional asset and a resource to their profession.

MANAGEMENT OF FUND DEVELOPMENT OFFICE OPERATIONS

Fund development office operations—leadership training, team building among volunteers, planning and marketing, market and prospect research, and performance evaluations—are just as essential to prepare and meet goals and objectives as are the individual fund development methods used for solicitation. There is a trend toward more staff solicitation, perhaps growing out of the staff's success with direct mail, grantsmanship, and planned giving. Staff should not do all the asking, but how is a balance maintained between staff and volunteer solicitation? Guidelines and "rules of operation" are needed to help everyone work together toward the same goals of institutional advancement. Budget preparation and supervision; staff hiring, training, and evaluation; space and equipment needs, suitable to get the job done; and the overall image of the office charged with both raising funds and managing funds raised—all need continuing attention.

Few people brag about the quality of their office operations. Success as a manager of fund development includes success as a manager of the fund development office. This office coordinates every form of solicitation and all volunteers, donors, and prospects. Like any other department, it must also direct its own daily activities and routine functions with a high degree of measurable success. The fund development manager, then, has an obligation to attend to the wants and needs of the office, which includes giving credit where it is due.

In a manner hard to understand, too many advancement managers withhold oral expressions of approval. It is a fact, scarcely to be contested, that advancement personnel work in arenas in which appreciation is rare, disappointments frequent. Despite the fact that most managers of the advancement function have been promoted from staff positions in advancement (in which they have coped with failures, "noes," and discouragement), the mantle of authority, once draped, often brings with it amnesia about the value of commendation and the emotional support it provides for those who have met discouragement, rejection, or disappointment. Words of encouragement from the boss mean a great deal and often motivate a staff member to double and redouble efforts.[13]

Basic management practices associated with annual giving, gifts from institutions, and major gift programs were presented in earlier chapters. Exhibit 6.4 shows the distribution of basic functions when an office is served by a 3-person or a 13-person staff. Certain areas of emphasis in office management are essential to success in daily operations: program budgeting, technology and change, gift processing and reporting, management of funds raised, volunteer training, and donor recognition. Each is given more attention in the following sections.

Program Budgeting

The budget for fund development assigns to each invested dollar an expected rate of return of 400 percent, or a cost-effective ratio of 80 cents profit for every 20 cents invested for mature programs (three years or more of continuous operation). Fund development offices should be recognized as "profit centers," not "cost centers." The fund-raising cost guidelines presented earlier (Chapter 2) recommend individual program measurements as the test for performance because each fund-raising method performs differently. The positive relationship between budget and results should be reported, using the nine-point performance index to demonstrate growth, profitability, and productivity, and to encourage volunteers and donors to continue their growth, progress, and performance that comes from their efforts and commitment. If one or more fund-raising activities are performing above or below expectations, all indicators should be carefully studied to understand what's working and why, before adjusting the budget up or down.

Technology and Change

Computers, a wide variety of software applications, e-mail, the Internet, facsimile machines, beepers, cell phones, compact discs, and video- and

---

[13] Day, *The Effective Advancement Professional*, 28.

EXHIBIT 6.4 Basic Functions of the Fund Development Office

General Duties	Office Staff Assignments	
	3-Person Office*	13-Person office[†]
Leadership and direction	Fund raiser	Fund raiser/leader
Fund raising	Fund raiser	Fund raisers (3)
Office supervision; budget and personnel management	Secretary	Office manager
Secretarial tasks	Secretary	Secretaries (3)
Gift processing, donor records, pledge billing	Gift records clerk	Gift records clerk
Thank-you letters and cards on all gifts received	Gift records clerk	Acknowledgment clerk
Research and files control	Gift records clerk	Research clerk
Computer records, data input and control	Gift records clerk	Electronic data processing (EDP) coordinator
Mail, phone, visitors	Secretary	Receptionist
Supplies, equipment, storage	Secretary	Office Manager
Mail list preparation, maintenance, control	Secretary	EDP coordinator
Mail assembly and distribution	Everybody	Nearly everybody
Personnel training and skill development	Secretary	Office manager
Dedications, receptions, benefit events	Everybody	Fund raiser (1) and office manager
Plaques, awards, honors	Fund raiser	Fund raiser (1) and office manager
Coordination of all support groups	Fund raiser	Fund raiser (1) and one secretary

*Fund raiser, gift records clerk, and secretary.
[†]Fund raiser/leader, fund raisers (3), secretaries (3), office manager, gift records clerk, acknowledgment clerk, research clerk, EDP coordinator, receptionist.

audiotape are all now in use at every fund raising office. These modern tools enhance communication and every fund-raising staff must learn to utilize them well. The benefits are greater efficiency, productivity, more accurate data, and better management of greater numbers of donors, volunteers, and prospects. In general, contacting people is faster and easier. Not every organization will itself be technologically up-to-date. The financial investment is much greater than buying computers and installing software; computers must be serviced, maintained, and kept in daily operation. Staff need to be trained and kept current; they also quickly become dependent on technology. Previous office support systems (typewriters, donor record cards, paper files, etc.) are soon eliminated. Despite their advantages, modern tools have drawbacks; the following is a short list of problems associated with modern technology:

- There is simply too much information available.
- Advancement officers depend on relationships, created and nurtured, to do their jobs; computers add little to the relationship-building, cultivation, or solicitation process.
- Means and ends are different realities.
- Information systems technology, as represented by both hardware and software, is always changing; no matter what the institution acquires today, it is almost immediately obsolete."[14]

Office technology is not the only thing that changes. Fund development managers must keep current with changing accounting standards and audit guidelines on how to record and report contributions plus changing tax laws and their increasingly complex regulations that govern not-for-profit management including several areas specific to fund-raising practice: conflict of interest, gift substantiation, intermediate sanctions, planned gift values, public benefit tests, quid pro quo rules, revised IRS Form 990, and more.

Gift Processing and Reporting

Each contribution received must be recorded as official revenue to the organization, to comply with Internal Revenue Service (IRS) and American Institute of Certified Public Accountants (AICPA) guidelines for gift accounting and reporting. Each gift also needs deposit, data entry, fund accounting, and acknowledgment. No matter how many solicitation programs are being offered, a single processing procedure should be used

[14]Ibid., 141–142.

to handle all replies with efficiency and to eliminate errors in bookkeeping. Each staff member who handles gifts needs extremely careful instruction. Good working relationships with finance, business, and accounting staff should be established. Gifts are not secret transactions within an organization; but details about who gives, how much, and for what purpose are unavailable as public information. Regular reports on results should group the data by source, purpose, and method used to raise the money. (See Exhibits 3.18, 3.19, and 3.20.) Both the number of gifts and total revenue should be tallied in reports for public use. Formal financial statements, audits, and summary reports required by federal, state, and local authorities must be prepared and submitted by deadlines. These reports become public documents, available to anyone who requests them. Proper handling and accounting ensure that each donor is thanked, that donors receive proper gift substantion for income tax purposes, that the funds are used correctly, and that reports on all solicitation activities are accurate. These data can be significant for management decisions about current performance and for future planning.

Management of Funds Raised

Consistent with sound business and accounting practices in handling gift revenues is the need to be prepared for cash management, entry of pledges as receivables, and reliable pledge-billing procedures. There must also be short- and long-term investment of funds held, administration of charitable trusts, pooled income funds and other forms of planned giving, and a balanced management of funds held as endowment. Most often, these activities are guided by finance and investment committees and follow board-approved policies and procedures. Fund development staff have the responsibility for proper deposit of all funds received as well as their correct use in accordance with donors' wishes, especially when they are restricted and special-purpose funds. Fund raising includes responsibility for what happens to the money after it arrives. Each gift should be traceable along its path to utilization and details on its use should be reported to donors at least once a year including, where possible, evidence of measured benefit delivered to the community as a result.

Volunteer Training

Identifying, recruiting, training and developing, and rewarding volunteers are duties of the fund development office. Volunteer training is essential to help find all the volunteers needed, to prepare an adequate supply of experienced volunteers for future assignments, and to find candidates for leadership positions that are critical to success. Volunteers do not deliver themselves ready-made for the work asked of them; they must be trained to support the organization's many programs according to its culture and style. Without them, programs quickly wither and can die.

Donor Recognition

Fund development staff should assume responsibility for donor recognition, donor relations, and donor communications. Donors require and deserve continued attention, and the management of their fair and equitable treatment is an obligation vested in the fund development office. After a proper "thank-you," their friendship and good will must be preserved. Each method of fund-raising produces a separate opportunity to thank donors, but the methods used should be coordinated and consistent.

If fund development programs are to enjoy high regard among volunteers and donors, these management areas must be given time and attention. Confidence in office operations is as important to public trust as are the methods of solicitation used to raise money. It is also important to recognize that the "things that go bump in the night" can happen to any fund-raising program and disrupt its best efforts (see Exhibit 6.5). Nevertheless, persistence in following proven methods, securing quality leadership, and adequate support to the process will win against nearly all odds.

Overall Cost-Effectiveness Evaluation

A sample nine-point performance analysis has been offered for each of the fund-raising methods discussed in Chapters 2 through 5. Following that precedent this chapter will discuss and offer a sample evaluation of the overall fund development program to demonstrate how the several methods contribute to a larger success than the cost-benefit ratio of any one year's performance. Fund raising might be defined as a variety of loosely knit activities conceived to raise money, received with suspicion, and delivered without precision. Yet, it works. But does it work with effectiveness as well as efficiency? Can it demonstrate productivity as well as profitability. Can it predict future performance? Answers to these questions are necessary for two key reasons: (1) to preserve public confidence

EXHIBIT 6.5 Mistakes to Avoid in Fund-Raising Work

- Assuming that board members will give and that face-to-face personal solicitation is not necessary
- Naively assuming that Murphy's Law will never stake a claim in your office
- Not sending thank-you letters to donors within 24 to 48 hours
- Not calling a donor who has returned a $50, $75, or $100 gift in response to a mail appeal, to say thank you
- Not stopping periodically to evaluate the progress in the matter of acquiring, renewing, and upgrading gifts
- Not evaluating all aspects of your program at least once a year
- Not hiring a competent consultant to perform a periodic full program audit
- Urging donors to give *this* year, before tax laws change and giving is made less advantageous (What will your story be next year?)
- Submitting to the popular belief that a recession is a bad time to request gifts and not asking
- Not setting a regular date and time to meet with the chief executive to discuss program progress and review problems
- Not suggesting solutions to those problems, for review by the executive
- Not making your own gift, pleading that you are underpaid and that that constitutes your gift
- Not reading books, periodicals, and occasional papers about various aspects of your profession
- If you are an executive director, assuming that fund raising is not part of your responsibilities and not making yourself available to your development staff for periodic conferences and the solicitation of special prospects
- If you are a board member, seriously believing that occasional attendance at board meetings represents your total responsibility, that mission and vision are buzz words, and that giving and asking and attention to the nonprofit's financial condition are someone else's concern (and then boasting to friends and associates that you understand the meaning of stewardship and trusteeship)
- If you are a development officer, entering the profession to earn a good living and not to give of yourself as a servant leader in dedication to the public good

(continued)

EXHIBIT 6.5 (continued)

- Believing in the fable that funds can be raised without a serious examination of all facets of the program planned for annual fund, capital campaign, or endowment and planned-giving fund raising. Shooting from the hip in this activity is foolhardy—and perhaps the worst, most damaging mistake a not-for-profit can make

Reprinted with permission from Rosso on Fund Raising: Lessons from a Master's Lifetime Experience *by Henry A. Rosso (San Francisco: Jossey-Bass, 1996), 37–38.*

in giving and volunteering, and (2) to provide reliable forecasts for financial planning. The fund-raising program also should be able to demonstrate its ability to accomplish the following secondary objectives:

- Enhance the image and reputation of the organization it serves
- Advance its marketing, promotion, and community relations efforts
- Increase public confidence and trust in the organization and its leadership and management
- Achieve a higher level of effectiveness and efficiency in the quality of its programs and services offered for public benefit, including its solicitation practices.[15]

A sample year-end gift report for a fund development program is shown in Exhibit 6.6. Results are included from all methods of giving. An interpretation of these data follows:

1. Five methods of annual giving are in operation and produced $302,100 in gross revenue at a direct cost of $40,000. Adding labor/payroll and nonpayroll costs (direct and indirect overhead expenses), the cost-benefit ratio is 34 percent.
2. Four areas of major giving also were active and produced $301,000 in gross revenue at a direct cost of $11,315. After labor/payroll and non-payroll costs, the cost-benefit ratio is 9 percent.
3. In combination, $603,100 was raised at a cost of $131,115 for a cost of fund raising of 22 percent overall, and a return on expenses of 360 percent.

Based on these data only (which exceeded the approved budget by $2,365, a variance of 1.8 percent), was this program successful? How is

[15]James M. Greenfield, *Fund-Raising Cost Effectiveness: A Self-Assessment Workbook* (New York: Wiley, 1996), 246.

EXHIBIT 6.6 Year-End Gift Report

	Gift Amount	Budget Approved	Budget Expended	Cost of Fund-Raising (%)
A. Annual Giving Programs				
Direct mail (acquisition)	$35,500	$14,500	$14,798	42
Direct mail (renewal)	76,500	1,500	1,620	2
Membership dues	48,500	550	585	1
Benefit events (3)	59,600	20,000	21,747	36
Volunteer-led solicitations	82,000	1,200	1,250	2
Subtotal	$302,100	$37,750	$40,000	13
Direct Costs: Annual Giving				
Labor/Payroll		$62,000	$63,050	
Nonpayroll costs		37,750	40,000	
Subtotal		$99,750	$103,050	34
B. Major Gifts Programs				
Corporations	$45,500	$3,500	$3,250	7
Foundations	65,000	3,500	2,015	3
Individuals	145,500	3,800	4,200	3
Bequests received	45,000	200	1,850	4
Subtotal	$301,000	$11,000	$11,315	4
Total	$603,100	$48,750	$51,315	9
Net Income	$471,985			
Direct Costs: Major Giving				
Labor/Payroll		$18,000	$16,750	
Nonpayroll costs		11,000	11,315	
Subtotal		$29,000	$28,065	
C. Expense Summary (A + B)				
Direct Costs		$80,000	$79,800	
Indirect Costs/Overhead		$48,750	$51,315	
Total		$128,750	$131,115	22
Return				360

Reprinted with permission from Fund-Raising Cost Effectiveness: A Self-Assessment Workbook *by James M. Greenfield (New York: John Wiley & Sons, Inc., 1996), 249.*

success measured? The cost-benefit ratio for both annual giving and major gifts are within Council of Better Business Bureau (CBBB) and National Charities Information Bureau (NCIB) guidelines of 35 and 40 percent respectively. Certainly, if this program can maintain a return of 360 percent each year, it is a winner! Probably no other department within the organization can claim such a level of productivity. Exhibit 6.7 provides a sample three-year summary that helps us understand the progression and consistency inherent in most fund-raising programs (year 3 includes results from the previous exhibit; year 4 is an estimate of the coming year's results, based on those of years 1, 2, and 3). What do these figures suggest?

1. A significant growth in number of donors from 1,478 in year 1 to 4,879 in year 3 suggests acquisition is a major commitment and helps to explain expenses in year 3 for direct mail acquisition ($14,798) and benefit events ($21,747) (amounts found in Exhibit 6.6), which consumed 91.4 percent of that year's annual giving budget.
2. Average gift size further confirms the commitment to annual giving, because the average has declined from $196 to $124. Correspondingly, the average cost per gift has declined from $73 to $27.
3. An equally impressive growth in income received can be seen, from $289,330 to $603,100 compared with budget increases from $107,565 to $131,115.
4. Cost of fund raising has declined from 37 to 22 percent, with a corresponding increase in the return from 169 to 360 percent.

EXHIBIT 6.7 Three-Year Summary Analysis with One-Year Forecast

	Year 1	Year 2	Year 3	Est. Year 4
Participation	1,478	3,315	4,879	5,000
Income	$289,330	$431,150	$603,100	$660,000
Expenses	$107,565	$118,325	$131,115	$135,000
Percent participation	0.064%	0.095%	0.102%	0.100%
Average gift size	$196	$130	$124	$132
Net income	$181,765	$312,825	$471,985	$525,000
Average cost per gift	$73	$36	$27	$27
Cost of fund raising	37%	27%	22%	20%
Return	169%	264%	360%	389%

Reprinted with permission from Fund-Raising Cost Effectiveness: A Self-Assessment Workbook *by James M. Greenfield (New York: John Wiley & Sons, Inc., 1996), 256.*

5. The most telling figure for the organization is the increase in net income from $181,765 to $471,985 to be used to meet priority needs.
6. The forecast for year 4 is positive in all respects, based on solid performance and growth along with increased efficiency as well as effective management of fund-raising activities.

What data are missing from this analysis to achieve a comprehensive understanding of this organization's performance? It would be helpful to know (1) how many people were asked to give, (2) how many new-versus-old donors made these gifts, (3) how many prior donors did not renew, (4) whether upgrading was offered to annual donors, (5) whether the three benefit events were first-time efforts or were in their third year, (6) how many major gift proposals are outstanding, (7) how many proposals are in preparation, (8) how many new, planned gifts were executed and what their values were, (9) how much history preceded these results. Add to these questions a few about the fund development office staff, to learn (1) how many years of experience they have, (2) whether a capital campaign is coming, in progress, or just concluded, and (3) whether raising endowment funds is a priority. Finally, what about the organization itself? It is important to know (1) what type of charitable mission it serves, (2) where it is located, (3) what its image, reputation, and competition are, (4) who its board members and CEO are, as well as their tenure and involvement, (5) what state its financial condition and reserves are in, and how its endowment is performing, and (6) what its master plan for the future consists of. Each of these criteria are important to the success of the overall fund development program and should be included in measurement of its performance.

Setting Performance Standards

Without accurate records and reports, careful analysis of results, and an understanding of the many factors that influence success, an organization cannot predict future performance in fund raising any more than, without those prerequisites, it could predict the future performance of its own programs and services. Not-for-profit organizations are not the same in how they conduct fund raising, nor does fund raising perform the same for every organization. In the absence of any established external standards, an organization can use its own experience as the guide for setting its performance standards. Thus, if an organization has three or more years of experience and complete records of its results, these three years are a good indicator of performance in the fourth year. When applying performance standards an organization should be flexible and take into account the effect this standard giving program can have on the results of another. For example, if a major capital campaign is begun, prior experience will help predict what potential may exist for major gifts; prior annual giving results also will serve as an indicator of lost revenue as annual donors are redirected to the capital campaign objectives. Some past results will be misleading because of atypical gifts. Arrival of a major bequest can make for a striking bottom-line performance in one year, resulting in misleading analysis from observing bottom-line data alone. The same gift is not likely to be repeated the following year and must be removed from future forecast estimates. The value of a performance standard is that everyone knows and appreciates the effort required to produce fund-raising results. A valid standard releases donors, volunteers, and staff from excessive and unrealistic expectations and allows them to concentrate on what they are doing well and encourages them to continue their improvements.

Growth in giving is measurable, and its analysis yields reliable data upon which to forecast likely outcomes and against which to monitor performance. Thus growth is often the primary performance standard. The following comments, are based on the sample rate of growth analysis shown in Exhibit 6.8:

1. The increased number of participants, at a cumulative rate of growth of 31 percent over three years, confirms the importance of assessing success in raising friends and building relationships along with raising money.
2. Income received grew at 26 percent in this period while expenses increased at half that rate, or 13 percent.
3. Average gift size declined slightly from $331 to $318, an indication of the current commitment to acquire and renew new donors. It also suggests more effort in upgrading current donors is required along with more emphasis on major gift activities.
4. Average cost per gift declined by 15 percent, from $86.01 to $73.29, as did the cost of fund raising by 11 percent, suggesting a level of efficiency is being achieved.
5. Return on investment increased by 16 percent, from 285 to 333 percent, suggesting a positive trend but also limited by the necessary investment of budget in acquisition.

EXHIBIT 6.8 Report on Overall Rate of Growth in Giving Using Nine-Point Performance Index

	Two Years Ago	Last Year	Annual Rate of Growth (%)	This Year	Annual Rate of Growth (%)	Cumulative Rate of Growth (%)
Participation	1,355	1,605	18	1,799	12	31
Income	$448,765	$507,855	13	$571,235	12	26
Expenses	$116,550	$123,540	6	$131,850	7	13
Percent participation	39%	44%	13	52%	18	31
Average gift size	$331	$316	−4	$318	0.4	−4
Net income	$332,215	$384,315	16	$439,385	14	30
Average cost per gift	$86.01	$76.97	−11	$73.29	−5	−15
Cost of fund raising	26%	24%	−6	23%	−5	−11
Return	285%	311%	9	333%	7	16

Reprinted with permission from Fund-Raising Cost Effectiveness: A Self-Assessment Workbook by James M. Greenfield (New York: John Wiley & Sons, Inc., 1996), 272.

RELATED ORGANIZATIONS: MORE THAN RAISING MONEY

Solicitation needs to be straightforward insofar as who is asking and for what purpose. When more than one organization related to the parent is involved, each activity needs to be in order so that all the requests are coordinated. Solicitations must function legally and be within accounting guidelines. Many not-for-profit organizations have one or more related organizations attached to them, such as a college alumni association, a hospital auxiliary, or a museum or theater guild. The nature of these relationships is often quite structured, but the organizations enjoy varying degrees of independence in their operations. Some have their own separate tax-exempt status, board of directors, and fund-raising programs. Others use the name of the parent corporation and share common operating procedures and rules, but they function somewhere between semiautonomous and downright independent, with separate names and volunteer leadership. Coordination, cooperation, and communication are essential among all these related organizations, and can be effected because each subsidiary functions in the name of and on behalf of the parent. Consolidated accounting procedures are essential. All funds raised must first be reported by each tax-exempt subsidiary and then be reflected in the consolidated financial statements of the parent. Combined results must be reflected in audits and annual filings to the IRS, and to state and local authorities. These documents are available to the general public upon request.

Separate from these legal and accounting requirements, every person and every entity involved, no matter how independent it is from the parent corporation, must operate within the purview of the board of directors, chief executive officer, and fund development office of the parent corporation. The controlling factor is the use of the official name of the parent, which holds the original charter and without which all the others would have no reason to exist. Internal or external fund development operations by any subsidiary organization, whether related to the parent's purposes or not, must be within the administrative control of the parent. The control is even tighter for funds raised in the parent's name. Donors contribute on the assumption that the funds will be used for the charitable purposes described in the mission statement of the parent corporation. No matter which part of the parent organization donors have supported, they may enjoy a charitable contribution deduction from federal and state taxes.

These relationships are usually friendly and supportive but, as within families, there can be areas and periods of conflict. The fund development process requires observance of essential areas of operation such as

343

prospect control, events scheduling (calendar control), accounting for and transfer of funds received, election of boards, officers, and committees, donor recognition, and newsletters and annual reports. Most important of all, a spirit of coordination, cooperation, and communication must exist so that all these enterprises continue to serve the best interests of the parent corporation.

Related organizations permit many opportunities for volunteers, donors, and prospects who choose to be involved to build on their interest and support. There is a need to recruit and train those willing to work and to plan for their progress toward future leadership roles. A supply of new suspects and prospects must constantly be identified and brought into some part of the organization to begin their support of the institutional priorities needing their help in future years.

Four management areas can assist in understanding the parent-subsidiary relationship and the ways in which all related organizations serve the fund development process. They are as follows: ownership and authority, setting goals and objectives, financial accounting and reporting, and (lastly) donor relations.

Ownership and Authority

Tax-exempt status is the key element in the relationship, and this privilege is usually located in the parent corporation. One or more subsidiary organizations may have their own tax-exempt status, but their articles of incorporation will identify the "corporate member" that elects each subsidiary's board of directors. Most often, the parent board has this authority. Financial reporting requirements are linked to tax-exempt status. The authority of the parent also determines policies and procedures, including guidelines for all fund development practice, annual goals, and objectives and priorities for funds raised.

A related organization may have its own subsidiaries. For example, a college is parent to an alumni association, which may have several "freestanding" chapters spread across the country. Or a multi-hospital corporation may control three hospitals and two nursing homes, coordinating all its fund development through a single hospital foundation. The alumni association and the hospital foundation can be separately incorporated and have their own Code Section 501(c)(3) tax-exempt status; their chapters and separate fund development offices may operate their own affairs and elect their own boards of directors, committees, and volunteers. These separate fund development efforts are carried out by what the public might assume is a wholly separate organization. Because all fund raising conducted is for the ultimate use of the parent, the link to the parent should be visible and should be used to add credibility to every solicitation. Unless great care is taken to assure the public of an interlocking relationship and the flow of money to the parent for charitable purposes, the confusion and complexity associated with related organizations can deter giving.

Setting Goals and Objectives

One means to unite several dedicated groups is through the annual preparation and submission of goals and objectives developed according to common guidelines and deadlines and submitted together for review and approval by the parent organization. Use of a standard form for setting goals and objectives for both new and repeat fund-raising programs has considerable value (see Exhibit 6.9). These goals can be shared with everyone involved in the preparation process. Publication of the individual and collective goals and objectives will provide volunteers and donors with a larger perspective, the "big picture." Such communications will help to allay fears about "control" and instill an appreciation of the significance and greater potential of the combined efforts, which are much greater than the capacity of any one subsidiary acting alone. Related organizations benefit from some cooperation and coordination of otherwise separate activities, especially when membership and volunteer recruitment, leadership development, and events scheduling are being done within the same geographic area and are communicating with the same audiences. Competition among related organizations can be healthy and productive if adequate communication is maintained among all those involved. Competition can be destructive if any group feels threatened in its ability to carry out its own mission and purpose or is deemed less important than others. The parent corporation must provide equal support and encouragement to all related organizations working in its behalf. Arbitration and negotiation are the business of governments in their relations with other nation-states; they are not the strategies and tactics of raising friends and funds for charitable purposes.

Financial Accounting and Reporting

Donors must be completely confident about where their money goes and how it is used. These facts must be communicated by all the related organizations that may handle any of the parent's funds. Each subsidiary may keep its own books, elect a treasurer, open bank accounts, and control its

EXHIBIT 6.9 Sample Form for Setting Goals and Objectives for New and Repeat Fund-Raising Programs

Solicitation Activity: _____

_____

Current Chairperson
And Vice Chair(s): _____

_____

_____

Proposed Next Chairperson
and Vice Chair(s): _____

_____

_____

1. Description of the Solicitation Activity:

2. The Primary Purposes/Goals/Objectives:

3. Proposed Date(s) and Schedule for Planning Preparation, and Implementation:

4. Estimate of Volunteers and Staff Required:

5. Analysis of Prior Experience and Results with Nine-Point Performance Index:

6. Estimated Budget (worksheet attached):

7. Forecast on One-, Two-, and Three-Year Performance:

Reprinted with permission from Fund-Raising Cost Effectiveness: A Self-Assessment Workbook *by James M. Greenfield (New York: John Wiley & Sons, Inc., 1996), 268.*

own finances to some extent, but corporate policy should require that all funds raised and received be reported to the subsidiary's board and committees and to the parent organization. Disclosure within each group is important for many reasons, accountability being the primary one. Individual gift reports demonstrate progress and success. The results of each related organization should be shared with all the others, to reveal the progress and success of everyone involved, all of whom are working to benefit the parent. Audit and accounting guides require extensive care in handling of all dollars contributed in the name of the parent corporation. Master files on all donors should be maintained in the central fund development office so that each donor receives full credit and a proper "thank-you" for every gift, no matter which activity or group did the solicitation. Frequent financial statements and the annual audit will disclose all details, including all temporarily or permanently restricted funds that require separate handling and reporting, the cost of fund raising for *each* activity, and how all funds raised were spent for charitable purposes. The first two pages of IRS Form 990 represent the accounting required of all not-for-profit organizations and their related organizations. Each organization and all of its volunteers must appreciate that failure to observe correct deposit and reporting procedures for every gift dollar can result in the loss of tax-exempt status for the parent corporation.

Donor Relations

Donors respond to requests for gift support even when they may not understand what part of the organization has asked them to give. They trust they are supporting the mission, purpose, goals, and objectives of the named organization represented to them. The recipient must treat them and their money properly. This duty includes proper stewardship of their funds and appropriate recognition for their generosity. Related organizations can establish their own donor recognition practices and maintain regular communications with all their donors. When results are reported to the parent, donors may enjoy added benefits and privileges offered by the parent. This practice is especially valuable when cumulative giving records are kept; donors are credited for every gift they make, no matter how many times they give to one or more of the related organizations that ask them for money. Volunteers are sometimes surprised to learn that "their" donors give in several other ways to the same organization during the same year. Each related organization should feel partially responsible for the continued good faith and confidence of any repeat donor because each gift is another expression of personal support for them all.

THE FUTURE: FULL OF CHALLENGES

The horizon is always full of challenges and opportunities, often embodied in the same situation. This section is not an attempt to forecast the future but only to highlight certain changes that have been and will be influential to program decisions. Internal Revenue Service publication 1391, issued in June 1988 (based on a 1967 Revenue Ruling), asked not-for-profit organizations to inform donors who buy tickets to special events or benefits how much of their ticket price is actually deductible (the rest cannot be claimed as a tax deduction).[16] Not-for-profit organizations had to change their wording on invitations and "thank-you" letters and their practice of crediting donors for gifts at the full ticket price. Other challenges are likely to be added in the future.

Some changes can have a positive effect, and being alert to them allows early implementation of their benefits. Organizations themselves need to make some changes, whether challenged by outside forces or not. Improved management skills are needed. Cost-effective analysis must become more widespread, to achieve better use of available resources. Increased attention must be focused on alternative sources of revenue.

The basic daily challenge is to be a catalyst for decisions affecting the management and conduct of fund development. Fund development should be looked upon as one of the solutions to fiscal problems, as a source of reliable and additional revenue, even as an institutional resource. Funds raised are still considered something "extra" in some settings; they are absolutely necessary dollars. They represent help, whether to balance the operating budget or to close the gap of the ever elusive margin of excellence. The organization's case statement must define its need for understanding, participation, and support. Philanthropy is more and more a necessity; gift dollars have outgrown the "nice to have" category. Dependence on contributions and on volunteers and pressure to raise gift income to higher levels have increased. Organizations must retain their own commitment to expand, to do more, and to grow, even when faced with less revenue. The means to grow can come from greater public gift support. Successful solicitation programs can ensure that an organization succeeds in meeting its goals and objectives and fulfills its mission and purposes. Being alert to changes can enhance management of those programs.

---

[16]"Deductibility of Payments Made to Charities Conducting Fund-Raising Events," Internal Revenue Service Revenue Ruling 67–246 (June, 1988).

EXHIBIT 6.10 Challenges to Fund Development Professionals

Access	Ethics
Accountability	Giving is voluntary
Caring	Loyalty and integrity
Charitable purpose	Not-for-profits making profits
Certification	Outcomes measurement
Coalitions and collaboration	Privacy rights
Commerciality	Professional conduct
Communications	Professional (paid) solicitors
Community	Public benefit tests
Compensation	Public confidence and trust
Competition	Quality reporting
Cost-effectiveness	Research on philanthropic practice
Cultivation	Scams, scandals, and fraud
Culture	Telemarketing
Disclosure	Vision and values
Diversity	Volunteers
Education and training	Women in philanthropy

Exhibit 6.10 lists in alphabetical order some challenges that may require modifications to organizations' behavior and management practices. Each is described in the following sections.

Access

More often than not, access to services is a problem for the people who need them. Today there are more people than ever standing in longer lines, facing shortages of food and housing, being referred to other sites, sometimes meeting with outright denials. All this in a nation where economic times are better than ever. Government has consistently reduced spending for human services (a policy called "devolution") in the 1990s while the huge government deficit inherited when the decade began has all but been eliminated. The expectation that not-for-profit organizations will be the government's safety net is a fiction made more unbelievable by congressional tax reform measures to reduce the incentives for private giving! Too many agencies and institutions, never flush with enough money, are on fiscal short rations to survive; they may still be here but access to them has decreased. Where in their mission statement does it say a positive bottom line is their purpose for being? Where does it say that America's rich tradition of philanthropy has to exist using minimal facilities with staff working long hours at low wages trying to deliver quality services to people in need? Only a few of America's more than one million not-for-profit organizations are financially healthy. A breaking point is coming when this valued system will collapse under the sheer weight of people in need with no other place to go.

Accountability

One of the biggest challenges facing America's not-for-profit organizations is accountability. How do they answer to the call to demonstrate the relevance of their mission, validate their vision, explain their fiscal conservatism, prove the public benefit they render, defend their management practices, and explain their fund-raising expenses? Janne G. Gallagher and Bruce R. Sievers suggest that the answer lies in standards set by the not-for-profit industry itself, not in government-imposed restrictions:

> In fact, despite a few well-publicized cases to the contrary, there is little evidence of significant wrong-doing or irresponsible behavior by non-profit organizations. Nor is there a lack of accountability. The real problem is the growing tendency to confuse the accountability standards for government agencies with those for private organizations that work toward the public good. The standards for one set of organizations are different—and should be different—from the standards of the other. . . . It is inappropriate and ultimately counterproductive for government, in the name of accountability, to impose substantial restrictions on non-profit groups' private operations. . . . Indeed, self-accountability is a vital goal for the field and should be encouraged through the promulgation of accountability standards and effective management practices by professional associations and non-profit policy groups.[17]

Results of performance reviews must be subject to open and full disclosure because not-for-profit organizations depend on the public's confidence and trust in what they say and what they do with "their money." Results can be measured and monitored and the conclusions publicized, but organizations must go beyond minimal reporting standards. They must also be willing to share operating details as well as sensitive information including fiscal decisions, in order to keep a sometimes skeptical, even cynical, public willingly supporting their mission and vision by giving of their time, talent, energy, wealth, and work. There is increased in-

---

[17]Janne G. Gallagher and Bruce R. Sievers, "Charities and the Shibboleth of Accountability," Editorial in *Chronicle of Philanthropy*, July 16, 1998, 56–57.

terest in how all the monies received are used, no matter the source, to benefit the community.[18] The public wants to see results as measurable outcomes. Fiscal reports are of particular interest; they must be meticulously correct, clearly presented, easy to read, accurate, and fully accessible to the public. The conduct of everyone associated with a not-for-profit organization must be impeccable at all times, not only to validate their levels of expertise and competency, but to be blameless in their personal conduct. Everyone, employees as well as board members and management staff, must be able to demonstrate a serious commitment to a high quality of performance. In summary, there can be nothing private about a public benefit corporation, including the conduct of its board members, managers, donors, and employees engaged in support of its mission, vision, and values to benefit others.

Caring

While the word *care* does not appear in the mission statement of every not-for-profit organization, it is implied without exception. The purpose of charitable enterprises is to help others or to advance a cause on behalf of others. Those who would abuse this basic intent for personal gain care not at all about anyone but themselves, although they may pretend otherwise. *Philanthropy* means "love of humankind," an active expression of honest concern for others. *Altruism* is the practice of unselfish concern for the welfare of others (as opposed to *egoism*). Active practice is required; it has been said that "fund raising is a contact sport." Charitable actions demonstrate an honest spirit of goodwill toward others. Such actions are of noble purpose, convey high worth, and add dignity to those in need. Whatever the form or method used, it is the selfless action of caring that we humans can demonstrate to one another and for all living things, including this fragile planet, that makes us unique on this earth.

Charitable Purpose

Not-for-profit organizations currently enjoy four special privileges under the law provided they demonstrate a charitable purpose. These areas, like the four legs of a table, are the exemption from income, sales, and property taxes plus the charitable contribution deduction. Some states are

---

[18]See "Donors Want to Know Where the $$ Goes!" by Bruce Campbell, *Fund Raising Management*, 29 (July 1998): 40–42.

EXHIBIT 6.11 Pennsylvania's Institutions for Purely Public Charity Act

---

Characteristics of a "Pure Public Charity"
(for Hospitals, as Defined by the Commonwealth of Pennsylvania)

	Score				
	Low				High
1. Advance a charitable purpose	1	2	3	4	5
2. Render gratuitously a substantial portion of its services	1	2	3	4	5
3. Benefit a substantial and indefinite class of persons who are legitimate objects of charity	1	2	3	4	5
4. Relieve government of some of its burden	1	2	3	4	5
5. Operate entirely free from private motive	1	2	3	4	5
Totals:					

The above law, Institutions for Purely Public Charity Act, was amended in November 1997 to provide three additional tests to retain tax-exempt status:

1. The institution must provide uncompensated service equal to at least 75 percent of net operating income but not less than 3 percent of total operating expenses.
2. Compensation and benefits of any director, officer, or employee shall not be based primarily on financial performance of the organization.
3. The institution must relieve some governmental burden, such as providing service that would otherwise be the government's responsibility.

---

moving to restrict these benefits, however. The Commonwealth of Pennsylvania has codified charitable purpose for hospitals in the Institutions for Purely Public Charity Act (see Exhibit 6.11). Furthermore, in 1997, three stiff requirements were added for organizations that wish to retain tax-exempt status. Hospitals that fail to comply may lose their exempt privilege or pay a tax or assessed fee tied to a ratio of a quantified measure of community benefits delivered compared with gross revenues received. The intent behind this law appears to be to raise money for state and municipal services (e.g., fire and police protection) rather than to advance the delivery of human services to those in need. Should this policy spread to other states, it will cost more than any taxes or fees; it will undermine the public's confidence and trust in the ability of charitable organizations' ability to render public benefits.

Certification

Every fund-raising executive should be in serious pursuit of his or her certification as a competent professional. Certification is an objective validation of personal accountability to our craft and all those we serve—our donors and volunteers as well as our organizations and clients—and of our commitment to professional performance to the best of our ability. The Certified Fund Raising Executive (CFRE) Professional Certification Board, established by NSFRE and AHP in 1996, represents the consolidated or "baseline" level of self-credentialing. To earn the CFRE citation requires five to eight years of fund-raising employment; submission of an application reporting positions held, funds raised, continuing education, and public service; and passing a four-hour, 200-question examination. Two advanced levels of certification also are available: NSFRE's Advanced Certified Fund Raising Executive (ACFRE) and AHP's Fellow (FAHP). Requirements for them are similar to those for the CFRE with the following additions: eight or more years experience, at least one CFRE recertification, a second four-hour examination, and an oral defense of examples of current work. The advanced level is not for everyone but the baseline credential should be every professional's minimal commitment to his or her craft.

Coalitions and Collaborations

The speed of everything except making baby elephants continues to accelerate. The delivery of services, whether to the few or the many, is rendered more complex to understand and made more difficult to effect. No single organization can hope to address more than a portion of one major problem, such as the AIDS epidemic, child health, or hunger, be it at the local, national, or global level. Resources are too limited. The best solution is joint enterprises that can effect change, enterprises that bring together organizations from the business, government, and not-for-profit sectors as partners. These partnerships will work because they engage the best minds of all three worlds, all working together for common purposes. Each sector brings a separate strength and ability to help define problems and to design and achieve solutions. The public prefers to see its time, energy, and money go as far as possible to address the needs of more people rather than less. More important to the future of not-for-profit organizations, the larger should help the smaller, the strong the weaker, the more experienced the newcomer. Because the resources available for charitable work are limited, coalitions of funds, talent, energy, and volunteers must become more acceptable within organizations as well as outside their walls. Without true partnership efforts involving the resources of the entire community, the most serious issues of our day will only stammer and stutter in our consciousness and never truly be resolved.

Commerciality

Many areas of not-for-profit enterprise have become businesslike. Today it is difficult for people to tell the difference between for-profit and not-for-profit entities. America's hospitals are but one highly visible example. A rash of acquisitions, buyouts, and mergers in the 1990s among for-profit hospitals and not-for-profit chains has caused this confusion. For-profit multi-institutional systems now operate clinics, nursing homes, rehabilitation centers, and hospices as well as hospitals in numerous states. They employ thousands of people, have billion-dollar operating budgets, possess significant reserves, and even have their names listed on the stock market. And by their profit margins, they demonstrate a high level of effectiveness and efficiency. To be fair, there has been enormous economic pressure on all hospitals to merge and to position themselves as strategic marketing units in order to survive and continue to provide quality services. In the midst of so much commercial-seeming activity, the public is hard pressed today to recognize its community hospital as for profit or not-for-profit and committed to charitable purposes. This perception destroys the reason to give. Weakened requests are more likely to go unopened and unanswered unless public confusion is replaced with public confidence and trust again.

Other not-for-profit entities such as museums and thrift stores, even Goodwill Industries and the YMCA, engage in highly visible (and perfectly legal) for-profit enterprises as a source of additional revenue. Critics (usually for-profit competitors) claim this activity blurs the not-for-profit and for-profit distinction and is materially disadvantageous to business enterprises. For example, a similar if not identical business such as a gift shop, recycling or thrift store, or fitness center does not have the tax-exempt privileges of a museum, Goodwill, or YMCA. The income, sales, and property tax-exempt privileges of not-for-profit organizations make competition unfair, especially when the not-for-profit entity can charge a lower price for the same service because it also can seek gifts to support its programs. At risk, should these sources of revenue be challenged in court, is not the loss of exempt privilege but paying taxes on the income. And although the intent of such enterprise is to earn money for charitable purposes, the court challenge may result in the loss of more than the amount of the taxes. These same dollars would have served those in need.

Communications

In today's global society, the sum of human knowledge is doubling every four years. More people are accessing this information, thanks to computers and satellites, which enable instant communication with just about anywhere in the world. But the *art* of communication between people is suffering from this information overload. "Sound bites" do not provide real information but are used for emphasis, perceived verification, and less than the whole story. News sources, in their race to be "first" with any story, have become lax in verifying their facts. Television programs not only showcase sex and violence but do so with vulgar language and incorrect grammar.

Not-for-profit organizations cannot hope to compete financially with commercial and government uses of communications systems. They must learn how to use these tools in select ways by investing in their knowledge and expertise to remain current as well as visible. One by-product of so much data is saturation—the public "tunes out" the variety of audio and visual communications. Getting a message delivered is tough and takes new knowledge plus special skills, repetition, and real money to invest in multimedia strategies (i.e., using mail, radio, telephone, fax, the Internet, advertising, video, cable and commercial TV *together*). Because money always will be scarce for this area, which is often perceived as unrelated to mission-oriented programs and services, not-for-profit organizations must be selective, employ competent staff, invest in a highly coordinated way, stay the course, monitor the results, and remain flexible. Modern communications are driven by public receptivity and responsiveness. That mood can change rapidly and leave a new marketing campaign in the dust, regarding it as "old fashioned" and "out-of-date." Such campaigns are ineffective and a poor use of scarce dollars.

Community

Some 180 years ago, Alexis de Tocqueville made several (wise) observations on the nature and spirit of Americans in their still-new country—specifically he noted how citizens acted together to address community needs without any state or federal support or encouragement. Perhaps the only vestige of this practice we can claim today are "grassroots" organizations who are noisy, focus on local needs (even at the city block level), organize citizens to action, take on issues, and address problems left unresolved or unattended by government. Robert Putnam in his now-famous commentary, "Bowling Alone," observed our failed community action practice and laid the blame on excessive hours spent watching television. The reality of gangs, violence, self-absorbed people, failed schools, teen problems, and declining church membership and attendance are ample evidence of our failed communities. Because most not-for-profit organizations were founded to serve the breadth of community needs, they still represent our best hope to provide the leadership to regain citizen respect for and a willingness to participate in their communities.

Compensation

The debate on paying not-for-profit executives escalated in the 1990s following disclosure of several fiscal excesses, beginning with James and Tammy Fay Bakker's abuse of PTL Ministries money for personal purposes. Just as notable was United Way Chief Executive William Aramony's $483,0000 salary and benefits package, which included New York and Florida apartments plus trips on the *Concorde*. Both Jim Bakker and Aramony landed in jail as a result. These revelations were treated inaccurately by the media as fund-raising scandals; they were improper use of funds raised, not illicit solicitation practices. Congress has attempted to set a salary ceiling for all not-for-profit executives. One bill proposed a limit of not more than $100,000 per year, another a ceiling not to exceed that paid a junior member of the House of Representatives. At this writing, no ceiling has yet emerged as law, but the issue has been reinforced by the 1996 Tax Reform Act ("The Taxpayer Bill of Rights 2") that gives the IRS the power of "intermediate sanctions." One area included in the IRS regulations covers how to identify "excessive compensation."

The compensation method for professional fund-raising executives is a separate as well as sensitive issue. Some board members still believe these employees are salespeople and can be motivated to work harder to bring in more gifts if personal, private-gain incentives are their compensation method. But this theory is contrary to the nature of not-for-profit organizations. Commissions and percentages have the potential to harm fund raising at all levels and to decrease, not increase, gift revenue. Consider just two scenarios: First, most organizations depend on volunteers to help raise money. How long will volunteers solicit their friends and neighbors if the fund-raising staff receive a commission or percentage of the funds they raised? Second, donors' confidence and trust in the organizations they support depends greatly on the use of their money for charitable purposes. How long will donors give if they know the fund raiser asking for their gift will receive part of it and is motivated to get as much money as he or she can? Private gain is incongruous with charitable giving at every level and should be avoided without exception. Each of the professional trade associations representing fund raisers of all types has a strict code of ethical conduct and standards of professional practice that expressly prohibit membership and certification for anyone who accepts a percentage or commission method of compensation.

Competition

The opportunities for one organization's volunteers, donors, or staff to speak against another's to gain favor are few, thankfully. Such practices do not serve the public or philanthropy well at all. However, competition does exist for funds, friends, community leaders, donors, and volunteers. And it becomes conspicuous when organizations appeal to the same publics at the same time for support. This form of competition is healthy because it requires each request to be of high quality and for a verifiable need. However, this same public can become resentful from too much solicitation by mail, phone, or other means. Too many requests of the public are beyond the control of any one organization; just one request too many will tip the scale. Organizations must work smarter to control the use of their own lists and the timing of their requests so as not to overburden their constituents. Each has a variety of opportunities and means to increase its share of current and future leaders, members, donors, volunteers, and new friends. The best way to grow is to demonstrate respect for others' work as well as for each donor and volunteer who will help. Just how the continuous recruitment of new friends is done will be the key to each institution's success. Careful work is required along with a steady investment of time and effort; the rewards will be there and communities served will be the beneficiaries.

Cost-Effectiveness

Considerable effort still needs to be put into establishing cost-effectiveness standards for fund-raising methods as well as performance guidelines for overall fund development programs. At present, neither standards nor guidelines exist. Some measurement standards have been promulgated by the Council of Better Business Bureaus and the National Charities Information Bureau. These "watchdog" agencies suggest a combined expense for management and administration plus fund-raising costs of not more than 35 percent or 40 percent respectively. But separating these two broad areas of operations from direct program and service expenses is the first challenge; the second is distinguishing fund-raising costs from management and administration. All must be done *without* precise guidance from either the Financial Accounting Standards Board (FASB) or the AICPA, whose work in this area is incomplete.

Some in the field think that performance analysis can be applied across all organizations, but that is a difficult translation since fund-raising practices, while similar in form, do not perform the same for all organizations any more than program and service performance are identical. Comparative analysis between organizations, even between those of like nature (colleges, hospitals, museums, etc.), is difficult and often is misleading. This is especially true when simple bottom-line analysis is attempted. Variations from organization to organization in solicitation techniques, demographics, access to funding sources, pledge payment schedules, history of active fund raising, unscheduled bequest receipts, capital campaign status, volunteer performance, and many more factors make fair and equitable performance comparisons nearly impossible. This is especially trying for those board members, executive staff, donors, volunteers, and others who seek some benchmark data for assurance that their solicitation programs are within boundaries of acceptable practice. The best answer is for organizations to measure their own performance for a minimum of three years and use that to establish their own standards. In the meantime, the question of fund-raising expenses will remain a thorny issue for every not-for-profit organization and its fund development staff today.

Cultivation

Too often fund development staff and volunteers concentrate on solicitation more than cultivation. Granted, repeated requests, or solicitations, are part of the design of the annual giving programs described in Chapter 3, but gifts of size from corporations, foundations, and especially individuals are not easily repeatable and require time to develop. Sometimes the pace of activity or the pressure to produce cash by deadlines or achieve dollar goals can cause a hasty ask of an unprepared prospect. Donors need time to make an important (big gift) decision. It is this period of deliberation, called cultivation, that is reserved as a time for "wooing" the prospect. The objective is to provide information, encourage involvement, verify interest areas, and invite active participation leading to an important investment decision. Cultivation is both a strategic and artful process that requires skill plus patience and perseverance. The goal is to persuade but remember that making a gift is the donor's decision, not ours. Our role is to be a catalyst, to facilitate the process leading to a favorable decision, and to be sure to ask when the time is right. And, lest we forget our manners and our professionalism, if the donor's decision is "no," we should maintain however much interest and attention is warranted to keep the door open for another opportunity in the future. It is truly bad manners to "drop" the prospect just because he or she declined to make a gift when asked. If we judged the prospect as qualified and worthy of attention in the first place, he or she remains so and should still be treated with respect in order that the cultivation can continue.

Culture

Each not-for-profit organization, no matter its size, has an internal culture. This style of "the way we do things," or manner of operating, can emanate from the founder or a board member but most often comes from the CEO. If the CEO comes to work at 9:00 A.M. and stays until 6:00 P.M., that pattern is likely to be copied by other managers. If the chairman of the board begins meetings on time, most board members will make the effort to be prompt. Culture plays a role in fund raising, too, in the form of the personality or style of key people in the organization who meet with donors and prospects. Some CEOs are friendly and outgoing, even gregarious; meeting people is a pleasure for them. They enjoy it, and it shows. But it is also exhausting. Other CEOs are less outgoing; the necessity to meet and talk with strangers is difficult. This style shows too and is equally exhausting. But both personalities can be successful at fund raising. For example, the fund raiser can arrange settings and circumstances to use the gregarious CEO with impact, such as seating select guests at the CEO's table following a full receiving line where he or she meets all the guests. Likewise, the fund raiser can increase the comfort of less outgoing CEOs by employing smaller gatherings and private dinners. Donors as well as volunteers are quick to tune in to institutional culture and the personal style of its key leaders.

Disclosure

Nothing makes a not-for-profit organization more nervous than being asked to explain itself. What is it doing? Whom is it serving? Its reason for being is not difficult to explain, and most can and are willing to share this information in detail. Where they have problems is with questions about decision-making processes, including board nominations, and about how they use their funds. Not-for-profit financial operations are different from for-profit practices. Revenue flows in from contributions, gifts of property, dues and memberships, proceeds from benefit events, and bequests—sources that are foreign and unavailable to any for-profit firm or corporation. Expenses are expressed in programs and services given to the public for free, not in the manufacture and sale of products for sale. More difficult to understand, from the corporate point of view, are the absence of the profit motive, the drive to earn money from operations, and the need to satisfy stockholders. Not-for-profit organizations pay first allegiance to their mission, vision, and values statements. Philanthropy and altruism are principles, not products. To overcome its fear of disclosure, then, the organization should go on the offensive. Explain why its mission was adopted. Educate others about how public needs are met through not-for-profit organizations designed to deliver services. Share where the income comes from and where the expenditures go; if people want to learn and understand, they will accept information with an open mind.

The 1990s ushered in the "age of accountability" and not-for-profit organizations were invited (even required) to disclose details about their internal operations. Regardless of who or what caused it—a doubting public, media coverage of scandals and abusive practices, political motives, or other causes—this need to explain has increased. Open and full disclosure helps the public to understand better what its charitable institutions and agencies are trying to accomplish, why they believe their work is needed, how they go about their business, and how they measure success. Most organizations have written, revised, and updated their statements of mission, vision, and values to provide better answers. But some remain reluctant to open their doors (and especially their books) to the public, whom they are founded to serve. If questions are about compensation of the five highest paid employees, that information is public knowledge (see Section IV, IRS Form 990, the annual tax return filed by all not-for-profit organizations). If questions are about quantity and quality of service, many not-for-profit organizations are accredited, provide program details to government sources, and offer their own reports on community needs and how they attempt to meet them. The lesson to be learned is that information made available to the public upon request is a positive strategy. Whatever the inquiry, organizations can accept the guidance that "there is nothing private about a not-for-profit, public-benefit corporation."

Diversity

A continuing challenge for each not-for-profit organization is reflecting the diversity of its constituency on its board and among its management staff, volunteers, donors, professional staff, and support employees. Two obstacles must be overcome. First, to be a donor requires a certain financial ability that not everyone has. Therefore, fund raising is discriminatory out of necessity. Second, the diversity of many organizations' current board members and employees does not reflect that of their constituencies. Organizations also do not have easy access to community leaders within these diverse groups. Conversely, these leaders are too often spread thinly among many organizations, including their own. In other cultures not evolved from the Western civilization path, traditions of philanthropic practice are different and an adjustment to current patterns will be required to compete successfully with other, established charities. It is incumbent upon America's not-for-profit organizations and fund-raising professional trade associations to reach out to all their constituents. They must define places to allow wider participation, provide easy access to their institutions and membership, offer orientation and training on not-for-profit operations, invite personal involvement with programs and services, and teach that volunteerism benefits everyone in the community. Should these organizations fall short or worse, fail to try, then in all likelihood they cannot succeed in their mission.

Education and Training

Board members, executive and management staff, donors, and volunteers, along with fund-raising staff at all levels, need access to education and training in the management of not-for-profit organizations. Too many men and women come to work with high desire and serious intentions but without any instruction or experience in the nature and purpose of the organizations they serve, the tradition of philanthropy, or the management skills required to direct those organizations. Moreover, they know even less about how fund raising is conducted and how to supervise it. Here is one example. Do you think you know how to organize and manage a not-for-profit organization? If you do, pay a visit to each of the following: a food distribution center, a thrift store, a symphony orchestra, a performing arts center, and a United Way office. What you will find is that each is quite a different enterprise to be managed. You will also find that each is alike in being volunteer intensive. The ability to manage volunteers to perform jobs as demanding as those of actual employees without monetary reward is an art. If you wish to serve and serve well, avail yourself of the education and training programs in not-for-profit management now widely available.

Ethics

The decade of the 1990s witnessed increased attention to ethical standards and guidelines for professional practice in fund raising. To their credit, all of the fund-raising trade associations and their leaders have made ethical conduct a priority with their members and have increased public awareness of the principles they advocate. Many of these principles are uncontested, but one has been the focus of controversy—compensation. As noted earlier in this chapter, professional standards advocate that fund raisers, both employed staff and professional consultants, be paid only a salary or fee, and not on a commission or percentage basis. However, some board members and volunteers whose own for-profit business pays its employees in this fashion all the time have challenged this principle. Providing employees with compensation as an incentive to raise more money, they argue, is the way to increase fund-raising results. The traditional method to raise more money has always been for board members to join with staff. This issue is not easy for everyone to understand but the arguments against commissions and percentages are the correct policy. Bonuses are another issue. A bonus payment is acceptable if overall performance is the measure, the practice is consistent throughout the organization, and the bonus paid is not based exclusively on funds raised. One other compensation issue relates to the professional or "paid" solicitor and is discussed later in this chapter.

The public in general is unaware of the ethical principles that do guide professional practice, and that lack of knowledge does not work in favor of public confidence and trust by donors and volunteers. One way to increase the public's awareness is to publish guidelines for not-for-profit organizations, as the Maryland Association of Nonprofit Organizations and the Minnesota Council of Nonprofits both have done. The Maryland Association's guidelines for ethical behavior by charities contain 8 "Guiding Principles" and 55 "Standards for Excellence." The Minnesota text offers 90 "Standards for Excellence." Not-for-profit organizations that wish to be certified by the Maryland Association must submit an application with supporting documentation and pay a fee. Once approved, their certification remains in effect for three years, after which they must reapply.[19] Language for these two principles and standards texts was taken from documents already developed and used by the following organizations: American Association of Museums, American Cancer Society, Council of Better Business Bureaus, Council on Foundations, Evangelical Council for Financial Accountability, InterAction, National Charities Information Bureau, and the NSFRE. The use of such measures by state authorities, currently a voluntary process, could be a burden for not-for-profit organizations if they must comply. Those that do complete their certification will be permitted to use this "seal of approval" in all their marketing, communications, and fund-raising messages—a great aid to increasing public confidence.

Giving is Voluntary

Lest we forget, public participation in not-for-profit organizations is a voluntary act. Bob Payton's definition of philanthropy as "voluntary action for the public good" is quite accurate. There are times when volunteers in their enthusiasm want to do something that others, especially staff, believe is misguided or doomed to failure. This is a difficult situation to address with success. At other times, fund-raising professionals find it hard to motivate donors as well as volunteers to participate adequately or in a timely manner. As fund raisers, we need to remember that our information is more complete and our motives, although correctly self-serving, are more focused than those of many donors. Our communications must make the argument repeatedly that the value of our organization and carrying out its mission, vision, purposes, goals, and objectives is focused on one cause—to meet public needs. The means to that end includes the active participation of the public, whether they give only

[19]Stephen G. Green, "State Associations Draft Ethical Standards to Bolster Trust in Charities," *Chronicle of Philanthropy,* July 16, 1998, 44–45.

time, energy, talent, and a willingness to work, or whether they give resources—treasure, true wealth, or in a generous spirit, whatever amount they can afford. We also must remember and share this mantra with all who are willing to help: Charitable work is not about us, nor money, nor time, but what volunteers acting together with organizations with money and time can do for others.

Loyalty and Integrity

Loyalty and integrity applies first to fund-raising staff, then to volunteers and donors. All three are influenced by commitment and longevity. The loyalty exhibited by staff must be greater than agreeing to abide by the organization's policies and procedures and adhering to its mission, vision, and values. They also must give their loyalty to their colleagues at all levels, most notably their supervisors and those they supervise. As public spokespersons for the organization, the loyalty of fund-raising staff is on display to the entire organization—its board, administration, professional staff, employees as well as its clients, patients, customers, volunteers, donors, and prospects. This same virtue applies to volunteers and donors, too, but to a lesser degree—in that they are not paid to work on behalf of the organization. For them, loyalty and advocacy are a matter of personal choice.

Integrity applies first to confidentiality required of staff with access to personal giving records and personal data used in prospect research and cultivation strategies. Integrity also applies to volunteers who commit to a task in front of their peers—one hopes that they do not turn to staff later and direct them to take care of their assignment. Also, the knowledge volunteers gain from one organization ought not to be used for personal gain at another. Donor integrity is no less important, for in promising to make a gift or pledge, it is incumbent upon them to fulfill it to the best of their ability. Should any of these participants fail their tests of loyalty and integrity, the organization is harmed somewhat, but its clients, patients, and customers are harmed more.

Not-for-Profits Making Profits

The public often does not understand that not-for-profit organizations, to be successful in carrying out their mission, must be well led, well managed, and well financed. As not-for-profit institutions and agencies grow they become better known in the community. Many are the largest employers in the community and could qualify as a Fortune 500 or 1000 company on the size of their operating budget. Just as any other organization, they must manage their annual budget successfully, which means they need to "make money" on daily operations. "Profit" is not a bad word for a not-for-profit organization; it is a sign of success, which most people can understand and appreciate. What is not as well known is what use is made of these revenues. The answer is that they are consumed by the organization in the next year's operating budget, are invested for future use, and are spent on equipment and facilities. They are not used to declare dividends and pay stockholders; there are no dividends or stockholders. As has been noted earlier in this text, federal law also allows not-for-profit organizations to engage in a limited amount of for-profit enterprise, because the use of any and all profits remain controlled by the not-for-profit organization for charitable purposes. Income tax is paid on the proceeds under Unrelated Business Income Tax rules. Despite their end use for charity, these for-profit efforts have crossed over into the area of regular business enterprises areas and earned the concern (and wrath) of small and large business owners, whose businesses have to compete with not-for-profit organizations that enjoy "unfair advantages" due to their tax-exempt privileges. The outcome may be more limits to what not-for-profit organizations can do, or increased UBIT taxes, or a complete restriction from such enterprises, all of which will reduce or eliminate a source of alternative revenue for annual operating purposes (only four sources are available: profit from operations, revenue from for-profit efforts, use of endowment and other investment earnings, and cash from contributions—to borrow money for annual operating purposes is never recommended).

Outcomes Measurement

Can a not-for-profit organization demonstrate that it is making a difference? Can it prove that it is fulfilling its mission by measuring the results of its programs and services? Is it effecting change, being a benefit to community residents, improving the quality of life, and more? Outcomes measurement is not about quantity as in counting how many people were helped or how much mail was distributed advocating a cause. It is more a measure of both the quality and quantity of programs, of whether they have made a positive difference. According to a United Way publication,

"Benefits may relate to knowledge, skills, attitudes, values, behavior, condition, or status. Examples of outcomes include greater knowledge of nutritional needs, improved reading skills, more effective responses to conflict, getting a job, or having greater financial stability. . . . Outcomes are benefits or changes for individuals or populations during or after participating in program activities. They are influenced by a program's outputs. . . . They are what participants know, think, or can do; or how they behave; or what their condition is, that is different following the program."[20] Outcomes measurement is now an imperative for all not-for-profit organizations, which must learn how to perform this difficult but not impossible task. Public benefit testing areas can be identified and matched to the mission, purposes, goals, and objectives of every organization, and the results should be reported annually and widely in a spirit of full and open disclosure. To do so is to fulfill the mission. To fail to conduct these essential measurements and public benefit tests may result in a loss of tax-exempt privileges.

Privacy Rights

Traditional prospect and donor research methods served fund-raising programs quite well for decades before the advent of electronic access to more complete information about people, corporations, and foundations. New methods of research will also serve us well. However, the current ease of access to data must be accompanied by an increased awareness of the privacy rights involved. Just because you have access to volumes of personal details about someone does not give you license to use that information in an unethical manner. In addition, organizations are expected to honor an individual's request to be left alone or to be removed from a mailing or telephone list. According to the Direct Marketing Association's (DMA) "Privacy Promise," based on rules that direct mail consultants are required to observe to remain DMA members, the client relationship on this matter will be guided by this precept: "The client still has the last say in terms of whether or not they follow these guidelines. Our obligation is to make a strong suggestion, and then document it if they refuse."[21] Both DMA members and not-for-profit organizations are encouraged to observe these four requirements:

---

[20]United Way of America, *Measuring Program Outcomes: A Practical Approach* (Alexandria, VA: United Way of America, 1996), xv, 2.

[21]Lee W. Robbins, quoted in Beverly Goodman, "Shielding the Donors: DMA's Privacy Plan Due This Month," *NPT's Direct Marketing Edition* (July 1998): 8.

- Organizations must provide notice as to how they use consumer information for marketing purposes.
- They must also provide an opportunity for recipients to opt out, or refuse, further mailings.
- They must maintain and use an in-house name suppression file.
- They must run their mailings through the DMA's suppression lists when prospecting for new customers.[22]

Privacy is perhaps the second-most privileged attribute each of us possesses, with freedom being the first. That the business of fund development is primarily friend raising and relationship building has already been noted. Respect for the rights of others is the beginning of a proper relationship; it must be accompanied by an equal and even greater respect for the personal and private information available to fund-raising staff and volunteers about individuals, corporations, and foundations.

Professional Conduct

It follows privacy rights that all individuals engaged in fund-raising work are called to a high standard of personal and professional conduct. They feel daily pressure to raise more money, increase the number of donors and their gift amounts, improve volunteer performance and their commitment, and more. To be true to this calling is to forego certain personal rights, including the right to step out of character at any time. As fundraisers we hold a 24-hour-a-day job, seven days a week. We are never "off duty" in the sense that we do not continue to represent our employer and its mission and values at the end of a work day. We also live in the same community as our donors and volunteers and will see them and be seen by them any time we are away from work. We are not invisible. Professional behavior is a personal responsibility. Observance of professional standards of conduct reinforces the validity of the organization's own message about respect for others, which is an integral part of its culture of caring for others. Personal behavior exemplifies how fund development ought to be performed and sets the standard for newcomers in the organization to follow. Professional conduct gives leadership, accountability, and maximum levels of performance to the entire fund development process.

---

[22] Beverly Goodman, "Shielding the Donors: DMA's Privacy Plan Due This Month," *NPT's Direct Marketing Edition* (July 1998): 8.

Professional (Paid) Solicitors

If standards of professional conduct apply to traditional fund raisers, then expectations of ethical conduct apply to those who choose to engage in this work as "paid solicitors." It is neither illegal nor unethical to engage in a business that uses traditional solicitation methods to raise money for not-for-profit organizations. Not-for-profit organizations can choose to hire firms who then hire solicitors and pay them on a commission or percentage basis to solicit the public. However, problems arise when an individual chooses to use these same trusted methods for fraudulent purposes. Several fraud cases are brought each year across America against people who abuse the public and unsuspecting not-for-profit organizations for personal and private gain. The harm they do to public confidence and trust is immeasurable. It should be noted that organizations engaged in this kind of fund raising and the people they hire can neither be members of the professional fund-raising associations nor be a Certified Fund Raising Executive (CFRE). Each member of American Association of Fund Raising Counsel (AAFRC), AHP, CASE, NSFRE, National Catholic Development Conference (NCDC), and similar societies, are prohibited from any form of commission or percentage fund-raising practices.

Public Benefit Tests

State, county, and municipal governments are increasingly demanding that not-for-profit organizations demonstrate that they are providing public benefit to the communities they serve in exchange for their tax-exempt privileges. At issue in most instances is government's need for revenue. Legislators and other government officials are quite willing to sacrifice a principle or tradition that is not their own to justify this policy revision. Their reasons include changing public needs, increased cost of public services (police and firefighters), use of water and sewer services, and more; plus they argue for applying a fair-share distribution of costs philosophy to assess not-for-profit organizations from previously exempt status. The property owned by churches, schools, hospitals, museums, Boy and Girl Scout councils, and others is not inconsequential. The funds at issue are not small, given property tax rates, nor do these organizations have much in the way of excess funds for this purpose every year. To invite volunteers and donors to help raise these funds through contributions is an unlikely alternative. Should public benefit testing spread beyond those states currently piloting the program, and should it survive court tests of the principles of tax-exemption, every organization may feel the demand for its share of community services expense. At issue on the other side is whether government can manage its resources better.

Public Confidence and Trust

Fund raisers face no greater challenge in their day-to-day work than preserving the public's confidence and trust in what they say and what they do with its money. The public today has grown skeptical in nearly all aspects of daily life; few people today express blind faith in anything or anyone. Yet not-for-profit organizations perform good works daily. They solve problems; effect change; cure ills; clothe the homeless; feed the hungry; comfort the abused; educate and develop children's minds and morals; inspire art, music, and theater appreciation; teach people to read and speak languages; conserve and preserve the environment; and more. Some of these works are public services that government and business have abandoned; others are designed as working partnerships between government, business, and not-for-profit organizations. Most community residents are unaware of the extent of services provided daily; they may know only of those they have personally experienced and that experience may not have been satisfactory every time. To regain the public's confidence and to make it more aware of not-for-profit activities is an enormous challenge to every not-for-profit organization. To accomplish those goals, each organization must pay attention to all that is said and done in its name. It must also help its employees understand that their commitment to quality service to everyone with whom they have contact is imperative, and will demand an even higher level of personal and professional conduct than they are already maintaining. This task is not easy, is not accomplished overnight, and is never going to go away. Therefore, organizations' commitment to quality of service and their respect for those whom they serve is the most direct method to preserve the image and reputation they seek.

Quality Reporting

Not-for-profit organizations can demonstrate that they are seriously engaged in their mission and performing their duties well by being open and releasing public reports. It is perfectly acceptable to "brag up" your accomplishments but you must have a record of performance to back up any claims. Quality reporting is not as easy as public reporting might sound. Here are two examples: First, if a college shares data on first-year students' academic performance with the originating high schools, do those schools use these records in public announcements to demonstrate the success of their college admission curriculum and counseling? Probably. Will they use it if their success rate is poor? Not as likely. Second, hospitals must file statistics with several authorities on the mortality and morbidity of their patients, which is public knowledge made even more public when released to the media. Those with above average results will want to use this information as quality indicators. Will those with below average results be willing share them?

Quality reporting demands that the performance of not-for-profit organizations be open and available to the public. Informed and responsive organizations also appreciate that open and full disclosure of financial details can increase public confidence and trust. This fiscal disclosure includes their annual tax return (IRS Form 990), a compendium of financial information that is not easy to interpret whether or not the organization is successful in meeting public needs. For too many years, most not-for-organizations have not taken preparation of their annual tax return seriously, but they must begin to do so. The IRS Form 990 is the *only* uniform public reporting document required of every not-for-profit organization operating in America. Only religious organizations and entities with less than $25,000 in annual revenues are excused from filing it. These performance details must be made available upon request, according to the 1996 Tax Reform Act, either by phone, mail, e-mail, or facsimile; refusal to do so violates the law and will bring penalties. Copies of every organization's Form 990 are now accessible on the Internet as well.

Research on Philanthropic Practice

Professional research studies on the wide spectrum of entities and enterprises belonging to the not-for-profit sector were sparse before the 1990s but have now begun in earnest. More than 40 colleges and universities have formal not-for-profit management and philanthropic studies programs, offer degrees and certificates, and sponsor research projects led by academicians. Another 200 offer courses relating to not-for-profit management and philanthropic practice within an existing curriculum. Individuals, corporations, and foundations have begun to provide funds to support philanthropic studies. All this is evidence that research is gaining momentum. Outside formal educational settings, organizations like Independent Sector, the Foundation Center, the Conference Board, the National Center for Nonprofit Boards, and others are sponsoring research projects around the world to study the functions and services provided by not-for-profit organizations. Several publishers and professional associations have invested their own resources in a stream of textbooks, resource manuals, and workbooks in the field. All of these efforts have added substantially to the body of knowledge and made the field more accessible to the public. Much more remains to be done. The challenge is to offer some guidance or structure to the process so that critical issues as well as basic theory can be defined and developed alongside the applications of professional practice based on experience in the field.

Scams and Con Artists; Fraud and Abuse

Since the world is not yet perfect, incidents of fraud and abuse of public confidence and trust in not-for-profit organizations and in the methods used to solicit gifts will continue. The few who would trade upon public trust are not deterred much by legislation and regulation. Of equal concern are those who, while few in number, would use for their own benefit the funds given them for charitable purposes. Laws against both forms of fraud are on the books and are adequately enforced.

Scams and con artists are much harder to police because they seldom have any link with a not-for-profit organization. They are in "business" and they solicit money by mail, telephone, or other means in the name of a charity but keep the money and use it for their own purposes. Unfortunately, the public cannot easily see whether their appeal is legitimate and begins to suspect everyone who writes or calls asking for support. Door-to-door salespeople have all but disappeared because the method is no longer profitable. But door-to-door solicitation continues; so do sidewalk and mall and airport personal solicitations. Who can tell on sight whether their appeal is for legitimate charitable purposes or for the private gain of the solicitor, who also may be dressed in religious garb? The challenge is to provide public education about proper fund development methods and legitimacy tests. Volunteers, donors, and prospects must understand that their actions are to demonstrate professional conduct and that they should avoid areas where the public is suspicious and distrustful.

Telemarketing

Technological innovations in mass communications are quickly put to wide use, including in public solicitation for charitable purposes. Telemarketing in all its forms (telephone, fax, e-mail, and direct mail) uses every available public communications channel today, singly and in combination as multimedia advertising, promotional, and sales programs. These messages join an already impressive stream of information that is growing daily. The challenges to not-for-profit organizations are twofold: being able to afford the cost, and being able to be seen and heard. How much time, effort, and money should an organization devote to mass communications using currently available technology? Can this task be hired out to professionals, or should the resources be brought inside the organization for better management and at less cost? Can these activities be justified when they require funds that otherwise could be spent on programs and services to meet public needs? There is also cause-related marketing to consider. It offers the option to partner with a for-profit business and take advantage of its experience and talent plus its much larger advertising and communications budgets, but its downside is being associated with the for-profit enterprise.

Vision and Values

Not-for-profit organizations tend to underutilize their statements of vision and values. Most people have heard *about* the mission statement (and more than a few board members and employees can recite it, if it is short enough), but is the public sufficiently familiar with its message? Most are too wordy and lack precision in their explanation of why the organization exists and what it does. Do you know the vision and values statements of your favorite organizations? A vision statement is important because it provides a direction for the future, a set of objectives the organization is striving to achieve, whether it is increasing the number of clients, patients, or customers served or improving the quality of its programs—noble and notable goals and worthy of study should they see the light of day. Values statements are important because they state the virtues that the organization and its employees strive to attain in order to achieve their mission and vision. That its values have been articulated in a formal statement means the organization is committed to supporting them with incentives and opportunities in their employee relations programs that encourage and enable everyone involved to serve their clients, patients, and customers with personal attention and respect. To a large degree, vision and values statements are examples of an organization's culture and reflect the expectations of all who choose to work there.

Volunteers

Volunteers are essential to every not-for-profit organization. Some come to you on their own; others you actively recruit. They serve in a multitude of ways from the top to the bottom of the organization, and all are valuable. Not because they are "free help," but because they share in the organization's commitment to help others. The first requirement in forming a not-for-profit, public benefit corporation is to recruit voluntary board members, who become responsible for the health and welfare of the organization itself. Other volunteers are recruited to fill out the board's committees, often with nonboard members (who are, in fact, recruits for board service later on). The programs and services provided are also avenues for voluntary service. Depending on the organization and its needs, there may be hundreds of volunteers working for it daily, providing valuable services to its clients, patients, and customers. Each organization faces the task of using its volunteer corps wisely: "Engaging volunteers in appropriate and meaningful ways must be the biggest challenge faced by not-for-profit organizations. Enabling is the way to answer the challenge. The big question is, what are the meaningful and appropriate activities volunteers can do? Philanthropic organizations continually wrestle with this. Often staff and volunteers disagree about what is meaningful and appropriate involvement. Through enabling, your volunteers and staff decide together."[23] Churches offer volunteer opportunities as collection takers, altar boys and girls, and leaders for bible readings, as well as opportunities to serve in choirs, or in guilds that decorate and maintain the facilities. Hospital auxilians perform innumerable services as information greeters, book distributors, gift shop operators, and office workers, performing duties that otherwise would require hiring more employees. Theater volunteers collect and sell tickets, usher you to your seat, and perform a variety of necessary tasks behind the curtain. Boy and Girl Scout councils depend on parents for multiple services that benefit both volunteer and youngster. The list is endless.

[23]Simone P. Joyaux, *Strategic Fund Development: Building Profitable Relationships That Last* (Gaithersburg, MD: Aspen, 1997), 178.

Fund-raising volunteers are the arms and legs of a development program and are an excellent means to recruit community residents to become engaged in "their" charitable organization of choice. Many volunteers are engaged in direct solicitation while others are busy with every facet of benefit event planning and production. Others prefer to assemble invitations and stuff envelopes. Still more provide advice and counsel on planning, marketing, and communications strategy, or help with investment policy or reviewing life-income contracts for planned giving donors. Leadership in all areas where volunteers are engaged also is essential. Volunteer leaders and workers must be recruited and trained, encouraged and supported, evaluated and rewarded in order for an organization to achieve progress.

Women in Philanthropy

Philanthropy has become feminized. Women represent the majority of volunteers as well as employed fund-raising professionals (accounting for 60 percent or more of association memberships). The field offers opportunities for satisfying work as well as new career options that contain the flexibility necessary for a woman to work and maintain a home and family. The demands of fund raising fit well with a woman's natural ability to engage people in social settings, to cope with diverse personalities, and to nurture relationships. The field is open equally to men and women with no formal training or prior experience although women more often have had direct contact with the job's duties and responsibilities as volunteers. There are, unfortunately, equity issues yet to be resolved regarding gender and compensation gap, and the work brings with it the challenge of dealing with frequent travel and the necessity of changing jobs to gain wider experience and increased responsibility.[24]

Women as donors and volunteers also represent a large part of the future of not-for-profit organizations. Women now control or will control decisions on the distribution of the bulk of an estimated $10 trillion in wealth and assets over the next 15 to 20 years, for the simple reason that women outlive men. Women as philanthropists already have established themselves by their personal leadership and their major gifts. They are dedicated, passionate advocates for a mission or cause and are equally ca-

---

[24]See Kelly, *Effective Fund-Raising Management,* 89–102, for a thorough presentation on the feminization of philanthropy. See also Duronio and Tempel, *Fund Raisers: Their Careers, Stories, Concerns, and Accomplishments,* 24–43, 61–68, 178–180, for details on career options, demographics, salary, titles, work weeks, and more.

pable of asking others for money—big money to support the organizations they represent. Women's participation is guided by the following precepts: Create, Change, Connect, Collaborate, Commit, and Celebrate. Both men and women need to understand these attributes in detail and appreciate in full.[25]

MEASURING SUCCESS

Sometimes it helps to see things from other perspectives. You can measure the true success of your fund-raising program by evaluating it through the eyes of donors, volunteers, the organization, and fund-raising staff. Here are the goals that each of those four evaluators might hope to achieve:

Success as Measured by Donors

- Be accepted and appreciated
- Respond positively; perform a duty
- Respond satisfactorily; receive spiritual reward
- Fulfill personal aspirations; be involved
- Assuage guilt; help others in need
- Be noticed; achieve status
- Be invited to do more
- Receive donor benefits and personal gains
- Overcome fear and anxiety
- Receive tax deductions

Success as Measured by Volunteer Solicitors

- Confirm true value of one's assistance
- Build personal confidence
- Build a willingness to volunteer again
- Be personally motivated to make own best gifts

[25]Sondra C. Shaw and Martha A. Taylor, "Women as Philanthropists: Leading the Transformation in Major Gift Fundraising," in *Developing Major Gifts,* ed. Dwight F. Burlingame and James M. Hodge. New Directions for Philanthropic Fundraising, no. 16. (Jossey-Bass, 1997), 66–69. See also Taylor and Shaw, *Reinventing Fundraising: Realizing the Potential of Women's Philanthropy* (San Francisco: Jossey-Bass, 1995), 83–100, and "Career Women: A Changing Environment for Philanthropy" *NSFRE Journal* 16 (Fall 1991): 43–49.

- Achieve more results than could provide alone
- Enable and encourage advocacy of the cause
- Be publicly recognized for high performance
- Be part of a successful team effort

Success as Measured by Not-for-Profit Organizations

- Help to fulfill the mission and vision
- Tell donors they are appreciated for who they are and confirm their value for what they have done
- Identify and recruit volunteers who will ask their friends for money
- Identify and recruit leaders who are able to direct others to perform a similar assignment when asked
- Ask current donors to increase their level of giving
- Identify major gift prospects among individuals and organizations
- Operate at a reasonable, cost-efficient budget level

Success as Measured by Fund Development Staff

- Successfully manage the solicitation process
- Successfully manage volunteer-donor exchange
- Successfully manage donor research data into an action plan with a cultivation and solicitation strategy
- Successfully build confidence of volunteers and donors
- Convert goals and objectives into programs and services that benefit others in need
- Successfully manage the continuing donor relationship
- Achieve personal goals and objectives

THE LAST WORD IS STILL RECOGNITION

When all else is said and done, everyone should be thanked again for all they have done to help the organization succeed in its mission to benefit others. Board members, donors, support group officers and members, capital campaign and annual giving campaign volunteers, benefit event volunteers and ticket buyers, the people who make commemorative gifts, the chief executive officer, chief financial officer, and other management staff, the fund development staff, the people across the hall who answer the phones when the staff are away, the housekeeping staff who empty the wastebaskets—*everyone*. Next, a letter should go to all clients, vendors, professional colleagues, and even competitors whose good work made everyone work harder. Together, all of them increased public understanding and support of the role of philanthropy in the community.

There are four major areas where attention to donors always deserves a priority: gift acknowledgment, donor relations, donor recognition, and rewards. This text concludes with some final advice on those who make fund development so worthwhile.

Gift Acknowledgment

How many ways can an organization say "Thank you"? Word processing programs simplify sending to the majority of donors each year letters that look and sound like they have been individually prepared. What is essential is that every donor gets a written acknowledgment signed by a hand, not a machine, and usually mailed within 48 hours after receipt of his or her gift. Several letters, or templates, can be prepared to have on hand for replies to every donor in whatever method of solicitation is used. The message in each letter is appropriate to the size of the gift, discusses the purpose or project he or she has chosen to support, and acknowledges accurate compliance with the donor's wishes. Different people will author these letters, depending on who directed the original solicitation. Higher authorities should acknowledge larger gifts, and the leadership gifts deserve at least two letters from the most senior people in the organization. These letters can be rewritten periodically, to keep their message fresh to repeat donors. Individual acknowledgment letters should go to donors who make a special or a more complicated gift such as stock, an appreciated asset, real property, or a planned gift. Each of these letters can be tailored to the conditions and details surrounding the gift. The text should assure the donors of the organization's complete and accurate understanding of their wishes for the use of their money, and a correct document for their use in filing tax returns should be provided.

Donor Relations

Donor relations begins with each donor the day his or her first gift is received. Giving is a habit; it needs to be nurtured and supported. Donors are an organization's best prospects and its relations with them never end until they stop giving; even then, their names are kept on the mailing list and they are asked again and again, to try to renew their interest. At some point, any further communications are neither worthwhile nor cost-effective, and the name should be moved to the prospect or suspect file. Some offices keep every prior donor on their mailing list forever because of a tale of a donor who had made a $25 gift 25 years before leaving a million dollars to the organization in a will. The assumption is that the donor made the bequest because the name was never taken off the mailing list. Sending mailing after mailing to everyone who ever gave a $25 gift does not make good management sense today.

Communication, the science of donor relations, begins with the first thank-you letter. The intent of continuous communication is to keep donors informed about the progress of the organization, made possible in part by their help, to solicit continued giving, and to invite active participation as volunteers. Managed communication is required and is fairly easy to set up. Donors of gifts under $100 receive an invitation to join the $100 annual giving club with all its benefits and to receive the annual newsletter that appears just prior to the time of their renewal solicitation. Donors of gifts of $100 to $999 receive all the annual giving club privileges plus the quarterly newsletter, invitations to special and benefit events, and commemorative giving materials. Donors who give four times a year for a total of $100 receive this same level of communication. Donors of gifts of $1,000 or more receive all these materials and are inducted into the donor recognition program. They are also designated for attention (personal solicitation) by the annual giving committee, are invited to the annual meeting, and begin to receive a sequence of planned giving materials if they are age 55 or older. Communication plans are designed to inform and educate donors about programs and services, future plans, and special priorities of need and good works. These messages also support donor retention by reporting how important donors are treated. Their "warm feelings" about giving should be enhanced. They should be invited to make other gifts during the year for special projects and then asked to repeat their annual gift, perhaps with a slight increase. Communication can be added at each donor's gift level, to provide more information and to stimulate more involvement and participation. All these messages should be timed carefully with other activities. Added avenues of association can be offered, in an effort to improve the opportunity for personal contact. The real objective is to try to get to know donors as people and to let them get to know the organization well.

Donor Recognition

In addition to solid acknowledgment and communications plans, the organization must have a comprehensive guide for recognizing all donors in a fair and equitable manner. Guidelines are important; major donors must be given appreciation that is commensurate with their generosity. Certain recognitions should be reserved for higher levels of attainment—individual or cumulative gifts that meet the established thresholds (see Section J in Appendix A). Guidelines are usually designed to match cumulative giving totals and to express thanks in a conspicuous way. A main donor wall can honor both the most faithful supporters and those who have given the most money. Individual recognition also can be located within the facilities and matched to those programs and services sponsored by the donor. An extra measure of pride of association with this service is rendered in full public view. Other naming opportunities can be added for administrative positions, endowed chairs, and permanent funds, all to express appreciation.

A well-written policy and procedure statement will guide an organization in responding to each donor who becomes qualified. The guide should include a description of all details. Uniformity has great merit when managing this program. Every donor will appreciate whatever is done to honor them. Some may ask whether they received everything their gift entitled them to and were treated the same as all other donors. Creativity is needed in donor recognition so that each occasion is made personal and special for each donor. Guidelines also should state any limits in recognition of generosity.

Rewards

Recognition for donors can also include direct benefits that reward them for their generosity. Donor clubs are useful ways to manage donor relations, recognition, and rewards. Election to the President's Club, Century Club, Society of Fellows, The Ambassadors, or Heritage Society is tied to gift size. A memento that reflects this association will help cement the relationship and stimulate its renewal. Benefits such as VIP parking, special seating at events, a lunch with the president, and identification cards add both personal and special features to this relationship. Another form of appreciation can be gifts such as paperweights, silver display boxes, or small art objects. These should always be presented in person, to allow the best opportunity for expressing appreciation and getting to know the donor.

Volunteers also must have a program of recognition and rewards. A separate program and materials are appropriate and need not match the cost of what donors receive. The point when rewarding volunteers is that their hard work and results deserve some attention. Victory celebrations are the traditional occasions for thanking donors and rewarding volunteers. Plaques and other forms of recognition can be given on these occasions. T-shirts are more proper during a campaign. A nice present such as a watch, clock, or similar item can be useful as well as visible. The message is that they are not forgotten.

Donors and volunteers may be candidates for honors and awards conferred by others, and should be nominated when appropriate. Several communities now participate in National Philanthropy Day programs at which local donors, volunteers, corporations and foundations, and even fund development executives are honored for their contributions. Other organizations offer "Woman of the Year" and "Man of the Year" honors. Whether they win or not, they will appreciate being nominated.

Six months after everyone's attention has long since been drawn to other things, donors and volunteers should be sent a brief note that simply says, one more time, "Thank you for all that you do for us." A phone call or a birthday or anniversary card will go a long way. Making friends is a full-time job. Donors and volunteers are the best friends an organization can ever hope to have; they should be loved over and over, forever.

Appendix A: A Manual of Fund Development Policy and Procedure for Not-for-Profit Organizations

CONTENTS

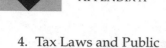

A. AUTHORITY FOR FUND DEVELOPMENT

1. *The Importance of Philanthropy.* The several benefits enjoyed by [name of organization] under the law include active support and voluntary contributions from individuals, corporations, foundations, government, associations, and societies. Positive relationships among all these parties are essential to the mission of this organization, especially its financial stability. Responsibility for preservation and enhancement of philanthropy shall be retained by the Board of Directors and carried out as herein defined.

2. *Board of Directors.* The Board has the authority and stewardship responsibility for all methods and techniques of fund-raising activity; for all forms of contributions received; for professional staff, consultants, and vendors required; for investment and management of all funds raised; and for disbursement of contribution revenues in exclusive support of the mission of this organization.

3. *Board Committee on Fund Development.* This committee of the Board of Directors is charged with leadership and direction of fund raising toward the objectives of (a) defining and developing programs asking for public support, (b) active solicitation in all forms, and (c) maintaining positive relations with donors.

4. *Department of Fund Development.* Under the chief development officer, this department is responsible to the President/CEO and the Committee on Fund Development for day-to-day management of all fund-raising activities. Professional and support staff will provide leadership, management, and direct support to fund-raising programs; acknowledgment of all gifts and maintenance of donor records and

recognition; deposit and accounting for all gifts received; supervision of the annual budget; and direction of all employees, consultants, and vendors hired.

5. *Related Organizations.* By authority of the Board of Directors, related organizations whose purpose is to develop gift revenue for this organization shall be authorized to use the name and tax-exempt privileges granted this organization, and shall be subject to the policies and procedures of the Committee on Fund Development. Accounting for all income of and expenses incurred by related organizations shall be made to the Office of Fund Development and leadership of the related organization.

6. *The Role of Volunteers.* Active volunteer participation in the fund development program is essential to its success. The roles of volunteers shall be defined as to level of responsibility, period of service, reporting relationships, staff support, and other details as required. A volunteer recognition program shall also be provided to honor the service given by those who lead and assist this organization.

7. *The Rights of Donors.* The value of past, present, and future donors shall be preserved and respected at all times in concert with the Donor Bill of Rights. The privileges and benefits accorded donors are defined in Honors and Recognition (Section J).

B. MANAGEMENT OF FUND DEVELOPMENT ACTIVITIES

1. *Goals and Objectives Established by the Board of Directors.* The priorities for public participation and support shall be established by the Board of Directors and carried out by the Committee on Fund Development and related organizations through the Department of Fund Development.

2. *Job Description for Director of Fund Development.* The Committee on Fund Development and President/CEO shall define the duties and responsibilities of the Director of Fund Development and shall participate in the hiring and performance evaluation of occupants in this position.

3. *Public Solicitation Programs.* All fund-raising activities shall be approved by the Committee on Fund Development and the President/CEO for approved priorities only. Goals and budgets associated with their achievement shall be prepared in advance of active public solicitation.

4. *Priority and Project Management.* Each fund-raising priority shall be managed as a separate fund-raising project. The assistance of volunteers, staff, and budget shall be organized to meet project deadlines and objectives. Fund development volunteers, staff, time, and budget shall be authorized only for approved priorities. Overlapping priorities shall be resolved by the Committee on Fund Development.

5. *Procedures for Approval for Gift Solicitation.* All priorities for fund development shall be defined, within procedures established by the President/CEO, for submission to the Board of Directors for approval, including budgetary authorization. Those programs appropriate for fund-raising support shall be so identified, and evaluation shall be performed by the Committee on Fund Development to assess anticipated public support and budget and staff and volunteer requirements for successful solicitation.

6. *Prospect Reservation.* Prospective candidates deserve considerate treatment at all times. When more than one approved project may qualify for the attention of the same prospect, the prospect reservation procedures shall guide resolution of the timing and period of reservation of its solicitation completion. This procedure will ensure that dual solicitation of prospects will be avoided and that prospects already assigned to approved projects shall have first priority.

7. *Use of Consultants and Vendors.* Professional assistance may be retained or purchased to support fund-raising activities. Each such association shall be guided by a written contract or memorandum of agreement in keeping with this organization's policies. The recommendation by the Committee on Fund Development and approval of the Board of Directors shall be required prior to entering into any contract or agreement.

C. PUBLIC SOLICITATION PROCEDURES

1. *Correct Legal Name.* All charitable contributions, regardless of value, form, or designated use, shall be made only to this organization, using the proper legal name of this corporation. Questions about methods of giving, timing, assignment, purpose, or about the value, designated use, and so forth, shall be directed to the Department of Fund Development, as shall all questions about legal forms for gifts, gift substantiation and their tax consequences, and donor recognition.

2. *Use of Organization Name for Fund Raising.* The use of the name of this organization for any fund-raising purpose by any other organization or entity *shall* require prior approval of the Committee on Fund Devel-

opment, acting on recommendations from the Department of Fund Development.

3. *Commercial Coventures and Charitable Sales Promotions.* Joint ventures for public marketing and solicitation with business or commercial organizations shall be defined within applicable state and federal laws and regulations. Each such association shall be guided by a written contract or memorandum of agreement approved by the Board of Directors upon recommendation of the Committee on Fund Development. The commercial partner involved shall disclose all income and expenses associated with each of these promotions. The uses to be made of proceeds from each joint venture shall be in keeping with the mission statement of this organization.

4. *Tax Laws and Public Reporting Requirements.* Voluntary contributions to not-for-profit organizations are endorsed by federal and state governments, which provide substantial tax deductions for donors. The Board of Directors will, at all times, comply fully with its obligations to fulfill applicable tax laws and public reporting requirements. Public report documents shall be available the same day a request is made in person, or within 30 days of receipt of a written, e-mail, facsimile, or telephone request, as required by law.

5. *General Fund-Raising Guidelines.* Donors and prospects shall be encouraged to support approved priorities and established programs at all times, in order that the most urgent requirements of this organization may be met to the greatest extent possible. Donor wishes will be considered to the extent possible, so long as their intended use of funds is in keeping with the mission statement. Resolution of donor wishes outside approved priorities and established programs shall be by the Board of Directors upon recommendation of the Committee on Fund Development.

6. *Joint Fund-Raising Programs.* Joint fund-raising activities between programs within this organization shall be encouraged because they provide donors and prospects with more opportunities to address approved priorities.

7. *Calendar for Solicitations.* Each 12-month period contains limited time available for fund-raising activities. Coordination and cooperation are required in planning each solicitation, to respect the rights of donors and to avoid creating the appearance of confusion and competition among the public. Each fund-raising program requires time for its own fulfillment and must also respect the preferred periods when other fund-raising programs shall be scheduled. The calendar for solicitation shall be reviewed and approved by the Committee on Fund Development at the beginning of each fiscal year. Modifications to the calendar

will be resolved by the Committee based on recommendations of the Department of Fund Development.

D. FORMS OF CONTRIBUTIONS

1. *Types of Gifts.* Besides *monetary gifts* in the form of cash, checks, money orders, and the like, *nonmonetary gifts* may be accepted, such as (a) bonds and securities, (b) real property, (c) tangible personal property, (d) gifts-in-kind to be used in the form in which they are given, (e) royalties, copyrights, and trademark rights, (f) mineral rights, and (g) insurance policies naming this organization as beneficiary in whole or in part.

2. *Unrestricted and Restricted Gifts.* Gifts with no stipulation by the donor as to their purpose or use are *unrestricted.* Gifts given and accepted for a specific purpose, as designated by the donor as a condition or so directed by this organization, shall be *temporarily restricted.* Such gifts are only to be used for the purpose intended, and their status is to be disclosed in financial and audit statements in accordance with Financial Accounting Standards Board (FASB) and American Institute of Certified Public Accountants (AICPA) accounting standards and guidelines. Gifts given or so directed by this organization to be *retained* are considered to be endowment and are recorded and reported as *permanently restricted,* with only their investment and interest earnings available for use as determined by the Investment Management Committee.

3. *Appraisal Rules and Procedures.* Current Internal Revenue Service (IRS) regulations will be observed when calculating the charitable contribution value of gifts of property, including advice to such donors regarding these regulations and the reporting obligations both parties must observe. A list of qualified professional appraisers will be offered each donor for his or her independent use. Donors are obliged to pay for professional appraisals of their property. The appraised value thus certified will be entered in the donor's gift record and reported in IRS Form 8282 if sold within two years of the date of the gift. Official gift acknowledgment documents will refer only to the object given and appraised value.

4. *Special Handling of Select Gifts.* Commemorative gifts may be received in the form of "in memory of," "in honor of," or "on the occasion of" from any source. Separate gift acknowledgment procedures will reflect the special nature of these select gifts. Unless their use is specified by the donor or the person or family named, they shall be considered un-

restricted gifts. Commemorative gifts that qualify for Honors and Recognition also will observe the procedures described in Section J herein.

5. *Temporarily Restricted Funds.* A donor may deliver funds or property as a gift and specify a conditioned use over time, with such funds to be held for a fixed period until the condition is met. Among the conditions may be a specific event, decision, financial transaction, or time-defined future activity. During this interim, the Investment Committee may invest the funds; any earned income is usable by this organization until such time as conditions or maturation are achieved. After the condition has been met and the funds dispersed for the restricted purpose, the use shall be recorded and reported as an unrestricted expense in accordance with FASB and AICPA accounting standards and guidelines.

6. *Gifts in Trust.* This organization may accept gifts in trust, agreeing to hold and manage a donor's principal resources and assets in exchange for life income, after which the principal and future income become the property of the organization for use as designated by the donor. A donor may deliver funds or property in a trust agreement to provide income for his or her lifetime and the lifetime of a spouse or other designated beneficiary, in accordance with the operating procedures of the Planned Giving Program (Section K). Specific details regarding trust documents, tax consequences, and income projections shall be reviewed by legal counsel prior to completion. If this organization acts as trustee, the selection of investment manager and custodian, performance evaluation, and administrative/accounting services shall be directed by the Investment Committee and approved by the Board of Directors.

7. *Income-Producing Properties.* In instances where income-producing properties are gifted, the Investment Committee shall determine and report to the Board of Directors, in advance of acceptance, several details including unrelated business income tax implications, environmental analysis and toxic waste potential, operations and maintenance expenses, and salability of the property. If accepted, the Investment Committee shall provide guidance on operations and disposition of the property to resolution.

8. *Legacies and Bequests.* A donor may arrange in a Will or Living Trust that this organization be designated as a beneficiary to receive a direct gift from the Estate. A donor may also arrange, after the death of a named beneficiary, that the principal or some of the surviving Estate shall become the property of this organization. Any restrictions on the use of such income as specified by the donor shall be in keeping with the mission statement. Unless otherwise specified, the Board of Direc-

tors, on advice of the Fund Development and Investment Committees, shall consider all other legacy and bequest income as unrestricted endowment.

E. FUND-RAISING METHODS AND TECHNIQUES

1. *Procedures for Setting Goals.* Annual goals and multiyear campaign objectives shall be established by the Committee on Fund Development based on prior years' experience, estimated improvement based on economic conditions and campaign acceptance, established priorities of need, and budget appropriated, with approval by the Board of Directors. Fund development staff, time, and budget are reserved only for established priorities approved by the Board of Directors.

2. *Annual Giving Activities.* The several methods and techniques that solicit donors as well as prospects for support each year shall be coordinated by the Committee on Fund Development. A variety of solicitation programs may be offered, including but not limited to direct mail, memberships, benefit events, telephone and media appeals, personal solicitation, commemorative giving, and more.

3. *Procedures for Benefit Events.* Each special and benefit event shall be approved in advance by the Committee on Fund Development, based on the following criteria: (a) appropriate fit to the existing calendar of fund-raising activities, (b) recruitment of an adequate volunteer committee or sponsoring agency or organization, and (c) a budget reflecting income and expense plans projecting a minimum of 50 percent net proceeds as gift income to this organization. All event funds shall be administered by the Office of Fund Development; so also shall be all contracts and agreements for services required to support any event.

4. *Business, Corporation, and Foundation Relations.* These gift prospects are important resources and deserve careful consideration at all times. Direct contact with any business, corporation, or foundation for any purpose shall be only with prior approval of the Committee on Fund Development. Prospect reservation procedures shall apply at all times.

5. *Special Project Campaigns.* Separate solicitation programs may be developed to meet urgent priorities or to take advantage of unusual opportunities offered by donors that match well with current fund-raising program objectives. Each such special project campaign shall be approved by the Committee on Fund Development prior to initiation, based on (a) appropriate fit to the existing calendar of fund-raising ac-

tivities, (b) recruitment of an adequate volunteer committee or sponsoring agency or organization, and (c) a budget reflecting the expense required to achieve the income potential proposed with a minimum of 75 percent net proceeds as gift income to this organization.

6. *Multiyear and Capital Campaigns.* The Board of Directors may direct that a major fund-raising effort of a multiyear nature be conducted for urgent priorities, in keeping with long-range and strategic plans. Such campaign plans shall be developed by the Committee on Fund Development in concert with the Finance and Investment Committees and with thorough analysis of leadership and volunteer support, gift potential, internal capability, staff time and expense required, added budget requirements, and other preparations.

7. *Planned Giving Programs.* Public solicitation that offers forms of estate planning and planned giving shall be guided by the Planned Giving Policy (Section K) and administered by the Committee on Fund Development. This organization can act as trustee when accepting gifts in the form of charitable remainder trusts, charitable lead trusts, and pooled-income funds, in accordance with state and federal regulations, subject to approval of each gift by the Board of Directors.

F. GOVERNMENT GRANTS AND CONTRACTS ADMINISTRATION

1. *Authority and Supervision.* The President/CEO and the Sponsored Research Administrator are authorized agents for all grant and contract agreements. Each grant or contract application shall be approved by the President/CEO and Sponsored Research Administrator prior to submission.

2. *Office of Grants and Contracts.* The Office of Grants and Contracts shall provide resource services including the following: details on application requirements, budget preparation with appropriate indirect costs and fringe benefits, application preparation and review, final signature approvals, accounting reports and audits, and liaison to government agencies. Completed applications must be delivered to the Grants and Contracts Office at least five working days prior to the submission deadline.

3. *Grants and Contracts Officer.* The Grants and Contracts Officer is responsible for supervision of all grant and contract applications including budget review and approval, and for supervision of accounting for funds received and public reports required by these agreements.

4. *Institutional Review Committee (IRC).* An Institutional Review Committee shall be appointed by the President/CEO to be composed of nine members, three of whom shall be laypersons not employed by this organization. IRC duties include oversight and analysis of all work proposed and performed under grants and contracts as well as such other issues of ethics and professional conduct associated with any activity performed by this organization that is funded by government agencies and other revenue sources.

5. *Manuscripts and Articles.* Manuscripts, articles, and reports based on work performed under a grant or contract awarded this organization, or work identified with this organization by name, shall be reviewed by the Grants and Contracts Officer prior to submission for publication.

6. *Accounting, Reporting, and Audits.* The Chief Financial Officer will establish accounting procedures for administration of all funds received in a grant or contract agreement. Budget changes requested by the Principal Investigator shall be delivered to the Grants and Contracts Officer, who will negotiate with the agency for resolution. Requests for disbursement by the Principal Investigator first shall be directed to the Grants and Contracts Officer, who will verify the fund balance and expense to be in accordance with the approved budget. The Chief Financial Officer will supervise the preparation of all financial statements and public reports, including grant and contract audits, for submission to the granting or contract agency, in accordance with generally accepted accounting principles.

7. *Royalties, Copyrights, and Patents.* All royalties, copyrights, and patentable results from work performed under grant and contract agreements shall adhere to the Royalties, Copyrights, and Patents policy of this organization.

8. *Nongovernment Grants and Contracts.* Funds requested or received from nongovernment sources (e.g., corporations or foundations) that are, in fact, a formal agreement for specific work as defined in the application shall be administered by the Grants and Contracts Office in accordance with its operating policy and procedures, with support from the Fund Development Office as appropriate.

G. GIFT PROCESSING PROCEDURES

1. *Checks and Cash.* All gifts in the form of checks, cash, or credit cards received by any department shall be delivered *on the day they are received*

to the Department of Fund Development, which will process the gift. In instances where the use specified by the donor is unclear, these details shall be brought to the immediate attention of the Department of Fund Development by telephone before acceptance of any gift binds this organization to fulfilling the donor's wishes. If none are known, the gift shall be considered to be for unrestricted purposes.

2. *Gifts of Securities.* The transfer of securities certificates or their ownership to the name of this organization is especially sensitive and may only be accomplished as follows: (a) Ask the donor and his or her broker to call the Department of Fund Development for instructions on transfer to our agent, setting up a brokers' account, board authorization action, and other details. In instances where prior securities transfer have occurred with the same broker, the Department of Fund Development will proceed with transfer instructions. (b) Certificates belonging to the donor will be delivered only by certified or registered mail, or by hand. A stock power form, signed by the donor and naming the organization as transferee, shall be in a separate envelope using certified or registered mail. Disposition of the securities will be guided by policies established by the Investment Committee.

3. *Gifts of Personal Property.* Personal property may be accepted when (a) the property can be sold, or (b) the property can be used in keeping with the mission of this organization. Internal Revenue Service regulations require gifts other than cash or publicly traded securities valued in excess of $5,000 to be appraised by a certified professional appraiser, and a copy of the appraisal must accompany the gift. Cost of the appraisal shall be the responsibility of the donor. The gift value shall be the appraised value at the time of the gift. If the property is sold within two years of its receipt, IRS Form 8282 will be completed and submitted to the IRS.

4. *Gifts of Real Estate.* Real estate in the form of a residence, business, commercial building, undeveloped land, etc., may be accepted when (a) the environmental and toxic waste review is completed, *and* (b) the property can be sold in a reasonable time, *or* (c) the property can be used in keeping with the mission of this organization. A certified appraisal performed within 60 days of the gift date shall be provided by the donor. In most cases, real estate will be sold at current market prices through a broker hired by the organization. Properties with mortgages will not be accepted if the mortgage amounts to 50 percent or more of fair market value established in the appraisal. This type of gift will be governed by "bargain sale" rules.

5. *Gifts-in-Kind.* Gifts of material or products may be accepted when the form of the gift can be used immediately by the organization. Contri-

bution values shall be as allowed by IRS regulations. Credit for IRS approved gift values shall be added to the donor's gift history.

6. *Employee Gifts and Payroll Deduction.* Employees may make gifts at any time and may use payroll deduction to transfer their funds. Arrangements for the amount of the gift, frequency of deduction, and period when deductions are to begin and conclude are made by the employee, who shall be responsible for instructing the Payroll Office of these details in writing. The Department of Fund Development will provide sample language or a proper pledge card for these purposes.

7. *Fiscal and Calendar Year-End Procedures.* Gifts in any form received near the date ending the fiscal or calendar year may be credited to the prior reporting period if there is evidence that the donor intended to make the gift within this period, and the gift is received and processed within 10 days of the closing date for the fiscal or calendar year-end.

H. GIFT ACKNOWLEDGMENT PROCEDURES

1. *Official Acknowledgment.* All gifts, regardless of value, form, or designated use, shall be acknowledged by this organization with official correspondence. Acknowledgment represents to the donor this organization's acceptance of the gift along with its restrictions, and may also serve the donor as evidence to certify a possible tax-deductible event.

2. *Additional Acknowledgments.* Additional "thank-you" messages by volunteers and staff are encouraged and are dependent on the donor, size of the gift, or purpose, as determined by the Department of Fund Development. Details about the gift will be provided by the Department of Fund Development when additional acknowledgments are appropriate. Copies of additional acknowledgments shall be sent to the Department of Fund Development for retention in the donor file.

3. *Time of Acknowledgment.* Gifts must always be acknowledged as promptly as possible. Gift processing shall have as its first priority the timely acknowledgment of all gifts within 48 hours of receipt.

4. *Donor Records and Recognition.* The Department of Fund Development shall retain all correspondence regarding contributions, gift records, cumulative gift histories, and other data on donors' activity, which shall be confidential information for use only in support of fundraising activities. All recognition and reward accorded to donors by reason of their gift frequency, amounts, or cumulative total shall be in accordance with the Honors and Recognition guidelines (Section J).

5. *Gift Substantiation Rules.* IRS requires nonprofit organizations to disclose to donors of $75 or more *at the point of solicitation (invitation)* when the gift is related to a special or benefit event, the amount of the gift value that is *nondeductible* because of material goods (e.g., food and drink) consumed by the donor in exchange for their gift. Further, IRS requires of *all* contributions of $250 or more disclosure to the donor of the extent (value) of any benefits, including material goods, due to the donor in exchange for their gift, the value of any such benefits to be reported to the donor as *nondeductible*.

6. *Tax Records and Public Disclosure.* Gift acknowledgment correspondence is useful to donors for tax submission purposes. Donors may request verification of previous gifts for any purpose, which will be documented and released only to donors. Public release of details surrounding individual gifts shall be made only with the express permission of the donor, who shall be appraised of the purpose for such disclosure and given the opportunity for prior approval of the language to be used.

7. *Gift Reports on Results.* Public reports of gift results will not disclose gift amounts for individual donors. Gift reports will tally results by revenue sources, purposes or use, and fund-raising programs employed. Distribution of gift reports shall be limited to those who need to know these results.

I. ACCOUNTING FOR GIFT REVENUE

1. *Fiduciary Responsibility.* Each gift, regardless of value, form, or designated use, shall be accounted for at the time of receipt until used as directed by the donor in support of the mission of this organization. During such time as funds are retained, they shall be actively invested in accordance with procedures of the Finance and Investment Management Committees. The Department of Fund Development shall be responsible for any reports to donors on the use of their funds, to be accomplished in concert with operating managers and the fiscal/accounting department.

2. *Allocation to Restricted Funds.* Gifts received for restricted purposes (either temporarily restricted or permanently restricted) shall be separately accounted for, in order to maintain stewardship of these funds as donors direct. The segregation of these funds is to be performed by the fiscal/accounting department, who shall report to donors on their disposition and use by the departments and managers involved, through the Department of Fund Development.

3. *Expenditure Controls.* The uses of gift revenues, especially restricted gifts, shall be fully accounted for, beginning with their deposit to temporarily restricted fund accounts, stewardship, disposition reports, and with expenditures only as directed by the donor in keeping with the mission of this organization.

4. *Allocation to Endowment and Investment Earnings.* Funds restricted to endowment or so restricted by the Board of Directors shall be invested and accounted for in accord with policies determined by the Finance and Investment Management Committees. Investment earnings shall be used only for the purposes specified by the donor or Board, as directed by the Investment Committee.

5. *Investment of Funds.* All gifts received shall be invested until used in accord with donor wishes, using short-term or long-term investment plans as defined by the Finance and Investment Management Committees. Funds restricted to endowment or so restricted by the Board of Directors shall be invested and accounted for as directed by the Finance and Investment Management Committees. Investment earnings shall be used only for the purposes specified by the donor or Board, with amounts as resolved by the Finance and Investment Management Committees.

6. *Accounting Reports.* Regular accounting reports will summarize the status of all gift money, illustrating their present disposition by source, purpose or use, and fund-raising program originating the gift. These reports shall be prepared monthly and distributed to the Board of Directors and the Finance, Fund Development, and Investment Management Committees who shall review and approve them. Annual reports will be prepared as a summary of all fiscal-year activity.

7. *Audits and Tax Returns.* The Board of Directors will conduct an audit of all contributions received and held, which shall be conducted in accordance with generally accepted accounting principles. Public reports of financial details shall be prepared as required by federal and state regulations. Public reports of financial details shall be available immediately to the public if request is made in person or within thirty days after receipt of a written, e-mail, facsimile, or telephone request.

J. HONORS AND RECOGNITION

1. *Policy Concept.* Formal recognition of distinguished service to this organization, in the forms of gift support and voluntary time and talent, shall receive official consideration by the Board of Directors. The

qualifications, review and decision procedures, and methods of recognition to be followed in regard to gift support in its many forms, and as specified in this Section, are (a) the naming of buildings, property, or any space therein; (b) the naming of departments or titled positions, including chairs within this organization; and (c) the conferring of awards or citations on any individual, institution, association, or society for gift support or services rendered.

2. *Guidelines.* The Board of Directors, in concert with the Committee on Fund Development, shall assess each recommendation for honors and recognition. They shall consider the relationship between the honoree's qualifications and the size and scope of the project supported. Consideration in the conferral of honors and recognition will include (a) benefit to this organization, (b) visibility and prominence accorded to the honoree, and (c) use of honors and recognition to further the goals and objectives of this organization in financial gain and in public recognition and respect.

3. *Qualifications.* Individuals or institutions that make large contributions shall be qualified for honors and recognition. A gift of $25,000 or higher qualifies for such consideration and may include a single gift received, total giving over several years, or a pledge amount of fundraising goal achieved. Each such donor may be offered an appropriate form of recognition to be placed in the area selected or in the main donor recognition area, or a suitable dedication ceremony with a tour of the area identified for recognition included whenever possible. Gifts valued under $25,000 shall be recognized at the discretion of the Committee on Fund Development.

4. *Procedure for Approval.* Recommendations for honors and recognition shall be made to the Board of Directors after review and approval by the Committee on Fund Development, with adequate details on the individual or institution to be honored and the reasons for such action by the Board of Directors.

5. *Naming of Buildings or Space Therein.* All areas of this organization are subject to naming. Such identification will be appropriate in light of the gift or gifts received and will be sensitive to function and location and shall be consistent with internal graphics and signage procedure. Buildings, floors, and areas may be named as donors prefer when the extent of service and contribution merits such recognition.

6. *Naming of Endowed Chairs.* Endowed chairs represent another means to recognize major contributions to this organization. Endowed chairs may be named in honor of a present or former staff member, the donor, or someone the donor wishes to honor, and may be either a memorial or a living tribute to the honoree. A financial goal shall be set for each

endowed chair that is approved by this organization, and shall be based on a preliminary budget prepared for the use of a portion of the investment earnings in keeping with the mission of the organization.

7. *Naming of Departments or Title Positions.* Professional, scientific, and service departments and their administrative positions represent another means to honor a donor or someone the donor wishes to honor, or a present or former staff member. Such occasions occur especially when the personal contributions, service, and achievements of the honoree have been intimately associated with that department or its service or functional area.

8. *Awards or Citations.* This organization may establish and may confer at its pleasure such awards or citations upon individuals or institutions in recognition for either or both their voluntary service and contributions. These awards or citations may be given at such time and on such occasions as the organization's Board of Directors may determine. Recommendations for conferring an award or citation shall be made as defined in paragraph 9 below.

9. *Process for Recommendation.* Recommendations for honors and recognition are directed to the Committee on Fund Development, who shall confer with the Chairperson of the Board of Directors and the President/CEO before action is taken. In those instances where a present or former employee is nominated or a department or title position is proposed, the President/CEO shall confer with the department head most closely associated with the candidate, or the department head most closely associated with the title position, for advice in advance of forwarding the recommendation to the Board of Directors for its decision. In addition, adequate consultation with the honoree or his or her family or their representative(s) shall be conducted at the same time as other internal consultations, to be concluded to their satisfaction prior to presentation of these recommendations to the Board of Directors for action.

10. *Public Notice.* Honors and recognition decisions represent opportunities for public announcement. Agreement for such public notice shall be requested of each honoree, or his or her family or representative(s), in advance. Honorees shall have the opportunity to notify family and friends, and to invite their participation with the organization in any dedication ceremonies and receptions conducted in connection with the conferring of honors and recognition. Responsibility for coordination of such public notice shall be by the President/CEO and Director of Fund Development.

11. *Forms of Recognition.* Various forms of recognition shall be available in accordance with the wishes of the donor and with the concurrence of

the Board of Directors. Details as to form shall be included in recommendations submitted to the Committee on Fund Development. Forms of recognition may be among the following: donor walls, formal dinners, portraits, dedication ceremonies, receptions, plaques, gifts to donors and honorees, photo sessions, reports in the organization's publications, and other forms of recognition.

12. *Graphics Continuity.* Materials, typeface, and presentation forms shall be consistent with graphics standards established by this organization. The application of overall visual aids, signage, and graphics utilization shall be in accordance with graphics standards established by this organization.

13. *Renewed Solicitation.* The resolicitation of donors who have been accorded honors and recognitions shall be reviewed in advance by the Committee on Fund Development, and shall be based on submission of a strategic action plan for continued donor relations and the master gift plan defined for each such donor prior to consideration of another gift that may qualify for added honors and recognition.

14. *Donor Communications.* The Office of Fund Development shall monitor relations with all individuals or institutions accorded honors and recognition, in order to provide continued communications with this organization at a level satisfactory to these donors.

K. MANAGEMENT OF PLANNED GIVING PROGRAMS

1. *Programs for Solicitation.* The types of planned gifts to be offered, minimum gift amount, range for percentage payout, assignment as trustee, and administrative services shall all be defined by the Committee on Fund Development and approved by the Board of Directors, and shall include procedures for preparation and review of performance of planned gifts in force.

2. *Acting as Trustee.* This organization will prefer to act as trustee of charitable trusts, annuities and pooled-income funds with concurrence of the donor(s), and will provide (or arrange to provide) such investment, distribution, income tax, audit, and other administrative services as required of a trustee.

3. *Charitable Trust and Pooled Income Fund Management.* The Board of Directors, acting on recommendations of the Fund Development and Investment Management committees, will administer each charitable trust, annuity and pooled-income fund in which the organization is

acting as Trustee in accordance with guidelines established by the trust document, annuity contract or pooled-fund agreement, including investment strategies and payout rates. Investment managers will be selected by the Investment Management Committee, who will perform regular evaluations of investment performance and will report these results to the Board of Directors at least annually.

4. *Life Insurance Programs.* All life insurance programs offered as gift opportunities shall be defined by the Fund Development and Investment Management Committees and approved by the Board of Directors. Selection of agents, performance of due diligence, and supervision of policies in force shall be the responsibility of the Investment Management Committee, acting on recommendations from the Committee on Fund Development. Other life insurance gifts may be accepted, provided the policy is current and designates this organization as owner and beneficiary. If partially paid, the donor will be required to submit a written pledge to complete premium payments within eight years and to provide the original policy to this organization.

5. *No Commissions or Finder's Fees Paid for Planned Gifts.* It shall be the policy of this organization not to pay commissions or percentages associated with negotiation and acceptance of any form of planned gift. Further, the standards of professional conduct in this area shall be as published by the National Committee on Planned Giving.

6. *Wills and Bequests: Probate Procedures.* Sample texts shall be provided to all those who express an interest in naming this organization as beneficiary of a bequest. Sample texts shall be subject to approval by the donor's legal counsel. Donors who name this organization in their Will or Living Trust will be asked to provide a copy of their document or that section wherein this organization is named. It shall be the policy of this organization to closely follow to conclusion all probate proceedings where this organization is a named beneficiary.

L. INVESTMENT AND ENDOWMENT OPERATIONS

1. *Obligation of the Board of Directors.* All gifts to be invested or funds held as endowment shall be managed with professional assistance at all times with the express approval of the Board of Directors. The objectives in management of such funds shall be to preserve their current value and to generate earnings for current use by this organization. Supervision shall be by the Investment Management Committee, who

will establish investment guidelines, conduct performance evaluation, recommend distribution of earnings, and submit regular status reports on all invested funds.

2. *Selecting Professional Management Services.* The Investment Management Committee shall interview and recommend to the Board of Directors such professional managers, custodians, and performance evaluation services for all invested and endowment funds as are required, and shall conduct performance evaluations at least semiannually.

3. *Short-Term Money Management (under two years).* The Investment Management Committee shall recommend to the Board in concert with the Finance Committee how funds to be held for a brief period (under two years) shall be invested and managed, including the selection of professional managers and setting their investment guidelines.

4. *Invested Funds Management (two to five years).* The Investment Management Committee shall recommend to the Board in concert with the Finance Committee how funds that may be held for a period of up to five years shall be invested and managed, including the selection of professional managers and setting their investment guidelines. Funds to be held for more than five years shall observe endowment fund management.

5. *Endowment Fund Management.* Funds restricted to endowment or designated by the Board to observe endowment management shall be invested with professional managers and may include commingling such funds together for maximum benefit. Guidelines for investment shall consider current market conditions, preservation of principal, balanced fund strategies, and the annual income needs of this organization.

6. *Purposes and Uses of Earnings.* Investment earnings shall observe the use designated for any invested or endowment fund at its inception or may otherwise be used at the discretion of the Board of Directors. If a portion of earnings is not consumed or their use is not required, it shall be the policy of this organization to retain and reinvest all such funds.

M. CORPORATE MEMBER: THE SEPARATE FOUNDATION

1. *Corporate Member of the Foundation.* Any organization established in the form of a separate not-for-profit corporation in foundation form, whose mission is to assist this parent corporation, shall be as a related organization. The Corporate Member shall be the Board of Directors of

this organization, who shall approve the Articles of Incorporation and Bylaws and annually elect the Directors of each such related organization.

2. *Routine Operations and Information Reports.* The routine operations of the foundation shall be guided by its Articles of Incorporation and Bylaws. Information reports shall be made to this organization by the foundation President or other officer who shall be invited to regular meetings of the Board of Directors of the parent corporation. Reports shall include information about its activities in support of this organization, fund-raising programs, and financial results.

3. *Review of Annual Goals and Objectives.* The foundation shall prepare its annual goals and objectives in concert with the priority needs of this organization. These goals shall include projects identified for fund raising, estimated income, and operating budget and staff required, to be submitted to the Board of Directors of this organization for review prior to inception.

4. *Professional Staff Hiring Procedures.* Professional employees of the foundation, including employees of this organization assigned to foundation work, shall include in the interview and selection process the Chairman of the Board, Chairman of the Fund Development Committee, Chief Financial Officer, and the President/CEO. All employees shall observe the policies and procedures of the parent corporation at all times.

5. *Transfer of Funds Raised and Held.* The transfer of funds raised and held by the foundation shall be at the request of the President/CEO or Chief Financial Officer of the parent corporation or their delegates. Recommendations shall include the use or disposition of funds to be transferred for reports to donors. Each transfer shall be approved by the foundation board of directors and reported to the Board of the parent corporation.

6. *Nominations Process for Foundation Directors.* The Bylaws of the foundation specify that the Nominations Committee of the Board of Directors of the parent corporation shall identify, recruit, and nominate candidates for service on the Board of Directors of the foundation.

7. *Honors and Recognition by the Foundation.* Honors and recognition accorded to qualified donors and volunteers shall be conducted in concert with the parent corporation at all times, including the naming of any part of facilities, named positions, and the placement of donor recognition materials in or on buildings owned by the parent corporation. Honors and recognition accorded by the foundation shall otherwise be guided by the Honors and Recognition policy of the parent corporation (see Section J above).

8. *Annual Meetings and Annual Reports.* The foundation shall conduct its annual meetings and issue its annual reports in concert with the parent corporation at all times. A selection of foundation directors, volunteers, and donors will be invited to attend annual meetings of the parent corporation. Annual reports prepared for the two organizations may be separate or combined, as the two Boards may determine.

9. *Annual Audit Review.* Audits prepared for the foundation shall be conducted in accordance with generally accepted accounting principles. Selection of the firm to conduct the audit shall be made by the parent corporation and the report delivered to the foundation board and the board of directors of the parent corporation. Further, as accounting guidelines may direct, the financial experience of the foundation may also be reported in the consolidated audit of the parent corporation as a related organization.

N. RELATED ORGANIZATIONS: SUPPORT GROUPS

1. *Authorization to Exist.* Support group organizations may be formed either by this organization or its subsidiary foundation only with the approval of the board of directors of both organizations. The purpose of any such support group shall be in keeping with the mission, purpose, goals, and objectives of the parent corporation. Support groups may not be established as separately incorporated associations except in the form of a subsidiary foundation as defined in Section M above.

2. *Approval of Operating Rules and Procedures.* Support group organizations formed for fund development purposes shall be guided in their activities by written operating rules and procedures, which shall be approved by the parent corporation or its subsidiary foundation. Their operating rules and procedures shall include text reporting their formal affiliation, purposes, members, Board of Directors, election of officers and their duties, powers, committees, meetings, receipt of funds and assets and their disposition, rules of order, limitations on political activities, insignia, amendments, and the like.

3. *Use of the Organization's Name.* Support groups may act only in the name of the parent corporation or its subsidiary foundation, use their name in their communications, solicit contributions only for support of their mission and priorities of need, and otherwise support their purposes, goals, and objectives.

4. *Review of Annual Goals and Objectives.* The annual goals and objectives of each support group organization shall be prepared in coordination and cooperation with the parent corporation or its subsidiary foundation. Preparation of annual goals and objectives shall be defined and approved by the Board of Directors of each support group and reported to the Board of Directors of the parent corporation or its subsidiary foundation for review and approval.

5. *Nominations Process for Officers and Members of the Board of Directors.* A nominations committee shall be appointed by the Board of Directors of each support group who will conduct elections to its Board of Directors. Composition of each nominations committee will include the Chairman of the Board, Chairman of the Committee on Fund Development, and President/CEO of the parent corporation, along with similar representatives of its subsidiary foundation. Candidates for election shall be approved by the parent corporation and its subsidiary foundation in advance of their election.

6. *Professional Staff Hiring Procedures.* Professional staff hired to assist support group organizations shall be employees of the parent corporation or its subsidiary foundation. Representatives of each support group will be invited to serve on selection committees for the hiring of professional staff whose duties include staff management and support for these organizations.

7. *Control of Funds Raised and Held.* All funds raised and held by support groups shall be in the name of the parent corporation, or its subsidiary foundation, and shall be delivered to it upon receipt or following completion of the activity for which these funds were raised. Regular reports of funds raised and held shall be made to the Committee on Fund Development of the parent corporation or to the Board of Directors of its subsidiary foundation, which funds shall be included in their regular financial statements and annual audit report.

8. *Annual Meetings and Annual Reports.* Support groups shall conduct their annual meetings and prepare their annual reports as their Operating Rules and Procedures specify. Invitations to annual meetings shall include representatives of the parent corporation and its subsidiary foundation, who shall also receive their annual reports.

9. *Annual Audit Review.* Funds raised or held in the name of the parent corporation or its subsidiary foundation are the property of these organizations and shall be included in their financial statements and annual audit report. If support groups manage their own funds, their books and financial statements will be delivered annually to the parent corporation or its subsidiary foundation for review and to provide such information as is required for preparation of the annual audit

statement and IRS return. A report of each review will be delivered to the President of each support group.

O. DEPARTMENT OF FUND DEVELOPMENT

1. *Areas of Management Responsibility.* The Department of Fund Development reports to the President/CEO and is charged with management and staff support to the entire fund development program, including all employees, annual budget, donor records, and files. The definition and direction of fund-raising activities, recruitment and training of volunteers, accounting for all funds raised, and public reports shall be with the approval of the Committee on Fund Development and the Board of Directors.

2. *Approved Fund-Raising Programs.* Only those fund-raising programs and activities approved by the Committee on Fund Development shall be performed by this Department with the use of its employees and their time and with such budget funds as are made available. Any other program must first receive full and formal approval by the Committee prior to its implementation.

3. *Donor Relations and Communications.* This Department is charged with responsibility for the complete supervision of all records, personal relations, and communications with donors, including honors and recognition. This Department shall act as a resource to this organization on its formal obligations to donors at all times.

4. *Support Service.* The organization shall provide this Department with normal and routine support services, such as accounting, financial management, personnel, employee health, engineering, housekeeping, and so on, in the same manner as other Departments and assist in completion of its assigned duties, as appropriate.

5. *Job Descriptions and Hiring Practices.* All employees of this Department shall be guided in their daily duties by a written job description prepared for their position, as reviewed and approved by this organization. Salary levels, pay schedules, benefits, performance evaluations, and other matters relating to full- or part-time employment shall be consistent with personnel procedures of this organization, as shall be all hiring practices. Employees shall observe the same policies and procedures that apply to all other employees at all times.

6. *Budgets and Accountability.* Budget preparation and accountability for funds entrusted to the Department shall be performed by management staff of the Department in accordance with routine procedures of this

organization. Departmental managers are responsible for the correct expense of all funds provided for operating purposes in accordance with organization policy, and for verifying these details to the finance division as required.

7. *Records and Files.* All records of correspondence, gift transactions, and their related details will be maintained by the Department as sensitive information for such periods of time and in such form as is appropriate. The use and disclosure of any of this information shall be restricted to Department employees and such others who have a need to know in order to carry out their assigned duties. Donor gift histories shall be preserved for the life of the donor. Any record destroyed shall protect the sensitive nature of the contents until destruction is complete.

P. PUBLIC REPORTING REQUIREMENTS

1. *Internal Revenue Service.* Preparation of Internal Revenue Service Form 990 and other IRS documents associated with the conduct of public solicitation and acceptance of gifts of any type and form shall be completed on schedules provided and in accordance with current IRS regulations.
2. *State and Local Agencies.* Such other reports as may be required by state, county, local community, or other agencies shall be completed on schedules provided and in accordance with current regulations. Such permits, licenses, and fees that may be required along with public disclosure of tax-exempt certificates, audits, financial statements, and the like will be completed in accordance with current regulations.
3. *Public Requests for Information.* Any request in writing, asking for copies of public documents so defined by law, such as reports submitted to the IRS and local authorities, will be completed in accordance with current regulations and will be honored the same day a request is made in person, or within 30 days of receipt of a written, e-mail, facsimile, or telephone request, as required by law.

Q. APPROVALS, REVIEWS, AND AMENDMENTS

1. *Authority of the Board of Directors.* This Manual is authorized by the Board of Directors, acting on recommendation of the Committee on

Fund Development. It is designed to provide guidance and direction to all areas of fund development activity of this organization. Its contents shall be followed by all who accept appointment to voluntary and staff positions of this organization.

2. *Periodic Review and Reissue.* A review of this entire Manual will be conducted by the Committee on Fund Development every other year, with results reported to the Board of Directors. The purpose of this review will be to maintain an accurate relationship between the current practices of operating programs and the contents of this Manual. Any section or subsection may be examined at any time, as appropriate, with changes and additions proposed in accordance with the amendment procedures.

3. *Process for Amendment.* Changes to this Manual must be approved by the Board of Directors, who will act only on formal recommendations from the Committee on Fund Development. Proposals for amendment may be submitted in writing, at any time, by any participant in the fund development program who shall utilize existing committees, related organizations, or other appropriate and standing leadership structure for prior reviews and approvals leading to submission by the Committee on Fund Development.

Appendix B:
Reality Tests for
Cause-Related Marketing

Five areas of inquiry along with 20 questions to ask companies offering such a program.

Area 1. The corporate relations program
A corporate relations program for a not-for-profit organization can expect to receive annual gifts, benefit event support, special project grants, and capital campaign contributions. The traditional methods in soliciting such gifts involve building an informed relationship and mutual respect between the company and the not-for-profit organization.
1. How does the organization solicit this company now and has it received any prior contributions?
2. How does cause-related marketing fit into the organization's corporate relations program plan?
3. How else might the corporation and its employees help the organization first?
4. Does the organization have a written agreement with the corporation for this cause-related marketing program that meets all state and local requirements for such a commercial coventure?

Area 2. Donor recruitment
How will this program recruit new donors? The general public who participate in this cause-related marketing campaign must purchase the product first, not make a gift first.

5. Is there a tax deduction for the donor?

6. Is a "thank-you" letter sent to the donor from the not-for-profit organization?

7. Does the not-for-profit organization receive a list of "donors" from the company during or after the cause-related marketing campaign?

8. Will the organization be able to involve these new donors in other relationships, for example as volunteers, or with future gifts?

9. Can the organization rely on this relationship as a source of continuing corporate revenue?

Area 3. Exploitation

10. Did the company approach the organization or did the organization invite the company into this joint relationship?

11. Can every not-for-profit organization expect to be equally attractive to the objectives of this corporate cause-related marketing program?

12. Does the organization have any control over how the promotion is worded and how, when, and where the name of the organization will be used?

13. Does the organization have any liability or exposure regarding the product sold in the event of a consumer lawsuit?

Area 4. Accounting reports

An accounting of all income received along with expenses required to conduct this marketing campaign should be shared with the not-for-profit organization.

14. Will the organization receive any financial reports on the success of this project that will disclose the budget planned, expenses incurred, and all revenues received?

15. If the organization was offered and it has accepted a fixed amount as the gift due from this campaign, has the organization been informed of how such an amount was derived?

16. Has the organization and its corporate partner met all the state and local requirements for a charitable sales promotion?

Area 5. Ethical considerations

17. If it is the judgment of the organization that this cause-related marketing program is legal and ethical, how does it fit into the organization's plans for its overall fund development goals and objectives?

18. Does the organization know (or wish to know) whether the regular price for the product offered in the promotion has been inflated for purposes of this campaign?
19. Does the organization recommend accepting a cause-related marketing program as the basis of a normal proposal to solicit this company for a contribution to meet its priority needs?
20. Does the not-for-profit organization have the right to ask any company each of these 20 questions?

▼ Selected References

Abbin, Gerle M., Diane Cronwell, Marvin J. Dickman, Richard A. Helfand, Ross W. Nager, Joseph P. Toce, Jr., and Mark L. Vorsatz. *Tax Economics of Charitable Giving*, 12th ed. Chicago: Arthur Anderson, 1995.

American Association of Fund-Raising Counsel. *Giving USA: 1998*. New York: AAFRC Trust for Philanthropy, 1998.

Anderson, Albert. *Ethics for Fundraisers*. Bloomington: Indiana University Press, 1996.

Aston, Debra. *The Complete Guide to Planned Giving*, 2d ed. Cambridge, MA: JLA Publications, 1990.

Bendixen, Mary Anne, and Robert L. Torre. *Direct Mail Fund Raising: Letters That Work*. New York: Plenum, 1988.

Blazek, Jody. *Tax and Financial Planning for Tax-Exempt Organizations*, 2d ed. New York: Wiley, 1994.

———. *Tax Planning and Compliance for Tax-Exempt Organizations: Forms, Checklists, Procedures*, 2d ed. New York: Wiley, 1993.

Bowen, William G. *Inside the Boardroom: Governance by Directors and Trustees*. New York: Wiley, 1994.

Brakeley, George A., Jr. *Tested Ways to Successful Fund-Raising*. New York: Amacom, 1980.

Brentlinger, Marilyn E. *The Ultimate Benefit Book: How to Raise $50,000-Plus for Your Organization*. Cleveland: Octavia, 1987.

Briscoe, Marianne, ed. *Ethics in Fundraising: Putting Values into Practice*. New Directions in Philanthropic Fundraising, no. 6. San Francisco: Jossey-Bass, 1994.

Broce, Thomas E. *Fund Raising: A Guide to Raising Money from Private Sources*. 2d ed. Norman: University of Oklahoma Press, 1986.

Brody, Ralph, and Marcie Goodman. *Fund-Raising Events*. New York: Human Sciences Press, 1988.

Bryson, John M. *Strategic Planning for Public and Nonprofit Organizations*. San Francisco: Jossey-Bass, 1988.

411

Burlingame, Dwight F., ed. *The Responsibilities of Wealth*. Bloomington: Indiana University Press, 1992.

———, ed. *Critical Issues in Fund Raising*. The NSFRE/Wiley Fund Development Series. New York: Wiley, 1997.

Burlingame, Dwight F., and James M. Hodge, ed. *Developing Major Gifts*. New Directions for Philanthropic Fundraising, no. 16. San Francisco: Jossey-Bass, 1997.

Burlingame, Dwight F., and Lamont J. Hulse, ed. *Taking Fund Raising Seriously: Advancing the Profession and Practice of Raising Money*. San Francisco: Jossey-Bass, 1991.

Burlingame, Dwight F., and Dennis R. Young, ed. *Corporate Philanthropy at the Crossroads*. Indianapolis: Indiana University Press, 1996.

Burnett, Ken. *Relationship Fundraising: A Donor-Based Approach to the Business of Raising Money*. London: White Lion Press, 1992.

Burns, Michael E. *Budgeting Guide for Nonprofit Administrators and Volunteers*. New Haven, CT: Development & Technical Assistance Center, 1995.

Carlson, Diane M. "Mail and Phone Solicitation Offer a Winning Combination." *Association for Healthcare Philanthropy News* (February 1995): 5.

Carlson, Diane M., and William Freyd. "Telemarketing." In *The Nonprofit Handbook: Fund Raising*, 2d ed., James M. Greenfield. New York: Wiley, 1997.

Carlson, Mim. *Winning Grants Step by Step: Support Centers of America's Complete Workbook for Planning, Developing, and Writing Successful Proposals*. San Francisco: Jossey-Bass, 1995.

Ciconte, Barbara Kushner, and Jeanne G. Jacob. *Fund Raising Basics: A Complete Guide*. Aspen's Fund Raising Series for the 21st Century. Gaithersburg, MD: Aspen, 1997.

Connors, Tracy D. *The Nonprofit Management Handbook: Operating Policies and Procedures*. New York: Wiley, 1993.

———. *The Nonprofit Handbook: Management*, 2d ed. New York: Wiley, 1997.

Costa, Nick B. *Measuring Progress and Success in Fund Raising: How to Use Comparative Statistics to Prove Your Effectiveness*. Falls Church, VA: Association for Healthcare Philanthropy, 1991.

Council for Advancement and Support of Education. *Case Campaign Standards: Management and Reporting Standards for Educational Fund-Raising Campaigns*. Washington, DC: Council for Advancement and Support of Education, 1994.

———. *Case Management Reporting Standards: Standards for Annual Giving and Campaigns in Educational Fund Raising*. Washington, DC: Council for Advancement and Support of Education, 1996.

———. *Fund-Raising Standards for Annual Giving and Campaign Reports for Not-for-Profit Organizations other than Colleges, Universities, and Schools*.

Washington, DC: Council for Advancement and Support of Education, 1998.

Cutlip, Scott M. *Fund-Raising in the United States: Its Role in American Philanthropy.* New Brunswick, NJ: Rutgers University Press, 1990 (reprint of a 1965 work).

Dannelley, Paul. *Fund Raising and Public Relations: A Critical Guide to Literature and Resources.* Norman: University of Oklahoma Press, 1986.

Day, Duane L. *The Effective Advancement Professional: Management Principles and Practices.* Gaithersburg, MD: Aspen, 1998.

Dove, Kent. *Conducting a Successful Capital Campaign: A Comprehensive Fundraising Guide for Nonprofit Organizations.* San Francisco: Jossey-Bass, 1988.

Drucker, Peter F. *Managing the Nonprofit Organization: Practices and Principles.* New York: HarperCollins, 1990.

———. *The Drucker Foundation Self-Assessment Tool for Nonprofit Organizations.* San Francisco: Jossey-Bass, 1993.

Duca, Diane J. *Nonprofit Boards: Roles, Responsibilities, and Performance.* New York: Wiley, 1996.

Duronio, Margaret A., and Eugene R. Tempel. *Fund Raisers: Their Careers, Stories, Concerns, and Accomplishments.* San Francisco: Jossey-Bass, 1997.

Fink, Norman S., and Howard C. Metzler. *The Costs and Benefits of Deferred Giving.* New York: Columbia University Press, 1982.

Fisher, James C., and Kathleen M. Cole. *Leadership and Management of Volunteer Programs.* San Francisco: Jossey-Bass, 1993.

Fisher, Marilyn. "Ethical Fund Raising: Deciding What's Right." *Advancing Philanthropy* 2 (spring, 1994): 29–33.

Flanagan, Joan. *The Grass Roots Fundraising Book.* Chicago: Contemporary Books, 1982.

Frantzreb, Arthur C. *Not on This Board You Don't: Making Your Trustees More Effective.* Chicago: Bonus Books, 1997.

Freedman, Harry A., and Karen F. Smith. *Black Tie Optional: The Ultimate Guide to Planning and Producing Successful Special Events.* Rockville, MD: Taft Group, 1991.

Fry, Robert P., Jr. *Nonprofit Investment Policies: Strategies to Grow the Funds of Your Organization.* The NSFRE/Wiley Fund Development Series. New York: Wiley, 1998.

Gaby, Partricia, and Daniel Gaby. *Nonprofit Organization Handbook.* Englewood Cliffs, NJ: Prentice Hall, 1979.

Gee, Ann D., ed. *Annual Giving Strategies: A Comprehensive Guide to Better Results.* Washington, DC: Council for Advancement and Support of Education, 1990.

Geever, Jane, and Patricia McNeill. *The Foundation Center's Guide to Proposal Writing*. New York: Foundation Center, 1993.

Golden, Susan L. *Successful Grantsmanship: A Guerrilla Guide to Raising Money*. San Francisco: Jossey-Bass, 1997.

Gooch, Judith Miricl. *Writing Winning Proposals*. Washington, DC: Council for Advancement and Support of Education, 1987.

Grace, Kay Sprinkel. *Beyond Fund Raising: New Strategies for Nonprofit Innovation and Investment*. The NSFRE/Wiley Fund Development Series. New York: Wiley, 1997.

Grasty, William K., and Kenneth G. Sheinkopf. *Successful Fund Raising: A Handbook of Proven Strategies and Techniques*. New York: Charles Scribner's Sons, 1983.

Gray, Sandra Tice. *Everyday Ethics: Key Ethical Questions for Grantmakers and Grantseekers*. Washington, DC: Independent Sector, 1991.

———. *A Vision for Evaluation*. Washington, DC: Independent Sector, 1993.

Greenfield, James M. *Fund-Raising Fundamentals: A Guide to Annual Giving for Professionals and Volunteers*. New York: Wiley, 1994.

———. *Fund-Raising Cost Effectiveness: A Self-Assessment Workbook*. The NSFRE/Wiley Fund Development Series. New York: Wiley, 1996.

———, ed. *Financial Practices for Effective Fundraising*. New Directions in for Philanthropic Fundraising, no. 3. San Francisco: Jossey-Bass, 1994.

———, ed. *The Nonprofit Handbook: Fund Raising*, 2d ed. The NSFRE/Wiley Fund Development Series. New York: Wiley, 1997.

Gross, Malvern J., Jr., Richard F. Larkin, Roger S. Bruttomesso, and John J. McNally, ed. *Financial and Accounting Guide for Nonprofit Organizations*, 5th ed. New York: Wiley, 1995.

Gurin, Maurice G. *Confessions of a Fund Raiser: Lessons of an Instructive Career*. Washington, DC: Taft Group, 1985.

———. *What Volunteers Should Know for Successful Fund Raising*. New York: Stein & Day, 1991.

Hall, Mary S. *Getting Funded: A Complete Guide to Proposal Writing*, 3d ed. Portland, OR: Continuing Education Publications, 1988.

Harr, David J., James T. Godfrey, and Robert F. Frank. *Common Costs and Fund-Raising Appeals: A Guide to Joint Cost Allocation in Not-for-Profit Organizations*. Landover, MD: Nonprofit Mailers Federation and Frank & Company, 1991.

Harris, April L. *Raising Money and Cultivating Donors through Special Events*. Washington, DC: Council for Advancement and Support of Education, 1991.

Hasselbein, Frances, Marshall Goldsmith, and Richard Beckhard, ed. *The Leader of the Future*. San Francisco: Jossey-Bass, 1996.

Hasselbein, Frances, Marshall Goldsmith, and Richard F. Schubert, ed. *The Community of the Future.* San Francisco: Jossey-Bass, 1998.

Herman, Robert D., and Associates. *The Jossey-Bass Handbook of Nonprofit Leadership and Management.* San Francisco: Jossey-Bass, 1994.

Himmelstein, Jerome. *Looking Good and Doing Good: Corporate Philanthropy and Corporate Power.* Indianapolis: Indiana University Press, 1997.

Hodgkinson, Virginia Ann, and Murray S. Weitzman, ed. *Giving and Volunteering in the United States: Findings from a National Survey.* Washington, DC: Independent Sector, 1994.

————, ed. *Nonprofit Almanac 1996–1997: Dimensions of the Independent Sector.* San Francisco: Jossey-Bass, 1996.

Hopkins, Bruce R. *Charity, Advocacy, and the Law.* New York: Wiley, 1992.

————. *A Legal Guide to Starting and Managing a Nonprofit Organization*, 2d ed. New York: Wiley, 1993.

————. *The Tax Law of Charitable Giving.* New York: Wiley, 1993.

————. *The Law of Fund Raising,* 2d ed. New York: Wiley, 1996.

————. *The Legal Answer Book for Nonprofit Organizations.* New York: Wiley, 1996.

————. *The Law of Tax-Exempt Organizations*, 7th ed. New York: Wiley, 1997.

Hopkins, Bruce R., and D. Benson Tesdahl. *Intermediate Sanctions: Curbing Nonprofit Abuse.* New York: Wiley, 1997.

Howe, Fisher. *The Board Member's Guide to Fund Raising.* San Francisco: Jossey-Bass, 1991.

————. *Welcome to the Board: Your Guide to Effective Participation.* San Francisco: Jossey-Bass, 1995.

Huntsinger, Jerald E. *Fund Raising Letters: A Comprehensive Study Guide to Raising Money by Direct Response Marketing.* Richmond, VA: Emerson, 1985.

Independent Sector. *Daring Goals for a Caring Society: A Blueprint for Substantial Growth in Giving and Volunteering in America.* Washington, DC: Independent Sector, 1986.

————. *Ethics and the Nation's Voluntary and Philanthropic Community: Obedience to the Unenforceable.* Washington, DC: Independent Sector, 1991.

Jenkins, Jeanne B., and Marilyn Lucas. *How to Find Philanthropic Prospects.* Ambler, PA: Fund Raising Institute, 1986.

Johnston, Michael. *The Fund Raiser's Guide to the Internet.* The NSFRE/Wiley Fund Development Series. New York: Wiley, 1999.

Jordon, Ronald R. and Katelyn L. Quynn. *Planned Giving: Management, Marketing, and Law.* New York: Wiley, 1994.

Josephson, Michael. *Ethical Issues and Opportunities in the Non-Profit Sector.* Marina del Rey, CA: The Joseph & Edna Josephson Institute for the Advancement of Ethics.

Joyaux, Simone P. *Strategic Fund Development: Building Profitable Relationships That Last.* Aspen's Fund Raising Series for the 21st Century. Gaithersburg, MD: Aspen, 1997.

Kelly, Kathleen S. *Effective Fund-Raising Management.* Mahway, NJ: Lawrence Erlbaum, 1997.

Kihlstedt, Andrea, and Catherine P. Schwartz. *Capital Campaigns: Strategies That Work.* Aspen's Fund Raising Series for the 21st Century. Gaithersburg, MD: Aspen, 1997.

Kiritz, Norton J. *Program Planning and Proposal Writing.* Los Angeles: Grantsmanship Center, 1980.

Klein, Kim. *Fund Raising for Social Change.* Inverness, CA: Chardon Press, 1988.

Kotler, Philip, and Alan R. Andreasen. *Strategic Marketing for Nonprofit Organizations.* 3d ed. Englewood Cliffs, NJ: Prentice Hall, 1987.

Kovener, Ronald R. *Accounting and Financial Reporting Issues Related to Fund Raising.* Falls Church, VA: Association for Healthcare Philanthropy, 1993.

Kuniholm, Roland. *The Complete Book of Model Fund Raising Letters.* Englewood Cliffs, NJ: Prentice Hall, 1995.

Lane, Frederick S. "Enhancing the Quality of Public Reporting by Nonprofit Organizations." *Philanthropy Monthly* (July 1991): 3–38. Reprint of report of the Nonprofit Quality Reporting Project, Baruch College, City University of New York.

Lautman, Kay, and Henry Goldstein. *Dear Friend: Mastering the Art of Direct Mail Fund Raising.* 2d ed. Washington, DC: Taft Group, 1991.

Lefferts, Robert. *Getting a Grant in the 1990s: How to Write Successful Grant Proposals.* New York: Simon & Schuster, 1990.

Leslie, John W. *Focus on Understanding and Support: A Study in College Management.* Washington, DC: American College Public Relations Association, 1969.

Levy, Barbara R., ed. *The NSFRE Fund-Raising Dictionary.* The NSFRE/Wiley Fund Development Series. New York: Wiley, 1996.

Levy, Barbara R., and Barbara H. Marion. *Successful Special Events: Planning, Hosting, and Evaluating.* Aspen's Fund Raising Series for the 21st Century. Gaithersburg, MD: Aspen, 1997.

Lindahl, Wesley E. *Strategic Planning for Fund Raising.* San Francisco: Jossey-Bass, 1992.

Martin, Del. "The Development Audit: Providing the Blue Print for a Better Fund-Raising Program." *NSFRE Journal* 15 (Autumn 1990): 28.

Marts, Armaud C. *Philanthropy's Role in Civilization: Its Contributions to Human Freedom.* New Brunswick, NJ: Transaction Press, 1991.

McLaughlin, Thomas A. *Streetsmart Financial Basics for Nonprofit Managers.* New York: Wiley, 1995.

McLeish, Barry J. *Successful Marketing Strategies for Nonprofit Organizations.* New York: Wiley, 1995.

Meador, Roy. *Guidelines for Preparing Proposals,* 2d ed. Chelsea, MA: Lewis Publishers, 1991.

Merlyn, Vaughan, and John Parkinson. *Development Effectiveness: Strategies for IS Organizational Transition.* New York: Wiley, 1994.

Miner, Lynn E. and Jerry Griffith. *Proposal Planning and Writing.* Phoenix: Oryz Press, 1993.

Mixer, Joseph R. *Principles of Professional Fundraising.* San Francisco: Jossey-Bass, 1993.

Moerschbaecher, Lynda. *Marketing Magic for Major/Planned Gifts.* Chicago: Precept Press, 1996.

Murray, Dennis J. *The Guaranteed Fund-Raising System: A Systems Approach to Planning and Controlling Fund Raising,* 2d ed. Poughkeepsie, NY: American Institute of Management, 1994.

New, Anne L. and Wilson C. Levis. *Raise More Money for Your Nonprofit Organization: A Guide to Evaluating and Improving Your Fundraising.* New York: Foundation Center, 1991.

New, Cheryl, and James Quick. *Grantseeker's Tool Kit: A Comprehensive Guide to Finding Funding.* New York: Wiley, 1999.

Nichols, Judith. *Targeted Fund Raising: Defining and Refining Your Development Strategy for the 1990s.* Chicago: Bonus Books, 1991.

———. *Pinpointing Affluence: Increasing Your Share of Major Donor Dollars.* Chicago: Bonus Books, 1994.

———. *Growing from Good to Great: Positioning Your Fund Raising for BIG Gains.* Chicago: Bonus Books, 1995.

———. *Strengthening Fund Raising through Evaluation.* Chicago: Bonus Books, 1998.

O'Connell, Brian. *America's Voluntary Spirit: A Book of Readings.* New York: Foundation Center, 1983.

———. *Philanthropy in Action.* Washington, DC: Independent Sector, 1987.

———. *Budgeting and Financial Accountability.* Washington, DC: Independent Sector, 1988.

O'Neill, Michael. *The Third America: The Emergence of the Nonprofit Sector in the United States.* San Francisco: Jossey-Bass, 1989.

———. *Ethics in Nonprofit Management.* Institute for Nonprofit Organization Management, University of San Francisco, 1990.

Panas, Jerold. *Mega Gifts: Who Gives Them, Who Gets Them.* Chicago: Pluribus Press, 1984.

————. *Born to Raise*. Chicago: Pluribus Press, 1988.

Pappas, Alceste T. *Reengineering Your Nonprofit Organization: A Guide to Strategic Transformation*. New York: Wiley, 1995.

Payton, Robert L. *Philanthropy: Voluntary Action for the Common Good*. New York: Macmillan, 1988.

Perlman, Seth, and Betsy Hills Bush. *Fund-Raising Regulation: A State-by-State Handbook of Registration Forms, Requirements, and Procedures*. New York: Wiley, 1996.

Pidgeon, Walter P. *The Universal Benefits of Volunteering: A Practical Workbook for Nonprofit Organizations, Volunteers, and Corporations*. The NSFRE/Wiley Fund Development Series. New York: Wiley, 1998.

Prince, Russ Alan, and Karen Maru File. *The Seven Faces of Philanthropy: A New Approach to Cultivating Major Donors*. San Francisco: Jossey-Bass, 1994.

Raybin, Arthur. *How to Hire the Right Fund-Raising Consultant*. Washington, DC: Taft Group, 1985.

Roberts, Mary Lou, and Paul D. Berger. *Direct Marketing Management*. Englewood Cliffs, NJ: Prentice Hall, 1989.

Rosso, Henry A. *Rosso on Fund Raising: Lessons from a Master's Lifetime Experience*. San Francisco: Jossey-Bass, 1996.

Rosso, Henry A., and Associates. *Achieving Excellence in Fund Raising: A Comprehensive Guide to Principles, Strategies, and Methods*. San Francisco: Jossey-Bass, 1991.

Scanlan, Eugene A. *Corporate and Foundation Fund Raising: A Complete Guide from the Inside*. Aspen's Fund Raising Series for the 21st Century. Gaithersburg, MD: Aspen, 1997.

Schmaedick, Gerald L. *Cost-Effectiveness in the Nonprofit Sector*. New London, CT: Quorum Books, 1993.

Schwartz, John J. *Modern American Philanthropy: A Personal Account*. New York: Wiley, 1994.

Seltzer, Michael. *Securing Your Organization's Future: A Complete Guide to Fundraising Strategies*. New York: Foundation Center, 1987.

Seymour, Harold J. *Designs for Fund Raising*. New York: McGraw-Hill, 1966. (Paperback edition: Ambler, PA: Fund Raising Institute, 1988.)

Shannon, James P. *The Corporate Contributions Handbook*. San Francisco: Jossey-Bass, 1991.

Sharpe, Robert F., Sr. *Before You Give Another Dime*. Nashville: Thomas Nelson, 1979.

————. *The Planned Giving Idea Book*. Nashville: Thomas Nelson, 1980.

————. *Planned Giving Simplified: The Gift, the Giver, and the Gift Planner*. The NSFRE/Wiley Fund Development Series. New York: Wiley, 1998.

Shaw, Sondra C., and Martha A. Taylor. *Reinventing Fundraising: Realizing the Potential of Women's Philanthropy.* San Francisco: Jossey-Bass, 1995.

Smith, Bucklin and Associates. *The Complete Guide to Nonprofit Management.* New York: Wiley, 1994.

Solomon, Lester M. *America's Nonprofit Sector: A Primer.* New York: Foundation Center, 1992.

Stern, Gary, and Rebecca Andrews. *Marketing Workbook for Non-Profit Organizations.* St. Paul: Amherst H. Wilder Foundation, 1991.

Stern, Susan (with John L. Schumacher and Patrick D. Martin). *Charitable Giving and Solicitation.* New York: Prentice Hall/Maxwell MacMillan, 1990.

Teitell, Conrad. *Deferred Giving.* Old Greenwich, CT: Taxwise Giving, 1991.

Teuller, Alden B. *The Planned Giving Deskbook.* Rockville, MD: Taft Group, 1991.

Tracy, John A. *How to Read a Financial Report: Wringing Vital Signs out of the Numbers,* 4th ed. New York: Wiley, 1994.

Trenbeth, Richard P. *The Membership Mystique.* Rockville, MD: Fund Raising Institute, 1986.

Van Til, Jon, and Associates. *Critical Issues in American Philanthropy.* San Francisco: Jossey-Bass, 1990.

Warner, Irving R. *The Art of Fund Raising,* 3d ed. New York: Harper & Row, 1990.

Warwick, Mal. *Revolution in the Mailbox.* Baltimore: Fund Raising Institute, 1990.

———. *You Don't Always Get What You Ask For: Using Direct Mail Tests to Raise More Money for Your Organization.* Brakeley, CA: Strathmoor Press, 1992.

———. *The Hands-On Guide to Fundraising Strategy and Evaluation.* Gaithersburg, MD: Aspen, 1997.

Weinstein, Stanley. *The Complete Guide to Fund-Raising Management.* The NSFRE/Wiley Fund Development Series, New York: Wiley, 1999.

Weisbrod, Burton A. *The Nonprofit Economy.* Cambridge, MA: Harvard University Press, 1988.

White, Douglas E. *The Art of Planned Giving: Understanding Donors and the Culture of Giving.* New York: Wiley, 1995.

Williams, M. Jane. *Big Gifts: How to Maximize Gifts from Individuals, with or without a Capital Campaign.* Rockville, MD: Fund-Raising Institute, 1991.

Young, Dennis R., and Richard Steinberg. *Economics for Nonprofit Managers.* New York: Foundation Center, 1995.

Zeff, Robbin. *The Nonprofit Guide to the Internet.* New York: Wiley, 1996.

Index

Page numbers followed by (ex) refer to exhibits.

INDEX

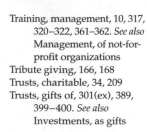